WILLIAM DARGAN
An Honourable Life
1799–1867

A portait painting of Dargan in 1854, by George Francis Mulvany,
first Director of the National Gallery of Ireland (courtesy CIÉ).

WILLIAM DARGAN
An Honourable Life
1799–1867

Fergus Mulligan

THE LILLIPUT PRESS
DUBLIN

Published in 2014 by
THE LILLIPUT PRESS
62–63 Sitric Road, Arbour Hill
Dublin 7, Ireland
www.lilliputpress.ie

ISBN   978 1 84351 630 9

1 3 5 7 9 10 8 6 4 2

A CIP record for this title is available
from The British Library.

Set in 9 pt on 14 pt Trump Mediaeval by Marsha Swan
Printed by GraphyCems in Spain

Contents

List of abbreviations

BBC&PJR	Ballymena, Ballymoney, Coleraine and Portrush Junction Railway
B&BR	Belfast & Ballymena Railway
B&CDR	Belfast & Co. Down Railway
BJR	Banbridge Junction Railway
B&LJC	Birmingham & Liverpool Junction Canal
CB&PR	Cork Blackrock & Passage Railway
CIÉ	Coras Iompair Éireann
DART	Dublin Area Rapid Transit
D&BJR	Dublin & Belfast Junction Railway
D&DR	Dublin & Drogheda Railway
D&ER	Dundalk & Enniskillen Railway
D&KR	Dublin & Kingstown Railway
DL	Deputy Lieutenant
D&WR	Dublin & Wicklow Railway
DW&WR	Dublin Wicklow & Wexford Railway
EGM	Extraordinary general meeting
GSH	Great Southern Hotels
GS&WR	Great Southern & Western Railway
ISER	Irish South-Eastern Railway
KJR	Killarney Junction Railway
L&BR	Liverpool & Bury Railway
L&CR	Londonderry & Coleraine Railway
L&ER	Limerick & Ennis Railway
L&FR	Limerick & Foynes Railway
L&MR	Liverpool & Manchester Railway
L&NWR	London & North-Western Railway
MGWR	Midland Great Western Railway
M&LR	Manchester & Leeds Railway
N&AR	Newry & Armagh Railway
N&ER	Newry & Enniskillen Railway
NW&RR	Newry Warrenpoint & Rostrevor Railway
P&DR	Portadown & Dungannon Railway
RAIS	Royal Agricultural Improvement Society
RDS	Royal Dublin Society
RE	Royal Engineers
RHA	Royal Hibernian Academy
RHSI	Royal Horticultural Society of Ireland
RIC	Royal Irish Constabulary
TCD	Trinity College Dublin
T&KR	Tralee & Killarney Railway
UCD	University College Dublin
UR	Ulster Railway
W&LR	Waterford & Limerick Railway
W&TR	Waterford & Tramore Railway
WWW&DR	Waterford, Wexford, Wicklow and Dublin Railway

Preface and Acknowledgments

Over many years I've studied the life and career of William Dargan, developing a great admiration and genuine respect for the kind of man he was and his achievements, even though he died eighty-five years before I was born. His way of living and working are admirable and were always marked by a sense of decency and fair play. Also the scale of his achievements in developing the dormant Irish economy through transport infrastructure and many other enterprises has to a large extent been forgotten. Behind this cold economic terminology is the reality that Dargan provided many thousands with a livelihood, especially during the dark days of the Famine. However, we should not confuse humanitarian qualities with softness: Dargan could display steel-like attributes when necessary.

The example of a life well lived is relevant in all eras but especially so in difficult times such as the present. Openness, honesty and fair dealing are universal, timeless qualities and comprise a valid role model for anyone in business even if they have been clearly absent from many of our financial and political institutions in recent years. The life of William Dargan has a resonance and a relevance even for our day.

Sometimes he has seemed a hard man to track down. On occasions I found myself in libraries, archives or company record repositories, trawling through a vast, almost indecipherable nineteenth-century minute or letter book trying to locate a vital piece of information on a Dargan project secreted somewhere within.

A board or committee meeting's 'rough minutes', as they were called, the first draft, written in haste in spider scrawl and without an index of course are often the only company records to survive. To the occasional alarm of other researchers I've tried communicating with Dargan at such times, appealing to him to help me find the right page along these lines: 'If you want me to write your life story, you'd better help me.' Then, as people used to do in a former era when seeking guidance from the Good Book, I would open the huge volume of minutes at a random page. And there, every single time, without fail, guaranteed, would be … nothing of any use or interest whatsoever.

Despite Dargan's lack of celestial cooperation in the area of research he would still be the first person in my line up of historical guests at an imaginary dinner party and my list of questions to him would be as long as the phone book.

The Greatest Train Journey of All

In researching Dargan I've sometimes thought of life as a train journey. When you first step aboard, the train seems to be full of old people and it moves very slowly. It makes lots of stops and you have to stand as all the seats are occupied. But at each station some people get off and others get on, so that at times the train can seem crowded but at others quite empty and you have no trouble finding a seat. As the journey continues the average age of the passengers appears to decrease and at the same time the train starts to speed up. After a while you look around the carriage and realize not only are most passengers younger than you but you're actually one of the oldest. Occasionally you seek out a friend or a relation only to discover they got off several stations back.

And then suddenly it's your stop. No matter that there's something you just have to do, there are people you meant to contact, you really want to finish the book you're reading or you'd rather chat to your fellow travellers than face the disruption of alighting at a strange station in the middle of nowhere. It'd be much easier if this was the terminus and everyone alighted together but your journey isn't like that and the fact that lots of others before you have left the train at their destination is little comfort. Your ticket is only valid as far as here, so leaving everything including the comfort and warmth of the train behind you, reluctantly, you get up from your seat, walk to the door and step from the train onto a darkened platform. You've never felt so completely alone and barely notice people at the carriage windows waving goodbye as the door behind you swings shut and the train moves off slowly into the night. You have no choice but to turn and face … what? This is where my imagery fails.

If you've tried to lead a decent life, and even if you've failed, you've nothing to fear when you leave the train, no matter what awaits you on the platform. And that's one of the reasons I wrote this book about William Dargan: to present a pen portrait of someone who was honourable, fair-minded and hard-working, a man who changed the face of Ireland and left the world a better place than he found it.

Buíochas

Lots of people helped with this book and I received great encouragement from many different quarters. My friend Martin Nevin of the Carlow Historical and Archaeological Society, who was enthusiastic from the start about a life of William Dargan, has done much to research and preserve the memory of Dargan in his native county and farther afield and has always been most generous in sharing his time and his knowledge.

Prof. Louis Cullen was very supportive and would often greet me with an interrogative: 'And how is Mr Dargan?' before gently demolishing my excuses for not completing this book. Prof. David Dickson, my PhD supervisor at Trinity College Dublin, always encouraged me to publish, while the Dargan family, the most patient people on the planet, were ever supportive and encouraging. While researching in the Public Record Office of Northern Ireland I often met the late Herbert Dargan SJ, one of William's great-grandnephews, then based in Belfast. His brother, the late Dan Dargan SJ, lived in retirement in Ranelagh and would occasionally phone me to suggest a possible research area and to inquire directly how the book was progressing. Their niece, Mary Dargan Ward, who rightly has immense pride in her great-great-granduncle, has always been positive and interested in nuggets of information I managed to discover about her illustrious ancestor.

Grants from the Grace Lawless Lee Fund at Trinity College Dublin helped greatly when travelling to the UK for research purposes. At a recent critical stage, when the writing molehill was truly a mountain, I spent two very pleasant weeks during a cold, crisp winter at Villa Palazzola in the Alban Hills outside Rome where free of all distractions and excuses the peace and calm of that beautiful place were so conducive to writing. My thanks to Mgr Nicholas Hudson and Joyce Hunter for facilitating those productive visits. I am grateful to Geraldine Finucane, Group Secretary and the Board of CIÉ for allowing me to reproduce the fine portrait of Dargan by George Mulvany, and to Olivia O'Leary, a famous Carlovian like Mr Dargan, for performing the launch.

My brother, John Mulligan, willingly drove me around Anglesey to locate Mr Dargan's early handiwork in north Wales and we spent many pleasant hours with

Tara Dog exploring and photographing Dargan's canal in Staffordshire and visiting the church at Adbaston where he and Jane were married. Among people deserving a special mention are: Dr Andy Bielenberg, University College Cork, Bruce Bradley SJ, John Callanan, Engineers Ireland, Prof. Ron Cox, Trinity College Dublin, the late Dr Maurice Craig, Kevin Curry, Brian Donnelly, National Library of Ireland, Brian Gilmore, Rob Goodbody, the late Charles Hadfield, Richard Harrison, Mary Kelleher former RDS Librarian, Barry Kenny, Iarnród Éireann, Kathleen Kinsella, Bray, my cousin Dr John Logan formerly of the University of Limerick, the late Lord Meath, Jenny Muddimer, St Michael's church, Adbaston, Frederick O'Dwyer, Cormac Ó Grada, University College Dublin, Sr Maire O'Sullivan, Mount Anville convent, Ray O'Sullivan jnr Genprint, Joanna Quinn, RDS Library, Peter Scott Roberts, Holyhead Maritime Museum, Alexander Smeaton, Dublin City Libraries, the late Mark Tierney OSB, Glenstal Abbey, Ray Thomas, St Mary's church, Market Drayton, Dr W.E. Vaughan, Trinity College Dublin and Gerard Whelan, RDS Library.

That the writing of this book took so long is no-one's fault but mine and the fact that that some people in the above list have gone to a better place shows how extended its gestation has been.

I also want to thank the staffs of the following archives, libraries, companies and institutions who willingly provided access to records and archival material in their care: Allied Irish Bank Archives, Bank of Ireland, Belfast Harbour Commissioners, Bray Heritage Centre, British Library, London, British Library of Political and Economic Science, London, British Newspaper Library, Colindale, Caledon House, Co. Tyrone Carlow County Library, Carlow Historical and Archeological Society, Coras Iompair Éireann Archives, Cork City Archives, Department of the Environment, Belfast, Dublin Chamber of Commerce, Dublin City Archives, Dublin Diocesan Archives, Dublin Port Archives, Fingal County Council Archives, Engineers Ireland, Glasnevin Cemetery Archives, Glenstal Abbey Archives, House of Lords Record Office, Institution of Civil Engineers, London, Irish Architectural Archive, Irish Railway Record Society, Kilruddery House, Linen Hall Library, Belfast, Liverpool Record Office, Market Drayton Library, Shropshire, Marsh's Library, Dublin, Merseyside Maritime Museum, Mount Anville Archives, National Archives Dublin, National Archives London, National Gallery of Ireland Archives, National Library of Ireland, Picton Library, Liverpool, Probate Registry, York, Public Record Office of Northern Ireland, Religious Society of Friends, Dublin and London, Royal Archives, Windsor Castle, Royal Dublin Society Archives, Royal Irish Academy, Royal St George Yacht Club, Salt Lake Family History Centre, Utah, Shropshire County Record Office, St Alban's parish, Merseyside, St Patrick's College, Carlow, Trinity College Library and Manuscript Room, Ulster Folk and

Transport Museum, University College Dublin Library, Wicklow County Library.

A glance at the contents will indicate that this book covers Dargan's life in a thematic way focusing on the major projects he undertook and the key events of his life. In doing so it is broadly but not strictly chronological. I hope this book will encourage others to come forward with their research findings and new information about Dargan the man. All the usual E&OE apply and all amendments and updates about William Dargan will be gratefully received at fmcomms@indigo.ie.

For years when pointing out a building, a canal, a railway, a road or a viaduct my children's eyes would glaze over as they intoned in a monologue: 'Yeah, yeah, Mr Dargan built it.' And so I dedicate this book to my wife Eveleen and our children Matthew, Clare and Conor, who have tolerated if not shared my interest in William Dargan's life.

Fergus Mulligan
1 April 2013

PUBLISHER'S NOTE

The Publisher would like to thank for their painstaking work his editors Djinn von Noorden and Fiona Dunne, and Marsha Swan for her typesetting and page design.

WILLIAM DARGAN

An Honourable Life

1799–1867

ONE

Introduction

William Dargan is arguably the greatest Irishman of the nineteenth century. His name is often recognized yet his life and achievements are still only vaguely acknowledged. In the Republic there is one bridge named after him, the slightly overstated Luas bridge at Dundrum, despite calls to name it after a local politician from people who do not realize it is already called Dargan Bridge. For some time his name and dates on the bridge plaque were incorrect; they have since been corrected.

Forty metres from where I write is the embankment of a railway line Dargan built 160 years ago, still solid as ever and now a busy rail corridor for the Luas. That is a fair achievement by any reckoning and hard evidence of just one of his great achievements.

The major event in nineteenth-century Ireland was without doubt the Great Famine of the 1840s. No one is sure of the full extent of the deaths during and after an Gorta Mór: the authorities kept few records of pauper deaths, and a million dead and two million emigrants is probably as close as we can get to horrible reality. Two of the leading figures of nineteenth-century Ireland, Michael Davitt who founded the Land League and Charles Stewart Parnell, were both born in 1846 at the start of the Famine, while Daniel O'Connell, the Liberator, died in 1847 just as it reached its peak. By contrast Dargan's career as an engineer and entrepreneur was at its pinnacle in the years just before, during and after the Famine. At this time he claimed to have 50 000 people working on his various projects; possibly an exaggeration to include subcontractors he employed. But even if the figure is halved, it means 25 000 men earned a living on Dargan projects and if each supported four other people (a modest estimate), 100 000 relied on wages from William Dargan to survive during the bleak years of the 1840s. He gave this economic lifeline to so many people who would otherwise have starved.

Political figures, especially those who died for freedom, tend to be better remembered in Ireland than the few who employed the destitute and advanced the economic development of the country. One of the aims of this book is to show just how unique was Dargan's contribution to Ireland and to suggest that he, as much and probably more than any other figure in nineteenth-century Ireland, deserves that overused and sometimes abused title of patriot.

Dargan's Key Principles

Although most of Dargan's own records, accounts and business papers have not survived and there are irritating gaps in his curriculum vitae it is still possible to say a lot about the man and his business methods. He came from a modest farming background in Co. Carlow and his transition from an ordinary rural upbringing to becoming one of the richest men in Ireland was phenomenal. What marks Dargan out from many other successful entrepreneurs and industrialists is that he achieved this great success using his own talents and skills, with the benefit of some useful contacts at the start of his career but without inherited wealth and most important without exploiting his workmen. His success was built on his reputation: the companies that gave him contracts and the men he employed trusted him to behave fairly. This is not to say he did not have difficulties with some projects or that every one was a total success but his sense of business ethics and fair dealing put him ahead of many of his rivals. This is a hard role to adopt in any era but even more so at the dawn of the industrial revolution.

Dargan's decency towards his men won their loyalty and was a major factor in his being able to complete his projects satisfactorily. He paid wages on time but if his men went on strike (combination being an illegal act at the time) he could be ruthless, dismissing the strikers or in some cases prosecuting them. If a client treated him badly or refused to pay what he felt he was due he was very direct in saying as much and taking every step to recover what he was owed. Underneath that genial benevolence was a layer of steel.

An example of this forthright management style is the way Dargan handled the widespread system known as 'truck', on-site provision shops run by some contractors. Such hucksters often sold over-priced, shoddy goods, including alcohol

4

and food items and by extending credit ensured their labourers were caught in a perpetual web of debt. Dargan recognized truck had some benefits for men working far from any town but the risks and problems outweighed the potential benefits and so he did not permit it. However, when building a section of the line to Cork in 1845 a Dublin paper criticized the wages he paid and accused him of exploiting his own men with truck. His letter unequivocally refuted the allegation, adding that over fourteen years as a contractor he had paid his workmen £800,000 in cash (see Chapter 5).[1] Dargan was clearly irritated by the accusation and his trenchant response is eloquent in its denial of the charges and his statement of policy as regards his workmen. It also indicates his financial muscle: £800,000 was a very large sum. There were no further such accusations against him.

This fairness and transparency in relations with his employees is mirrored in Dargan's dealings with the companies who awarded him civil engineering contracts. Construction projects can be complicated and not every job went smoothly. However, Dargan managed to complete most of his contracts on time and within budget and even when this was not the case, measured negotiation nearly always resolved any major issues, with one or two notable exceptions.

An engraving of William Dargan by W.I. Edwards for the 1853 Catalogue to the Industrial Exhibition based closely on the portrait by George Mulvany.

A Giant Among Men

Dargan accomplished an extraordinary amount of work in his lifetime. He is known today mainly as a railway contractor (or civil engineer) and the mark he left on the country is huge. He built around 830 miles of railway in Ireland (1335 kms), a staggering amount, plus sections of line in Lancashire and Yorkshire. Before any railway opened in London he built the first public passenger railway in Ireland, the Dublin & Kingstown, now the DART line between Pearse Station and Dun Laoghaire. Farther afield, anyone travelling by train to Wexford, Waterford, Cork, Killarney, Tralee, Limerick, Athlone, Galway, Longford and Belfast is travelling on lines built wholly or mainly by William Dargan. We can add to this list other branch lines (most now closed) such as Cavan, Foynes, Tramore, Passage and several out of Belfast including Newtownards, Banbridge, Armagh, Ballymena and Portrush. Although the railway network in the north has been decimated and only a few of Dargan's lines there remain open, without Dargan's industrial muscle, who knows how long Ireland would have had to wait before these lines were built?

Yet Dargan did much more than just build railways. After constructing the road between Howth and Dublin – the final link in Telford's great highway from London to Dublin – he built several canals, among them a section of the Newry Navigation with its magnificent locks, the Kilbeggan branch of the Grand Canal and the entire Ulster Canal connecting Lough Neagh to Lough Erne. He then ran barges on the Ulster Canal, which fed into the cross-channel port at Newry and from there ran steamers to Liverpool. He attempted to develop the linen and sugar industries, growing flax and sugar beet, he invested in hotels, he changed Bray from a wretched fishing village into a thriving, fashionable seaside resort, he reclaimed vast sloblands on the Foyle and in Wexford, turning them into fertile farmland, he ran a thread mill in Chapelizod, which at one time employed 900 people and he built canals and a brace of major railways in England.

The creation of the National Gallery of Ireland is largely the result of public demand for an expression of gratitude to Dargan for his work in proposing, building and funding entirely on his own the Art-Industry Exhibition of 1853. It was held on Leinster Lawn on ground now occupied by the Gallery.

In contrast to this great catalogue of achievements Dargan was a genuinely modest man. The Victorians had a distressing fondness for excessive rhetoric that often verged into humbug: the successful completion of a railway line elicited a squadron of public and private individuals eager to claim the credit. The celebratory dinner always included many tedious speeches and toasts to everyone from the monarch down to the station cat. Despite being the key person who brought the line into existence both literally as its builder and sometimes the chief financer,

Dargan was usually among the last to speak. More often than not he simply stood up, wished the company every success, and sat down again. This was typical of the man: he was paid to do a job and he was glad it turned out well. Subsequently he declined many offers to take a seat in Parliament and steadfastly refused public honours, culminating in his courageous direct refusal of a baronetcy from Queen Victoria when she called to his house for tea one afternoon in 1853.

Given the nature of his work all over Ireland it is not surprising Dargan moved around a lot. The compilation of his addresses below taken from correspondence and various directories shows how much he travelled in the course of his career. Until 1851 some served as both home and office. All dates are approximate and overlaps are evident.[2]

Table 1.1: MAN ON THE MOVE: DARGAN'S ADDRESSES

Home/office

8 Lr Merrion St, Dublin	1831–2
7 St Andrew St, Dublin	1832–3
Salthill House Hotel	1833–4
Caledon, Co. Tyrone	1833–9
34 Anglesea St, Dublin	1834–6
8 Lr Merrion St, Dublin	1836–7
34 Anglesea St, Dublin	1837–8
121 York St, Belfast	1841–6
31 Upper Abbey St, Dublin	1846–8
81 Ann St, Belfast	1846–8
137 York St, Belfast	1850
19 Collingwood St, Belfast	1850

Home		Office	
Maryville, Raheny	1851–2	1 Lr Dominick St, Dublin	1851–2
Mount Anville, Dublin	1852–65	74 Harcourt St, Dublin	1853–60
Bray Castle, Killarney, Bray	1865–7	Chapelizod Flax Mills	1853–64
2 Fitzwilliam Square E, Dublin	1863–7	62 South William St, Dublin	1861

A Famous Son of Carlow

Some years ago the Old Carlow Society decided to raise a plaque to the county's most famous son and asked me to write the text and to unveil the plaque, a surprise and a great honour. The ceremony took place on the platform of Carlow station in September 1993 in the presence of William's great-grand-nephew, the late Fr Daniel Dargan SJ and Mary Dargan Ward. It was a wonderful occasion and passing through Carlow station it still gives me delight to see the plaque on the station wall honouring this great man.

TWO

Dargan's Early Life
and Career

William Dargan was born at the cusp of the nineteenth century on 28 February 1799, a year after the bloody rebellion that took place throughout south-east Ireland. Dargan family tradition has it that two of William's uncles, Thomas and Michael Dargan, were involved in that fatal and informer-blighted uprising and were tricked into going to Carlow town where the yeomanry, with their trademark brutality, seized and hanged them.[1] The name Dargan comes from the Irish Ó Deargain, the red-headed one.

Dargan's Accent: Follow Me Up to Carla'

Despite the absence of recording equipment in the nineteenth century we can, with a degree of accuracy, hazard a guess as to William Dargan's accent. Take the train from Heuston Station towards Waterford along the line he built so well and alight on the platform at Carlow. Walk down the town and stop in Main Street and wait till you see two local people aged forty-five or over and listen to their chat. If they're Carlow people and they haven't lived away from the town for any length of time, chances are you're hearing an accent very similar to William Dargan's.

Dargan's Birthplace

Co. Carlow was and remains a prosperous part of the country with good farmland and a number of fine country houses. Some details of Dargan's family background were published in *Carloviana*[2] with the location of the grave of William's father in Killeshin cemetery. Patrick Dargan died in 1833, aged seventy-seven, and William's mother, Elizabeth, who died aged forty-two in 1813, is also buried in this grave, as are four of William's youthful siblings reflecting the high child mortality rates in those days. Among his other surviving brothers and sisters were Mary, Thomas, James, Elizabeth, Selina who is mentioned in his will (see Chapter 9) and Michael. Apart from his brother James who worked with him as a railway engineer little is known about this group. Similarly the family religion is uncertain; the fact that so many of his relations entered the priesthood, combined with events at the end of his life, make it likely he was born a Catholic.

Press Coverage in 1799

Finn's Leinster Journal, *one of the few local papers in Ireland at the time of Dargan's birth, was published twice weekly in Kilkenny and circulated in Co. Carlow. The issue for 27 February to 2 March 1799 unsurprisingly has no mention of Dargan's birth: the son of a tenant farmer would not merit inclusion. It did, however, carry London gossip, news of local outrages, continuing efforts to stamp out the 1798 rebellion and the winning numbers of the 'English Lottery' with substantial prizes of £20,000, £10,000, £500 and £50.* Plus ça change.

William's parents, Patrick and Elizabeth Dargan, were said to be relatively well-off tenant farmers with a holding of around sixty-one acres at Springhill and Ballyhide, Queen's County (Laois).[3] In 1819 Patrick transferred the sixty-one-acre tenancy to his sons Thomas and William.[4] The question of William's birthplace remains disputed as both Laois and Carlow claim him. The plaque unveiled at Carlow station by the Old Carlow Society states he was from Carlow while a similar but contradictory plaque at Portlaoise station claims him for Laois.[5]

In later years *The Irish Times* cited his birthplace as Carlow, a location firmly rejected by the editor of the *Carlow Sentinel* who said Dargan was born at 'Spring Hill in the Queen's County',[6] close to where Martin Nevin of the Carlow Historical and Archaeological Society places it.

Those industrious genealogists, the Church of Jesus Christ of Latter Day Saints (aka the Mormons), have listed Dargan's birthplace in their universal *International Genealogical Index* as Ardristan near Tullow, Co. Carlow. It is quite possible Dargan's family moved from there when he was an infant, even to several different locations. One move may have been to Graiguecullen, a suburb of Carlow town west of the River Barrow and therefore in Co. Laois. Another possibility is that William may have lived with some of his relations. It was not uncommon for large families to divide their children among other family members to share the burden of rearing them.

Martin Nevin has made great efforts to locate the Dargan homestead but even he can only locate it approximately. The most likely location and the place where he grew up (but not necessarily where he was born) is in the townland of Ballyhide, Killeshin, Co. Laois, west of Carlow town and the River Barrow on the slopes of the Slieve Bloom mountains. It is possible the family lived in Crossleigh House, Ballyhide. The evidence for this claim is a land purchase Dargan made in 1850 through the Encumbered Estates Court of 101 acres owned by Lord Portarlington for £2114 9s. 3d., a substantial sum even for a man as wealthy as he had become by then.[7] The land is good quality and the map accompanying the deed shows it is about half a mile wide and a quarter deep, divided into approximately seventeen small fields with two small houses.[8] By 1825 the tithe records do not list a single Dargan living in Ballyhide.

The Text on the Dargan Grave at Killeshin

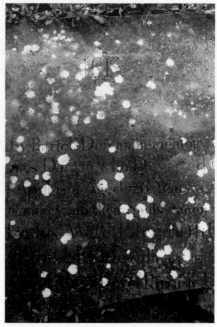

IHS Gloria in Excelsis Deo Erected by Patrick Dargan in memory of his mother Giles Dargan who departed this life the 24th of April 1801 aged 76 years. Lord have mercy on their souls. Amen. And also his wife Elizabeth Dargan who departed this life December 24 1813 aged 42 years. And of the above Patrick Dargan who departed this life March 12 1833 aged 83 years. And of his children Michael Laurence Bridget and Patrick who died young.

The Dargan family grave at Killeshin graveyard, Co. Laois. William's parents Patrick and Elizabeth Dargan and several of his infant siblings are buried here. Photo: Fergus Mulligan

The Barrow bridge at Carlow town with the distinctive castle that once guarded the river crossing. Dargan would have passed over this bridge many times.

Crossleigh House, Ballyhide. Co. Laois, where Dargan may have spent his early years.

The deciding factor must be that he described himself as from Carlow on more than one occasion, for example before a House of Commons parliamentary committee in 1845: 'Q. I believe you are a native of the County Carlow yourself? A. I am.'[9] In summary, it is therefore likely that Dargan was born near Tullow, Co. Carlow, and moved to Graiguecullen, Co. Laois, outside Carlow town at an early age and then spent most of his youth at Ballyhide, also Co. Laois.

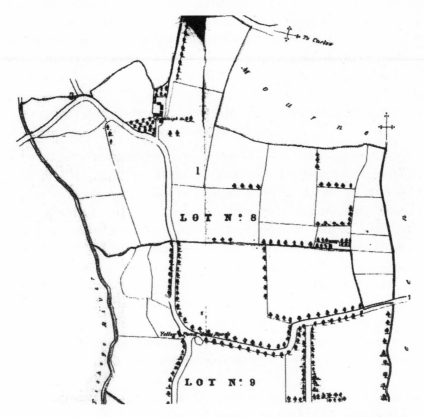

Encumbered Estates Court map showing the lands Dargan acquired when he bought his homestead in 1850.

Patrick Dargan's holding was part of the estate of Lord Portarlington whose seat was Emo Court. From later events it appears William attracted significant patronage and that he and his family were well regarded by their landlord.

William was one of a large family. His brother James worked as a railway engineer and married Jane Walsh in the Anglican church of St Philip, Liverpool on 7 September 1839. He died in Limerick in 1854, aged forty. James had a son, also called James Dargan and another railway engineer and it is from him that William's great-grand-nephews, the three Jesuit Dargans, were descended down to William Dargan SJ, Herbert Dargan SJ and Daniel Dargan SJ, all deceased, as well as Mary Dargan Ward, keeper of the surviving family records.[10]

A useful and rare source on Dargan's early years is a manuscript version of the *Handbook of Contemporary Biography* published soon after 1853, in which the subjects edited or rewrote their own entry.[11] The handwritten author proof corrections survive in the British Library and we can be reasonably certain that Dargan made these corrections himself. The entry states that Dargan went to school in

13

Graiguecullen.[12] He was said to be of strong physique, very speedy in drawing up a contract and could complete calculations rapidly and accurately; all characteristics that would serve him well in his later career. A government report throws some light on the possibilities.[13]

The Best Days of His Life: What Kind of Schooling Did Dargan Have?

The Appendix to the Second Report of the Commissioners of Education Inquiry Information provides data on schools in Carlow and Laois in the early nineteenth century. Though published in 1824, about ten years after Dargan finished his schooling, the report reveals a great deal about education in that era. Graiguecullen, east of Carlow town, had five stone-built schools, all fee-paying: three Catholic and two Protestant, with pupil numbers ranging from sixteen to seventy. The income of the master or mistress is recorded (£10 to £35 p.a.) but the only mention of a curriculum in the Appendix is whether or not the scriptures were read to the pupils. There is also an entry for Evaton, 'a spacious mansion', probably Everton House at Kelleskin (Killeshin) civil parish, a private RC boarding school with thirty-three male pupils under Master George Alexander Lynch, which cost £3000 to build. His income was a staggering £1280 p.a. By contrast, Master Patrick Byrne ran a school at Ardristan, east of Carlow, possibly Dargan's birthplace. He taught thirty-eight RC boys and girls in a 'miserable mud cabin', surviving on an income of just £4 p.a.

On leaving school, probably in his early to mid teens, it is believed Dargan spent some time working on his father's land and that his first job was in the Carlow county surveyor's office.[14] There were reports of a career setback, possibly an unsuccessful application for a job with the Carlow Grand Jury, the body responsible for a wide range of public works in the county.[15] At this point two influential patrons, John Alexander and Sir Henry Parnell MP, enter Dargan's life, possibly through the efforts of Lord Portarlington, the family's landlord.

John Alexander ran his successful mills at Milford, Co. Carlow, once very extensive according to the 1840 travel diaries of Mr and Mrs Hall.[16] The ruined building still stands in a picturesque location on the River Barrow from which it drew its power. Somehow Alexander came to hear of the young Dargan and seeing his talents decided to help the young man at the start of his career.

The Milford mills complex owned by John Alexander's family was once one of the largest in Ireland. This derelict building is one of the few survivals of this vast enterprise.

Milford, the small station south of Carlow town, closed in 1963.

Telford's Great Road from London to Dublin

It is easier to establish the nature of the support William Dargan received from Sir Henry Parnell, MP for Queen's County (Laois), a major political figure at the time and an uncle of Charles Stewart Parnell. Parnell the elder spotted the talents of the young Dargan around 1819 and found a job for him on Telford's great road. It is quite possible that Alexander referred Dargan to Parnell, knowing of his involvement in public roads.

As a government minister Parnell travelled often to London via Holyhead, 'the barbarous little hamlet' as F.R. Conder described it, enduring the hazards of the mountainous track taken by the mail coaches across north Wales into the English midlands and on to London. Samuel Smiles described the road across Anglesey as a dangerous, 'miserable track, circuitous and craggy, full of terrible jolts, round bogs and over rocks'.[17] After braving another watery crossing of the Menai Strait the weary traveller faced the road across north Wales, which was 'rough, narrow, steep and unprotected, mostly unfenced and in winter almost impassable'. One coach in 1815 took forty-one hours to cover the 225 miles (363 km) from Holyhead to London.

This building at Holyhead was once the Eagle and Child Inn. In the early 1800s surveyors and engineers measuring sections of the Holyhead road used it as a common reference point in their journals.

This was the principal line of communication between the government in London and Her Majesty's Irish subjects. The problem was that maintenance of the Holyhead Road was the job of several turnpike trusts who levied tolls to cover the cost of road repairs. These trusts were notoriously corrupt and proceedings were speedy and secretive, with much jobbery, partial allocation and outright fraud, so that only a small part of the funds allocated trickled down to road repairs; hence their poor state.[18]

In 1814 Parnell wrote to Robert Peel complaining bitterly about the state of the road and the discomfort and dangers of the journey to London he and the other 13,000 travellers annually had to endure. The government appointed Parnell chairman of a parliamentary commission whose task was to prepare estimates and supervise construction of what was essentially a new road. The Commission entrusted the project to the great Scots engineer, Thomas Telford,[19] and the two men worked closely on it, becoming friends. Parnell was a frequent guest at Telford's engineering dinners held in his Westminster house.

Who You Know

There are several layers of connection here, all suggesting the contacts and support which helped Dargan in his early career and later when his business was thriving.

The Halls, who were friends of John Alexander of Milford, later became friends of William and his wife-to-be, Jane Arkinstall. William Fairbairn of Manchester (who built the 120 hp mill engine at Milford) was later a close friend and business associate of Dargan's and supplied many locomotives to him and the railway companies for whom he worked.

John Alexander became in time a director of the Irish South-Eastern Railway, which Dargan built through Carlow towards Kilkenny. Alexander was a relation of the Earl of Caledon (whose family name is also Alexander). Dargan had close links with Lord Caledon while building the Ulster Canal in the early 1830s.

Sir Henry Parnell, Charles Stewart Parnell's uncle, became Minister for War and later Paymaster-General in Lord Melbourne's government, becoming Lord Congleton in 1841. In later years, like other members of the Parnell family, he began to suffer bouts of insanity. These became increasingly serious and some time later hanged himself. 'That fatal strain again', as F.S.L. Lyons puts it.

We have an 1836 account directly from Dargan himself of his duties on the Holyhead Road from evidence he gave while enduring spirited parliamentary cross-examination about a bill to authorize the Dublin & Drogheda Railway.[20] He said he was an inspector of works and resident engineer under Telford rather than simply an overseer, as had been suggested by learned counsel, and was a works manager under one of three principal supervisors, William Provis. It was Provis' job to submit daily works journals to London for each section of the road under construction, information supplied by a number of inspectors, including Dargan.

These handwritten journals are still in existence and contain detailed information about the number of men and horses on site every day, the hours worked, the weather, tasks completed, overall progress and any unusual events.[21] More specifically Provis also described the job of a works manager like Dargan as logging time and materials used, deploying workmen, removing rubbish, checking bridges, drains and fences, keeping a daily journal and paying the men's wages. A works manager earned 24 shillings a week in the first year, rising to 27 shillings in the second year and 30 shillings thereafter. Provis and Dargan worked together on canals in the English midlands some years later and Dargan must have been fond of him because he kept a bust of his old boss in his Mount Anville house. An assistant of Telford's on the Holyhead Road was John Macneill, later to become a leading engineer in his day and first Professor of Engineering at Trinity College. Macneill earned 2½ guineas per day in Wales (£2 10s 6d), a substantial salary when the average wage for an unskilled labourer was just 1s 6d a day. He and Dargan worked on many projects together but their relationship was more professional than amicable.

Sir John Benjamin Macneill (1793–1880)

John Macneill, a leading nineteenth-century Irish civil engineer, was born at Mount Pleasant House, Dundalk, a fine house with 'something of the air of one of the smaller government houses of the British Raj', as Bence Jones describes it. (The building, called Mount Oliver, is now a religious institution.) After five years in the Louth militia, Macneill, like Dargan, worked with Thomas Telford on the Holyhead Road from 1826–33. The Drummond Commission appointed him to plan railway developments in the north of Ireland and his colleague Charles Vignoles did the same in the south. Macneill became the first Professor of Civil Engineering at Trinity College in 1842 but his interest lay more in building railways than teaching others how to build them.

He was involved in almost every major railway project in Ireland, working closely with Dargan on many of them, sometimes with sparks flying. They were not exactly friends, more like close colleagues. Like W.R. Le Fanu and other prominent engineers, Macneill was a freemason.

He was also quite litigious: in 1849 he sued Durham Dunlop, the editor of the influential Irish Railway Gazette, *for libel, not a wise move and one he was to regret. In later life Macneill went blind and lived in relative poverty in London. However, the story that he was reduced to selling matches on the city's streets is a myth. He died in a house on the Cromwell Road and is buried in Brompton Cemetery. Long unmarked, the Institution of Engineers of Ireland and Trinity College Dublin erected a plaque over his grave in 2001 (see p.204).*[22]

Apart from often having to make the journey to London, Parnell had a particular interest in road construction and wrote a book on the subject. He gave detailed technical instructions to the works inspectors on the Holyhead Road such as Dargan who were to supervise a foreman and a gang of labourers 'quarrying rock, gathering field stones, getting gravel, breaking stones, scraping the road, loading materials into carts and all works that are reducible to measure'.[23] Parnell opposed pitting contractors against one another since they would cut corners if the price was too low, leading to disputes, ruinous subcontracts and law suits.[24] Telford's instructions were equally clear. He insisted the surface had to be elliptical for drainage with a solid pavement of large stones laid close together, a binding of walnut-sized stones and a layer of gravel. He favoured employing women and boys to break the smaller stones and advised payment by piece-rate.

The Stanley Sands toll-keeper's house by Thomas Telford on Holy Island near Anglesey whose design resembles a traditional Welsh hat and provided a view of travellers coming in both directions. Dargan adapted a similar one-storey design for his lock-keeper's cottages on the Ulster Canal, see p.54.

The last section across Anglesey passes over the Stanley Sands to Holy Island and is closely identified with Dargan. Telford decided on a completely straight road from the Menai Strait to the Eagle and Child Inn, Holyhead at a cost of £52,221 12s 7d over four years.[25] In autumn 1821 work began on lot 8, the Stanley Sands embankment, which was 1100 yards long, 34 ft wide, 16 ft above the sands with a bridge on a rock outcrop for tidal flows.[26] By February 1822 most of the road across the island was complete and the embankment well in hand.[27] Provis reported the embankment was complete in summer 1823 and had opened with an elegant toll house and gates at the western end.[28] The Stanley Sands was Dargan's first major engineering project, a most useful training for his later work on the Howth road, the coastal route of the Dublin & Kingstown Railway and the Foyle and Wexford slobland reclamations. Ten years later, when tendering for the Dublin & Kingstown Railway, Dargan travelled with the company's engineer, Charles Vignoles, to view this work on the Stanley Sands in April 1832 (see Chapter 2).[29]

For Those in Peril: 1843

Although the completed road was a vast improvement Thackeray wrote an account of one disagreeable journey through Wales in his 1843 Irish Sketch Book*:*

> The coach that brings the passenger by wood and mountain, by brawling waterfall and gloomy plain, by the lonely lake of Festiniog, and across the swinging world's wonder of a Menai bridge, through dismal Anglesea to dismal Holyhead – the Birmingham Mail – manages matters so cleverly, that after ten hours' ride the traveller is thrust incontinently on board the packet, and the steward says there's no use providing dinner on board because the passage is so short.

Both Telford and Parnell were pleased with Dargan's input and happy to recommend the rising young engineer for other projects. He was now ready to return to Ireland and put that knowledge to good use in the next phase of his career.

The Colossus of Roads: Thomas Telford (1757–1834)

Born in poverty in Dumfriesshire, the son of a shepherd, this great engineer became an apprentice stonemason at fourteen before moving to London. As Shropshire county surveyor he built forty bridges and then worked on roads, harbours and canals, including the magnificent stone and iron viaduct carrying the Llangollen canal high over the River Dee valley.

Telford's greatest project was the London-Holyhead road, now the A5. Beyond Shrewsbury it was virtually a new road. The 1826 Menai suspension bridge was a triumph and his journals describe the heart-stopping tension as early one morning he watched the first raising of the vast iron link cables holding the bridge.

The poet Robert Southey assigned Telford the 'colossus' title; another was the 'Pontifex Maximus'. John Macneill worked closely with Telford on the Holyhead Road, as did Dargan in the later stages. Telford always wrote of Dargan in very warm terms. He was a poet in his own right and wrote his autobiography but never married and had no known family. He held regular all-male engineering dinners at his house, 24 Abingdon Street, beside the Houses of Parliament. He died there in 1834 of a 'bilious derangement', as his clerk described it.

With the highway open to Holyhead and the journey time by coach from London cut from forty hours to a more manageable twenty-eight, the final stage of the London-Dublin mail coach route was the road from Howth to Dublin. Although a difficult harbour to use, Howth was the main packet station until cross-channel ships transferred to Kingstown (Dun Laoghaire). Impressions of Howth at the time were almost as negative as those of Holyhead. An anonymous writer advised anyone travelling to this 'village of wretched thatched cabins' to bring 'a troop of horse to guard against robbers and a gunboat for protection against sea pirates'.[30]

In 1823 Telford ordered a detailed survey of the road from William Duncan (most likely Dargan), which found it was in a poor state and subject to frequent flooding from the sea but not as bad as the Holyhead road before completion.[31] Dargan rebuilt the entire road with a solid stone sea wall from Clontarf crescent to Sutton. It drew high praise from Telford and Parnell, who described it as 'in a perfect state ... a model for other roads in the vicinity of Dublin'.[32] Dargan's work is still visible in the low sea wall, which resembles the one he built across the Stanley Sands near Holyhead. Even better, Col. John Burgoyne of the Commissioners of Public Works, a man who would feature in Dargan's career when he began to build railways, persuaded the Treasury to award Dargan a premium of £300 for the quality of his work.[33] This was a large sum of money and apart from the confidence it expressed, gave Dargan the vital seed capital needed to set up his business in Ireland.

THREE

Dargan's First Contracts

With the Holyhead and Howth roads now complete, Dargan was beginning to make a name for himself as one of Telford's rising stars. As well as building roads Parnell had become interested in improving the Barrow Navigation, canals being one of the chief means of transporting goods and passengers in the pre-railway era. In 1824 the Barrow company offered Dargan the post of superintendent and he presented his resignation to Telford who replied warmly from Edinburgh that he was sorry to lose him and that his conduct was always 'perfectly satisfactory'.[1] Both Telford and Parnell advised him to take the job, which he did, but it is not known how long Dargan held it.

Dargan then began to work for a number of turnpikes. In late 1827 the Malahide Turnpike noted it had received 'a letter from a person of the name of William Dargan' in response to a press advertisement. Dargan said he would maintain the Malahide and Summerhill roads for five years, protect the footpath from Summerhill to Ballybough, provide a 'good, firm, even surface', fix the road from Fairview Crescent to Malahide with a footpath, all for £2000 with £500 for repairs and £900 for other improvements.[2] Not being prone to hasty decisions the trustees were still discussing his tender five months later and finally decided to award a basic maintenance contract worth just £30 to Thomas Carney.

Dargan was more successful in his native Carlow, becoming a surveyor on the Dublin-Carlow road. He calculated the job would take ten months and his estimate for the Castledermot to Carlow section is included with the plans deposited before parliament bearing his signature.[3]

At the 7 July 1829 trustees' meeting at Ball's Inn, Blessington, Dargan offered to act as clerk without an increase in his surveyor's salary of £100 p.a.[4] At the next meeting, 12 August 1829, the trustees ordered him to spend £134 on repairs at Tallaght, Dolphin's Barn and Poulaphouca. From then until 6 July 1830 the minutes are in his handwriting and signed by him.[5] Later he was ordered to erect milestones with corrected figures and sat on a committee to decide work priorities.[6] Dargan also invested in the turnpike: the next month he took a number of £100 debentures, to be partly repaid in road tolls and in July 1830 estimated repairs to one section at £150 13s 4d.[7] At this meeting Capt. Derenzy became overseer and replaced Dargan as clerk. The meeting also defined Dargan's duties as surveyor: to inspect the whole road once a month, account for expenditure and provide a quarterly estimate of projected work, the number of men needed and their wages. In 1831 he agreed to seek a government loan and provided a three-month estimate for a section near Carlow:

Table 3.1: DARGAN'S ESTIMATE FOR IMPROVEMENTS TO COTTSTOWN–PALATINE ROAD, 5 APRIL – 6 JULY 1831

Wages: ten labourers, thirteen weeks @ 6s 6d	£35 15s 0d
2000 tons broken stones @ 1s 8d per ton	£166 13s 4d
1000 tons gravel @ 10d per ton	£49 13s 4d
Fence at Saggart	£1 0s 0d
Total	£253 1s 0d

By autumn 1831 Dargan was beginning to reduce his involvement with the Carlow turnpike as he focused more on the Kingstown railway.[8] However, Dargan had a repair contract for the Circular Road, Dublin, running 5 miles 80 perches from Leeson Street and Kilmainham to Summer Hill, beginning on 1 December 1829, worth £28 11s 5d p.a. per mile with £150 annually for upkeep.[9] He attended thirteen board meetings over the three years and the secretary reported the materials he used were excellent.

The Dunleer turnpike contract, covering a section of the Dublin-Belfast coach road, was more controversial. The commissioners approved his plan to reroute one stretch near Balrothery to save costs after which Dargan won a year's contract for the Dublin-Swords road from 24 December 1828, worth £650, paid quarterly.[10] He received £81 in February and £189 16s in June 1829 but from then on relations deteriorated. In reply to a remonstrance about delayed repairs from William Robinson, Turnpike Secretary, Dargan wrote: 'The most satisfactory reply I could give you would be by getting to work quickly'.[11]

Robinson then said the Swords road was 'exceedingly bad' and needed Dargan's 'prompt exertions to put it in to passable repair, which I hope you will immediately attend to'.[12] A fortnight later Robinson was more insistent: the Dunleer road was in 'very bad condition' part of it being 'completely worn down' and if Dargan did not fix it his 'sallary will be withheld on next quarter's day'.[13] Soon after he added that sections at Drumcondra, the fifth milestone, Pennock Hill, Swords and the tenth milestone needed 'immediate and substantial repairs' while the Swords foot-path was 'in a ruinous state which I am sorry to say you have intirely neglected'.[14] Despite these complaints Dargan received £225 in May 1831, made improvements at Cloghran hill (for which he earned £65 6s 6d plus £100 for his main contract) and was asked to submit plans for Julianstown bridge and hill.[15]

Illness prevented him attending the meeting on 1 August 1831 but he wrote: 'As I am very much in want of money, you will greatly oblige me by having the amount of my quarter's contract forwarded to me by Mr Robinson.' This produced £250 a few days later.[16] Dargan missed the next meeting for more dramatic reasons: 'Some riots having occurred in Banbridge [cut] on the works carrying on there by me. I am obliged to be present this evening at the Investigation.' He concluded the works were now, hopefully, satisfactory and added: 'I want money very much.'[17] But a month later Robinson complained about the 'very bad order' of the Swords road, which was 'in a wretched condition for want of gravel', with similar problems at Balrothery, north of Gormanstown and north of Drogheda.[18] He said he would hire men if Dargan failed to remove piles of materials near Santry and clear the blocked water table at Swords. Not surprisingly matters came to a head and Dargan tendered his resignation on 21 November 1831. The Commissioners had expected his contract to run for three years from February 1830 and began proceedings against him estimating the urgent repairs would cost £400.[19] A year later, because there was 'no injury or loss sustained by the public' from his resignation, the Commissioners instructed their lawyer to drop the legal action.

This contract may have been troublesome because Dargan underestimated the work or he may have been distracted by his Banbridge and Kingstown railway contracts. Four years afterwards, he argued before a Lords Committee that he was free to end the contract at any time and when the Dunleer Trustees criticized his work unfairly and retained part of his fee, he did so. His response to them was: 'Now, gentlemen, I have kept the road in good order as far as I bargained, and now you have paid me, our engagement ceases.'[20] At the same parliamentary committee Mr Joy, counsel, argued that many of Dargan's contracts, the Kingstown Railway,

Ulster Canal, Dunleer road and Kilbeggan Canal were blighted by disputes and poor relations. Dargan countered that they were complex, demanding a flexible response from him to problems that were impossible to foresee, that costs overran and apart from the Kilbeggan Canal, he had concluded all these contracts amicably.

Canals in the English Midlands

One of Telford's last engineering projects before his death in 1834 was the construction of the appx. 40-mile (64 km) Birmingham & Liverpool Junction Canal. This was a slight misnomer as the canal was nowhere near either city but built to connect existing waterways. The canal cost over £800,000 in total and Provis and John Wilson won the substantial contract to build the 39 miles of the main line.[21] Dargan was by now quite well off as indicated by the fact that in 1826 he took twenty £100 shares in the company.[22] He described his duties a few years later to a parliamentary committee thus: 'I surveyed the principal portion of the Birmingham & Liverpool Junction Canal. I was then assistant manager for Mr Prowes [Provis] on these works and I contracted afterwards for some works on the Middlewich canal … [I was] three years surveyor, superintendent and contractor.'[23]

The deep cutting of the Birmingham & Liverpool Junction canal at Woodseaves has an unusual keyhole opening to reduce the dead weight of the filling on the whole structure. The Spectacle bridge between Ennistymon and Lisdoonvarna is similar to it.

A high bridge of mixed materials carries the road over the B&LJ Canal near Gnosall.

The second contract, with Dargan as assistant manager, proved difficult. At Woodseaves a mile-long cutting, 90-ft deep, a mile-long 50-ft embankment between Knighton and Sheldon and a 2-mile cutting at High Offley were very troublesome.[24] Worst of all was a mile deviation through Norbury Park, made at Lord Anson's behest: there were almost endless collapses until several years later a solid bank was built.[25] Vignoles admired the 'great canal excavations of Mr Telford' when he saw them in 1833.[26] Telford left his sick bed in London to inspect the works but died on 2 September 1834, six months before the opening and the first boat passed through the completed canal on 2 March 1835. Eleven years later Robert Scott MP described it as 'one of the best canals in the kingdom ... constructed on the best principles of canal-making'.[27]

Walking Dargan's Canal

In April 2011 I walked a delightful five-km stretch of the Birmingham & Liverpool Canal around Gnosall, Shebdon, Woodseaves and High Offley in Staffordshire This is now part of the Shropshire Union Canal, a popular and busy leisure waterway. Near Gnosall (pronounced 'Knows-all'), there is a long deep cutting and a tunnel through the sandstone with crudely finished walls and roof, unlike many of the pretty little road bridges, which have lovely curves of beautifully cut stone. The lack of finish suggests the company was under financial strain and had to economize. Another very deep cutting near Woodseaves has a high bridge with a curious keyhole.

Dargan also won part of the contract to build the 9¾-mile Middlewich Canal, a feeder branch of the B&LJC towards Manchester, which cost £129,000 and opened on 1 September 1833, eighteen months before the main canal.[28] It is uncertain how much of the contract work Dargan completed and his testimony suggests he worked on the main line before the branch.

Dargan's Wife

Dargan came back from the English midlands with more that just useful experience – he also acquired a wife. On 13 October 1828 he married Jane Arkinstall in the Anglican parish church of St Michael and All Angels, Adbaston, Staffordshire, which is close to the route of the B&LJ Canal. The curate who celebrated the wedding was Charles Thomas Dawes and the witnesses Sarah Arkinstall and William Arkinstall. Jane was born in Adbaston, the daughter of Thomas Arkinstall and Jane Elizabeth Armson.[29] It is tempting to read doctrinal significance into the fact that Dargan registered his home parish as St Thomas' Church of Ireland parish, Marlborough Street, Dublin and that he was married in an Anglican church.[30] It was the norm in those days for a wedding to take place in the bride's home parish and perhaps like many a young man he was not that concerned about religious faith.

We can presume that William met his future wife while working on Telford's canals. There is no mention of members of William's family being present nor of a honeymoon. The couple did not have any children.

Looking North

Returning to Dublin with his new wife, Dargan decided to focus his business efforts on Ireland, looking around for more substantial projects than simply fixing roads or building canal sections. The north-east of the country was then more developed than the rest of Ireland so it made sense for him to concentrate his energies there. He won a contract for major improvements to the centre of Banbridge, Co. Down, the first of several projects he undertook in the north. Between 1831 and 1833

Dargan built a new market house in the town (still standing), dug a deep excavation to lower the steep main street (590 ft long and 16 ft wide/180 x 5 metres) and built a granite arch across it with a carriage road on either side, at a cost of £19,000 plus £2000 for the market house.[31] These works completely changed the appearance of the town.

The pretty little Anglican church of St Michael and All Angels, Adbaston, Staffordshire where William Dargan married Jane Arkinstall on 13 October 1828.

The entry in the registry for the marriage of Dargan and Jane Arkinstall. Courtesy Staffordshire Records Office.

Dargan dealt with a local man on this project, William Reilly DL, advising him that it would give Banbridge a 'novel and interesting appearance'.[32] Others were not so enthusiastic: writing in the OS Memories of Ireland, Lt George Bennett RE said when he saw the cut in 1834 he thought while it was 'of great benefit to travellers, [it] is none to the inhabitants, indeed, on the contrary, and it is the subject of much complaint'.[33] More recently the market house was described as 'a foursquare-plus building of random blackstone with heavy granite quoins at the corners and to the central projection'.[34]

When all had been completed Dargan wrote to Reilly in February 1833 requesting payment, saying his plant and capital were all tied up and 'I am greatly in want of all the monies due me to get on with the [Kingstown] Railway.'[35] Two months later Dargan wrote again, from his new office at 34 Anglesea Street. He had 'much reason to regret having ever contracted for these works as I am considerably the loser by them' and a month later he was 'miserably in want of money' and 'it was a great hardship' that £700 was retained because part of the work was incomplete, a part that was not in the contract, according to Dargan.[36] By September 1833 all was finished but Dargan still had twelve months' unpaid bills and unless these were settled he would have to resort to 'some unpleasant means'.[37] He was paid, finally, but in the summer of 1834 as he struggled to finish the Kingstown Railway, referred to malicious gossip: 'Some parties who meddle more in my affairs than I wish, have represented to my friends that the cause of my not being sooner settled with at Banbridge was owing to the improper and defective manner in which the work was done,' a charge he stoutly denied.[38] Some years later he worked with Reilly again, improving Carnbane Hill on the Banbridge-Belfast road and again he had to wait some time before being paid.[39]

Kilbeggan Canal

Another troublesome watery project of Dargan's was an 8-mile (13 km) branch off the Grand Canal in Co. Westmeath funded by a £14,000 government loan.[40] He began work around 1830 on what should have been a straightforward job but problems arose right at the start. Initially Dargan took his own levels but the company insisted he use those prepared by its former engineer, John Killaly, even though Dargan reported there was an error of 20 inches (50 cm) in them, a miscalculation that would cost him dearly in extra work.

The Grand Canal Company eventually conceded there was an error but were not so keen to compensate their contractor for the cost of making good the resultant leaks and breaches. This was Dargan's version of events, given to a parliamentary committee in 1836: 'I thought, very naturally, that as I had more work to do in consequence of those errors, I had a right to be paid. I put forward my claim, and we disputed a long time about it, and the account was not settled. And I must say, for the purpose of keeping on good terms with the Canal Company, whom I respected, I gave up the entire sum.'[41] A job he thought would take a year took four and it was another two years before he reached a settlement of £2657, writing to the company in 1835: 'It may be understood that from and after Monday next I shall be relieved from any expence [sic] for maintenance or care of said canal.'[42] The branch closed in 1961, the entrance was dammed and the navigation drained. At the time of writing the harbour buildings and basin have been well restored but the navigation remains dry. A community employment scheme restored the canal and the masonry and warehouses are in pristine condition. All it lacks is water.

The years around Dargan's thirtieth birthday on 7 February 1829 were difficult and challenging in business terms. Before establishing his reputation he had taken on several projects, possibly underpricing them or employing less-than-professional subcontractors and then not giving the job his full attention. This suggests that although Dargan had acquired many skills from some outstanding engineers he was still learning. One factor was that in those days the roles of engineer and contractor were ill-defined and sometimes interchangeable.[43] Inadequate surveys and specifications by poorly qualified technicians and surveyors left the contractor responsible and he had to make good the deficiency or did not receive his fee.

Dargan was now ready to move on from small, troublesome road repair and canal contracts to a new kind of engineering project, one that would directly affect his fortunes for the rest of his life.

The First Passenger Railway in Ireland

Before the arrival of the railways, canals and horses and walking were the main means of transport.[44] Although proposals for a railway from Kingstown to the city reached the House of Commons as early as 1825[45] the first Irish railway act passed by the British parliament was for the Limerick & Waterford Railway in 1826, a time when water dominated transport with 487 miles of canals and waterways in use in Ireland.[46] When the cross-channel packet station moved from Howth to Kingstown, William Cubitt estimated the cost of a canal to the city at £270,000, with locks a further £50,000.[47]

There was derision from many quarters at the notion that Ireland could support even one railway – previous schemes had perished on the rocks of conservatism. The first proposal for a line between Dublin and Kingstown was as early as 1825, drawing opposition from assorted interests: cab drivers, cart owners and respectable Kingstown residents who feared an influx of the lower orders. Canal promoters suggested the main problem with a railway would be its excessive efficiency: goods delivered too quickly and in bulk would create a glut and ruin traders and merchants. Others dismissed any such objections as being a ridiculous sop to favour 'a few nursery maids descending from ... Kingstown to the sea at Dunleary'.[48]

The company set about raising finance with the capital for the Dublin & Kingstown Railway (D&KR) being £200,000 in £10 shares (about 25 million today). The petition to the Commons refers to a railway 'from, at or near Trinity College in the City of Dublin to the pier at Kingstown'.[49] Strong opposition at both ends of the line meant it was shorter than projected. Alexander Nimmo's construction estimate of 1831 was £103,000, revised a year later by George Stephenson to £90,000 plus £20,000 for buildings based on a long embankment from Westland Row to Serpentine Avenue whose arches he suggested could be used for artisan dwellings.[50] The £78,000 list of share subscribers included 'Wm Dargan, C.E.' of Merrion Street who subscribed £2000 to the new railway, a substantial sum and a marker of his confidence in the project.

The canal basin of the Grand Canal Kilbeggan branch, everything in place except water.

But public scepticism and opposition persisted. Trinity College decided to 'oppose a Bill about to be introduced for erecting a railway for steam carriages at the north end of the College and partly on College land'.[51] It forced the company to move its proposed terminus, probably designed by Vignoles, from a site near Thomas Clarendon's riding school, livery stables and knackers at 200 Great Brunswick (Pearse) St to its present location.[52] The Dublin Penny Journal journal described opposition to the whole railway project and the proposed central terminus site thus: 'Vague fears, misrepresentations, and other causes, created an outcry against such a proposition, and it was ultimately abandoned.'[53] John Macneill, who should have known better, voiced serious concerns about the D&KR's long-term viability: 'I must confess I have some doubts as to the ultimate success of the Rail Road, at least for another half century. I would by no means recommend a friend to take any shares.'[54] Ironically much of Macneill's later career focused largely on building and promoting railways.

Another group sceptical about the railway's viability was the office of the Commissioners of Public Works (CPW). Within days of the passing of the Kingstown Railway act, Thomas Pim, a director, wrote to the CPW to explain the line would give employment to hundreds of labourers, improve communications with Britain, boost exports and lead to the development of Kingstown harbour; tagging on a request for a loan of £100,000.[55]

Table 3.2: D&KR SURVEY OF VEHICLES USING THE ROCK ROAD, BLACKROCK, 1832

Vehicles	Nos	Average occupants	Total occupants
Private coaches	36,287	2	72,574
Hackneys	7272	4	29,088
Private cars	133,537	4	534,148
Public cars	186,108	4	744,432
Gigs	24,175	2	48,350
Saddle horses	46,164	1	46,164
Total	433,543		1,520,920

To support the company's application to parliament, Charles Vignoles, the chief engineer, took a vehicle survey on the Rock Road at Blackrock daily for eight and a half months up to April 1832 (Table 3.2). This showed over 400,000 vehicles used the road in that time. Vignoles averaged 4167 person-journeys per day, which he rounded to 4000 train fares at 6d, equalling £100 per day or £36,500 p.a. On

£500,000 capital less expenses and loan interest of £11,500, this would produce a return of 5 per cent or £25,000. This rosy scenario presumed of course there would be an almost 100 per cent transfer of traffic from road to rail, leaving the Rock Road deserted, an unlikely scenario.[56] However, when the Liverpool & Manchester Railway opened it registered a 500 per cent increase in passenger numbers over recorded road traffic. It seemed there was plenty of potential traffic for a railway in Dublin.

Charles Blacker Vignoles (1793–1875): An Unfortunate Engineer

Born in Wexford, Vignoles was a peppery character who trained, like Dargan, under Telford and then joined the British army, gaining valuable engineering experience in America and all over Europe. In 1825 he worked with the eminent engineer George Stephenson on the survey of the Liverpool & Manchester Railway. Among his European achievements was the bridge over the River Dnieper at Kiev. His military background helped when negotiating a Treasury loan for the D&KR with Col. John Fox Burgoyne who chaired the Commissioners of Public Works. He invented the flat-bottomed rail laid directly onto a sleeper without the use of a 'chair' to hold it in place. It is common in France and is known as the Vignoles rail.

Paying him a backhanded compliment, John Macneill wrote to Maj. Donald Macneill, another engineer, that if he came across Vignoles he 'need not shun his society' despite his French name but there was 'more information to be got from Mr [Alexander] Nimmo in half an hour than from him in a lifetime'. Olinthus Vignoles in his biography said his relation, known as 'the Colonel', was impetuous, imprudent and hot-tempered.

F.R. Conder, an engineering pupil of Robert Stephenson, graphically describes Vignoles' rages, with a dig at his French origins: 'He was chiefly known and dreaded by the staff … by his method of evincing displeasure when anything went amiss. It was a method often witnessed on the banks of the Seine, but which does not tend to get the greatest amount of work out of the educated Englishman. It consisted in gesticulating in the midst of the room, swearing in a loud scream … profusion of blasphemy, enforcing the volley of startling oaths by stamping on the floor, and finally plucking frantically at the hair.'

Vignoles' salary on the D&KR was a healthy £500 plus £3000 for surveyors, draughtsmen and model makers, though he was less than successful in managing his own finances. On his fiftieth birthday he wrote he had been an engineer for twenty years but was 'a poorer man than at my start. ... I have gained money but never had the art of keeping it'. Indeed he was known even by relations as an 'unfortunate' engineer. In later life he was the first civil engineering professor at University College London and then President of the Institution of Civil Engineers.

Dargan became heavily involved with the preliminary work on the D&KR, long before he won the contract to build it. He met Vignoles early in 1832 and the two worked well together. Dargan often travelled to meetings at Vignoles' offices at South John Street, Liverpool, where staff drew up plans for the railway. Vignoles promised the company he would spend a third of his time on the D&KR and in 1832 alone made forty visits to Dublin, sometimes staying for one day before heading back across the Irish Sea.[57] In April 1832 Dargan and he spent a week in Liverpool working on the railway plans after which Dargan took Vignoles to see his handiwork on the Stanley Sands embankment, similar to the proposed coastal route of the railway. Travelling back from Holyhead to Liverpool, Dargan paid £4 2s for inside seats.[58]

Many of the D&KR directors and investors were Quakers, who had the financial resources to complete such a revolutionary project. The Society of Friends played a key role in Dublin business and what Richard Harrison describes as the 'delicately balanced sectarianism' of Dublin commercial life.[59] They were a distinct grouping and most knew each other or were related by blood or marriage. The leading Quaker behind the D&KR was Thomas Pim along with James Perry (1794–1858), later a railway investor and a major influence on Dargan's career.[60]

Dargan was spending a lot of unpaid time on preliminary work for the D&KR: planning the route, dealing with landowners, discussing potential engineering problems, investing and helping to raise finance. Although all this diverted him from other revenue-earning projects it was a shrewd time investment. Cooperation with Vignoles and the directors of the company was a calculated risk but it would pay off handsomely if the line went ahead and if he won the contract. From his time in England Dargan recognized the future of transport lay with railways and if anyone could finance the first one in Ireland it would be the D&KR directors. Whoever succeeded in building the first line in Ireland would be leagues ahead of his engineering competitors as lines would likely spring up all over the country. It was a gamble that paid off handsomely.

Winning the D&KR Contract

In December 1832 the D&KR board presented Dargan with £50 in gratitude for his services.[61] This group was fair and reasonable but never profligate with company funds, so the services were doubtless considerable. Advertisements inviting tenders to build the line appeared in the press in Dublin, Liverpool, Leeds, Birmingham and London. When the directors opened seven tenders on 26 January 1833, Dargan's was the lowest at £83,000 (about 10 million today), £11,000 below the next lowest; the highest was £142,000. The company duly awarded him the contract and Vignoles and Pierce Mahony, the company's lawyer based in Dame Street, prepared the detailed legal document and the costs of almost every single item on the line.[62] The line was to open no later than 1 June 1834 with a penalty of £100 for every week over schedule and a bonus of £50 per week for early completion. Above all Dargan would not be paid for any extras. But as Olinthus Vignoles dryly observed, 'these stringent clauses did not prevent that gentleman claiming and receiving an extra sum of £26,000'.[63] Commenting on the fact that D&KR cost £63,000 per mile against the Manchester and Leeds at £50,000, Anthony Marmion remarked rather sourly: 'It is not, therefore, surprising to see the fortunes that have been acquired by Mr Dargan and others who had the early railway contracts.'[64] Building a public railway was venturing into unknown territory: no one in Ireland had done it before and it was rather more than making a road and placing a line of rails on top. The contract required guarantors but as Dargan said, the real security he offered was that he was paid only as he completed sections of the work.

Dargan had a clear advantage over his competitors in that he knew rather more than anyone else about the railway project and had been working closely for some time with senior figures in the company. However, there is no truth in the fable that when challenged at a dinner party he scribbled down a cost estimate for the D&KR on a slip of paper in a matter of minutes. In a business where accurate costing of materials and labour is vital it is certain he would never have used such slipshod methods. Furthermore, his wife Jane later rejected this suggestion with a dismissive 'False' written beside a newspaper account of the supposed instant calculation.

Having won the contract, the next hurdle was compulsory purchase of the land to build the railway, apart from the section on an embankment across the sea from Merrion to Blackrock. Dargan and Vignoles attended the numerous land valuation jury sittings that also determined decisions on trespass precautions, safety and train speeds. In the course of discussing the unfortunate death of Liverpool MP William Huskisson, which marred the opening of the Liverpool & Manchester Railway in 1830, Vignoles admitted D&KR trains might travel at speeds up to 30 mph (48 kph).[65]

Death on the Railway: William Huskisson MP

Huskisson's death at the opening of the first passenger railway, the Liverpool & Manchester in 1830, was a Titanic moment: the circumstances being these. The Duke of Wellington, British Prime Minister at the time, was also present and might be held partly responsible for one of the very first railway fatalities. The glory days of Waterloo and Napoleon's defeat were long past and although still powerful, Wellington was deeply unpopular for his rigid opposition to political reform. He and fellow Tory, Liverpool MP William Huskisson, leader of the more liberal wing of the party, had a bitter falling out over the issue.

On the opening day the inaugural train had stopped halfway at Parkside to take water. As Huskisson and his friends strolled along the track, Wellington gave him a faint regal wave from his carriage and opened the door. Huskisson and his colleagues saw the chance for a reconciliation and he rushed over. Someone then saw the Rocket *bearing down on the adjacent track and shouted to Huskisson to get into the carriage. Huskisson tried to scramble round the open door, stumbled and fell with his leg across the rail just as the* Rocket *reached that spot. He died that evening in Eccles from his injuries. Huskisson's death cast a shadow over railway optimism that must have touched Dargan and every other railway promoter.*

That day Wellington's train continued to Manchester where despite a heavy police and military presence it was met by a vast mob that roared and waved banners reading 'Remember Peterloo', hurling stones at the carriages. The Iron Duke beat a hasty retreat and following these two events the train returned to Liverpool with a lot less gaiety than it had when it departed.

The railway press of the time dismissed claimant landowners as greedy and obstructionist. Most land claims were settled easily, such as that made by the Pembroke Estate;[66] one or two were not. Dargan paid one Catherine Moran £5 for loss of land she had rented at Irishtown. William Hodgens of Newtownpark Avenue, a dedicated sea bather, showed Dargan an address he planned to publish that stated the railway would ruin all sea bathing by 'stilling the waters and allowing filth from the sewers and otherwise to deposit there'.[67] Dargan believed Hodgens would travel to London to oppose the railway and urged the company to settle quickly. In an era when the city's sewage was pumped untreated onto the shoreline there were real concerns about a railway being built across an embankment with the sea on either side, trapping sewage. The area on the landward side was later reclaimed to preserve what became Booterstown marsh and to create Blackrock Park. Meanwhile Hodgens' claim rose from £150 to £500 and then £800, which the board finally paid him.[68]

Resisting the Railway

Two of the most vehement opponents of the railway lived on the seafront in Blackrock: Lord Cloncurry of Maretimo House (now demolished) and Rev. Sir Harcourt Lees of Blackrock House, who managed to gain exemption from the compulsory land purchase orders applying to lesser mortals. In October 1832 Cloncurry wrote to the railway company: 'I continue to believe that the proposed undertaking does not hold out such national or other probable benefits as should induce me to make the contemplated sacrifices.'

The D&KR had to offer both parties increasingly generous inducements before gaining leave to proceed. The landowners drove a hard bargain and the final settlement involved the construction of 'a shortened tunnel, fishing and bathing lodges, a camera-obscura tower, a boat-slip with pier and harbour, and an iron-latticed bridge leading from the grounds across the railway to the sea, the whole of the buildings … being executed in the very best style of Italian architecture'.[69] The two gentlemen also agreed to accept sizeable monetary compensation: £7500 (Lees) and £3000 (Cloncurry). Some of the mainly derelict buildings are still visible from the Dart line south of Blackrock. Over the summer there were also complaints from delicate local residents that during meal breaks Dargan's men were prone to frolic in the sea au naturel.

An arched pedestrian side tunnel under the
Kingstown Railway near Pearse station

The remains of the temple-style bathing shelter that the railway company built near Blackrock at the behest of Lord Cloncurry.

A Dart train leaving Booterstown station on a stormy day. As an economy measure the line from Merrion to Blackrock was built across a sea inlet.

Starting on the Kingstown Railway

A month before he began to build the railway Dargan received the sad news that his father, Patrick Dargan, had died aged eighty-three on 12 March 1833. He was buried in Killeshin graveyard alongside his wife Elizabeth.

Dargan's men broke the ground at Salthill on 11 April 1833 and while excavating at Monkstown discovered a good supply of granite for use on the sleepers and the sea wall. Dargan leased Salt Hill House as his works headquarters for a year at a rent of £100. In May he had 1000 men at work with plans to employ 3000 by midsummer. There were problems, however: apart from a few brought in from England almost all the men were unskilled, lived in poverty and did not have the stamina for heavy physical work until regular wages and a better diet built up their strength. Low productivity meant unequal wage rates and within a fortnight there were stoppages by aggrieved workers with reports of intimidation and the presence of mounted police. A few days later groups of men demanding work brought the site to a halt, an area of contention being piece-rate wages. Dargan was paying out £1200 in wages every week; the daily rate was 1s 6d a day but the better men could earn 2s 6d. To put that in context: a large top-quality loaf of bread cost 7d so an ordinary day's work would buy two and a half such loaves. After resolving these problems another strike broke out the following month. The police arrested James Byrne, Simon Byrne and Christopher Murray, three of the combinators (labour organizers) and sent them for trial.[70]

Vignoles reported to the D&KR board in August 1833 that it must pay Dargan regularly as his men were moving 3000 cubic yards of material a day; he was spending £1200 weekly in wages and 'this great expenditure must be met by correspondent advances'.[71] With blasting and heavy excavation, accidents and injuries were common: labourers were considered to be working entirely at their own risk there being no employer liability. Within weeks rock blasting at Salthill injured a workman and during the summer rock falls badly injured several others. They went either to Baggot St Hospital or local dispensaries and the company reluctantly gave £5 to three such dispensaries, adding rather coldly that it was 'unable to dispense any portion of the Company's funds for such purposes, however meritorious they may be'.[72] It later mellowed and asked Dargan to approach Dr Murray of Kingstown and Dr Benson at Baggot St with a payment offer for treating its workmen.

The Commissioners of Public Works, whose loan made the project possible, reported very favourably on the works at the end of 1833, noting in particular that Dargan paid his men regularly every week.[73] Mentioning this in their report suggests it was rare enough. The Commissioners also referred to public concern about the risk of a railway running across the sea for 2½ miles (4 km). One account put this rather coyly: 'A smile will be raised at the recollections of the good-natured predictions of the direful and destructive effect of winter storms.'[74] These warnings were in many cases anything but good-natured and as events turned out, well founded.

This arched gateway is all that survives of the Salthill House Hotel where Dargan had an office during the railway's construction. The directors of the Kingstown Railway held a dinner here to celebrate the opening of the line on 17 December 1834.

Dublin and Kingstown Railway

Track layout, based on an original plan prepared by Charles Vignoles and drawn by Goerge Beaver under the direction of Thomas Woodhouse as an Appendix to the Second Annual Report of the Commissioners of Public Works, Ireland, 1833.

In line with practice at the time, Vignoles' track design of iron rails laid on granite sleepers was meant to create total rigidity but made for an uncomfortable ride. It also caused heavy wear on rolling stock and in time was replaced.

Dargan told a House of Lords committee in 1836 that the most expensive part of the works was not the troublesome sea embankment but the retaining walls near Westland Row (Pearse) station, which he assured the company would 'outlast the pyramids'.[75] This was an unfortunate boast: as Grierson noted most of these walls were inadequate, needing heavy tie rods to hold them together some years later and the masonry was poor quality 'probably owing to the haste with which it was constructed'.[76] The line was raised and today still runs above street level as far as Lansdowne Road with its distinctive overbridges, some quite low, and the neat little pedestrian arches demanded by Wide Street Commissioners. Dargan laid temporary rails at the end of 1833, setting them into granite blocks. Engineering practice at the time required total rigidity of track and trackbed so workmen drilled two 1-inch holes 6 inches deep into each granite block, sealing the hole with oak plugs. When the sleeper was in position they drove an iron spike into each plug causing it to spread and grip the sides of the hole. This secured the chair that in turn held the rail. The total inflexibility of the track caused heavy wear and tear on engines, carriages, rails and track and after three years Vignoles admitted he had made a mistake and relaid the line with wooden sleepers.[77] The granite blocks with their distinctive drill holes were reused and are still visible today on the sea wall from Merrion to Blackrock.

Vignoles and Dargan worked closely together and in November 1833 the company's senior engineer told the directors that he and Dargan were travelling to Liverpool to study engine and management methods on the St Helen's Railway. The two continued to meet regularly and one Sunday in December they walked the entire line together. Christmas Day was a normal working day for Vignoles.[78]

New year 1834 dawned and the company was anxious to fix a June opening date; but Dargan wrote that as he had been delayed fourteen weeks by Messrs Cloncurry and Lees he was now unreasonably expected to complete in twelve months what his contract required him to do in fifteen months. The only way he could keep to the original schedule was to take on more men and he would do this if the board gave him £50. The directors agreed to give him a £1000 bonus if the line was ready by 18 June 1834, dropping to £500 if it was delayed until 1 July with a weekly penalty of £100 for a later completion date.[79] Vignoles costed his plans for the Westland Row terminus at £1664 6s 5½d and the D&KR accepted Dargan's tender of £1700, less £600 for items such as earthworks.[80]

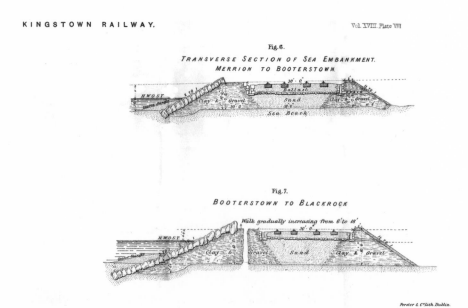

Engineer's drawings of sections of the sea embankment on the line between Merrion and Blackrock taken from the 1887 *Transactions of the Institution of Civil Engineers of Ireland*.

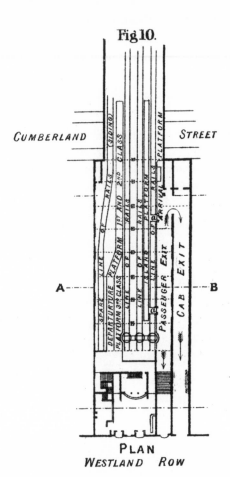

Fig. 10.

Vol. XVIII, Plate IX

NOTE. a. a. are Gangways between Arrival and Island Platforms.

PLAN
WESTLAND ROW

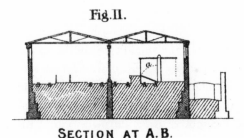

Fig. II.

SECTION AT A.B.

A plan of the terminus at Westland Row (Pearse) station as Dargan built it and before the loop line extension across the city built in the early 1890s. The station was and remains a compact space and to allow passengers to enter and exit speedily a series of wooden drawbridges could be lowered across the tracks and then raised.

By now Dargan was constructing the Ulster Canal and in the time-honoured tradition of builders was dividing his time between different projects, despite a clause in his contract forbidding such double-jobbing. The D&KR realised he was neglecting the railway and Vignoles' letter of 12 February 1834 has a distinctly frosty tone:

> *Sir,*
>
> *By virtue of the authority vested in me under your deed of contract with the company, I hereby give you notice and direction to commence <u>forthwith</u> working at the excavations and rock blasting through the lawns of Lord Cloncurry and Sir Harcourt Lees during the night <u>as well</u> as the day, taking proper care to have superintendents and sufficient fire grates.*
>
> *Should the Irish workmen or miners demur about working at night you can have no difficulty in procuring men from England or Wales.... I trust you will not put me to the necessity of any further trouble by hesitating to comply with this order.*
>
> *I am, sir, your obedient servant,*
> *Chas Vignoles, Engineer, Dublin and Kingstown Railway*[81]

The obedient servant was himself often absent from the works but despite this the two had a perfectly cordial meeting a few days later. There may have been a theatrical element in this missive, possibly for the benefit of the D&KR board. One thing is sure: the sound of rock blasting must have kept people in Blackrock awake for quite some time while at Seapoint Dargan was expected to use a diving bell to secure the track foundations.

Col Burgoyne visited the railway in May 1834 and Vignoles wrote with some glee how the two former soldiers used a heavy charge to bring down 200 cubic yards of sandstone cliff at Salthill at, he estimated, less than a penny a yard.[82] By now it was clear Dargan could not possibly finish the line by June and instead of relying on Vignoles' reports the directors took matters into their own hands, making weekly site inspections to assess progress and giving Dargan further instructions.[83]

Vignoles may not have been present as often as the company would like but he served in other ways. In July 1834 he called on the youthful future queen, Princess Victoria, at Kensington Palace to ask if she would perform the opening ceremony of the railway. He was unsuccessful, either because of fears for her safety in Ireland or, as Charles Forth wrote to Vignoles later, she was afraid of catching cholera in Dublin.[84] (Dargan was to entertain her to tea as queen some twenty years later.)

On 9 October 1834 the locomotive *Hibernia* made a trial run to Salthill hauling eight carriages packed with guests. Further trips followed and one train reached a speed of 60 mph, which must have been alarming for the passengers, few of whom would have travelled at much above 12 mph. However, the line was far from ready and dropping all inducements and threats, with a note of wearied acceptance, the directors asked their engineer when he thought the line might be finished.[85] Nature then intervened to delay matters further. On the night of 7 November the River Dodder flooded and swept away the railway bridge at Lansdowne Road. Dargan swiftly made good the damage and also repaired the sea embankments that had suffered storm damage.[86]

Open at Last

In a sudden and resolute decision, the board decided: 'That this railway be opened for the conveyance of passengers on Wednesday the 17th inst [December 1834] and that trains start from each end of the line every hour from 9 o-clock in the forenoon till 4 o'clock in the afternoon', but not on Sundays between 11 am and 2.30 pm.[87] The company carried its first mail consignment on 13 December (an important income source for all railways) and soon after there was a special train for the gentlemen of the press. Advertisements then announced the official opening for 17 December. The first class fare was a shilling, second 8*d* and third 6*d* with parcels being carried at 4*d* for the first cwt (approx. 50 kg) and a shilling up to 5 cwt (254 kg).

Geometrical Section of the First, Second, Third, and Fourth Class Carriages, with the Engine and Tender, passing Merrion, on their way to Kingstown.

A few months before the official opening *Hibernia* hauls a train of four carriages over the sea embankment near Merrion in 1834 with a dwelling-less view of Howth in the distance. At 18 ft (5.5 m) each carriage was tiny, while the fourth class carriage is essentially a goods wagon with seats. An engine crew of a driver and a fireman worked up to eighteen hours a day: note what appears to be a boy shovelling coal into the engine. This is one of a series of drawings that appeared in the *Dublin Penny Journal* prior to the opening of the railway. See illustration p.162 for a similar third-class carriage thirty years later.

At Dun Laoghaire station a long flight of steps, still in situ, leads from the platform to the original entrance with its fine Ionic columns. The building is John Mulvany's design and is now a restaurant.

The opening day was busy if low key, unlike almost every subsequent railway opening in Ireland. At 9 am *Hibernia* steamed out of Westland Row (Pearse) station with packed carriages. There were eight trains in each direction, plus an extra one from Kingstown, all full. Vignoles noted immense crowds burst the barriers in their eagerness to experience this amazing new form of transport and in total 5000 passengers travelled on the first day. The only unpleasant note was a foiled attempt to seize the cash box at Kingstown. That evening the directors sat down to dinner with Dargan and Vignoles in Marsh's Hotel, Salthill House, with the usual speeches, toasts and congratulations, all past differences forgotten.[88]

'May Success Crown Enterprise and Industry'

Two months earlier Dargan's workmen presented him with an inscribed silver cup. Grecian in style with coral edges ornamented by vine leaves and vine branch handles, it came from Law's of Sackville (O'Connell) Street and cost 36 guineas. The cup bore the following inscription: 'Presented to William Dargan Esquire, Contractor of the Dublin and Kingstown Railway, by the persons in his employment, in testimony of their respect. October 1834. May success crown enterprise and industry.' The cup's current whereabouts are unknown.

Vignoles' heartfelt comment on the opening of the line was: 'a delightful reward for the two years of incessant anxiety'. Although he did not hear the news for a few days, his wife, Mary, died on the opening day in Walton Lodge, Liverpool, an institution where she had been confined for some time.[89] Abandoning its earlier doubts the Public Works Commissioners thought the D&KR 'a very splendid work ... a great convenience as well as a source of enjoyment' for the people of Dublin'.[90] But John Macneill was still unconvinced: 'The Irish Railway opens this day. I understand the proprietors are much frightened at the cost and the probability of steam carriages running on the common road.'[91] The wife of Thomas Drummond, author of the *Railway Commissioners' Report* produced by Vignoles and Macneill, was a bit of a railway widow and less than impressed with it all, writing in 1838: 'My husband is in Dublin railroadsising ... The railway business will, I trust, soon be over.' And a month later: 'The horrid railroad report is finished. I suppose the Commissioners will be assailed with all sorts of abuse.'[92] The Kingstown line was a commercial success from the start: in the first year it made £6500 profit after all expenses and loan repayments, a trend that continued for many years.

An Early Trip on the Kingstown Railway

This description of a spin on the D&KR a few months before the official opening appeared in 'Thirteen Views of the D&KR', the Dublin Penny Journal *of 30 August 1834:*

> Hurried forward by the agency of steam, the astonished passenger glides, like Asmodeus, over the summits and the houses of our city – presently is transported through green fields and tufts of trees – then skims across the surface of the sea, and taking shelter under the cliffs, coasts among the marine villas, and through rocky excavations, until he finds himself in the centre of a vast port, which unites in pleasing confusion the bustle of a commercial town with the amusements of a fashionable watering place.

> Asmodeus, the demon of lust and gambling, flies through the night and lifts the roof off people's houses to spy on their nocturnal activities, a curiously voyeuristic analogy for the infant railway.

Some years after the opening an anonymous letter from someone in the D&KR to the *Railway Times* eloquently described Dargan's early construction problems. The line crossed seven city streets and then ran through 'lawn parks and villas, grounds for which we had to pay dearly indeed. From Merrion to Kingstown our works are in the sea, touching the shore only in two or three places, at each of which we interfere … with the villas of gentlemen … [and] had to pay very high both in works and money.'[93]

The terminus of the line as it opened was near the East Pier at Dun Laoghaire and there was intense opposition to it going any nearer the town from both Daniel O'Connell and Thomas Gresham. When this opposition was overcome the company asked Dargan to complete the half-mile extension to the bottom of Crofton Road and this time the Commissioners of Public Works gave a loan of £37,000 without hesitation. It opened in May 1837. A flight of steps led from the platform to the original station building elegantly designed by John Skipton Mulvany, now a restaurant. Mulvany also designed an extension to the Salthill House Hotel soon after he set up his architect's practice in 1836.

The D&KR was and remained a success as passenger numbers grew steadily. In the first six weeks it had almost 40,000 passengers and within seven years of the opening by 1842 it was carrying over 1.6 million passengers per year.[94] Despite the technical problems it was a triumph for Dargan, justifying his early commitment to the company and confirming the viability of railways. Even more important it established his reputation as the premier railway builder whose experience and training placed him leagues ahead of other contractors when submitting railway and other engineering tenders.

Finding Traces of the Kingstown Railway Today

Despite many changes over 180-odd years, including the arrival of the Dart, there are still quite a few original traces of Ireland's first railway. Dargan's Westland Row (Pearse) Station has been completely rebuilt and the site of the original D&KR platform is probably to the east of the northbound platform where a long incline, once used by horse-drawn carriages, leads down to Sandwith St. South of the station several of the overbridges with their pedestrian side tunnels are still extant: the one at Clanwilliam Terrace is particularly low.

Farther out, from Merrion Gates onwards, the old granite sleepers that held the rails have been recycled to make a sea wall, many with drill holes still visible, while Booterstown marsh on the land side of the railway is now a bird sanctuary. At Blackrock only the twin towers of the overbridge from Maretimo are still standing. Cloncurry's house has been demolished but travelling south there are some traces of the little harbour on the left.

Just before the west pier at Dun Laoghaire a pillar on the left marks the site of the original Kingstown station. From beyond the Coal Harbour the route of the line is visible on either side.

The Ulster Folk and Transport Museum has preserved a 3rd class, 35 seat D&KR carriage from the 1860s, no.48, which shows the Spartan travel conditions of the day. It had seats for thirty-five passengers and was open to the elements.

The Dalkey Tube

The Dalkey atmospheric railway was something of an oddity, a curious engineering experiment that in many ways was ahead of its time. It ran the 2 miles (3 km) from Dun Laoghaire up to Dalkey as an extension to the D&KR. Engineers Samuel Clegg and Joseph Samuda invented this novel system using vacuum propulsion and in 1840 built an experimental track near Wormwood Scrubs. There was no locomotive involved but a tongue attached to the carriage slotted into a valve opening in the top of a long tube laid between the rails. A steam pump at Dalkey sucked the air from the tube to create a vacuum, much to the abhorrence of nature, and when the pressure built up sufficiently, the driver released the brake and the force of the vacuum drew the train at some speed up the 1 in 115 incline to Dalkey. The air tube stopped 560 yards short of the terminus to prevent overruns and the train coasted to a stop in Dalkey. The return journey was made by gravity.[95]

John Macneill, Charles Vignoles and James Pim of the D&KR had seen the system operating near Wormwood Scrubs (Macneill had finally come round to railways) and being convinced of its great potential, secured a loan from the Commissioners of Public Works to cover the construction costs.[96] Several Kingstown residents opposed the further extension of the railway and as a result the company had to cover in large parts of the line with girders and plates as well as sinking it to make it even less visible. Dargan began work in the autumn of 1842 on a straightforward construction job. The first trial runs took place the following August. The line was narrow and ran through a deep cutting as it still does today and when inspecting it prior to its opening on 29 March 1844, apart from some operational changes Major General Charles Pasley thought it 'perfectly efficient and safe'.[97]

That same year the *Athenaeum* published a lyrical description of a journey on the Dalkey air-train:

> The distance was performed in somewhat more than about two minutes, or at the rate of forty-five miles per hour. This is a whirlwind pace. I seemed merely to get into the machine to get out of it, and had very little jaunt for my money (but 3d however), which reminded me of the poor cookmaid, who complained she had small enjoyment of her bed, as the night passed away before she had well laid herself down...[98]

HISTORY OF THE KINGSTOWN RAILWAY

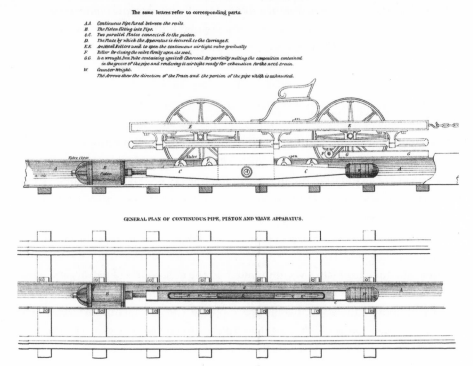

A drawing reveals the working of the unique track, piston, pipe and valve system as used on the atmospheric railway to Dalkey.

Moving into top gear, the writer judged this form of travel to be safe, clean and silent with just the 'rustle of autumn leaves swept forward by a low wind – very mysterious, and rather awful'. Passengers on a conventional steam train endured 'eternal puffing, panting, snorting, and fiery evominition'. But on the atmospheric there was no danger of being 'smothered and blinded with smoke, grit, gravel and coal dust' nor the hazards of a 'huge copper bomb-shell, ever ready to burst, and a furnace threatening to lick with its flamy tongues the whole wooden apparatus (human contents included)'.

George Irwin welcomed this new form of travel, noting that over 4300 passengers travelled on 12 May 1844, each paying an average fare of $2\frac{1}{2}$ pence. He observed: 'Were the valves and engines perfectly air-tight, a single stationary engine would give power to a line of one thousand miles as easily as to a line of one mile.'[99] There's the rub. With the technology of the time it was impossible to create a perfect seal as the train passed over the tube repeatedly and then closed the opening. It was said passengers could predict the arrival of a train by the hiss of air escaping from myriad tiny holes in the tube. Occasionally a strong wind could halt the downhill train some distance short of the Dun Laoghaire platform and any sort of breakdown closed the whole system. Popular lore also assigns blame to the coastal rats who allegedly developed a taste for the tube sealant.

The atmospheric railway ran successfully for ten years and there were plans to build part of the Cork line using it. However, in 1854 the D&KR decided to convert it to normal traction. The last air-train ran on 12 April and so this remarkable pioneering system came to an end.[100] Little remains of it today apart from a Dalkey road near the site of the pumping station named Atmospheric Road. It is still possible to see a short section of the Atmospheric route where the track runs parallel to the Dart line by walking along the Metals, a delightful pathway along the route of a tramway from the early nineteenth century that carried stone from Dalkey quarry down to Dun Laoghaire to build the harbour.[101]

FOUR

Northern Waters and Early Railways in Ireland and England

Just as he shrewdly predicted the future dominance of railways in transport, Dargan also recognized that the north of Ireland (an industrial area with pressing needs to transport the goods it produced) was the place to focus. This explains why many of his projects in the late 1830s were in Ulster, to the extent that for several years he maintained an office in York St, Belfast.

Connecting Lough Erne to Lough Neagh: The Ulster Canal

At almost the exact time Dargan began building the Kingstown Railway he also took on construction of one of the last canals to be built in Ireland. The Ulster Canal connected Lough Erne and Lough Neagh and allowed conveyance of goods from mid-Ulster to Belfast on the Lagan Navigation and to other ports such as Newry for onward shipment to England. The 46-mile (74 km) canal ran south-west from Charlemont on the River Blackwater south of Lough Neagh, through Benburb, Caledon, Midleton, Monaghan and Clones to join the Upper Erne at

Charlemont, the first lock on the Ulster Canal where it enters the River Blackwater. Adjacent to the lock are the walls of the original dry dock. Although derelict, there are regular proposals to reopen the canal as a north-south initiative.

Wattle Bridge near Belturbet. Telford, Dargan's earlier mentor, was the second engineer to survey the route in 1826 and Dargan the second contractor appointed. As in several other areas, Telford had a hand in Dargan winning the contract: 'I did all in my power to forward it,' he wrote in July 1833.[1] Another familiar face was James Perry (1794–1858), a D&KR director and an early managing director of the canal company; his influence is ever present in Dargan's career. The contract price was £154,385 8s 'of good and lawful money' but the final cost turned out to be £230,000.[2] Pierce Mahony was solicitor to this company as well as the D&KR.

From March 1833 to spring 1839 Dargan rented a house from the Caledon Estate in the Co. Tyrone town of that name and made it his headquarters. Although the rent was £18 per annum the house was in poor condition and he repaired it himself at a cost of £25, a sum he expected Lord Caledon would reimburse, without success.[3] Later the two set up the Ulster Canal Carrying Co. to convey goods on the waterway; Dargan bought it outright in 1843. Dargan chose a kinsman as his assistant, Patrick Moore, later a railway contractor in his own right, as well as his brother James Dargan. To begin the work he quite sensibly moved some of his skilled men and overseers from the Kingstown Railway to the Ulster Canal. This interrupted progress on the railway, greatly annoying the directors. This innocent move also led to a sectarian dispute, not for the first time in the history of Northern Ireland. At least one labourer, Thomas Clancy, was attacked and a local Protestant clergyman, Rev. Henry Kennedy, complained to Dublin Castle about bringing in Catholic workmen from outside the area. Lord Gosford in turn wrote to Dargan urging him to use fairness and avoid any act that would disturb the peace.[4] In fact only 60 of around 2000 men employed were from outside the area but absurdly their religion became a source of contention and it is believed Dargan received several anonymous letters threatening violence if he did not employ more workmen from one religion or the other.

A terrace of estate houses in Caledon, Co. Armagh, one of which Dargan rented from the Caledon Estate while building the Ulster Canal.

A simple yet beautiful lock keeper's cottage on the Ulster Canal near Benburb.

The route was a tricky one and in a bid to economize, the company inflicted fatal damage to the canal's viability by reducing the number of locks and their size. Most of the twenty-five locks were 56 ft long and 12 ft wide (approx. 17 x 4 metres) but the one at Wattle Bridge was a mere 11 ft 8½ inches (3.6 m) across, the narrowest lock in Ireland. Boats were becoming bigger and many were simply too large to use the Ulster Canal.

As Dargan continued to divide his time between Dublin and the north he received complaints from both companies. In April 1835 the canal Company Secretary, James McCleery, objected that Dargan was building the canal too close to the Blackwater and the consequent breaches would undermine the waterway. Two months later McCleery was even more direct about the poor quality of the masonry work on the bridges. It was 'for the most part of the worst description, such as a county Irish road maker might be ashamed of'.[5] The last may have been a sly dig at Dargan's earlier employment on the turnpikes. The lock wings and walls would not sustain the impact of boats, he said, and the root problem was Dargan's lack of supervision, in other words his frequent absences in Dublin. The works in the Benburb area were among the most difficult sections: there were seven locks in a 1-km stretch where the canal squeezed past the Blackwater on one side and a limestone gorge on the other. One engineer described the route thus:

> The course of this portion of the line lay along the bottom of a steep ravine in limestone rock, parallel with the channel of a mill-race adjacent to the river Blackwater; the mill-race was, therefore, diverted into the river between the first and fifth locks of the canal. ... The masonry was all constructed of limestone from an adjacent quarry ... The locks are 73 feet long, 12 feet wide and vary in rise from 6 to 11 feet. They are all constructed in ashlar masonry.[6]

Farther south the route was easier and Dargan's men reached here in 1838, building a short tunnel under Old Cross Square in Monaghan, still visible and still watered. But the company was struggling and both Lord Caledon and James Perry sought government support.[7]

Sections of the canal opened as they were completed: the 24 miles from Monaghan to Charlemont opened in 1839 and the navigation throughout on 19 May 1842. Boats ran daily from Belfast to Moy, Caledon and Monaghan. Dargan was soon the canal's best customer, making a determined effort to build up the human and freight traffic, a project 'in which I am greatly interested', he told Reilly.[8] He ordered a goods and passenger boat, *Grand Junction*, from Belfast boat-builders, Coates & Young, brought it in sections to Portadown and launched it there in July 1842. His other boats on Lough Erne were *Countess of Erne*, *Shamrock*, *Countess of Caledon* and *Countess of Milan*. There were agents and stores at Belfast, Newry, Portadown, Monaghan, Clones and most towns along the route and a quay at Portadown with a direct rail link. He then bought several more boats, running some as far as Belleek, sold 'artificial manure' from his depots and even lent the canal stores at Monaghan to Fr Mathew for a temperance meeting.[9]

But despite all his efforts the Ulster Canal was in serious trouble. Poor receipts, low water levels, tiny locks, the inadequacy of the connecting Lagan Navigation and the delayed plan to build a link to the Shannon (later to become the Ballinamore & Ballyconnell Canal) were crippling the waterway. The arrival of the railway to Monaghan and Clones dealt the final blow and in 1850 John Macneill suggested the best prospect was to convert the waterway into a railway, an idea Dargan had by then come to support.[10] The owners had no hope of repaying the state loans they received to build it and in 1851 the Exchequer Loan Commissioners seized the canal before leasing it to Dargan who was now involved in every aspect of its running. By 1853 he had around fifty boats running on it, two steamers sailing from Warrenpoint and Newry to Liverpool, three boats on Lough Neagh and one on the Erne.[11]

Relics of the Ulster Canal

In the mid 1990s I drove, walked or cycled almost the entire length of the Ulster Canal. Many sections are still visible though some have been totally reclaimed as farmland. The only trace of one part of the route north of the border is a bridge standing in total isolation in the middle of a field. Some of the locks are intact, many of the beautiful lock-keepers' cottages are still visible (though most are derelict), while the cut under Cross Square in Monaghan town is still watered.

The canal store at Clones opened as a tourism and heritage centre in 1996 and many of the derelict locks near Monaghan have survived. A small section of the waterway at Benburb has been restored and watered. This stretch, which was so difficult to build, now comprises a delightful woodland walk and at the Charlemont end the remains of a dry dock are clearly visible.

There are regular proposals to reopen the entire canal as a north-south project. Doing so would connect Lough Neagh with the Shannon via the Shannon-Erne Waterway and on to the Royal and Grand canals, a superb notion.

Dargan finally disposed of his interest in the Ulster Canal, selling it to the Dundalk Steam Packet Co.[12] When Macneill surveyed it in 1861 it was in poor condition: 'I have to report that the canal in its present state is totally useless, some levels are quite empty, others deficient of water. ... The various railways ... passing through the same district of country have rendered the latter entirely useless.'[13] He concluded the only option was to remove the lock gates, drain the waterway and convert it to grazing land, exactly what happened to large sections of the canal; it was officially abandoned in 1931.

In a curious way the unsuccessful Ulster Canal provides a direct link to Dargan and his work of 170 years ago. Because it functioned for such a short period the sections that are still extant, in particular the bridges, lock walls and the delightful lock-keepers' cottages, although abandoned are in many cases virtually unaltered.[14]

Mourne Mountains and Belfast Reservoirs

The demand for a steady water supply from factories and mills in the Banbridge area led to the construction of a 253-acre reservoir at Island Reavy, Co. Down to channel water to the River Bann in the dry season. Once again working with William Reilly, Dargan won the contract worth almost £15,000 and began work in autumn 1837.[15] Major leaks appeared in early 1839 attributable to an error in the mortar mixture made by the engineer, John Bateman. Dargan's men picked out the mortar, caulked with oakum and filled with roman cement. This worked well and soon after the supervisor noted there were no leaks whatever: 'If it were ink I would not find enough escaping to write my name.'[16]

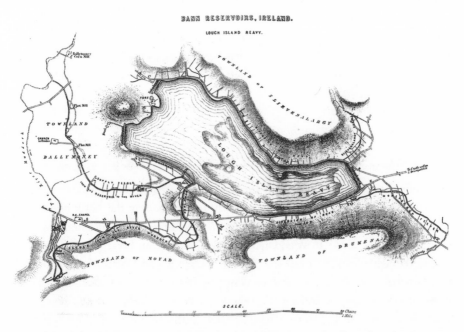

A plan of the Bann reservoir on Lough Island Reavy near Castlewellan, Co. Down.

A fine serving dish with the inscription 'Ulster Canal
Steam Carrying Company' with an illustration of PS
Hercules. The dish is in the Holyhead Maritime Museum.
(Photo: Christopher Day and Peter Scott Roberts)

To help meet Belfast's daily demand for six million gallons of water John
Macneill designed another reservoir at Solitude off the Antrim Road. He was also
engineer to the project, worth £8250, but left it almost entirely in the hands of
Dargan who began work in May 1841.[17] Harsh winters must have been expected
for part of his contract was to build a tower to store ice for sale to fishmongers. To
celebrate laying the first pipe Belfast Water Commissioners entertained Dargan's
220 men to ale and bread at Solitude House, 'which put them all in the best of good
humour – an excellent beginning', the Commissioners noted.[18] Dargan finished
the reservoir in the summer of 1843 though not before Macneill warned him the
fencing he put up was likely to be stolen 'in that part of the country'. Macneill
then told the board the works were 'perfect' and completed 'in a workmanlike
manner to my satisfaction'.[19]

Newry Canal and Steamers to Liverpool

Dargan further expanded his Ulster Canal Carrying Co. by running passenger and
goods steamers from Newry and Warrenpoint to Liverpool in the 1840s and 1850s.
He had up to six vessels, including the *Pearl*, the ill-fated *Sea Nymph* (see p.59)[20]
and the *Hercules*, a 148-ft wooden paddle steamer built in Liverpool in 1835 that
Dargan owned from 1851 until the mid–1850s. Holyhead Maritime Museum has
a rare memento of Dargan's shipping company: a superb meat platter used in the
galley of Ulster Canal Carrying Co. vessels for beef or mutton joints, suggesting
fine victuals were served in first class at least. In the centre of the large company
crest is an image of the *Hercules* under steam (see above).[21] The company's ships

provided a valuable service for some years and brought much business to Dargan's Ulster Canal Carrying Co. and indeed the Ulster Canal itself, which was his intention.

Death on the Mersey, 1846

Fog has always been a major threat to shipping and led to some major maritime disasters. In 1914, two years after Titanic *foundered, a collier rammed the* Empress of Ireland *in thick fog near Quebec. She sank within fourteen minutes killing 1000 people.*

A similar though smaller-scale tragedy occurred to one of Dargan's ships, the Sea Nymph, *an iron paddle steamer built at Greenock in 1845. On 25 May 1846 she was making passage from Clarence Dock, Liverpool to Newry under Captain Thompson with fifty deck passengers. In thick fog she cleared the Clarence Dock, sailing on the western side of the Mersey. Inbound from Sligo at the same time was the* Rambler *a vessel of the Glasgow and Londonderry SP Co. under the command of Captain McAllister carrying 250 passengers, mainly emigrants, and 300 animals. In poor visibility the* Sea Nymph *collided with the* Rambler, *holing her below the waterline. The collision caused the deaths of at least twelve passengers on the* Rambler *with many more injured, although neither ship sank.*

Small craft brought the remaining passengers ashore at Egremont. The dead were conveyed to St Alban's RC chapel, Liscard and buried the next day in a single grave. Fr Ambrose Lennon recorded them in the parish register as 'incogniti navigentes ex Hibernia' *(unidentified seafarers from Ireland). Eight names are recorded: Patrick Geoghagan, Martin and Brigid Ford, Patrick Lang, Brigid and Owen Furey, Patrick Charles O'Malley and Patrick Walsh. Interred with them were* 'quattuor cadavera incognita'.

At the inquest a week later both of the crews disputed events, as happens. The chief mate on the Rambler *said there was no rule about which channel vessels should follow while Samuel Easter from the Sea Nymph said he was only proceeding at four knots. The harbour master said Captain Thompson was at fault for sailing so close to the New Brighton shore that vessels entering the Mersey were in danger of running aground. The major cause of the collision was in fact that both ships had inadequate lights and lookouts for such poor weather conditions. The assessor, Captain Daniel RN, found both masters at fault, imposing a £200 deodand on the* Sea Nymph. *(Deodand: an archaic legal term for a fine imposed for causing a death, the money being donated to charity.)*[22]

Whatever about efforts to assign blame, the dreams of these twelve emigrants from the west of Ireland for a new life in America died with them that day in the cold waters of the River Mersey.

Sailors often consider some ships unlucky and the *Sea Nymph* falls into this category. Following the incident described, she collided with a schooner a few years later, again in the Mersey, killing the master, and a year after that she had a third accident in the same river at the entrance to Huskisson Dock, colliding with the *Connaught Ranger* inbound from Sligo, which was run aground at Egremont for repairs.[23] The Belfast SS Co. bought the *Sea Nymph* in 1853 and the government chartered her for war service in the Crimea. Reports of her demise were premature and she survived to bring him some gory trophies, among them several Russian muskets, 'a bloodstained bayonet ... bent by a cannonball' and a short sword 'with blood on the handle'.[24] She then sailed the Dublin-Holyhead route for the Chester & Holyhead Railway and after a long, eventful career was broken up in 1880. Dargan added several more ships on the route in the summer of 1851 including the 500-ton *Eagle*.[25] He sold the Ulster Canal Carrying Co. and its vessels to the Dundalk Steam Packet Co. in 1857

Dargan capitalized on his reputation for canal-building by taking a contract from the Newry Navigation Committee to develop this venerable waterway, arguably the first canal to be opened in Britain or Ireland (1741).[26] The job involved running it dry to widen and deepen the channel to take larger vessels and forming a junction between the old and new channels. A strike for higher wages led to stone throwing, riots and police bayonet charges with scathing comments from the press about the workmen's avarice: 'these gentlemen navvies ... have scarcely a bite to eat'.[27] The Newry Navigation letter books (appropriately showing water damage) record that by spring 1850 Dargan had nearly finished the job at a cost of £170,000, including the very handsome Victoria lock at Fathom.[28] The new canal and lock opened on 15 April 1850 with twenty-one vessels invited to make a trial run through the lock, among them the *Sea Nymph*, at the time in between collisions.[29]

Creating the Port of Belfast – Dargan's Island

Dargan is largely responsible for establishing Belfast as a major nineteenth-century port and shipbuilding centre. His contribution to its economic development is reflected in the naming of a cross-river rail bridge in recent years as the Dargan Bridge. The Dargan name is highly respected in Northern Ireland.

A painting by James Wilson of an emigrant ship leaving Belfast in 1852 shows the straight channel Dargan dug to help create the port of Belfast.

Belfast Harbour had for many years suffered from its geography: the awkward dog-leg approach, low water and inadequate quays made access difficult for shipping. The ubiquitous Telford suggested a ship canal leading to floating docks but a more feasible option was to cut a tidal channel through the flats and eliminate the two sharp bends in the river that caused the problem.[30] In 1839 the Belfast Ballast Board invited tenders from three companies, one of them Dargan's. The wording of the minutes suggests Dargan had tendered unsuccessfully against the contractor who won the original contract, a Mr Logan of Glasgow, but he died before starting work.[31] Macneill supported one of the other bidders but Dargan had a recommendation from Lord Caledon and an effusive reference from Col now Sir John Burgoyne: 'I believe Mr Dargan to be a man of much energy, zeal and intelligence, of thorough integrity, and a very considerable knowledge of the best modes of carrying out such undertakings as canals, railways, roads, bridges and harbour works.'[32]

All to the good but the fact that Dargan's tender of £32,500 was the lowest by £2500 probably carried more weight with the canny Belfast men.[33] Among his sureties was the omnipresent James Perry of Obelisk Park, Dublin (the house is now a residential home in Stillorgan). The mile-long Lagan cut was to run from Dunbar's Dock across the sloblands to Mile Water Perch. Dargan's method was to bank the ground and use a steam dredge to dig out the channel, dumping the spoil in the river on the Co. Down side. The amount of spoil produced was so great that

The entrance to Harland & Wolff's offices at Queen's Island, formerly called Dargan's Island, after its creator.

soon the pile was visible above the surface of the water and in time it grew in size to become an island of seventeen acres, described as 'a neat little island of sea-gathered soil'.[34] The Harbour Company planted trees and shrubs, laying out paths and making the island available for public recreation. It was known as Dargan's Island and became a much-needed public park and recreation centre with a crystal palace, an aquarium, a zoo and a place for concerts, fêtes, equestrian events, boat races and shows.[35]

In 1839 Dargan moved his office from Caledon to 121 York Street, Belfast, to be near his projects in the north-east and he completed the first phase of the Belfast Harbour works in early 1841.[36] So pleased was the Ballast Board that it decided to award him the contract for the second phase: 'a bargain should be made with a contractor without the formality of seeking tenders'.[37] This stage was similar to the first but the cost would be higher as interestingly Dargan estimated labour costs had increased by 16 per cent since 1839 and the works were more difficult. To un-water the cut he had to create two 150-yard dams. Working farther out in the channel it was not an option to wheel away the spoil so Dargan came up with an ingenious solution using fifty boats to shift the mud, which he filled with spoil at low water, then floated off on the tide to empty them further downstream.[38]

Work began in April 1847, an extremely busy time for Dargan as he was involved with several major railway projects at the same time. Among these were Thurles-Cork, Limerick-Tipperary, Belfast-Ballymena, Newry to Portadown and to Warren-point, Carlow to Bagenalstown and Liverpool to Bury. It called for a high degree of organization and management skill to keep these and several other projects going.

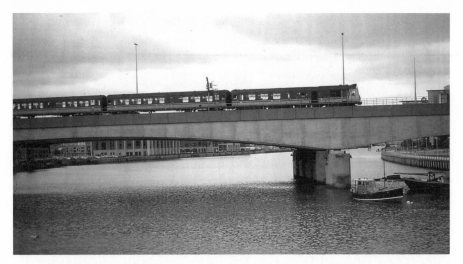

The Dargan Bridge, Belfast, opened by Queen Elizabeth, carries rail traffic across the Lagan.

By that summer there were 1500 men at work on the Lagan earning 10*s* a week and a newspaper of the time thoroughly approved of their regulated activity: 'Such a hive of beautifully organized labour we have never witnessed ... the distribution of the gangs, the unembarassing order of their work ... whereby all have free space for acting and could not shirk their duty, showed a masterly arrangement.'[39]

The Victoria Channel opened on 10 July 1849 with gun salutes, fireworks and a dinner for 250 in a marquee on Dargan's Island whose name had recently changed to Queen's Island in honour of Victoria's imminent visit. By 1864 the Crystal Palace built on the island to host soirées had perished in a fire and Messrs Harland & Wolff had begun to set up their shipbuilding firm on part of the island. By 1875 the remainder of the island was very neglected, the haunt of ne'er-do-wells and other undesirables and it was soon joined to the mainland. The area retained the name Queen's Island and became the home of the world-renowned builders of *Titanic*.

Floundering on the Foyle

Around this time Dargan took on a very difficult and complex project that brought him to the brink of ruin: the large-scale reclamation work he undertook on extensive sloblands on Lough Foyle. Once again John Macneill was the chief engineer and it was a project close to his heart. He was keen for Dargan to become an investor and to take on the £37,000 job to reclaim 2300 acres, which he did reluctantly in April 1841 and regretted ever after. The nature of the problems was complex:

several other contractors and subcontractors were involved, early partnerships ruptured and disputes, resignations and threats of legal action were commonplace with one contractor, Dimsdale, detained for a period in the Marshalsea. Unlike at Solitude Macneill was very much involved in every aspect of the works, sending letters, arranging meetings, visiting the site and finding himself in the sorry position of half contractor, half inspector of works.[40] All the while he urged Dargan to persevere, even though some days only 14 metres of ground were dug.

Endless accusations, disputes and legal actions meant unpaid bills and Dargan desperately tried to extricate himself from the mess; he was even more determined not to become involved in Macneill's plans for similar works on Lough Swilly. Tensions rose between the two men and at one point Macneill became quite incensed about Dargan's conduct: 'he does not seem to have much regard for his promises ... a man's word should be as sacred as his bond, in fact more so,' he wrote to a colleague and 'Dargan has behaved anything but well in the matter. He should not have deceived me,' he wrote in February 1842.[41] The precise nature of his complaints is unclear from the correspondence but it is clear the whole project was dogged with problems and difficulties.

The following summer Macneill was in London singing Dargan's praises for his work on the Foyle to the Devon Commission on Land in Ireland: this 'highly reputable contractor' had built a 3-mile (5 km) embankment and reclaimed 1000 acres of good quality land which was now dry and suitable for cultivation with work starting on another 800 acres.[42] He added that Dargan had invested £36,000 raised from friends including the very wealthy James Perry. This was a critical point. Dargan could not extricate himself from this contract, his plant and capital were tied up in it and as Perry told a Commons committee in 1846, Dargan asked him for financial help, which he gave as an investment, probably with little hope of a return. This unedited handwritten extract from the Committee's proceedings records Perry's exact words:

> I was a partner with Mr Dargan in two undertakings ... He had not a large capital and he got concerned in one undertaking particularly which I believe was the cause of his applying to me. This undertaking was the embankment of some sloblands and he had got into a litigation about it and he was unable to go on with the works without obtaining some assistance from some person or other and he then applied to me to come and look at the works and then he asked me whether I would assist him with money. I did assist him with money but our partnership was limited to that works.[43]

A major complicating factor in the various disputes was the diverse motives of several parties involved in the reclamation works. Among them were the promoters of the Londonderry & Coleraine Railway (L&CR) who planned to finance their line by selling reclaimed land. Dargan did not have a chance to tender for this line, which went to his rival Hemmings, one of the parties in dispute. As the legal cases rumbled on these and similar tactics led the Master of the Rolls to accuse the L&CR backers of 'fraud, deception and falsehood'.[44] Dargan was fortunate this crisis did not bring him down and although he managed to offload some of his holdings onto the noted English railway contractor, Thomas Brassey, it was several years before he was free of the fiasco on the Foyle.[45]

The last word goes to Thomas Carlyle who visited the reclamation works in August 1849 and in his jaundiced way advised travellers:

> Look in returning, at the attempted futility of an 'embankment of the Foyle'; Railway to Newtown Limavady was to embank Foyle; £80,000 (?) spent; no railway done, none was or is needed; no embankment, only heaps of barrows, waste flat diggings and some small patch of ground (inconceivably small) saved out of the wreck till new money be subscribed.[46]

Despite this by 1854 there were 800 acres under wheat and 100 under flax. Today the long sea embankment and the extent of the fertile land reclaimed by Dargan is best seen from the train travelling west from Magilligan towards Derry with flat cultivated fields stretching far into the distance towards the lough.

The First Northern Lines: The Ulster Railway

The second railway to open in Ireland after the Dublin & Kingstown was the Ulster Railway (UR) whose line ran south-west from Belfast towards Armagh. Dargan did not build the first seven-and-a-half-mile (12 km) section that opened in 1839. It is not certain if he tendered for it but as one of the few Irish contractors with railway experience it would be surprising if he did not. Also with several of his major projects in the north at this time, the Ulster Canal, the Banbridge cut and market house and the Bann reservoir and an office in Caledon and later Belfast, he was in a strong position to bid for it.

Dargan went on to win a succession of northern railway contracts and built the next 90 miles (145 km) of line radiating from Belfast. He was in England when the first section of the UR to Lurgan opened in November 1841 and missed the compliments paid him at a dinner in the Donegall Arms Hotel by the chairman, James Goddard, that he was 'never to cause the slightest trouble to the directors'.[47] He was thus well placed to win the next tenders and complete the route to Portadown in January 1842. Before it could open every line of railway had to pass a safety inspection, usually conducted by a Royal Engineers officer who made a report to the Commissioners of Railways. He had the power to demand improvements and prevent a line from opening if he thought it unsafe. Major General Charles Pasley, Inspector General of Railways, travelled from Portadown to Belfast in late 1843 and confirmed the line was 'in a safe and efficient condition, and the traffic well regulated'.[48] Lack of investment delayed the 11 miles (18 km) onward to Armagh but still the UR was able to pay an impressive 6 per cent dividend in 1845 that compares quite favourably to the steadily profitable Dublin & Kingstown's 9 per cent and the Dublin & Drogheda Railway's 5 per cent.

Returns Dargan made on the UR to parliament tell us a lot about his business operations at the time. His workforce of 1716 was made up of one secretary, thirty-six superintendents, two storesmen, one accountant, one cashier, two clerks, two artificers and 1671 labourers. Workmen earned 2s a day, 6d more than he paid on the D&KR seven or eight years before.[49] His only rivals in winning the tender at £88,000 for the line from Portadown to Armagh were the unscrupulous Thomas Jeffs and his brother from Scotland who so exploited and racked their workforce with the truck system that no matter how desperate for employment, many labourers refused to work for them and they suffered a succession of stoppages and strikes. This pattern repeated on the Midland Railway (see Chapter 5).

The Portadown to Armagh extension featured two level crossings with the distinctive names of Quakers' Crossing and Purgatory. When Captain John Simmons RE inspected he was complimentary about the quality of the masonry and the workmanship in general but found the rail fastenings poor, the bog embankment at Grange Road subsiding and more worryingly the absence of any signals whatever 'most dangerous'.[50] Such an economy on the part of the UR was unwise and hazardous and although Simmons allowed the line to open in February 1848 he imposed minor restrictions ordering the company to change the points layout at Portadown, run no more than one engine at any time on the line and keep speeds 'moderate'. Railway safety in those days was very much on a wing and prayer.

Armagh 1889 – The Worst Railway Accident in Irish History

As well as most of the line from Belfast to Armagh Dargan also built the first five miles from Newry towards Armagh. Completed some years later this section was the scene of the worst ever railway accident in Ireland when lax safety standards caused more fatalities than any other crash before or since.

On 12 June 1889 a Methodist Sunday-school excursion train with sixteen carriages and 940 passengers aboard, about 600 of them children, set out from Armagh for the seaside at Warrenpoint. The train was so overloaded that the small engine could not ascend a steep incline a few miles from Armagh and stalled. Unwisely the crew divided it, intending to take half the carriages to Warrenpoint and then return for the other half. This deactivated the vacuum brake system so that only stones under the wheels and a single handbrake held the isolated carriages. It is possible some of the youthful passengers may have tampered with this flimsy brake.

A backwards nudge from the engine as it started on the steep hill caused the rear portion of the heavy train to roll slowly back down the hill. The runaway carriages (locked as a misguided safety precaution) with their terrified and screaming occupants gathered speed until they were hurtling along at 40 mph into the path of the oncoming scheduled train heading for Newry. The driver of the latter was able to bring his engine almost to a stop but this did little to prevent the carnage as the wooden carriages smashed into the locomotive on a high embankment throwing it off the rails. In all, eighty-eight passengers died in the crash with many more seriously injured. The impact of the crash divided the Newry train and two sections in turn began to roll backwards, one almost catching up with the other before the driver and guard managed to apply the brakes preventing even more deaths.

Afterwards in response the Regulation Act (1889) compelled railway companies to install automatic continuous brakes on all trains, to inter- lock points and signals and operate a line block system that prevented a train from entering a section of track until another had cleared it.

Dargan offered to finance an UR extension to Monaghan to keep his men and plant busy but the Treasury refused the company a loan, ironically on the grounds that it would damage traffic on the already moribund Ulster Canal, which Dargan had also built.[51] However eight years later the UR gave him the contract worth £100,000 for the 16½ miles (26 km) to Monaghan; it opened in May 1858. He thus brought both canal and railway to the town and this completed the bulk of his work for the UR. It is likely he built many of the overbridges and the stations at Lisburn, Moira, Portadown and Armagh. Of these only the original signal cabin at Moira has survived with plans to preserve it.

Linking North and South

Three companies built the line from Dublin to Belfast: the UR, the Dublin & Drogheda Railway (D&DR) and the Dublin & Belfast Junction Railway (D&BJR),

all of these at least partly Dargan's work. The D&DR was Ireland's third railway, estimated by William Cubitt in 1836 to cost £650,000 to build over five years with a terminus in O'Connell St opposite the GPO.[52] Dargan put enormous effort into promoting the D&DR with a lengthy and gruelling appearance in 1836 before a House of Lords Committee of Inquiry into the railway.[53] Opposing counsel attempted to undermine his reliability as a witness and proponent of the line by questioning his skills and focusing on some of his less successful projects.

Having finally overcome his doubts about railways, John Macneill became engineer to the D&DR at five guineas a day. However, he had yet to grasp the finer points of railway operation as instead of the more obvious coastal route he advocated a circuitous inland one with four tracks: two inside for locomotive hauled trains and two outside for other trains, which he suggested could be pulled by men or horses.[54] With the 'most rigid economy in force' and despite Dargan's support of their case in Westminster, the company unwisely decided to award the first contract to a firm that soon withdrew and another to the disreputable Jeffs brothers. Inevitably Macneill had to admonish his resident engineer, George Hemans, about the Jeffs' substandard work, exploitation of their men and use of shoddy materials.[55]

One of Dargan's occasional contracting partners at this time was William McCormick, a man with a varied business career who later became an MP and won one of the early D&DR contracts in his own right. So keen was Dargan not to miss out to one of the eleven other bidders for section four (the seven miles/eleven kms north of Malahide) he offered to take almost half his £46,000 fee in shares, an offer the company had no trouble accepting. Still based in Belfast Dargan was much occupied finishing the Ulster Canal, as well as working on Belfast Harbour, the Bann works and the Foyle where he and the truculent Macneill were at loggerheads. He then won D&DR contract five on his own and contracts six and seven with McCormick.

Dargan at this time had up to 8000 men at work on the D&DR paying them 9s to 15s a week so that, as Macneill told the Devon Commission, 'he makes by a good man and loses by a bad one'.[56] Following a trial run to Drogheda for 550 people Major General Charles Pasley RE inspected and passed the line, staying at Macneill's house in Rutland (Parnell) Square where there was a buffet and a ball that evening. Earl de Grey laid the foundation stone at Amiens St (Connolly) station on 24 May 1844 enclosing coins of the realm ranging from a farthing to a sovereign, newspapers of the day, D&DR reports and a handwritten history of the railway – the latter being of necessity fairly brief. The earl then opened the railway and commanding the engineer to kneel, knighted Macneill on the platform. Grey then hopped on the first train, which left for Drogheda at 3 pm, passing over the very fine 11-arch viaduct designed by Macneill and built by Dargan over several roads and a river at Balbriggan in 1844. Dinner that evening was in the Malahide (Grand) Hotel in which Dargan later had a substantial interest.

Working together, Dargan and McCormick won the contract for the short Howth branch, which opened on 30 May 1847. During this time Dargan was heavily involved in the Great Southern & Western Railway to Carlow and he and McCormick were building the Liverpool & Bury Railway; not surprisingly Howth took almost two years to complete.

With the Ulster Railway and the Dublin & Drogheda Railway the third strand in the Dublin-Belfast link was the Dublin & Belfast Junction Railway (D&BJR) whose title was a misnomer, being located many miles from either city. Its line ran between Drogheda and Portadown of which Dargan built the sections from Newry to Portadown. Cash-flow problems meant the company was slow to pay its contractors so progress was minimal. At this point Dargan made what was then an unusual deal with the company: he offered to run all train services between Drogheda and Dundalk and handle repairs, maintenance and pay staff in return for 2s 6d per mile for each train run, a proposal that Macneill recommended warmly.[57] A shareholder queried the deal, saying English railways paid 1s 3d per mile and the MGWR 8¼d, to which Macneill responded that Dargan owned and serviced his own engines.

The Boyne viaduct at Drogheda designed by James Barton and John Macneill was a difficult piece of work that bankrupted the original contractor, William Evans of Cambridge. Dargan was fortunate not be involved.

The magnificent Craigmore viaduct north of Newry on the Dublin-Belfast rail line is arguably the finest railway structure in Ireland. Dargan built it to a design by John Macneill.

The major remaining gap in the route was the River Boyne at Drogheda. Without a bridge passengers going to Dublin had to detrain on one side of the river and either walk or take a hackney before facing the steep hill on the other side. The company complained it did not have the cash for such a major engineering project but John Grey Porter dismissed this excuse with a wry comment: 'Will the time ever come when it will not cost money?'[58] Thus matters rested with the Boyne a great divider, as it has been for many years.

There is no record of Dargan tendering for the Boyne viaduct but it would be surprising if he did not, even if he recognized how difficult a project it would be. William Evans of Cambridge, who built the Conway tubular bridge in north Wales, did win the contract and proudly showed W.R. Le Fanu round the works in 1852 but he was eventually bankrupted by the difficulties of the river crossing. A temporary line of rails allowed some trains to pass over to accommodate people going to Dublin to visit Dargan's 1853 Exhibition but the permanent structure was only completed in April 1855. James Barton, D&BJR engineer, designed it with input from Macneill. He was justifiably proud of this magnificent viaduct and showed a model of it at the 1862 exhibition in London.[59]

Even more impressive but less famous because of its remote location is the Craigmore viaduct north of Newry on the main Dublin-Belfast line. Designed by Macneill, Dargan built this most elegant structure in 1852 at a cost of £50,000. Each of the eighteen granite arches has an 18-metre span and rises 21 to 43 metres above the valley, making it the highest and the finest railway viaduct in Ireland. It tends to be overlooked because passing over it by train it is difficult to see what an amazing structure it is, striding in a giant curve across the valley like some great stone colossus. Also near Newry is another fine structure, a 13-metre-wide railway bridge over the Newry-Camlough road known as the Egyptian arch. Dargan also built this in a style similar to Mulvany's Broadstone station.

From Belfast to the Atlantic

Just before he finished the UR line to Monaghan, Dargan won the contract for the Belfast & Ballymena Railway (B&BR). The original contract deed written in legalese on a large vellum sheet is a rare survival with a wealth of detail; his Belfast offices at this time were at 81 Ann Street and he lived at 137 York Street.[60] At the first sod ceremony at Whitehead in November 1845 Dargan took his place in the shovel queue before all retired for dinner at the Commercial Hotel. Among the many speechmakers Dargan was third from last, just before toasts to the linen industry and the gentlemen of the press. By May 1846 Dargan had 4000 men and 500 horses working two eleven-hour shifts, the first from 1 am to noon, the other from noon to 11 pm. Masons earned 24s a week and labourers between 12s and 15s.

Although progress was good Captain R.M. Laffan RE was not impressed when he inspected the line, which did seem very inadequate: the ballast and trackbed were poor, there were no signals, mileposts or gradient posts and the stations remained unfinished. He refused to allow the line to open until Dargan made good the deficits, and it eventually opened in 1848.

The line north of Ballymena towards Derry was built by the Ballymena, Bally-money, Coleraine and Portrush Junction Railway (BBC&PJR), quite a mouthful but in reality not much more than an offshoot of the B&BR. Dargan invested so heavily in the line he was virtually its owner before it opened. Charles Lanyon was the engineer as he was on the B&BR and Dargan was there for the first sod ceremony on 21 December 1853, 'the observed of all observers'. Afterwards 150 sat down to lunch in the Portrush Hotel at a cost of 4s 6d a head, three days' wages for a labourer.[61]

Sir Charles Lanyon, 1813–89, Architect of Belfast

Charles Lanyon was born in Eastbourne and after a stint with the Commissioners of Public Works in Dublin moved to Belfast. As well as his railway work, Lanyon designed many of the city's finest buildings, among them Queen's University, the Linenhall Library, the Customs House, Crumlin Road Courthouse and Jail, Union Theological College, the Palm House in the Botanic Gardens and a number of banks and churches including Sinclair Seaman's Presbyterian Church. In later life he was Mayor of Belfast and an MP for the city.

He also designed the campanile in Trinity College Dublin and Castle Leslie, Co. Monaghan.

'The Regenerator of Ireland' and Portrush

A special train ran from Belfast to Portrush on 7 November 1855 and at Ballymoney, in the northern tradition, a number of decorated arches were thrown over the station road with these inscriptions: 'William Dargan: the friend of Ireland' and 'William Dargan: the man of the people'. At the dinner that followed in Ballymena his toast was first on the list, before the queen.[62] The directors were later somewhat testier, querying why Dargan had changed some station sites, demanding his help to make a lucrative deal with the post office, asking what he was doing to stop the spread of disease in Ballymoney and did he intend to keep them ignorant of the duties of their Traffic Manager, Thomas Higgins. But in time relations improved and when closing his accounts with the company he gave each director a medal inscribed 'Presented by William Dargan to ... an original promoter of the company', along with a free pass for life. The company later referred to Dargan as the 'regenerator of Ireland'.[63]

Dargan also built the Randalstown-Cookstown section of the B&BR. Apart from the fine eight-arch viaduct near Randalstown, designed by Lanyon and built by Dargan with basalt stonework piers and barrels completed in brick there is little of this branch in situ. More remarkable than the line's construction was the lengthy speech Dargan made at the opening in October 1856 on railway investment policy in Ireland, which articulates his confidence in the future of Irish railways and the role of Irish capital in their development. It is worth quoting at length.[64]

Dargan on Railway Investment in Ireland, October 1856

'We have now spent upon railway enterprise about £18 million of money in this country. £12 million of that have been eminently successful and realised a most remunerative return to the shareholders. £3 million are still struggling, but in the hope of success ... £3 million have also been spent and developed. And that being the result I think that I may without any invidious comparison explain how the matter stands.

'These £12 million have been in the management of our own individual people, our noblemen, our gentlemen, our men of business of

their own peculiar neighbourhood. The £3 million not productive but still paying from 1–3 per cent are under the management of our coun-trymen, but not yet fully developed. The £3 million, which produced nothing, is purely English capital and English management.

'But I do say it for this purpose: that since I was ten years old I have been hearing that we are unable to take care of ourselves, that we are unable to do anything for our own prosperity, and that we must have English capital, English judgement, English enterprise, English management, English everything. I am delighted and gratified that these Englishmen have come and spent their money among us. I would be greatly pleased if they had had a better result; but why I bring this subject particularly forward is with the knowledge that there is one great interest in which that doctrine so long maintained against us is totally and entirely disproved.'

Dargan showed a strong interest in developing the resort of Portrush as he later did for Bray. He opened the Antrim Arms Hotel with Turkish baths in the town (later the Northern Counties Hotel). He also worked with Lanyon on developing the harbour to make it suitable for steamers to and from Scotland at an estimated cost of £100,000. The hotel was badly damaged in the Troubles and has since been demolished. One of his final jobs as a director for the railway company was to witness its sale to the Belfast & Northern Counties Railway (B&NCR), signing the last entry in the minute books on 31 December 1860.[65]

Dargan took over some railway construction projects around the border area when the original contractors fell by the wayside. Macneill was engineer to the Dundalk & Enniskillen Railway (D&ER) when Dargan and his partner McCormick began work on the first ten miles in October 1845. At the first-sod meal in Dundalk Guild Hall there were wines, champagnes, port and sherry of the 'richest quality', notwithstanding the presence of the Temperance Band.[66] A year later the two partners took over the next ten miles from the ailing Coyle & Atkinson. When Dargan refused to pay a subcontractor on the grounds his work was second rate he found himself before the Queen's Bench sued for £30,000. His counsel argued that not keeping a copy of their agreement showed his client's trusting nature; the judge thought it more a sign of imprudence.

When the line opened in February 1849 Dargan ran the train services on a piece-rate basis, drawing a healthy income of £2400 in one six-month period. The relationship was of little benefit to the other shareholders, causing the chairman to make the slightly odd comment: 'It appeared now that Mr Dargan had walked into them instead of their walking into Mr Dargan.'[67] He was not involved in building the sections frther west and the company struggled to complete it using a succession of contractors. Capt. George Wynne RE refused to pass the section to Ballybay because it was unsafe and had no telegraph: 'the locomotive inspector had only a vague idea of my coming today – these Irish fellows!' he wrote.[68]

In the Newry area Dargan constructed two railways, the Newry & Enniskillen (N&ER) which later became the more modest Newry & Armagh (N&AR) and the Newry Warrenpoint & Rostrevor (NW&RR) whose name was equally overstated: it never got as far as Rostrevor. Heading slowly in much the same direction as the Dundalk & Enniskillen but by a more circuitous route was the N&ER whose progress was even more snail-like than the leisurely construction of its southern neighbour; Dargan was unlucky he ever became involved. He won the contract for the first five miles and Lord Newry turned the first sod at Moorevale on 17 August 1846, asking Dargan when he expected to start and not to use truck.[69] Dargan replied he did not rob his men and would have 600 at work the next day at 10s per week. He was as good as his word but then the combinators struck and unskilled N&ER labourers demanded 12s a week, the same as experienced Ulster Railway men. Dargan defused the situation by saying he paid by results and when they were on a par with the UR he would pay the same rates. Infighting between the directors and also between Dargan and the board over payments due were finally resolved after extensive negotiations.

Dargan's experience with the NW&RR was a little easier. This time Lord Newry's unsolicited advice was to urge Dargan to employ local men and ensure 'sobriety, regularity and good order' as if anticipating the grievances of locals who complained about the workmen who ventured forth after dark 'annoying peaceful inhabitants and causing alarm to all persons'.[70] One problem was the fact the board's base was in London. For example the directors ordered two engines, *Kingstown* and *Victoria*, which arrived long before the line was complete and then sold them to McCormick who in turn sold them to Dargan. Running a railway in Ulster from Pall Mall was no easy task. Dargan told a board meeting in London in May 1849 he was owed £14,000, adding philosophically: 'I presume this cannot be paid me in cash and there is, I suppose, no use in my proposing it.'[71] The press liked the line describing it as a 'pretty, bijou railway', the ballast 'the best we have seen in Ireland … like a garden walk ... superfluous to state that they are finished in his [Dargan's] best style'.[72] Weekly receipts at the opening averaged £60 per week, but notwithstanding the elegance and the scenery, had fallen to £36 at the year end producing losses of £30. The board implored a reluctant Dargan to take over running the railway, sending letters to 'the various points where he is likely to be'. He did so for five years but lost out financially on the transaction.

East Out of Belfast

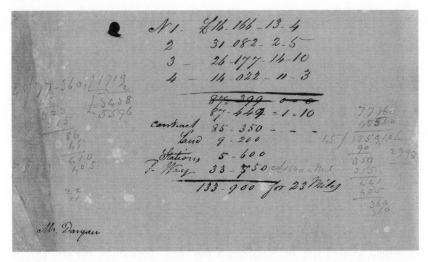

This enigmatic document is a rough cost estimate from c.1849 and bears Dargan's name but not his signature. It may relate to work on the Newtonards line.

The pattern of an enthusiastic start followed by slow payments from the board continued to be the case with the Belfast & Co. Down Railway (B&CDR). Dargan won the first contracts from Queen's Quay to Newtownards and Holywood, his price being half that of his nearest rivals. He began work at Comber on 28 April 1847 but the work was stop-start, as were the payments, while in effect Dargan was subsidizing the construction of the line, as he did with many others. This put great stress on his resources, plant and manpower. By mid July 1848 his men had rails laid between Queen's Quay and Holywood, which Captain George Wynne described in his report as 'complete and in fair order'.[73] The B&CDR had the good manners to recognize Dargan's input, reporting to the shareholders:

> They have been met, in the most liberal manner, by Mr Dargan, who has applied all his energies to the completion of his contract without at the same time calling for payment from the Board as rapidly as he was entitled to. It is necessary, however, that he should be supplied with some money during the course of the works.[74]

The line finally opened in May 1850. Work went ahead on the line to Newtownards, paid for in small irregular instalments, Dargan's demands often provoking special board meetings.[75] Newtownards opened on 6 May 1850 with 1000 passengers taking the thirty-five-minute journey. Queen's Quay station was demolished some years ago and all that survives of Dargan's work for the B&CDR is the short section to Holywood.

Hit and Miss at Queen's Quay Station, Belfast, 1848

The Belfast Newsletter *of 4 August described some ad hoc braking techniques used by trains entering Queen's Quay station: 'In order to save shunting, the engine was uncoupled when descending the hill and steamed in front into a siding, the train followed to the platform by its own momentum. Men working near the terminus assisted the brakeman, who stood on top of the carriage, to check any superfluous speed, by throwing stones and pieces of timber on the rails in front of the vehicles.'*

Uncoupling a moving engine was hazardous enough without throwing rubbish onto the track that could derail a train. It is unclear how long this dangerous practice continued, all with a view to saving a few shovelfuls of coal.

A similar construction pattern followed with the Banbridge Junction Railway (BJR), which started life burdened with the name Banbridge, Newry, Dublin & Belfast Junction Railway. For no discernible reason the detailed records, minute books and finance committee minutes of this insignificant branch are more complete than for almost every other much larger railway. It was a tardy, under-funded and troublesome little railway, which sought to benefit from its connection to the main Dublin-Belfast line. The directors visited Dargan in Dublin, urging him to send in his estimate straight away so the works could start immediately.[76] Construction followed the usual irregular pattern, complicated by the fact that the D&BJR was in the process of leasing the line even before it was built. It finally opened with a band at Scarva on 23 March 1859, five years after Dargan began work and not before his solicitors had threatened legal action if he was not paid.[77]

Dargan's name was initially linked with the 13-and-a-half mile Portadown and Dungannon Railway (P&DR) but the contract went to the English firm of Fox Henderson & Co who began work in 1855 but failed after a few months. The directors persuaded Dargan to take the job and he completed the line to Dungannon on 5 April 1858 where Lord Northland succeeded in locating the station well away from his estate and the town.[78] The company went on to extend to Omagh but Dargan was not involved.

Dargan's English Railways

A little-known facet of Dargan's career is that he and his sometime Drogheda Railway partner, William McCormick, took contracts to build two railways in the north of England: the Liverpool and Bury Railway (L&BR) and the Manchester &

Leeds Railway (M&LR). In the 1840s Britain was going through what was known as the 'railway mania', a period of frantic bubble investment that saw the launch of hundreds of railway plans and prospectuses. A few people made a fortune but many lost a great deal of money speculating in railway shares.

Although he was heavily committed to the Great Southern & Western Railway's route towards Cork, in September 1845 Dargan went to London with McCormick to negotiate on the first 14 miles (23 km) of the Bury Railway route from Boundary St Liverpool to Orrell. They were up against the heavyweights of English railway construction in the firm of Stephenson Brassey & Co. but won the contract for £228,000. They added they would build the whole line for £418,104, excluding the viaduct at Liverpool, to which the company agreed; Stephenson Brassey's bid was £447,744.[79] Once again John Macneill was one of two principal engineers with the ever-obliging James Perry as guarantor along with Henry Steel of Liverpool. In February 1846 the two sides signed the contract, which included a penalty clause of £400 for every week completion was late and a bonus of £250 per week if they finished early.[80] The foundation stone laid at Boundary Street contained the usual coins and newspapers plus a plate inscribed with the names of company officials along with those of Dargan and McCormick. A celebratory meal for the workmen followed in of all places the Great Howard Street workhouse, hardly a festive location.

The two contractors began work in February 1846 with much tunnel drilling at Walton and Billunge. The company showed a rare concern for its workmen whom it said were poorly accommodated, ordering the contractors to build a 'hut or cottage as experimental of the cost of such erections' while two scripture readers attended to their spiritual welfare.[81] It was more common for nineteenth-century railway navvies in Britain to receive a great deal more attention to their souls than their bodies.

The contract for the viaduct excluded from the original tender went to Dargan, McCormick and Samuel Holme, the latter being a Liverpool-based contractor who entertained his partners at a reception in Liverpool town hall.[82] He later became mayor of the city in 1852–3 and in 1867 travelled to Dublin for Dargan's funeral. The viaduct was troublesome for in March 1847 a structural weakness aggravated by heavy rains and possibly poor workmanship caused all twenty-one arches to collapse like a 'series of artillery charges' as a Liverpool paper described it.[83] Happily there were no injuries and the subcontractors responsible, Bullock & Evans, rebuilt it at a cost of almost £6000. By September 1848 the viaducts, tunnels, bridges and permanent way were almost ready but progress was at a price. Two workmen, Dennis Waterson and William Bradley (aged fifteen) died following surgery to amputate shattered limbs. This was the rarely costed price of heavy construction work.

By May 1847 3975 men were at work and around this time it appears that although the partnership continued McCormick took a more hands-on role in the L&BR while Dargan tended to focus on his many Irish projects. Captain George Wynne RE inspected the line in November 1848 prior to opening and pronounced 'unqualified satisfaction at the excellent manner in which the contractor has executed his work'.[84] With sixteen stations the line had cost £900,000 including land and at the regulation dinner in the Clarence Hotel, Bolton, McCormick alone was mentioned as contractor. The line opened on 20 November 1848.

The second railway contract the two undertook was exceptionally difficult: the trans-Pennine route of the Manchester & Leeds Railway (M&LR) was to link Liverpool with Hull and in the process Ireland with the continent. Before a shovel of earth was turned, Francis Whishaw described the challenges of this trans-Pennine line in his *Railways of Great Britain and Ireland* (1842): 'The line is literally studded with engineering difficulties from end to end, and those of no ordinary magnitude.'[85] Another writer at the time described the heavy works in the Calder Valley: by making 'embankments and cuttings, by removing rocks and building up arches, by occasionally diverting the river and the road and often crossing both, by piercing the hills with short tunnels ... a line has been constructed'.[86] Among the engineers was Charles Vignoles, who worked with Dargan on the Dublin & Kingstown Railway and Richard Osborne who also worked with him on the Waterford & Limerick Railway. Dargan and McCormick bid for a whole series of sections and won three of them at Cleckheaton and two near Bradford, worth a total of £412,000.[87] Once again it appears that McCormick was more actively involved than his partner.

The nature of the terrain and the works were such that injuries to workmen were frequent and often fatal. An 1846 House of Commons report on railway labourers noted that in the previous eight-year period the Manchester Royal Infirmary admitted fifty-two seriously injured M&LR men, thirteen of whom died.[88] Terry Coleman describes railway navvies of the time thus: 'They were heathens in a Christian country, they drank, had many women but few wives, broke open prisons and were not received in good society. It was fashionable to laud labour, but the men themselves could go hang, as some of them did.'[89] Life was indeed harsh and brief and they had little time for social or religious conventions; a common marriage ceremony involved the couple jumping over a broomstick in the middle of a crowd of revellers before being put to bed in the same room.[90] Thomas Carlyle, who expressed such a negative view of Dargan's Foyle reclamation works, was actually positive about Irish labourers working on the Manchester line: 'Not without surprise I find the Irish are the best in point of behaviour. The postman tells me that several of the poor Irish do regularly apply to him for money drafts, and send their earnings home. The English, who eat twice as much beef, consume the residue in whisky, and do not trouble the postman.'[91]

Captain Laffan RE passed McCormick and Dargan's sections of the line in July 1848 and May 1850 and the company agreed their final accounts in January 1851. A 2010 trip on the line between Leeds and Liverpool revealed some of the construction difficulties the contractors faced. The route twists and turns high above the valleys and has many tunnels as it runs through small neat towns, many with former mills and factories now adapted for various other uses.

FIVE

Rails into Munster and Connacht: The Peak of Dargan's Career

Until the mid 1840s, Dargan's career had focused on a series of quite small if commercially significant projects. It was now time for him to move into a different league. The largest nineteenth-century railway company was the Great Southern & Western Railway (GS&WR) with headquarters at Kingsbridge (Heuston) station. This is 'a delightful building, a renaissance palazzo, gay and full blooded, with fruit swags and little domed towers on the wings, a thoroughgoing formal composition, excellently articulated', as Maurice Craig described it.[1] Sancton Wood's design was preferred to one by John Mulvany, designer of the stations at Blackrock (being the oldest extant station in the Republic dating from 1841), Salthill and Dun Laoghaire as well as many other buildings throughout Ireland. Sancton Wood's work can also be seen at Inchicore Railway Works, Kilkenny, Portarlington ('his characteristically restless Gothic' as Jeremy Williams describes it)[2] and Portlaoise stations as well as Kilcroney House, Bray. Although Dargan did not construct the station building at Heuston he was the main contractor for the train shed.[3]

In 1836 Charles Vignoles projected a route to Thurles with a loose estimate: 'a million will accomplish all that is required and do it well' and a further £1.25 million to reach Cork.[4] The ever-present James Perry and John Macneill worked

The Dublin terminus of the GS&WR at Kingsbridge (now Heuston station) opened in 1846 and is seen in its grandeur in this fine watercolour dating from the early 1860s.
© Board of CIÉ, used with permission.

hard to promote the line, lobbying Robert Peel with costs and estimates for the first section to Cashel with a branch to Carlow, costed at £1.3 million or £11,000 per mile.[5] In time Macneill became engineer and Perry joined the board of the company. The focus on Cashel led to the route being called the Cashel line and its shares as 'Cashels'. Macneill told an 1844 House of Commons committee the terrain was easy, labour plentiful and the work could be completed in two years. Labourers in England, he said, earned 4s a day but in Ireland 'the men we shall employ will be glad to get a shilling ... I could have turned out any number, even at sixpence a day'; an exaggeration doubtless but necessary to loosen the Treasury purse strings and encourage private investors.[6]

As was common practice the company parcelled out the line in approximately ten-mile (16 km) sections and assigned each to different contractors as a way of testing their mettle. Dargan and William McCormick won the second section, Hazelhatch to Caragh, against competition from UK giants like Thomas Brassey.[7]

On 30 December 1844 the Duke of Leinster arrived at a field near Adamstown, dug six sods of earth, tossed them into a wheelbarrow and wheeled it off some distance. A dinner for the workmen followed but despite this auspicious start, delays, intimidation, strikes and accusations of exploitation marked the early months of Dargan's contract. In the first week a group of men urged those working near Lucan to strike for an increase from 9 to 12 shillings a week. Their motives are unclear, unless they hoped to be employed later at the higher rate or to take the jobs of strikers or combinators. The *Irish Railway Gazette* was apoplectic: 'a disgraceful proceeding ... for common labourers in Ireland, 1s 6d per day is not to be despised. Would to God every labouring man in Ireland had employment at such wages.'[8] Dargan began work on the second section, Hazelhatch to Caragh, on 1 February 1845 and Macneill assured the shareholders the workmen had now settled down. His reassurance was a little premature.

'Hedging, Heartless Adventurers'

In 1851 a leading English contractor, Samuel Morton Peto, spoke of how the problem of labour unrest affected Irish navvies working in England: 'Pay him well and show him you care for him, he is the most faithful and hardworking creature in existence; but if you find him working for 8d a day and that paid in potatoes and meal, can we wonder that the results are as we find them?'[9] An enlightened philosophy that Dargan embraced.

A great scourge for railway labourers everywhere was truck, the system of paying wages in kind or with tokens which could only be used to buy poor-quality, over-priced food and other goods and usually in tommy shops set up and run on site by contractors themselves.

Men building a railway often worked far from any town where they could buy their food and other supplies. Some contractors opened a shop selling items like bread, meat, potatoes and whiskey. This was sometimes useful and saved the men a long walk to the nearest town. Occasionally the good value on offer drew many local people to use the company shops. However, a number of unscrupulous employers exploited their workmen, charging inflated prices for third-rate goods and even paying them in kind or issuing vouchers, which could only be redeemed in their shop. Running up a tab, especially for whiskey, meant some workmen were permanently in debt to the contractor, their wages spent each week before they earned them. Some contractors, like the Jeffs brothers, made as much from this type of exploitation as they did from a construction contract and many would only employ men who bought from their tommy shops. For these workmen truck became a form of economic enslavement.[10]

As F.R. Conder relates, as well as 'ale in abundance, spirits, bread, meat, fat bacon, tobacco, shovels, jackets, gay crimson and purple waistcoats, boots, hats, and night-caps', one enterprising contractor in England went further to meet the men's needs, in particular their 'weakness for female society'. He brought prostitutes on site, providing them with food, clothes and housing. This helped the contractor to retain experienced workmen (and their money) who would otherwise, he says, be 'off on the randy' in nearby large towns and might not return. He then deducted the charge for these ladies' services directly from the men's wages.[11]

Within days of work starting at Adamstown, using heavily sanguineous imagery, the *Dublin Evening Mail* accused Dargan and McCormick of paying their men just 7*d* a day, 'a shocking state of things' and exploiting them using the truck system, 'that vampire that sucks the very life blood of the poor. ... This abominable system must not be permitted to drain the lifeblood of the country for the solace of hedging, heartless adventurers.'[12] Dargan's rebuttal of the charges in a letter to the papers two days later is a model of clarity and although brief says much about his employment policy.

> *Dublin, 19 February 1845*
>
> *Sir, I am the contractor for the second division of the Cashel Railway. I have never paid less than 1s 6d a day and always in cash, never goods. I have worked at public contracts for over 14 years and in that time have paid £800,000 in wages. I have never directly or indirectly used truck or allowed an employee to use it.*
>
> *I am, sir, etc.*
>
> *William Dargan*[13]

McCormick also replied to say no one in his employ earned less than 1*s* 4*d* and skilled men earned 4*s* a day. Two subcontractors ran shops at Adamstown and Ballyfermot, which gave such good value that local people flocked to them. But to avoid further misrepresentation he had ordered them to close, even though it meant greater hardship for his workmen.

Delays in gaining possession of land to build the railway and even more delays in the company paying its contractors' bills put pressure on Dargan during the summer of 1845 as the secretary paraphrased a letter he wrote to the board from London: 'Mr Dargan does not wish to be troublesome but desires, if possible, to keep his engagements with the Board and to avail himself of the advantages of the season.'[14] He added more directly that he and McCormick had spent £35,000 on materials and delayed payments were 'exceedingly annoying and inconvenient'. Part of his section of the line between Dublin and Kildare has been recently upgraded and an unfortunate effect is that many of the fine cut-stone bridges have been demolished to be replaced with double size but distinctly less elegant concrete structures.

Dargan and the Famine

The year 1845 marked the start of the Great Famine, although major food shortages leading to periodic hunger and even starvation were common before then. Crowds came from the worst-affected areas all over Ireland to the railway site looking for work and for many hundreds of starving people, finding work building the railway was their only chance of survival. The indifference of government figures and many newspapers has been well chronicled although it is equally well known the Society of Friends, so prominent in promoting and financing many railways in Ireland and Britain, were also much to the fore in famine relief efforts. On the other hand the *Irish Railway Gazette*, a useful recorder of railway developments, adopted an ostrich-like approach, saying in September 1845 that reports of potato blight and famine warnings were 'magnified to a much greater extent than warranted'.[15] Indeed the almost total absence of coverage of the Famine in newspapers like *Saunders News-letter* during the years 1845–8 suggested it was a unworthy of a news report. Such papers gave considerably more coverage of the trivial pursuits of the royal household than the mortality rate among the inmates of the Skibbereen workhouse.

Travelling around the country Dargan was very aware of the true level of distress. The GS&WR board had been critical of his lack of progress, suggesting Dargan was distracted by other projects and demanding to know why he was not harder at work. His response written on 17 June 1845 from his offices at 31 Upper Abbey Street stated the works were going ahead on all the sections where he had possession of the land and that he had no other projects on hand apart from the GS&WR. This was technically true but not literally so: he was close to completing negotiations for several major projects including the line to Galway for the MGWR. His letter to John Macneill paints a grim picture of his difficulties arising from not having the land to build the railway and the desperation of the destitute and starving who arrived on site looking for work:

> *31 Upper Abbey Street, 17 June 1845*
>
> *Sir, In reply to your letter inquiring why I am not proceeding faster with the works of the GS&WR, I beg to state that on every part of the line on which I have got possession of the land, the works are going on with the utmost energy and activity and so far from my time being engaged on other works I assure you I have not a single contract or piece of work on hands but those of the GS&WR Co and that I am and have been suffering great injury and inconvenience from being unable to get to work as I should do. ...*
>
> *All the assistants, overseers etc. are idling about and receiving wages from me. Add to this the immense numbers of unfortunate labourers from all quarters of the country, brought to the neighbourhood of the works by the expectation of employment, and in a state of utter starvation and wrackless misery.[16]*

This became a steady pattern: groups of destitute, semi-starving men arriving to demand work, which they were too weak to do and disrupting the works in their disappointment. The problem was the delay in the arrival of state loans to build the railway while at the same time the GS&WR had to convince shareholders to pay the next instalment on the shares they had purchased as an investment in a line that seemed to have ground to a halt. At this point Macneill as chief engineer should have intervened to insist the company meet its obligations to its contractors but he was busy with many other railway lines and his newly established chair of engineering in Trinity College.

With few other famine relief initiatives, there was heavy reliance on railway works and Dargan did more than his share to make up for the government's laissez-faire policy. At the height of the Famine he told Lord George Bentinck he could employ another 30,000 men if land and legal delays were overcome. Although a strong Tory, Bentinck's bill before the Commons in February 1847 proposed to spend £16 000 000 on building railways. He described other works as 'public follies' and the status of the half a million people employed as 'worse than idleness' although the daily wage paid on relief works such as roads was as little as fourpence a day, not enough to buy food for one person for that day. Such comments were unlikely to inspire further relief efforts and with strong opposition from key figures like Charles Trevelyan (see below), in due course Bentinck's railway bill was defeated.[17]

The same month the country was hit by gales and blankets of snow, reducing work hours on railway lines and adding to the suffering of famine victims. Illustrating this was the inquest in Mullingar on the body of railway labourer, Michael Kelly, which found he had starved to death. The British government sent James Walker to inspect the GS&WR works before authorizing another loan and he reported great destitution in Ireland, where the interior was 'virtually more remote than India or America'. But he had a high opinion of Dargan's work, 'a most efficient contractor' who paid good wages and employed almost 4000 men.[18] In truth railways could offer only limited famine relief: they employed the able-bodied, not the destitute or the starving and the lines were at this time far away from the worst affected areas of the west and south-west. The works were of their nature transitory, taking on local men at each stage, but as they progressed and the line moved on those formerly employed were left as badly off as ever. Nonetheless Dargan and other contractors kept many alive who would doubtless otherwise have perished.

God's Judgement on a Selfish, Perverse and Turbulent People

Charles Edward Trevelyan's title at the Treasury was Assistant Secretary but in fact he ran this important arm of government. He was in charge of the limited famine relief measures though he had no faith in public works, believing the Famine should be allowed to take its course and saw it as a 'mechanism for reducing surplus population'. He justified this Malthusian stance by calling on providence, saying that since the 'judgement of God sent the calamity to teach the Irish a lesson, that calamity must not be too much mitigated. ...The real evil with which we have to contend is not the physical evil of the Famine, but the moral evil of the selfish, perverse and turbulent character of the people.'

Trevelyan had no direct experience of the effects of the Famine, his first visit to Ireland being in October 1847 when he stayed at the Salthill Hotel (once Dargan's offices). His name is vilified in The Fields of Athenry, sung by Irish rugby and soccer supporters.

After a sluggish start the government rowed back on its laissez faire policy, rustling up £9.5 million for famine relief, a modest figure compared to the £69 million spent on the pointless and futile Crimean war a few years later.

Writing about the Famine in later years, Trevelyan declared it lasted only two years; 1846–7. But as Cecil Woodham Smith noted, people suffered even more in 1848 than they did in 1846: 'The famine was not "over", in the sense that an epidemic occurs and is over. The poverty of the Irish people continued, failures of the potato, to a greater or lesser extent, continued, and hunger continued.'[19]

Labour Troubles

Dargan kept his men at work as the line edged south-west and using a canal boat brought his materials on site to a store at Sallins. A few weeks after his exchanges with the GS&WR directors, he held a trial run on the nearly completed section using his own engine, The Lady Macneill, with a dinner that evening for his workmen. But when another strike broke out later in the summer Dargan decided to prosecute two of the ringleaders, Lord and Burgess, who appeared before the Athy petty sessions charged with the felony of combination.[20] His counsel said Dargan did not want to punish the men, just to check the spirit of combination, a crime at the time for which they could be transported. Their defence was that troublemakers had misled them, despite Dargan's liberality. He won the case with costs although prosecuting penniless labourers can hardly have been an economic exercise. The case suggests the pressure Dargan was under and the need to discourage others. A few weeks later McCormick arrived on site near Portarlington, another section for which the two partners had won the contract, to find the men playing cards and the gangers powerless; he fired 300 on the spot.[21]

The delightful station at Carlow, its tall chimneys and matching gable ends a mix of Gothic, Picturesque and Elizabethan styles; even the single oriel window on the first floor does not upset the composition balance. The stations on this line and the Craigmore and Boyne viaducts show that John Macneill was both a talented engineer and an imaginative architect.

Gauging the Difference

Ireland and England have different railway gauges (the distance between the rails). In 1840s England George and Robert Stephenson favoured 4 ft 8½ inches based on the Tyneside wagons they knew as young boys. I.K. Brunel built to a generous 7 ft while the Drummond Railway Commission chose 6 ft 2 in for Ireland, the gauge used in the first sections of the Ulster Railway while the Kingstown railway was built to 4 ft 8½.

To avoid ending up with a range of gauges the Board of Trade ordered railway inspector Major General Charles Pasley RE to make a recommendation for Ireland and he came up with a compromise of 5 ft 3 in, which it is to this day. At that very time England opted for 4 ft 8½ in, the standard now across most of the world. This might not seem a huge issue but those 6½ inches make a difference; all railway vehicles for use in Ireland have to be built to this unique gauge, an expensive exercise. By contrast the Luas tramway is 4 ft 8½ in. General Pasley did not do us a service in his Solomon-like judgement.

By the spring of 1846 Dargan was busy pushing the line towards Carlow, then the projected route to Cork and one of his engines, *Duchess of Leinster*, was making four-mile (6 km) runs near Athy, hauling works trains of 460 tons laden with rails and sleepers, a good test of the permanent way. Macneill continued to give the shareholders rosy progress reports, assuring them the workmen were 'contented and cheerful' and only occasionally lapsing into combination. One such eruption occurred when skilled masons struck for an increase from 4s 6d to 5s a day for building a bridge at Carlow, later known as Dargan's bridge. Dargan replaced them with ordinary labourers who completed the bridge in three weeks at the reduced cost of £611. He was no pushover.

A trial run from Dublin to Carlow took place in July 1846 and Major General Pasley approved the line soon after: 'One of the most substantial and best executed lines in the United Kingdom' was his verdict while Dargan's bridge was 'the finest bridge in the three kingdoms'; fulsome praise indeed.[22] On 3 August 1846 a special train brought the directors and friends to Carlow with a stop at the Curragh for lunch and the usual ponderous speeches and toasts.

Unveiling a plaque to William Dargan at Carlow station on 12 September 1993. The wording allows for the possibility that Dargan was born in either Carlow or Laois. *Left to right*, Martin Nevin of Carlow Historical and Archaeological Society and Fergus Mulligan.

Stations on the Carlow Line: A Delight to the Eye

John Macneill designed Athy, Carlow and Bagenalstown stations and it is quite likely Dargan built them. They are among the finest railway buildings in the country. Athy with its two-storey central block, single-storey pavilions, tall chimneys and steps that pierce the cast-iron balustrade leading down to the platform has a Victorian Tudor look. Carlow is even more elaborate, with single-storey wings and four tall chimneys. Bagenalstown (Muine Bheag) is a sheer delight: it is a wonderful Palladian building, a palazzola with pedimented residential area over corbelled entrances to the platform and two side wings, all balanced in perfect harmony. We can safely ignore the philistine comments of the Carlow Sentinel *at the time the line opened, the paper describing these three stations as 'gloomy-looking edifices' whose 'taste partook of barbarity'.*

The Leading Irish Engineer

August 1846 marked a watershed in Dargan's career. McCormick left to concentrate on his career in England, making over his Irish projects to Dargan. At the same time the GS&WR decided to employ a single contractor to complete the 80 miles (130 km) from Thurles to Cork. Their choice of Dargan was no surprise and made him the undisputed king of Irish civil engineering contractors.

With the focus of his operations shifting south, Dargan moved to the north Dublin suburb of Raheny, to a house called Maryville, which stood near Sybil Hill at the edge of what is now St Anne's Park. (Nothing remains of it apart from a small section of red-brick wall near the park.)

Dargan made a start at Mallow in November 1846 on the contract that was worth £600,000 (equivalent to at least 76 million today), by far the largest railway contract ever undertaken in Ireland up to then.[23] Along with Macneill he was now working closely with W.R. Le Fanu who came to know him well and whose diaries and other writings shed a great deal of light on Dargan's GS&WR work. For example on one of his many visits to Cork the two breakfasted together before spending the day on site with Dargan's assistant and later occasional partner, Edwin Edwards. Le Fanu's diary entries are a mix of the informative and the mundane: '13 September 1846, Champagne with Dargan and Macneill'; '6 October 1846, Meetings with Dargan on gradients. Got hair cut'.

Riding the *William Dargan*

The William Dargan *was a large powerful works engine used by Dargan along with the much smaller* Lady Macneill, *named after John Macneill's wife. Before the line to Cork opened, Le Fanu tells of a hair-raising journey on the roughly laid temporary single track between Limerick Junction and Charleville in the late 1840s. He instructed Dargan's employee, Robert Edwards ('a wild, reckless young fellow he then was') to have the* Lady Macneill *ready to take him back to Charleville at 8 pm, which he did, but Le Fanu did not turn up until 8.30 pm. Le Fanu takes up the story.*

> *We got up on the engine and started, Edwards driving at a great pace. 'Better not go so fast, Edwards' said I; 'the road is very rough, and we'll be off as sure as fate.'*
>
> *'I know the road is rough,' said he; 'but it's better to run the chance of being killed that way than to be surely killed the other way if we go slow.'*
>
> *'What other way?' I asked.*
>
> *'Why,' he said, 'I told the "William Dargan" to start from Charleville, with a rake of empty wagons, exactly at nine o'clock, if we weren't in before that, and if we don't run fast she'll be into us, and send us to glory.'*
>
> *'Better go back to the junction, and wait till she comes,' I suggested.*
>
> *'Never fear,' he said. 'It's only twenty miles; I'll do it in time.'*
>
> *So on we went, the engine jumping, and every minute swaying from side to side; two or three times I was certain we were off the line.*

They made it with seconds to spare, arriving in Charleville as the William Dargan *was pulling out of the station.*[24]

Both Le Fanu and Macneill were active freemasons, as were many professional men, railway directors and the gentry at the time and it is tempting to speculate whether Dargan frequented his local lodge, certainly it would have helped his business. However, the worshipful brethren have always been somewhat reluctant to throw open their membership lists so there is no known evidence Dargan ever joined. Against his membership is his very strong reluctance to become involved with any partisan, sectarian or political grouping; the balance of probability is that he was not a freemason.

Dargan's Labour Policy

The section of line from Kildare to Maryborough (Portlaoise) opened in June 1847. As noted, the routine at celebratory dinners at the time was to deliver many tedious speeches and toasts, verbosity and hot air – we know this because newspapers reported them verbatim. Dargan rarely said more than a few words on such occasions but this time, at the obligatory lunch at McEvoy's Hotel, Portlaoise, he spoke at greater length than usual on his labour policy as he had done at Portrush (see Chapter 4). He said the GS&WR had spent £1.2 million on construction from 1844–6 and he and other contractors employed 13,407 men on its lines, 12,006 labourers, 1001 tradesmen and 400 foremen.[25] He himself employed no less than 50,000 men in various projects across the country, possibly including those working for his subcontractors. Of considerable interest is his comment that by acting fairly towards his own men he promoted his own interests, an enlightened approach that was unusual for the day and contrasts with Macneill's philosophy shared with a House of Commons Committee in 1844, as mentioned earlier. However, the company warned Dargan that parliament was still considering whether to allocate further loans for railway construction and that he should not take on any more men but in fact be prepared to lay off those he had.

Dargan's Engines

In the course of his engineering career Dargan owned or leased many locomotives, among them the aforementioned William Dargan, *probably built by the Liverpool firm of Bury Curtis Kennedy in the 1840s, as was the* Duchess of Leinster. *The* Lady Macneill *was a product of Sharp Bros, Manchester, while other engines such as* Kingstown, Victoria *and several unnamed ones came from Grendons of Drogheda or Forresters of Liverpool. The wear and tear on a contractor's locomotive was heavy and in many cases when a line was completed Dargan sold on the engine to the contracting railway company, such as the Waterford & Tramore, the Dundalk & Enniskillen and the Newry Warrenpoint & Rostrevor railways.*[26]

Maryborough to Ballybrophy opened on 1 September 1847 and happily the anticipated £500,000 state loan materialized. Dargan was keen to make a start on the tunnel that runs into the Cork terminus, which he knew would be tricky and time consuming. Tunnelling is a hazardous business and involved excavators working in darkness with dirty air and foul water. Injuries were common. Four shafts were dug into the earth (later used as air holes) to lower the workmen in large buckets to dig out the spoil, which was raised to the surface in the same buckets. The walls were then lined with Youghal bricks.

With the Famine reaching its peak in 1847 the human devastation was unmeasured if not immeasurable. As autumn turned to a particularly severe winter Dargan considered suspending all works, those months of short daylight hours and atrocious weather being considerably less productive than the rest of the year. However, when his resident engineer, J. Rutledge, told him of the great hardship this would cause he agreed to maintain them over the winter. Rutledge estimated Dargan lost £2–3000 by this act, describing him as an excellent employer who had done 'more to protect the rights of labour in Ireland than any other man'.[27]

'Blood-Stained Tipperary'

As on most lines, injuries and fatalities were common. One workman named Brophy died and another was badly injured when struck by Dargan's ballast engine, the *Buffalo*, near Ballybrophy in September 1847. Industrial troubles too were never far away, often requiring police protection on site to keep the works going. Before long these tensions escalated into two murders. The first occurred at Ballybrophy on 13 November 1847 and the victim was Michael Smith, a supervisor of Dargan's, killed with a hatchet blow to the head.[28] Resident engineer J. Rutledge described what happened. A group of destitute men arrived on the site and despite being told there was no work for them, insisted on building a ramshackle road leading away from the railway. There were no wages for them at the end of the week and in their fury they turned on the unfortunate Smith. It is hard to imagine the misery that led them to such desperate actions.

A second murder under similar circumstances took place a few weeks later: this time the victim was John Rourke, a ballast inspector, killed near 'blood-stained Tipperary' as the *Irish Railway Gazette* called it in its melodramatic fashion. With equal hyperbole in July 1848 a journalist from Liverpool reported Thurles station in flames and miles of track torn up but an eye witness around the same time told the *Liverpool Chronicle* he saw nothing more in the town than a troop train heading south.[29] This was a period of revolution in parts of Europe and of William Smith O'Brien's abortive rebellion that ended in the somewhat farcical siege of the widow McCormack's house in Ballingarry, Tipperary.[30] F.R. Conder whimsically outlined the perceived dangers faced by his fellow English railway engineers working in Ireland, rooted in the 'inherent tendency of the Celtic race to conspire'. Above all they needed a fire-proof house and bullet-proof skin and must avoid affronting Sir Lucius O'Trigger as letters of complaint are delivered to overseers and employers using 'that postal service which is native to Ireland – that is to say, by being nailed by a knife to the door'.

Two other works-related deaths occurred the following year: a ganger named Dooley was shot by unknown assailants and a workman was killed when he fell 30 ft down the shaft of the Cork tunnel.[31]

The line to Limerick Junction opened on 1 July 1848 with lunch at Dundrum Park and as Le Fanu records in his diary, after 'plenty of champagne' he and Dargan went on to Tipperary for tea. A little farther south Macneill solved the problem of boggy land near Lisduff with the novel but hardly long-term solution of laying fir trees to create almost a floating trackbed. Around this time Dargan agreed to build the stations, offices, railway houses and goods sheds between Limerick Junction and Cork. The line opened to Buttevant after Christmas 1848 and Captain John

Simmons RE gave his blessing to the section to Mallow saying it was 'sufficient in every way'.[32]

In August 1849 Simmons' engineering colleague, Captain George Wynne, observed the arrival of four trains at Limerick Junction, long renowned for its intricate layout that required each train to engage in much shunting to and fro. But they did so, Wynn noted, 'without confusion'. Curiously the complex manoeuvres at Limerick Junction lasted another hundred years requiring every train to make at least one reversal and sometimes two.

Dargan hosted a lunch for the railway directors at a Mallow hotel where the chairman, Edward McDonnell, described him as 'an excellent contractor' and a man of 'integrity, ability and untiring zeal'.[33] It is worth noting that Dargan had agreed to accept £10,000 due him from the company in five-year bonds. Dargan had by now a reputation for being quite a heavy drinker, Le Fanu commenting in his diary that one evening he ordered ten dozen bottles of champagne and they spent the evening with George Ilberry, GS&WR general manager, 'drinking each other's health and such like fooling'.[34]

Captain Laffan commented that the works were heavy on the Mallow to Kilbarry section, the location of a temporary terminus pending completion of the tunnel. The viaduct at Mallow cost £14,000 and there was an 88-ft-high (27 m) embankment with one cutting through almost a mile of rock. He reluctantly passed the line with restrictions, noting the track was irregular in parts and only in fair order.[35] Work continued slowly on the tunnel with several further accidents: in March 1850 an explosion killed two workmen and injured ten, three of them critically; Le Fanu witnessed the carnage. Although far advanced in the tunnel excavation six months later Dargan agreed on final settlement of his bills at £40,000 and also that the company would take over completion of the tunnel.[36] For a time work stopped completely although it was discussed often, such as over a dinner in the Imperial Hotel, Cork, where Dargan often stayed. That evening, 20 March 1853, Le Fanu commented Dargan was 'gloriously drunk'.

Many people expected Dargan to retire on completion of the Cork line and indeed the line to Galway, which he also built a few years later, but that was not the nature of the man and he went on to work on many other railways and projects.

South from Carlow

The Irish South-Eastern Railway (ISER), the promoter of a line from Carlow to Kilkenny, was only nominally independent. Its sizeable neighbour, the GS&WR, held half its capital, ran its trains and in time absorbed the company. Once again

Bagenalstown is one of John Macneill's stations, its exquisite balance of twin platform entrances, round windows and side pavilions show the influence of Palladio. The design carries through onto the platform side of the building.

John Macneill and James Perry were active in promoting the line and the contract went to Dargan for an extremely modest £2800 a mile; £10–11,000 per mile would be more common.[37] He began work on 14 January 1847, just after starting the long Thurles-Cork section and the Cork tunnel. Dargan was a busy man, at the same time he was building several other lines: Drogheda to Portadown, the Liverpool & Bury Railway, Limerick to Tipperary, Belfast & Ballymena Railway, Newry to Warrenpoint as well as reclamation work on the Foyle and in Wexford.

Rattling Down to Carlow

In the 1990s security on Iarnród Éireann was somewhat looser than it is today and when travelling by train I often asked the driver if I could travel with him in the cab. I was hardly ever refused and made many fantastic journeys on Dargan's lines such as Dublin to Belfast, Waterford to Limerick and Dublin to Cork. Two such trips stand out, one on the goods-only line from Drogheda to Navan and Kingscourt: at each of the many level crossings one of the crew got down to open the gates, the long gypsum train went through and we waited while he closed the gates again and caught up with us.

Another memorable journey was Dublin to Bagenalstown. Passenger carriages ride smoothly but a heavy, elderly locomotive running on old track made it a bone-shaking journey for anyone in the driver's cab at the time. As we turned off the Cork line at Cherryville Junction heading for Dargan's home county of Carlow the driver increased his speed. The locomotive bucked and shook and rattled, swinging from side to side. The noise in the cab became intense and we had to shout to make ourselves heard. Within ten minutes the speed indicator stopped working but the driver, being an old hand, wasn't surprised and could assess his speed accurately. It will be a relief to know that track, rolling stock and driver comfort have improved hugely since the 1980s.

In April 1847 Dargan laid the first stone of the very fine Barrow viaduct south of Bagenalstown, designed by Macneill with five arches of limestone over the river and two over land. Carlow to Bagenalstown opened on 24 July 1848 and two years later work resumed south of Bagenalstown. On 14 October 1850 Dargan attended a dinner in the Clubhouse, Kilkenny with the engineers and directors of the ISER, GS&WR and Waterford & Kilkenny Railway to discuss the opening, which took place on 12 November. He was at yet another dinner in Freemasons' Hall where McDonnell, the GS&WR chairman, mentioned rather indiscreetly that his £40,000 bill was settled, proposing a fulsome toast to one whose 'intelligence and perseverance' made the project such a success. 'His enterprise was an honour to his country and a credit to himself' and he was 'true to his word, faithful to his promise and very well regarded by those whom he employed'.[38] The ISER closed its accounts with Dargan although he continued to attend its meetings and became a director in April 1852. The table below shows the completion rate for railways in Ireland, many of them Dargan's work.

**Table 5.1: TOTAL MILEAGE OF RAILWAYS OPEN IN
IRELAND FOR YEARS 1836–50**[39]

1836	6	1841	13½	1846	65
1837	6	1842	13½	1847	120
1838	6	1843	31	1848	209
1839	6	1844	31	1849	361
1840	13½	1845	65	1850	475

South from Cork

Around the time Dargan was finishing the Cork line in the late 1840s he fell into completing a 6-mile (10 km) suburban line, the Cork Blackrock & Passage Railway (CB&PR), running south-east from the Munster capital. He had submitted his tender a few years before with an estimate of £70,000 but according to Le Fanu 'Dargan was not in for it' and the contract went to the Dundalk-based Moores brothers for the considerably lower figure of £37,000.

Industrial troubles were not exclusively Dargan's for within days Moores' workmen downed tools optimistically demanding a 250 per cent increase from 1s 4d a day to £1 a week, and to emphasize the point pelted the unfortunate brothers with stones. They modified their demands to 12s a week and no superintendence, so they could 'idle their time as they had previously done on public works', as the *Irish Railway Gazette* put it in its cranky way. The paper proposed that any man refusing 1s 4d a day should be put on a treadmill and fed gruel and water.[40]

· The Moores' troubles proved enduring and in June 1849, having completed half the line as far as Toureen, they signed over their contract to Dargan who agreed to make a substantial shares purchase to finance the rest of the construction. Macneill was the engineer and announced Dargan would also run the train services with the involvement of John Dawson of Phibsboro, the firm that built the Dargan Saloon (see Chapter 6). Trial runs took place in May 1850 and the line opened on 8 June 1850 with ten trains in each direction daily. Although a director and much involved in the railway there were limitations in that the Bank of Ireland retained Dargan's CB&PR shares against his heavy borrowings and in May 1857 he had to obtain its proxy form to vote at a half-year meeting. The Bank of Ireland featured prominently in Dargan's commercial life, sometimes sympathetically, often less so.

Dargan showed his ongoing interest in matters maritime when the railway company began running steamers from the berth at Passage to Cobh, the terminus of a projected line from Cork (not built by Dargan). He also acquired the Cork River Steamers Co. in May 1856 in partnership with some of CB&PR directors.[41] He resigned from the railway board in November 1857 and many years later the company extended the line to Crosshaven, converting it to narrow gauge. The line closed in 1932, a good deal earlier than many others throughout the country.

An Unfortunate Railway: Linking Waterford and Limerick

Several engineers kept a diary, journal or letter book of their projects including Charles Vignoles, William Le Fanu and John Macneill but unfortunately not Dargan (or else they have been lost). These records give invaluable information on the day to day problems and successes encountered while working on a project, sometimes intermingled with totally mundane matters. One of the more detailed but sadly least reliable diary accounts of railway engineering and Dargan's methods is that kept by Richard Boyse Osborne who was resident engineer under Vignoles as chief engineer and over Dargan on the line from Waterford to Limerick for the aptly named Waterford and Limerick Railway (W&LR).[42] Curiously the very first act for a railway in Ireland was for one following the same W&LR route surveyed by Alexander Nimmo in 1826 and passed by parliament eight years before the Dublin & Kingstown opened.[43]

Osborne was born in England and worked in North America, specializing in bridge construction. He said Vignoles interviewed him for the job at his Trafalgar Square offices after inquiring about his experience and his ancestry. At the first W&LR general meeting in 1845 Vignoles told Dargan he had a good chance of winning the contract and he did indeed win that for Limerick to Tipperary against few if any other competitors.[44] At the turning of the first sod at Boher on 15 October 1845 Dargan spoke briefly, gave a 'large sum of money' to a group of locals and £5 to James McCormack, the tenant of the field to 'entertain his neighbours' with dinner for forty afterwards in Cruise's Hotel, Limerick. Within a fortnight 300 men were at work near Limerick, earning 9s a week in winter, 10s in summer. In what was becoming a standard pattern, 500 men disrupted the works demanding employment and only dispersed when seventy-five started on the job and the rest were promised work as soon as Dargan had the land. An interesting sidelight to this issue is that it is one of the few existing references to the involvement of Dargan's brother, James, with his more famous sibling. Osborne wrote: 'Jas Dargan, the brother and chief foreman of the contractor noted the names of the men lucky enough to be employed.'[45]

Osborne was not an easy man to work with and Dargan, Vignoles and the company chairman had many difficulties with him. Similar to his adventures on the Foyle reclamation Dargan found himself caught between several warring parties, making his position as contractor almost impossible. Osborne's diary entry describes an 1845 incident:

> Mr Vignoles and Mr Dargan, the great Irish Contractor, were ... ready to inspect the plans and profiles. (No other contractor was allowed to bid.) They

arranged the price to the satisfaction of both. I had prepared the work to be let under the schedule of prices as by our American system. Dargan did not wish to take work under that plan but I carried my point with Vignoles.[46]

There are many discrepancies between Osborne's version of events and dates and those in the company minutes and the press of the day, but as he wrote large parts of his diary late in life this may account for the inaccuracies and his attempts to justify his own shortcomings. Nonetheless the company advertised as far afield as Liverpool for the next section, Tipperary to Waterford, and gave the contract to Hammond Murray Patterson who were not long for the commercial world and expired soon after they had won the 26-mile (42 km) contract from Dublin to Enfield on the line to Galway. In the meantime land claims and labour troubles delayed Dargan further: his men stopped work in February 1846, demanding a rise of 2s a week, and having spent over £150,000 up to that year the company was in financial difficulties.[47] It did not help that a bridge built by the unfortunate Osborne, 'a beautiful piece of work', collapsed in August 1846. By contrast the directors thoroughly approved of Meagher's bridge, near Limerick, which Dargan had built. It was an 81-ft structure of wood and iron, made in Limerick.

A stormy W&LR shareholders meeting later that year questioned the competence of both Vignoles and Osborne and challenged the high legal and engineering costs as well as the endless works delays. When Lord Glengall turned the first sod of the Tipperary-Waterford section near Cahir in March 1847 Osborne wrote that the delays were not Dargan's fault nor that of his 2000 men and that they would work night shifts if necessary. By this time Vignoles had been fired for absence from the job, which was probably understandable, but it was difficult for him to be available constantly for a stop-start project like this. It was equally problematic for Dargan who could not keep men and plant idle while the company scrambled around looking for funds and someone to blame. Osborne too was under threat over disagreements about gradients, masonry and work methods and his general competence. An endorsement by the Drainage Commissioners did little to assuage the criticisms of the W&LR board.[48]

The company was now in severe financial difficulties and met the Lord Lieutenant to seek state aid. Dargan too was threatening to withdraw because the railway could not pay him except with almost worthless shares. Osborne's version is different, claiming Dargan resigned after a row between the two engineers and that James Dargan urged the workmen to 'live quietly in their boarding houses' until work resumed. This was highly unrealistic: what were they to live on? Osborne thought well of Dargan despite their differences of opinion and saw his departure as part of a conspiracy to attack him: 'The abandonment of Dargan's contract failed to cripple me, as expected, and the work with little loss of time went on at the same prices!'[49] This is pure fantasy: Dargan's contract was not cancelled, the works definitely did not go ahead and the company fired Osborne in November 1847.

Osborne gleefully describes his own dismissal, an incident that says much about him and the W&LR. On being summoned to the company's offices in Waterford to receive his marching orders, a senior official, Saunders, told him the company was unable to make the final salary payment due him. Osborne said he would take a cheque in the belief at some stage the funds would be there to meet it. Then using alleyways and short cuts he knew, he strode swiftly through the city to the company's bank and cashed the cheque. As he was leaving the bank a messenger from the W&LR was arriving with instructions to stop the payment.[50] Dargan must have found it hard to deal with such chicanery.

Captain Simmons inspected Limerick–Tipperary in April 1848 and passed it despite expressing concern about the very narrow cuttings where land slips posed a real hazard. He also queried the unprotected crossing at Tipperary; Dargan was at the same time building the GS&WR from Thurles south to cross the W&LR line at Limerick Junction and this opened a few months later.

The W&LR had agreed Dargan should build the Tipperary-Waterford section, despite Osborne's certainty he had gone and an equal lack of clarity how it was going to pay for it. However, there was increasing annoyance from the shareholders regarding the long delays. One proprietor, Maj. John Kennedy, felt so strongly he wrote and published a pamphlet in Calcutta on what he saw as the source of the company's woes. There were, he said, too many sharp curves on the line, steep inclines that were heavy on fuel and locomotives, badly located stations, poor ballast, extravagant station buildings, timber bridges and double instead of single tracks.[51] There is a grain of truth in all these accusations, as a run on the line even today will show. Kennedy's criticism of Dargan's role is even more trenchant and he urged the company to free itself from 'the ruinous contract by which Mr Dargan claims we are bound to him' for Tipperary-Cahir. Dargan's cost estimate of £57,000 should have been £28,000, according to Kennedy. This costing was wishful thinking: hardly any single line was built for less than £11,000 a mile so this figure would not produce three miles even with the most stringent economies.

A year later a weary company told its even wearier shareholders Dargan would complete the line from Tipperary as far as Fiddown, eight miles from Waterford, for £400,000, a hefty sum and a good deal higher than the one Kennedy projected. His offer depended on a state loan materializing but he did promise to make up any capital shortfall. There were just 300 men working in October 1850, rising to 800 the following summer near Cahir. There Dargan built a fine viaduct over the Suir with three spans, two outer wrought-iron and plated box girders on masonry abutments to a design matching the nearby station by William Fairbairn of Manchester from whom Dargan ordered many of his locomotives. The bridge with castellated towers at each end opened in 1853 and had two tracks originally but was later singled. It was the scene of a serious accident in December 1955 when a beet train ran through the buffers and fell through the gap on the bridge where the rails had been lifted. Both driver and fireman were killed.

Dargan built the very fine pioneering box girder bridge carrying the Waterford-Limerick line over the River Suir just west of Cahir station. This painting shows a detail of a corner of the bridge. Painting by Alice Coyle.

Dargan completed the last section to Newrath near Waterford and then handed it over to the company. The line opened on 11 September 1854. The extent of Dargan's involvement with this company, even more impecunious than most, is significant. He was, as in several other instances, contractor and financier, three of his engines were a major part of its fleet and he ran its train services. Seven months' receipts amounted to £12,643 of which he received £8808 and the balance went to the W&LR. This degree of commitment put severe financial pressure on him, major player as he was, when the Royal Bank of Ireland asked the GS&WR to guarantee a number of his W&LR shares presented as collateral for a loan.[52] Understandably Dargan sought to protect his investment by proposing himself for W&LR board membership but one shareholder was outraged at the notion of a contractor with a large unsettled account 'becoming a director and paying himself his own account to my cost'.[53] This criticism failed to recognize that the company did owe Dargan a substantial sum and that given his reputation he was unlikely to bankrupt the company to gain a partial payment. Further economies followed such as a cut in wages and directors' fees.

In the summer of 1854 Dargan was busy connecting the W&LR with the Kilkenny line, sorting out a subsidence at Dunkitt and reusing building materials from the Dublin Art-Industry Exhibition (see Chapter 6) to build the main station at Waterford. It was said to preserve some of the features of Sir John Benson's design for the Leinster Lawn Exhibition building. Unfortunately the station was demolished some years ago to be replaced with a building of little merit. Some of the original Exhibition ironwork is still in place supporting the platform roof.

James Dargan, William's brother, who worked with him as an engineer on the W&LR died in Limerick on 1 September 1854, aged thirty-nine. In his will dated 29 March 1852, James had £800 in cash and 'linen, plate, household furniture and other chattels'. All this he left to his brother William, Thomas Edwards of Moat (sic) and James Boland of Athlone in trust for James' wife, also called Jane Dargan, neé Walsh. James mentioned that William had just bought the family homestead at Ballyhide and had promised it to his son, also called James Dargan. However, James junior did not receive the 101 acres at Crossleigh as William Dargan sold the land to Maj. Gen. Henry Thomas on 16 May 1854.[54]

A Self-Contained Seaside Line

The coastal town of Tramore (aptly, Trá Mor, the great strand), has always been a popular resort for the people of Waterford and surrounding areas, so that a short railway to it could be fairly sure of paying its way. Its viability was helped by the fact that once again Dargan agreed to finance most of the construction cost by taking a large number of the 4800 £10 shares as payment and accepting bonds for any bills outstanding on his £41,500 contract after completion. This was a hard offer to refuse. Le Fanu defended the Waterford & Tramore Railway (W&TR) bill several time before House of Commons committees and in time became engineer, walking the entire 7¼ miles (12 km) of the route in April 1852. In December the company signed the contract with the 'philanthropic and successful promoter', as the Mayor of Waterford described Dargan.[55] Work began in February 1853 but a month later there were reports of labour shortages, allegedly because there were no more able-bodied men in the local workhouse.

Railway Vandalism on the Tramore Line

Le Fanu tells of riding a works engine just before the Tramore line opened when he saw a boy of about ten placing a massive stone on the rails just ahead. The iron guard in front pushed the stone aside and he and the driver stopped the engine to give chase to the boy.

> We led him back, weeping piteously, and took him up on the engine. He besought us not to kill him. We told him we would not kill him, but that we would bring him into Waterford, where he would be tried, and undoubtedly hanged next morning for trying to kill us. When we had gone about half a mile we stopped and let him off; and didn't the little chap run! He evidently feared lest we should change our minds again and deliver him up to the hangman.[56]

Construction was straightforward enough and the single line opened on 5 September 1853 with healthy passenger numbers right from the start requiring ten trains in each direction daily. Dargan supplied three Bury engines to run them but being past their best they were unequal to the task and were replaced.[57] Since the company still owed him a large amount it made him a director in March 1856, the same year he used W&TR bonds to raise loans totalling £12,800 from the Bank of Ireland. The fact that there was no quibble suggests the bank rated W&TR stocks a lot higher than it did W&LR shares. Soon after William Malcolmson, chairman of the latter company, bought Dargan's 1500 Tramore railway shares and replaced him on the board.[58]

The line needed fairly heavy renewal just five years after it opened: the company raised and re-ballasted the trackbed, completed major repairs to the turn-tables at each end and relaid the road to Tramore station. Either Dargan's work was not to his usual standard or twenty heavily laden trains daily took a heavy toll on the line. It closed in 1961.

Dargan on Holiday: Railing to the Kingdom

The first railway penetration of the Kingdom of Kerry took place in early 1846 when William Le Fanu prepared the estimates for the Killarney Junction Railway (KJR) between the Cork line at Mallow and Killarney, which was already developing into a popular tourist destination. Le Fanu's opinion of the first section, fortunately not built by Dargan, was damning: 'the works are very badly done – the masonry execrable'.[59] Construction stopped completely until Dargan came to the rescue once again. The two met in Mallow and then went to Cork on 1 September 1851 to study the estimates and to dine together. Three days later the KJR board met in Killarney and agreed to assign the contract to Dargan; work began under his trusty manager Edwin Edwards in spring 1852. After several meetings with Dargan in Dublin and Killarney, Le Fanu plotted a two-mile route deviation, which he said saved the company £70,000.[60]

From 22–25 July 1852 Dargan combined work with pleasure while staying at the Victoria Hotel, Killarney. Le Fanu, Dargan and 'his three young ladies' the Misses Maine, Allen and Haslam (his wife Jane's niece), went on a tour of Cork and Kerry. There is no mention of Jane. This is the only recorded occasion that Dargan took a holiday and therefore worth examination. It is only known because Le Fanu wrote of it in his diary. On 23 July the group explored Killarney and the Gap of Dunloe and the next day Muckross and Glengarriff, taking a boat to Bantry. The following day they went to Gougane Barra and on to Cork while some of the party, including Dargan, explored West Cork.[61]

Back to work in Killarney on 6 April 1853 Dargan told GS&WR chairman McDonnell that the first section of the KJR was almost ready and on 5 May, 20 miles (32 km) opened between Mallow and Freemount, for once with little ceremony. With 300 men working day and night the line was ready to be opened by the Lord Lieutenant when he arrived by special train in July 1853. The following year Dargan offered to take 2600 £10 shares in the company to raise capital in this line. The builder, as one newspaper described him, was 'the Peto or Brassey of Ireland, who from small beginnings has risen to be the foremost man in the material and practical progress of his country'.[62]

The extension of this line farther west to Tralee fell to the Tralee & Killarney Railway (T&KR) with Lord Carlise turning the first sod at Killarney on 19 September 1855. There were three cheers for the line and three more for the taking of Sebastopol, the Crimean war being then at its height. As was the norm nothing further happened for six months or so during which time the board met at Kingsbridge (it was from the start closely linked with the GS&WR as was the Killarney Junction Railway) and Dargan took the contract for £58,000, beginning work on 2 May 1856. Edward McDonnell, GS&WR chairman, also chaired the T&KR and urged shareholders to meet their calls (for interim payments on their shares) so Dargan could keep his 350 men at work.

Railway Hotels in Galway and Killarney

Railway companies built a number of de luxe hotels close to their stations to serve passengers and to boost tourism traffic. One of the first in Ireland, the Railway Hotel, Galway, now the Meyrick, was built by Dargan to a design by John Mulvany and opened in the summer of 1852. At one time you could walk directly and very conveniently from the platform into the hotel lobby as is possible at London Victoria.

The Railway Hotel, Killarney, opened on 11 July 1854 with 100 beds and is directly opposite Killarney station. A centenary GSH booklet from 1954 describes the hotel and its affluent Victorian guests:

> *Solid, luxurious in its jewel-like casing, it provided the proper background for the stately crinoline-and-antimacassar period. Victorian characters straight out of the novels of those years – and frequently engaged in writing them – paraded solemnly across its halls and drawing rooms, slept voluminously in its feather-stuffed four posters and dined almost gluttonously from its heroic table d'hôte.[63]*

A wages row broke out a few months later. In summer the men earned 10*s* a week with forty-five minutes for breakfast and half an hour for dinner (lunch) but in the winter the rate fell to 9*s* for the shorter hours with thirty-minute and fifteen-minute meal breaks. If work finished at 1 pm the men only earned 6*d* and up to 4.30 pm the rate was a shilling. The *Munster News* observed this was not Dargan's style and the row may have centred on the actions of a subcontractor he employed.[64] The regular delays in gaining land access and finance followed for over a year until the line eventually opened on 16 July 1859, the day after Captain Ross passed it. Le Fanu attended the opening dinner in the Railway Hotel, having just returned from London where he and most likely Dargan were at a Commons committee hearing on the Wicklow Railway. In 1860 the GS&WR absorbed both the KJR and the TKR.

Limerick Lines

Dargan built two lines at the western end of the W&LR, before it began extending up the west coast towards Sligo. One ran south-west to the port of Foynes and the other north to Ennis. Sir Matthew Barrington of Barrington's Hospital fame who lived at Glenstal Castle before it became a Benedictine monastery promoted a line to Foynes in the hope of beating Galway in the race to become the favoured transatlantic port in Ireland. Foynes never became the gate for Atlantic shipping that Barrington hoped it would, but in the twentieth century it was the base for a flying boat service between Ireland and North America.[65] Like the Tramore line Le Fanu was again engineer and Dargan was a major investor, having the largest individual holding of 1300 shares. All three men were heavily involved in aspects of the line and in a number of other ways: Le Fanu later married one of Barrington's daughters.

The night before the first sod ceremony of the Limerick & Foynes Railway (L&FR) on 29 September 1853 there was a banquet in Cruise's Hotel, Limerick and Le Fanu wrote in his diary: 'Dargan got very drunk. To bed 3 am'.[66] Nonetheless Le Fanu was up at 7 am to travel to Foynes for the ceremony, taking a steamer back to Limerick. It's not certain whether Dargan made it or not. As was often the case the initial sod-turning did not mean work started immediately and it was some months before the company signed a contract with Dargan.

In due course his foreman, named O'Brien, arrived at Adare on 5 May 1854 (along with a number of skilled workmen from the Dublin & Wicklow Railway that Dargan was building at the time) and almost immediately a number of violent incidents erupted as locals imagined they were being deprived of work.[67] Such a reaction was understandable but misguided as experienced men were needed at the start to supervise and train new workmen. A more serious assault followed, leaving six of Dargan's stonemasons in Barrington's Hospital. Two men were arrested and from then on an RIC sergeant and ten constables guarded the site.

This IOU for £500 made out to Lord Dunraven on 6 July 1858 bears Dargan's signature and has his office address, 74 Harcourt Street. Adare, the seat of the Dunravens, is on the line to Foynes and the date coincides with the time Dargan was building this branch line.

When Captain H. Tyler arrived in April 1855 for the usual inspection of the first section he noted a few problems. He described the approach to the fifteen-arch Robertstown viaduct at Foynes as incomplete and 'treacherous': the trackbed needed attention, the fencing along the line was inadequate and Foynes lacked a signal and that vital piece of station furniture, a clock. Tyler also criticized the absence of a telegraph system, insisting that operations be strictly controlled. Dargan planned to run ballast trains to work on the line in between passenger services but Tyler stipulated they must be in a siding at least fifteen minutes before any passenger train was due or else run at night. Despite these significant reservations and on the understanding they would be remedied, Tyler passed the line to open, an indication of the easier safety standards of the day.[68]

By July 1856 Dargan held £33,000 in L&FR shares and was owed a large sum of money, a fairly common pattern. Le Fanu told the board Dargan could not continue with the works until he was paid, its response being to raise £42,000 in preference shares.[69] The plan succeeded and work resumed slowly over the winter of 1856, with the added annoyance of the collapse of a metal bridge at Attyflin. Rathkeale to Askeaton opened on 11 May 1857 and Captain Tyler made his third appearance on the L&FR at the end of April 1858 to pass it to open.

Shannon Steamers

Dargan always recognized the traffic potential from linking train and boat services and Foynes presented the perfect opportunity. After the L&FR opened he began running steamers across the estuary of the Shannon between Foynes and Kilrush. He chartered the *Koh-i-Noor* and then bought the 191-ft *Kelpie* in 1858, to channel passengers onto the railway, which was not paying its way. This caused some concern to the proprietors who were vocal at the half-year meeting on 29 September 1860 in their objections to a directors' payment of £687.[70] The *Kelpie* was by contrast a success: despite competition from a City of Dublin SP steamer in the first few months she carried 14,000 passengers and earned £80 a week, almost a third of the L&FR's total receipts. As with the Tramore railway Dargan sold his railway shares to William Malcolmson in 1861 and as he began to wind down his business affairs disposed of the *Kelpie* around the same time. Her luck ran out when she was sunk in 1862 during the American Civil War while engaged in the lucrative but high-risk activity of running the Union blockade against the Southern states, a highly effective blockade stretching from the mouth of the Rio Grande to Chesapeake Bay.

North of Limerick Dargan rescued the Limerick & Ennis Railway (L&ER) in September 1856 when the appointed contractors, Johnson & Kinder, fell by the wayside.[71] At that stage five miles were ready for track and the materials for the Shannon bridge at Islandpoint had arrived at Limerick by ship from Scotland. Dargan agreed to complete the line in eighteen months for £53,000 plus 300 shares and signed a bond for £100,000 with Barrington & Jeffers, solicitors. This firm drafted and executed his will ten years later. Edwin Edwards, Dargan's manager, was busy all along the line the following year but within a few months the works had ground to a halt. James Pratt, resident engineer, told a half-year meeting Dargan planned to open the entire line by August 1858. But when Col Yolland RE inspected the timber Shannon bridge he called for a number of changes, eventually insisting on an iron replacement. A year later the colonel was still not happy and delayed passing Clare-castle to Ennis for several weeks.[72] Despite these setbacks the line did eventually open and Dargan tried to reassure the beleaguered shareholders in November 1859 by telling them a railway doubled its traffic every seven years.

Glenstal Castle

Dargan also worked with the Barrington family as a consultant on the rebuilding of their home, Glenstal Castle, Co. Limerick. It was to be Norman Revival with some folly-like features. Thomas Deane worked on it as early as 1839 as had William Bardwell, who strove for a twelfth-century look. He carved an inscription on the turret 'Bardwell me fecit' with the year 1839 cut so that it might be mistaken for 1139.[73] In October 1846 Dargan employed architect John Kelly to supervise the works. He worked on the estimates with Kelly and was often on site though in March 1847 he had a bad cold and his doctor advised him to 'go home to Belfast and rest for 7–10 days'.[74] There was little progress to show when Kelly suggested to Dargan they halt the works in August 1848 after a wet summer. Kelly's relations with Dargan and Barrington were difficult, much of it to do with money, and Dargan sought estimates from two other builders to finish the castle.[75] Towards the end of the year this phase of the works was drawing to a close though Kelly complained he had been 'most shamefully treated' and faced insolvency. The works continued in stages with several different builders for several years, by which time Dargan was no longer involved.[76]

Tullamore and Fermoy

Dargan completed two other branch lines for the GS&WR around this time, the first off the Cork line from Portarlington to Tullamore. This was sensitive since the GS&WR was seen to be invading the territory of the Midland Great Western Railway and Dargan was committed at that time to build a large section of the Galway line for that company. He began work on the contract, worth £30,000, in May 1858, a good five years after winning it and nine months later had 1580 men at work, some by moonlight. Captain H.W. Tyler RE passed it to open on 30 September 1859.[77]

The Fermoy branch was trickier for Dargan and his colleague Edwin Edwards, although he employed subcontractors for the Kilcummer and Carrickabrick viaducts, the firm of Andersons completed the ironwork and John Cunningham did the masonry.[78] Carrickabrick was a large structure, bigger than the Mallow viaduct and longer than the Chetwynd viaduct built many years later on the Bandon line. The Fermoy line opened on 17 May 1860 and cost £110,000 including bridges and stations. When Dargan settled his accounts in June this effectively ended his direct contract work with the GS&WR.

The Line to Galway: Midland Great Western Railway

Tucked away between the Four Courts and the North Circular Road in Dublin is a large Egyptian-style granite building, the Broadstone. This was once the terminus and head office of the second-largest railway in Ireland, the Midland Great Western Railway (MGWR), known as the Midland. The building's solid, square design suggested safety and financial reliability and the company was keen to inspire both. The station is the design of John Skipton Mulvany, 'a chaste and truly noble erection ... combining in its details the peculiarities of the Egyptian and Grecian style of architecture', as an 1850 company guide described it, while Craig said it was 'the last building in Dublin to partake of the sublime ... it is hard to praise it too highly'. Lamenting its closure in 1937 he added: 'Its lonely grandeur is emphasized now by its disuse as a terminus ... much of the poetry of travel perished when the Broadstone was abandoned.'[79] Midland trains ran to Galway, Sligo, Mayo and Cavan and some described it as the most Irish of the large companies, whatever that means. Dargan worked closely with the company's chief engineer, George Hemans, whose appointment was largely through the influence of the ubiquitous James Perry, a director of the MGWR among many other companies. As he often did, Dargan was an early investor in a railway from whom he sought contracts and by 1845 held seventy-seven shares valued at £1500.[80]

The first Midland section in 1845 was the 26 miles (42 km) to Enfield alongside the Royal Canal, a difficult stretch on account of the soft, boggy terrain. Dargan's

108

tender at £77,000 was the fifth highest so the ill-fated firm of Hammond Murray Patterson won it with an estimate of £41,553. They went out of business before starting work, after which the MGWR was imprudent enough to give the contract to the next in line, the brothers Jeffs. Dargan was very preoccupied with the GS&WR at this time and as events unfolded, fortunate not to win this section. In line with the usual pattern, the MGWR struggled to stay afloat through these early days via loans from the directors and shipping companies and paying for goods and services with shares and debentures.[81] As the Jeffs worked towards Mullingar, in due course they fell out both with each other and with the company, suing it for monies they claimed were owed. This cleared the decks for Dargan to make a strong bid for the 76 miles (122 km) from Mullingar to Galway; opting for reliability and honest dealing the company wisely accepted his tender of £500,000 with the help of a state loan to the railway of the same amount.[82] There were bonfires in Galway and the bells of St Nicholas' church rang out when news of Dargan winning the contract reached the city.

The monolithic Egyptian style façade of the Broadstone station on Constitution Hill near the King's Inns is the design of the talented architect John Mulvany. It was once the headquarters of the Midland Great Western Railway and like every other railway terminus in Dublin it was remote from the city centre. It closed in 1937 and is now a Bus Éireann depot.

Ireland's Most Afflicted Station: Broombridge

The MGWR's line to the west once started from the Broadstone terminus and closed in 1937 but retains some very fine original features. The route runs through a long deep cutting under the North Circular Road to emerge beside the Royal Canal at Liffey Junction, once a busy point for transferring cattle to the nearby markets.

The next station on the line to Maynooth is Broombridge, arguably the most distressed station in Ireland. Every single thing in, on or near it has been vandalized out of existence. Name boards are long gone, fireproof metal seats have been uprooted and show attempts to set them alight, fences torn down, lights smashed and even stone flags jemmied out of the platform. The long narrow field alongside is popular with car thieves and joyriders who leave evidence of their leisure activities in the shape of half-a-dozen or more burnt-out cars. A stranger alighting here in error might think they were in a post-apocalyptic nightmare.

As if it hasn't suffered enough the station name, Broombridge, has been rendered into dog-Irish: Droichead na Scuab. Broom is a plant with bright yellow flowers and scuab does indeed mean broom, but of the domestic sweeping variety. So the current Irish name means 'the Bridge of the Sweeping Brush'.

But Broombridge has one redeeming historic feature. The bridge at the west end of the station has a plaque to commemorate the thunder-clap insight of mathematician Sir William Rowan Hamilton of Trinity College Dublin. In 1843 while walking with his wife along the Royal Canal from his house at Dunsink Observatory he had a flash of genius, discovering quaternion equations.

He was so anxious not to lose the idea that he scratched the formula into the stonework of the bridge. He was forgiven this antisocial act and a stone plaque replaced his early artwork. It has this inscription: 'Here as he walked by on the 16th of October 1843 Sir William Rowan Hamilton in a flash of genius discovered the fundamental formula for quaternion multiplication $i^2 = j^2 = k^2 = ij = -1...$' The rest is illegible as the plaque has been vandalized.

After ten years wrestling with the problem Hamilton realized that in constructing algebra, maths had to move from three real numbers to four and that the algebra of quaternions was not commutative: a x b was not equal to b x a.

His discovery opened up a host of mathematical possibilities. NASA applied Hamilton's work on cone-theory to calculate the trajectory of

Apollo 11 on its journey back to Earth from the Moon and it is used today in satnav devices. He was also an amateur poet and a friend of William Wordsworth, who stayed with him at Dunsink.

The cash-strapped company relied optimistically on the state loan to cover the construction costs and by agreeing to take £130,000 of his fee in bonds, shares and debentures, Dargan was effectively subsidising the construction of the line to Galway, something he had done many times but which few, if any, of his competitors could do. Building lengthy lines for the two largest railway companies at almost the same time, Thurles to Cork and Mullingar to Galway demanded close attention and was a high financial risk. The plant, manpower and organizational skills needed to complete the two were enormous and if Dargan failed on either, the negative effects on his business and his reputation would have lasted years. Thomas Jeffs had no such concern for his firm's reputation and when he heard Dargan had won this large contract again sued the MGWR for £20,000, eventually winning £4500 in damages plus 6d costs from the Queen's Bench in June 1853; Dargan was summoned as a witness.

X marks the spot. Near Broombridge station in 1843 William Rowan Hamilton had a flash of genius, discovering quaternion equations. His insight helped to put astronauts on the Moon and guides errant motorists to their destination through the use of a satnav device. This plaque records the place where Hamilton scratched the formulae into the stonework of the canal bridge so he wouldn't forget it.

Up to 1937 most Dublin-Galway trains travelled via Mullingar and Moate on the line built by Dargan to Athlone. John Mulvany designed Mullingar station and since this 48–km route closed in 1987 the abandoned western platforms have had a neglected appearance. There is a case today for reopening the branch: around 24 Galway and Mayo trains daily crowd onto the 62 km single track between Portarlington and Athlone; one stoppage and everything comes to a halt. An expanded Connolly station or use of the Phoenix Park tunnel could route some trains to the west via Mullingar and Moate.

Dargan used various means to deliver his materials on site, bringing them by waterway via the Grand Canal to Ballinasloe, past the location of his unhappy experience with the Kilbeggan Canal branch (see Chapter 3) and even by sea to Galway. One sea delivery came to grief: the *Mary of Cork* ran aground on Mutton Island and *HMS Shearwater* came to the rescue. But rather than aiding her and offering assistance, as is the code of the sea, the naval vessel claimed her and her cargo of Dargan's railway materials as salvage.[83]

The Dargan Saloon

One of the finest railway carriages ever built in Ireland, still happily in existence, is the Dargan Saloon. *This is a delightful six-wheeled 31-ft (9 m) luxury carriage, which Dargan built for his personal use as a travelling office, meeting room and bedroom. Prior to this he would have travelled by horse in all weathers to inspect his far-flung engineering projects, staying in lodgings in remote locations. Using one of his own locomotives he could now travel in comfort by train to the railhead in a carriage where he had his own private accommodation.*

Dublin coachmaker John Dawson built it in 1844 with upholstery by the local firm of Robert Mitchell & Co.[84] It has decorated panels and bow glass windows at each end. It is easy to imagine the coach parked in a siding in a remote corner of Connacht and the occasional late-night party with plenty of good claret for senior MGWR officials and Dargan's colleagues such as Le Fanu, Edwards or Vignoles.

When he finished the Midland line to Galway Dargan presented the carriage to the company, which used it for the directors and as a state coach for VIP visitors. Among these in 1879 and 1880 was the Empress Elizabeth of Austria who travelled in it from the London & North Western Railway station at Dublin's North Wall to Kilcock and then Summerhill for month-long hunting trips. She needed her own train as the party arrived with over thirty servants and forty tons of luggage.

Joseph Tatlow, later general manager of the Midland Railway, describes how the board travelled in it in style to the 1891 Ballinasloe horse fair, an important event in the railway's calendar. A lavatory was added in 1904. The coach is a magnificent piece of work, beautifully restored and on public view in the Ulster Folk and Transport Museum at Cultra outside Belfast.

The Dargan Saloon in very handsome MGWR livery settles into its new home at the Ulster Folk and Transport Museum outside Belfast. Photo: Ulster Folk and Transport Museum.

By September 1849 Dargan had 600 men at work between Athlone and Ballinasloe with the colourful cleric Rev. Peter Daly turning the first sod at Renmore (further details of his diverse career below). The guardians of the Mullingar workhouse seized the opportunity to put sixty-five paupers to work on the line and by the following March Dargan had 6000 men, rising to 8500 in the summer and falling again to 1050 in September. He won the contract to build the Galway terminus and the adjoining hotel, both designed by John Skipton Mulvany. The hotel, known up to recently as the Great Southern and now the Meyrick, has a rather severe but imposing appearance in a dominant position overlooking Eyre Square. It opened in 1852, one of the first railway hotels in Ireland, boasting sixty-nine bedrooms, four dining rooms, two coffee rooms and a hundred gas lights.

For a terminus the station is much less impressive than the hotel, being functional and minimalist with a single platform under a rather dingy shed. The side projection of the building where it merges into the hotel resembles the Broadstone or Athlone (MGWR station) but is largely invisible because of its cramped location and the awkward side entrance onto the platform where train passengers compete for space on the narrow pavement with those waiting for buses to all parts of the country. Many of the intermediate stations on the Galway line have much more interesting features, such as Mullingar, Athlone and Athenry, all of them designed by Mulvany.[85]

John Skipton Mulvany, 1813–70: Dargan's Architect

A gifted, prolific architect, Mulvany is considered by some to be the Gandon of his day. Prof. Albert Richardson, author of Monumental Classical Architecture of Great Britain and Ireland, *has high regard for his work: 'Ireland has produced many buildings of renown, but few with the genius of J.S. Mulvany.' His portfolio includes Broadstone, Dun Laoghaire, Blackrock, Athlone and Galway railway stations, the former Railway Hotel, Galway, the Royal St George and Royal Irish Yacht Clubs and Brighton Vale, Monkstown. He tendered unsuccessfully to design Kingsbridge (Heuston) station and although John Macneill favoured his proposal the contract went to Sancton Wood.*

Like Dargan, Mulvany maintained close business links with the Quakers of Ireland, initially via his father's friendship with James Perry. Mulvany designed Perry's grave in Mount Jerome in the style of a miniature Broadstone. He also remodelled Mount Anville for Dargan and almost certainly designed his grave in Glasnevin. Like Dargan, Mulvany was a little ambivalent when deciding whether to be a Catholic or a Protestant and like him he was fond of a glass or two: he died of cirrhosis of the liver aged just fifty-seven.

MIDLAND GREAT WESTERN RAILWAY OF IRELAND.

OPEN TO GALWAY.

TIME and FARE TABLE for DECEMBER 15th, 1853.

Miles from Dublin	DOWN TRAINS.	Daily						Sunday	
	Hours of Starting.	7 . 0 Morn.	10. 30 Morn.	4 . 0 Aftern.	5 . 0 Aftern.	MAIL. 7 . 15 Even.	10 . 0 Night	10. 30 Morn.	MAIL. 7 . 15 Even.
	STATIONS.	1, 2, 3, Class.	1, & 2 Class.	1, 2, 3, Class.	1, 2, 3, Class.	1 & 2 Class.	Goods &c.	1, 2, 3, Class.	1, 2, Class
	TRAINS LEAVE	H. M.	H. M.	H. M.	H. M.	H. M.	H. M.	H. M.	H. M.
—	DUBLIN, at	7. 0	10. 30	4. 0	5. 0	7. 15	10. 0	10. 30	7. 15
4½	*Blanchardstown,*	....	*10. 40	....	* 5. 10	—	....	*10. 40	—
7	*Clonsilla,*	* 7. 20	10. 50	* 4. 20	5. 25	—	....	10. 50	—
9	*Lucan,*	....	*10. 55	* 4. 25	* 5. 33	7. 36	....	*10. 55	7. 36
11	*Leixlip,*	....	*11. 0	* 4. 32	* 5. 40	7. 42	....	*11. 0	7. 42
15	MAYNOOTH,	7. 40	11. 16	* 4. 42	5. 54	7. 52	10. 45	11. 16	7. 52
19	KILCOCK,	7. 50	11. 25	* 4. 52	6. 6	8. 2	11. 0	11. 25	8. 2
21	*Ferns Lock,*	....	*11. 30	4. 58	....	—	....	*11. 30	—
26½	ENFIELD,	8. 5	11. 45	5. 10	6. 30	8. 20	11. 35	11. 45	8. 20
30½	*Moyvalley,*	....	*11. 55	* 5. 22	....	* 8. 28	....	*11. 55	....
36	HILL OF DOWN	8. 20	12. 15	5. 37	....	8. 40	12. 10	12. 15	8. 40
41½	KILLUCAN,	8. 35	12. 35	* 5. 55	....	8. 52	12. 35	12. 30	8. 52
50	MULLINGAR arrives at		12. 50			9. 15		12. 52	9. 15
	leaves at	8. 55	12. 55	6. 25	....	9. 20	1. 10	1. 5	9. 20
58	CASTLETOWN,	9. 15	1 15	6. 50	....	9. 38	1. 40	1. 25	9. 38
62	*Streamstown,*		* 1. 22	* 7. 0	...	—	2. 0	* 1. 32	—
68	MOATE,	9. 35	1. 35	7. 15	....	9. 58	2. 40	1. 45	9. 58
78	ATHLONE, arrives at	10. 0	2. 0	7. 45			3. 30		
	leaves at	10. 20	2. 10		....	10. 22	5. 45	2. 15	10. 22
91½	BALLINASLOE,	10. 55	2. 40	....	....	11. 5	6. 25	2. 45	11. 5
101½	WOODLAWN,	11. 30	3. 20	....	....	11. 26	7. 20	3. 20	11. 26
113½	ATHENRY	12. 0	3. 50	....	....	11. 53	8. 5	3. 50	11. 53
121	*Oranmore,*	*12. 20	* 4, 15	....	....	12. 10	8. 40	* 4. 15	12. 10
126½	GALWAY,	12. 40	4. 30	....	....	12. 30	9. 15	4. 30	12. 30
		P. M.	P. M.	P. M.	P. M.	night.	A. M.	P. M.	night.

With 2nd & 3rd Class, Athlone to Galway.

Stations	FARES — PASSENGERS. 1st Class. s. d.	2nd Class. s. d.	3rd Class. s. d.	4th Class. s. d.	CARRIAGES. Two wheels. s. d.	Four wheels. s. d.	HORSES. One Horse s. d.	Two Horses. (If one Property.) s. d.	Three Horses. (If one Property.) s. d.
DUBLIN, at	—	—	—	—	—	—	—	—	—
Blanchardstown,	0. 10	0. 8	0. 4	0. 3	—	—	—	—	—
Clonsilla,	1. 0	0. 10	0. 7	0. 5	—	—	—	—	—
Lucan,	1. 3	1. 0	0. 9	0. 6	—	—	—	—	—
Leixlip,	1. 6	1. 3	0. 10	0. 7	—	—	—	—	—
MAYNOOTH,	2. 6	2. 0	1. 3	0. 10	5. 0	9. 0	5. 0	9. 6	13. 6
KILCOCK,	3. 0	2. 6	1. 6	1. 1	7. 0	11. 6	7. 0	11. 6	16. 0
Ferns Lock,	3. 6	2. 8	1. 8	1. 2	—	—	—	—	—
ENFIELD,	4. 0	3. 6	2. 2	1. 7	9. 0	13. 6	9. 0	15. 0	20. 0
Moyvalley,	4. 8	4. 0	2. 6	1. 10	—	—	—	—	—
HILL OF DOWN	5. 8	4. 10	3. 0	2. 2	12. 0	18. 6	12. 0	21. 0	28. 0
KILLUCAN,	6. 8	5. 8	3. 5	2. 7	14. 0	21. 0	14. 0	24. 0	32. 6
MULLINGAR	8. 0	6. 8	4. 2	3. 0	17. 0	25. 0	17. 0	30. 0	40. 0
CASTLETOWN,	9. 0	7. 6	4. 10	3. 4	19. 6	30. 0	19. 6	35. 0	49. 0
Streamstown,	10. 0	8. 3	5. 0	3. 6	21. 0	32. 0	21. 0	37. 6	52. 0
MOATE,	11. 0	9. 0	5. 6	3. 9	22. 0	34. 0	23. 0	41. 0	56 6
ATHLONE,	12. 6	10. 0	6. 0	4. 0	26. 0	39. 0	26. 0	47. 6	64. 0
BALLINASLOE,	15. 0	12. 0	7. 0	4. 6	31. 0	46. 6	31. 0	55. 6	76. 6
WOODLAWN,	16. 0	13. 3	8. 0	5. 0	34. 0	51. 0	34. 0	61. 0	84. 6
ATHENRY	18. 0	14. 6	9. 0	5. 4	38. 0	57. 0	38. 0	68. 6	94. 0
Oranmore,	19. 0	15. 3	9. 6	5. 9	40. 0	60. 0	40. 6	73. 6	100. 0
GALWAY,	20. 0	16. 0	10. 0	6. 0	42. 6	63. 6	42. 0	76. 6	106. 0

Miles From Galway.	UP TRAINS.	Daily						Sunday.	
	Hours of Starting.	MAIL. 12.0 Night.	8 . 0 Morn.	8 . 15 Morn.	8 . 30 Morn.	12 . 0 Noon.	4 . 0 Aftern.	4 . 0 Aftern.	MAIL. 12 . 0 Night.
	STATIONS.	1 & 2 Class.	1, 2, 3, Class.	1, 2, 3, Class,	1, 2, Class.	Goods, & 2, 3, & 4 Class.	1, 2, 3, Class.	1, 2, 3, Class.	1, 2, Class.
	TRAINS LEAVE	H. M.	H. M.	H. M.	H. M.	H. M.	H. M.	H. M.	H. M.
—	GALWAY,	12. 0	....	....	8. 30	12. 0	4. 0	4. 0	12. 0
5½	*Oranmore,*	12. 15	....	....	* 8. 45	*12. 20	* 4. 15	* 4. 15	12. 15
13	ATHENRY,	12. 30	....	....	9. 5	12. 55	4. 34	4. 34	12. 30
25	WOODLAWN,	12. 57	....	....	9. 40	1. 45	5. 4	5. 4	12. 57
35	BALLINASLOE,	1. 26	....	....	9. 55	2. 25	5. 21	5. 21	1. 26
48½	ATHLONE, arrives at	2. 0	....	....	10. 20	3. 20	5. 55	5. 55	2. 0
	leaves at	2. 5	8. 0	....	10. 30	3. 40	6. 15	6. 15	2. 5
58½	MOATE,	2. 22	8. 25	....	10. 55	4. 25	6. 38	6. 38	2. 27
64½	*Streamstown,*	—	* 8. 40	....	*11. 10	* 4. 55	* 6. 57	* 6. 57	—
68½	CASTLETOWN,	2. 45	8. 50	....	11. 30	5. 15	7. 7	7. 7	2. 50
76½	MULLINGAR, arrives at	3. 7	....	....	11. 50				
	leaves at	3. 12	9. 10	....	12 0	5. 45	7. 25	7. 30	3. 12
85	KILLUCAN,	3. 31	9. 30	....	12. 18	6. 15	7. 49	7. 49	3. 31
90½	HILL OF DOWN	3. 44	9. 42	....	12. 32	6. 40	8. 3	8. 3	3. 44
96	*Moyvalley,*	—	* 9. 55	....	*12. 49	....	* 8 19	* 8. 19	—
100	ENFIELD,	4. 6	10. 5	8. 15	12. 55	7. 20	8. 30	8. 30	4. 6
105½	*Ferns Lock,*	—	*10. 20	* 8. 30	* 1. 7	....	* 8. 45	* 8. 45	—
107½	KILCOCK,	4. 23	10. 25	8. 36	1. 11	7. 55	8. 53	8 53	4. 23
111½	MAYNOOTH,	4. 32	10. 40	8. 50	1. 22	8. 15	9. 4	9. 4	4. 32
115½	*Leixlip,*	4. 41	*10. 50	* 9. 5	1, 32	....	* 9. 18	* 9. 18	4. 41
117½	*Lucan,*	4. 46	*10. 55	* 9. 11	1. 37	....	* 9. 24	* 9. 24	4. 46
119½	*Clonsilla*	—	*11. 0	9. 17	* 1. 42	....	* 9. 32	* 9. 32	—
122	*Blanchardstown,*	—	*11. 10	* 9. 25	....	....	* 9. 41	* 9. 41	—
126½	DUBLIN,	5. 15	11. 30	9. 45	2. 0	9. 0	10. 0	10. 0	5. 15
		A. M.	A. M.	A. M.	P. M.	P. M.	P. M.	P. M.	A. M.

Stations	FARES. — PASSENGERS. 1st Class. s. d.	2nd Class. s. d.	3rd Class. s. d.	4th Class. s. d.	CARRIAGES. Two wheels. s. d.	Four wheels. s. d.	HORSES. One Horse. s. d.	Two Horses (If one Property.) s. d.	Three Horses. (If one Property.) s. d.
GALWAY,	—	—	—	—	—	—	—	—	—
Oranmore,	1. 0	0. 9	0. 6	0. 3	4. 6	6. 6	2. 0	3. 6	5. 0
ATHENRY,	2. 0	1. 6	1. 0	0. 8	4. 6	6. 6	4. 6	8. 6	11. 6
WOODLAWN,	3, 6	2. 9	2. 0	1. 0	5. 6	8. 0	8. 6	16. 0	22. 0
BALLINASLOE,	5. 0	4. 0	3. 0	1. 6	11. 6	17. 0	11. 6	21. 0	29. 0
ATHLONE,	7. 6	6. 0	4. 0	2. 0	16. 6	24. 6	16 6	30. 0	41. 0
MOATE,	9 0	7. 0	4. 6	2. 3	20. 0	29. 6	19. 6	36. 0	49. 0
Streamstown,	10. 0	8. 0	5. 0	2. 6	21. 0	31. 6	21. 0	38. 6	52. 6
CASTLETOWN,	11. 0	8. 6	5. 2	2. 8	23. 0	34. 6	23. 0	42. 0	57. 6
MULLINGAR,	12. 0	9. 4	5. 10	3. 0	25. 6	38. 6	25. 6	46. 6	64. 0
KILLUCAN,	13. 4	10. 4	6, 7	3. 5	28. 6	42. 6	28. 6	51. 6	71. 0
HILL OF DOWN	14. 4	11. 2	7. 0	3. 10	30. 6	45. 6	30. 6	55. 0	76. 0
Moyvalley,	15. 4	12. 0	7. 6	4. 2	—	—	—	—	—
ENFIELD,	16. 0	12. 6	7. 10	4. 5	33. 6	50. 0	33. 6	60. 6	83. 6
Ferns Lock,	16. 6	13. 4	8. 4	4. 10	—	—	—	—	—
KILCOCK,	17. 0	13. 6	8. 6	4. 11	36. 0	54 0	36. 0	64. 6	89. 0
MAYNOOTH,	17. 6	14. 0	8. 9	5. 2	37. 6	56 0	37. 6	68. 0	93. 6
Leixlip,	18. 6	14. 9	9. 2	5. 5	—	—	—	—	—
Lucan,	18. 9	15. 0	9. 3	5. 6	—	—	—	—	—
Clonsilla	19. 0	15. 2	9. 5	5. 7	—	—	—	—	—
Blanchardstown,	19. 2	15. 4	9. 8	5. 9	—	—	—	—	—
DUBLIN,	20. 0	16. 0	10. 0	6. 0	42. 6	63. 6	42. 0	76. 6	106. 0

NOTE.—When the Time in the Table is marked thus [*] the Train will only stop to set down Passengers, when application has been made to the Guard at a preceding Station; or take them up when the Station Master shews the Red Signal. *Flag Stations are printed in Italic.*

The Goods Trains cannot be insured to arrive punctually at the Stations, but will be as nearly punctual as possible.

N.B.—The times of Arrival of the other Trains at the various Stations named are not guaranteed.

Communication between Galway, Ballinasloe, Athlone & Mullingar with England, via Holyhead

First and Second Class Passengers can now be Booked through by this route to the following Stations on English Railways, at the subjoined Rates, which include the Sea Passage money between Kingstown and Holyhead, as also the Fares on the Dublin and Kingstown Railway:—

	LONDON		BIRMINGHAM		MANCHESTER		CHESTER OR LIVERPOOL	
	1st Class.	2nd Class.	1st Class.	2nd Class.	1st Class.	2nd Class.	1st Class.	2nd Class.
	£ s. d.	£ s. d.	£ s. d.	£ s. d.	£ s. d.	£ s. d.	£ s. d.	£. s. d.
To or From GALWAY, and	3. 16. 0	2. 14. 0	2. 18. 0	2, 0. 0	2. 4. 0	1. 16. 0	2. 0. 0	1. 11. 0
" BALLINASLOE and	3. 13. 0	2. 11. 0	2. 14. 0	2. 0. 0	2. 0. 0	1. 12. 0	1. 15. 0	1. 7. 0
ATHLONE and	3. 11. 0	2. 9. 0	2. 12. 0	1. 18. 0	1. 17. 0	1. 10. 0	1. 12. 0	1. 5. 0
" MULLINGAR and	3. 8. 0	2. 6. 0	2. 8. 0	1. 16. 0	1. 13. 0	1. 6. 0	1. 8. 0	1. 1. 0

The Single Journey Tickets are only available on the day of issue and the two following days. The journey may be broken at Dublin, Holyhead, Bangor, Crewe, or Chester.

RETURN TICKETS ARE ISSUED AT ABOUT A FARE AND A HALF.

Those to and from London are available for 14 days after the date of issue, *i.e.* the journey must be completed within the 15 days. Those to other Stations are available for Seven days after the date of issue, completing the journey within the Eighth day.

DEPARTURES OF THE STEAM BOAT FROM KINGSTOWN FOR HOLYHEAD:—
9 . 0 a.m., Sundays excepted.
First and Second Class by Express Trains between Chester, Birmingham, and London.

Mondays, Wednesdays, and Fridays, a Steamer leaves KILLALOE for ATHLONE to meet the 4 . 0 o'clock UP Train, (Dublin, 10 . 0 p.m.), and Returns from Athlone every alternate day, Steamer leaving at 10 . 30 o'Clock, Morning.

The MGWR announces it is open for business to Galway in 1853 with a wealth of information on trains, fares for all four classes and up to three horses plus rates from Galway to London, all squeezed onto one small flyer. Fourth class travel to and from Galway was restricted to occasional goods trains, took over eleven hours and cost six shillings. This was the equivalent of four days' wages for a labourer.

COACHES, CARAVANS, OR CARS,

Run (Sundays excepted,) from the following Trains from Dublin:—

From Mullingar Station,
7 : 0 a.m., Down Train

Boyle, Longford,
Ballymahon, Mohill,
Ballinamore, Moyvore,
Ballymote, Newtownforbes,
Carrick-on-Shannon, Rooskey,
Colooney, Rathowen,
Dromod, Sligo,
Drumsna, Tubbercurry,
Edgeworthstown,

From Athlone station
7 . 0 a.m., Down Train, to

Balaghy, Foxford,
Bangor, Killalla,
Belmullet, Loughglesun,
Ballymoe, Nockeroghery,
Ballyaghadereen, Parsonstown,
Ballina, Roscrea,
Roscommon,
Castlerea,
Dunmore, Swinford,

From Athenry station
7 . 0 a.m., Down Train, to

Balla, Dunmore,
Ballygass, Foxhall,
Balindine
Castlelbar Hollymount,
Claremorris, Tuam.
Dangan, Westport,

Galway station
7 . 0 a.m., Down Train, to

Ballinrobe, Kilmain,
Ballinahinch, Moycullen,
Claregalway, Outerard,
Clifden, Roundstone,
Flynns, Recess or Glendalough.
Headford.

from Oranmore station.
7 . 0 a m. Down Train, to

Ardrahan, Kilcolgan,
Clarenbridge, Limerick.
Ennis, Newmarket,
Gort,

from Mullingar station,
10 : 30 a.m. Down Train, to

Coolamber, Killeshandra,
Cavan, Longford,
Carrick-on-Shannon Newtownforbes,
Dromod, Rathowen,
Drumsna, Rooskey,
Edgeworthstown, Street
Granard,

From Galway station
10 . 30 a.m., Down Train, to

Claregalway, Tuam,

From Athlone Station.
10 . 30 Down Train, to

Roscommon.

From Athenry Station.
10 . 30 a.m., Down Train, to

Tuam.

From Woodlawn Station.
10 . 30 Down Train to

Loughrea.

From Moate Station,
10 . 30 Down Train to

Cloghan, Ferbane, Birr.

Ferns Lock station
4 : 0 p.m. Down Train, to Trim,

and Athboy.

Enfield Station
4 : 0 p.m. Down Train, to
Edenderry.

Killucan station
4 . 0 p m., Down Train to
Castletowndelvin, Castlepollard,
Oldcastle.

From Mullingar station.
4 . 0 p.m. Train, to

Ballinaleck, Edgeworthstown,
Rathowen, Longford.

From Castletown station,
4 . 0 p.m. down Train to
Kilbeggan,
Returning for the
8 . 15 a m. Up Train.
Job Cars in attendance on all other Trains, *Mail* excepted.

From Mullingar station
7 . 15 p.m., Down *(Mail)* Train

Boyle, Edgeworthstown,
Ballaghadreen French Park,
Ballaghy, Foxford,
Ballina Killalla,
Belmullet, Lanesborough,
Bangor, Longford,
Ballymote, Newtownforbes
Carrick-on-Shannon, Rooskey,
Colooney, Rathowen
Crossmolina, Sligo
Dromod, Strokestown,
Drumsna, Swinford
Dromore West Tulsk
Elphin, Tubbercurry.

From Athlone station
7 . 15 p.m., Down *(Mail)* Train,

Ballymore, Roscommon.
Castlerea,

From Ballinasloe station
7 : 15 p.m. Down *(Mail)* Train

Ahascra, Moylough,
Banagher, Portumna,
Birr, Roscrea,
Eyrecourt. Templemore,
Mountbellew,

From Oranmore station
7.15 p.m. Down *(Mail)* Train, to

Ardrahan, Kilcolgan,
Ennis, Limerick,
Gort,

From Galway station.
7.15 p.m. Down *(Mail)* Train, to

Ballinahinch, Outerard.
Claregalway, Roundstone,
Clifden, Recess or Glendalough.
Flynns,
Moycullen, Tuam.
Maam,

From Athenry station,
7 . 15 p.m. Down *(Mail)* Train, to

Ballina, Loughrea,
Belmullet, Newport,
Castlebar, Roundfort.
Hollymount. Tuam, Westport.

Rates for Parcels.

All Parcels and Packages, under 56lbs. weight each, are conveyed by Passenger Trains, (exclusively,) and charged at Parcel Rates; and all Packages and Parcels weighing from 56lbs. to 112 lbs. are likewise forwarded by Passenger Trains and charged at Parcel Rates, *if* "PER GOODS TRAIN" be not distinctly marked upon them.

VAN GOODS' PARCELS from 56 lbs. and upwards are conveyed by Passenger Trains at 25 per cent over Goods' Train Rates, particulars of which can be had at all the Station Parcels intended to be so conveyed should have the words "VAN GOODS' PARCEL" legibly written on the directions.

Parcels under one lb. 8d. each for any distance,—From 1lb. to 7lbs.		From 7lbs. to 14lbs.	From 14lbs. to 28lbs.	above 28lbs.
For any distance not exceeding 50 miles	0s. 8d. each	0s. 10d. each	1s. 0d. each	0½d. per lb. extr
50 do. and not exceeding 80 miles	0s. 10d. do.	1s. 2d. do.	1s. 4d. do.	0½d. do.
80 do. and upwards	1s. 2d. do.	1s. 6d. do.	1s. 8d. do.	0½d. do.

The above Rates to include all charges for Collection and Delivery in Dublin, Mullingar, Athlone, Ballinasloe, and Galway.

Parcels may be booked at 27 MERCHANTS' QUAY, and 25 BACHELORS' WALK, and at ALL THE STATIONS on the Line.

Mr. Bianconi's Coach Parcel Rates.

	From 1lb. to 7lbs	*Above 7lbs.*
For any distance not exceeding 25 Miles	0s. 6d	0½d. per lb. extra.
25 and not exceeding 50 Miles	0s. 9d	0½d. per lb. extra.
50 and not exceeding 85 Miles	1s. 0d	0½d. per lb. extra.
85 and upwards	1s. 0d	1d. per lb. extra.

Goods over 56lbs weight 30 per cent. off the above Rates.

LUGGAGE.

First Class Passengers are allowed personal LUGGAGE		150 lbs.
Second Do.	Do.	100 lbs.
Third Do.	Do.	60 lbs.
Fourth Do.	Do.	None.

Which is understood to be Personal Baggage, & not Merchandize. All excess beyond these weights will be charged for any distance not exceeding 50 miles, 0¼d per lb.; 50 miles and not exceeding 100 0½d. per lb.; 100 miles and upwards, 0¾d. per lb.

SUBSCRIPTION TICKETS are issued to ALL Stations, between Dublin and Maynooth.

First and Second Class Return Tickets are issued, enabling persons to travel between all Stations, to go and return the same day, at a Fare and a-Half. Those issued for any distance over 50 miles will be available for Return on the following day,

And those issued on SATURDAY and SUNDAY, beyond 50 miles, are available up to and for MONDAY.

PASSENGERS to ensure being Booked should be at the Station TEN MINUTES earlier than the time mentioned in the foregoing Tables.

Passengers cannot be Re-Booked at Road-side Stations to proceed by the Train in which they have arrived.

Passengers are Booked at intermediate Stations ONLY on condition of there being room in the Train

Passengers are required to have a legible address on each article of their luggage, and to see it placed in the Train.

Passengers are subject to a Penalty of Forty Shillings for riding in any of the Company's Carriages without having first paid the Fare and obtained a Ticket.

Passengers will be required to exhibit their Tickets previous to the starting of the Train.—Tickets not transferable.

Passengers' Tickets must be given up when demanded, and if not produced the whole Fare will be charged from the Terminus.

Children in arms, and under 3 years of age, travel free—3 years and under *Twelve* at Half-price.

Persons travelling in their own Carriage to pay First Class Fare in addition to charge for Carriage, and their Servants Second Class Fares.

Carriages must be at the Termini 20 minutes before the hour of starting.

Cars are in attendance on the arrival of each Train, at Dublin Terminus. Fare to or from any part of the City, 6d.

Grooms in charge of Horses, and riding along with them, travel free,

Trucks, or Horse Boxes, cannot be ensured at intermediate stations, unless bespoke the day before.

Entire Horses are charged *each* as half a Horse-box.

GOODS TRAINS run each way every day, (Sunday excepted); and Special Trains run every WEDNESDAY with CATTLE for Dublin Market, full particulars of which can be had at the Stations.

A Cloak & Luggage Room is provided at the Terminus—Charge 1d. for each Article.

DOGS.—Any distance under 20 miles, 6d.
20 do. and under 50 miles, 1s. 0d.
50 do. and under 80 do., 1s. 6d.
80 do. and upwards, 2s. 0d.

Dogs will not be permitted to accompany Passengers inside the Carriages, and they must be provided with collars and chains, otherwise the Company will not be responsible for their safety.

Smoking strictly prohibited in all the Carriages.

No Servant of the Company allowed to take gratuities from Passengers on pain of dismissal.

By Order.
HENRY BEAUSIRE, *Secretary.*

Dublin Terminus, December 15th, 1853.

Printed by W. Leckie, 59 Bolton-street, Dublin.

[*Over.*]

The reverse of the same flyer lists times for horse-drawn connecting coaches from various stations, parcel and goods rates. First class passengers could bring up to 150 lbs (68 kg) of luggage, second class was allowed 100 lbs (45 kg), third class had 60 lbs (27 kg) and fourth class, zero.

At 10 pm on a cold, wet evening in July 1851 Dargan's men connected the last rails on the line to Galway on the Shannon bridge at Athlone, built by Charles Fox and John Henderson, the Birmingham firm that built Paxton's Crystal Palace Exhibition Hall in Hyde Park, London (see Chapter 6). A few days later Dargan travelled with Captain Laffan as they inspected the line in a small train, possibly the Dargan Saloon, drawn by two engines, *Juno* and *Pelican*.[86] Company engineer George Hemans and Dargan had been conducting their own tests, running heavy trains over the Athlone viaduct and then across Lough Athalia on the approach to Galway. Laffan described both structures as of 'great magnitude' and offering 'perfect security' and he passed the line to open without hesitation.[87]

Ballinasloe Fair

This was an important event in the Midland Railway calendar and brought the company a lot of business, mainly of the four-legged variety: in 1860 alone 80,000 sheep and 20,000 cattle passed through the Fair, many by rail. So great was the business done that each year a large force of railwaymen headed by the chairmen and several of the directors descended on the town for the week along with dormitory coaches for the staff.

Joseph Tatlow from Sheffield was General Manager of the Midland and wrote an account of the Fair in 1891:

> *To be able to entertain friends and customers of the company was ... the main reason why the directors passed the fair week at Ballinasloe. Their hospitality was not limited to invitations to dinner, for guests were welcomed ... to breakfast and lunch and light refreshments during the day. It was an arrangement which gave pleasure to both hosts and guests. ... A good dinner solves many a difficulty, while the post-prandial cigar and a glass of grog, like faith, removes mountains.*

The approach to Galway station over Lough Athalia

An aerial view of Galway station around the 1970s. In the foreground is the former Great Southern Hotel designed by John Mulvany and built by Dargan. The lobby, greatly altered, retains a fine marble fireplace with MGWR crests on the surround. Passenger access to the station is to the left of the train sheds in a congested space that doubles as a bus terminus. In the top left hand corner a locomotive is parked at the start of the scenic line that once ran out to to Clifden; it closed in 1935.

Travelling West in 1853

The 1853 timetable leaflet (pages 115-6) issued two years after the route to Galway opened contains a great deal of information about MGWR services. There were five passenger trains and one goods train daily in each direction, the fastest journey time being five hours and fifteen minutes for the 126 miles (203 kilometres). The horse-drawn mail coach took approximately sixteen hours.

Single fares were £1 in first class, 16s in second, 10s in third and 6s in fourth. The latter passengers travelled in goods wagons, some with seats. Sending your horse to Galway cost twice the first-class fare, £2 2s, as did two-wheel carriages, but four-wheelers cost £3 3s 6d. Grooms travelled free. Accompanying passengers could travel inside their own horse-drawn carriage perched on a wagon if they so chose, which can hardly have been very comfortable, but they had to pay the first class fare as well. Dogs were confined to the guard's van and interestingly there was a smoking ban in all train carriages. Return tickets were 'about a fare and a half'.

The MGWR was quite forward looking in that as one visitor, Francis Head observed in 1852, the company operated some very comfortable wagons lits. Curiously the only train where they could be of use was the daily mail train out of Galway at midnight which arrived in Dublin at 5.15 am. Passengers could also book a through ticket from Galway to London for £3 16s one way.

With only a single line complete Laffan advised opening the second line as speedily as possible, more to reduce delays and fuel loss as trains waited for a section of the line to clear than for safety reasons. Ironically the Galway line was singled again in the 1920s and remains largely so today, even though trains to the west now travel from Heuston via Portarlington. Distance posts on the line are still in miles to this day and measured from the Broadstone via Mullingar, not from Heuston via Portarlington.

The Next Parish: Sailing from Galway to America

The railway line to Galway opened on 1 August 1851 and at the opening dinner the Midland's engineer, Hemans, generously attributed his success in completing the route satisfactorily to Dargan's 'talents, energy and industry'. Responding, Dargan wished the railway every success and then touched on a topic dear to the hearts of the directors: Galway's potential as the main port for transatlantic traffic between Britain, Ireland and America.[88] As early as 1836 Charles Vignoles proposed a 200-mile (320 km) railway from Dublin to Valentia to connect with ships sailing to Halifax and St John's. Almost every coastal town on the west coast, Cobh, Valentia, Foynes, Limerick, Galway, Westport, Sligo, Burtonport and Derry, had at some stage been proposed as the gateway to America.[89] The idea was to shave a day or two off the unpleasant Atlantic crossing by offloading passengers, mail and goods onto trains in Ireland. Thus the MGWR greatly welcomed Hemans' timely report on the benefits of Galway docks and the ease of a link to Dublin and Kingstown for onward shipment to London and mainland Europe.

At this time Dargan chaired the Dublin Steamship Association and was involved with the European and American Steam Co. set up in 1851 to promote shipping services to the US.[90] He was already running steamers from Newry to Liverpool (see Chapter 4). Recognizing the need for a deepwater pier suitable for large ships Dargan had offered to build a pier at Galway for £80,000. The Steam Co.'s prospectus estimated that London passengers using Galway could shorten their Atlantic crossing by two days and 400 miles (640 km) while Galway-London would take eighteen hours and Galway-Paris thirty hours. There was a strong Quaker presence in the company including Thomas Pim of the Kingstown railway, Thomas Bewley and James Perry. The offices were at 31 Eden Quay, Dublin.[91]

The progress of the shipping line, like an Atlantic crossing, was far from smooth. Press advertisements announced the departure of the paddle steamer *Viceroy* under Captain Robert Ewing from Galway to New York on 1 June 1850, a year before the railway opened. The sailing was first class only (no steerage for emigrants) and the fare was £25 to include provisions but not wine or liquor. Viewed at anchor near Mutton Island it was clear the *Viceroy* at 800 tons was tiny, being built for the Dublin-Glasgow route in 1846; the north Atlantic was a different kettle of fish.[92] After an eventful journey through storms, fog and icebergs and with a handful of passengers on board she arrived in Halifax on 11 June and in New York a few days later. The *Viceroy* set sail for Ireland at the end of June but ran aground in fog off the coast of Newfoundland. Attempts to re-float her were unsuccessful and she was wrecked. Happily there was no loss of life and all her cargo was removed safely.

A year later the *Galway Mercury* made a premature announcement of the arrival of the *SS North America* with 150 passengers but her owners sold her before she sailed. The press was miffed: 'Mr Dargan and his subordinates have been working like slaves and all for the mere purpose of accommodating a few American speculators ... a disgrace to the species and a dishonour to the country which gave them birth.'[93] Despite these setbacks Dargan attended at least two meetings in Dublin in August 1851 to promote the shipping line and Pierce Mahony, its legal advisor, wrote from London that the project was still alive, despite 'impudent notification ... from some Dublin papers– the *Express* – but it has done no harm'.[94] Dargan was also at a meeting in the Mansion House that voted to send Hemans and Perry to London to seek £85,000 in state aid for Galway harbour. Mahony wrote to Jane Dargan citing Lord Clarendon's low opinion of people in Galway 'that far corner of civilization' where 'defence associations and brawling patriots never gave them a day's wages'. But a 'true patriot' like Dargan had 'the genius to conceive, the head and the hand to exercise and the heart to enjoy all that is useful to Ireland'.[95]

There now bursts onto the scene a most interesting character, Galway priest Fr Peter Daly, who features prominently in the story of the Galway vessels.[96] The nub of the problem with making the city a packet station was this: Galway was well positioned between America and Britain and Europe and now had good rail links but the harbour was unsuitable and sometimes dangerous and the cost of developing it for transatlantic shipping was prohibitive. Little happened for several years until John Lever, a Manchester industrialist, ran a number of sailings in 1858. The *Prince Albert* brought 800 passengers to Galway in July 1858, departing again on 27 July with forty first-class, sixty second-class and 540 third-class passengers, reaching Cape Race after six-and-a-half days. The *Pacific* sailed for New York on 24 August 1858 with 190 passengers and a cargo of Guinness, Jameson whiskey and Irish linen, returning in October 1858.[97] Shipbuilder William Malcolmson of the Waterford & Limerick and Limerick & Foynes Railways became chairman of the Galway Line in 1860 even though he had an interest in promoting Foynes as a transatlantic port; Dargan had worked closely with him when building both railways. The 3000-ton *Hibernia* made one of the last sailings from Galway to New York on 10 January 1864, by which time Dargan had ceased his involvement with the Galway Line.

Fr Peter Daly (*c.*1788–1868) – A Turbulent Priest

Like some renaissance cardinal, the Rev. Peter Daly had a varied career as entrepreneur, venture capitalist, politician, lobbyist, rackrent land-lord, chairman of Galway Town Commissioners, prominent member of Galway Harbour Commissioners and Lough Corrib Navigation Trustees (where he ran a steamship named **Father Daly***), builder and inveterate promoter of the Galway Line and the Midland Railway, member of the Gas Board and occasional cleric and parish priest of Moycullen. He was energetic, outspoken and ambitious and had unfulfilled aspirations to be Bishop of Galway but clashed often with his bishop and with Cardinal Paul Cullen. He also brought the Sisters of Mercy to Galway and supervised the soup kitchens they set up in his various properties during the Famine.*

'I have no politics ... but my Packet Station' he told a promotional meeting and his committee chartered the first vessel to sail between Galway and America – the ill-fated **Viceroy** *that foundered off the coast of Newfoundland. At a meeting in April 1853 Daly sought Dargan's support for developing the packet station, asking if he could make the necessary harbour improvements for £120,000; apparently Dargan later revised this upwards to £150,000. Captain Washington RN thought £300,000 was a more realistic figure.*

In his seventies, Daly went to London in 1861 to lobby the prime minister, Lord Palmerston, threatening that the Irish MPs *would bring down his minority government if he did not support the Galway Line.*

Daly didn't bother with the formality of seeking the MPs' support before his meeting so his actions caused them some annoyance. Daly's portrait hangs in the chamber of Galway Council.

Imagine how the west of Ireland might have been transformed in the post-Famine years if Dargan's plan had materialized and if rebuilding the harbour and clearing the channel had not been such a huge task. Galway could have become a major port on the north Atlantic well into the twentieth century. Cobh, for example, prospered for many years as a transatlantic port, with 50,000 passengers using it as late as 1950.[98]

Isambard Kingdom Brunel (1806–59), An Eminent Engineer

Brunel was a brilliant, eccentric engineer, much involved in railways, particularly the English Great Western and various marine projects. His father, also a distinguished engineer was French and sent his son to schools in Hove and Caen, despite being held for a time with his children in a debtors' prison.

Brunel's main project in Ireland, the cliff railway line from Bray to Greystones, was and remains a troublesome if beautiful stretch. The line weaves in and out of tunnels, abandoned sections showing where the sea and rock falls have forced the route inland at great expense. It was not Brunel's finest project.

Once when performing a party trick with a sovereign he accidentally swallowed the coin, which lodged in his throat causing him enormous distress and pain. He eventually devised and built a Catherine-wheel-like apparatus to spin his body and hold it upside down; the coin fell out and he recovered completely.

An unfortunate maritime investment of Dargan's was in Brunel's ill-fated ship, the Great Eastern, the largest vessel afloat, intended for the Atlantic route. By 1853 Brunel had persuaded a number of his railway contractor colleagues, including Thomas Brassey, Samuel Peto and Dargan, to take 1000 shares each in his company.

The scheme was not a success and the Great Eastern ended her days moored on the Mersey serving as a wretched floating advertisement for Lewis' department store in Liverpool. All lost heavily on the venture. Curiously the last ship of the Galway Line, Hibernia, worked as a cable-layer alongside the Great Eastern, until wrecked off the coast of Brazil in 1877.

Longford and Cavan

Against several other bids the MGWR had no hesitation accepting Dargan's tender to build these two branches for £146,751 with 5000 £20 shares. Lord Farnham turned the first sod on 13 September 1853. The Longford branch left the Galway line at Mullingar where George Wilkinson, the architect of Harcourt St station who made his bread and butter building workhouses and mental hospitals, designed a fine Y-shaped junction building as well as most of the stations on the Sligo line, clean, elegant limestone structures such as Dromod and Carrick-on-Shannon. Beyond Mullingar, Hemans, the company engineer, and Dargan faced some difficult terrain. The line runs around the edge of Lough Owel and early in 1854 a section of track sank beneath the waters of the lake. (You might think Dargan had learned by now to avoid laying a track bed across water.) However, Dargan's foreman, a Mr Connolly, devised a large trawling device that he used to drag the lake and retrieve sleepers and rails, which he duly relaid. Hemans wrote a detailed account for the Institution of Civil Engineers of Ireland of this and other construction problems where the line ran across bog 70 ft deep in parts.[99] These problems were overcome and Mullingar to Longford opened on 8 November 1855 with intermediate stations at Multyfarnham and Edgeworthstown built to Wilkinson's design.

The purpose of extending to Cavan was to feed into traffic human and hoofed from the north-east, in particular via the Ulster Railway from Belfast with the prospect of connection to the planned transatlantic port at Galway. The Midland's route to Cavan opened on 8 July 1856. There the company built an unusual station, Wilkinson again, whose two bay platforms terminated facing each other, divided by a pedestrian pathway, the signal cab being squashed in between the main station building and the goods store. Some of these buildings have survived but the platforms are long gone.

These lines north of Mullingar had two other station curiosities: Clonhugh House just north of Mullingar was the home of George Forbes, Earl of Granard, who had a small private station built near his house and enjoyed the luxury of having Dublin-Sligo trains stop on request. It closed in 1947 but the platform and station house, now a private residence, are still there. Farther to the north-west trains to Cavan left the Sligo line at Inny (formerly Cavan) Junction. Named after a nearby river, Inny Junction was totally isolated with no town or village nearby and no road access. Trains stopped there infrequently and only for service reasons so that anyone alighting in error who let their train depart without them would face desert-like isolation. There is no longer any trace of Inny Junction.

This was Dargan's final contract with the MGWR and having successfully completed substantial projects for the two major railways in Ireland, the GS&WR and the MGWR, he was now at the very peak of his career.

Cutting corners is not always a good idea, especially across water: while Dargan's men were building this line north of Mullingar a section of track disappeared beneath the waters of Lough Owel.

Longford station on a quiet day in July 1970 when the signalman had plenty of time to chat to a youthful photographer sporting a brand new Ilford camera. Along with Cavan, Longford marks the north-western limits of Dargan's railway construction.

Clonhugh, south of Multyfarnham, was the private station of the Earl of Granard who lived at nearby Clonhugh House. The halt closed in 1963.

Like many companies, the Midland Railway issued a small number of free passes to important figures. This one dating from 1916 is signed by the General Manager of the time, Joseph Tatlow.

SIX

The Darganaeum: The 1853 Dublin Exhibition and the National Gallery of Ireland

The earliest exhibitions date back to the eighteenth century and one of the most successful, the Crystal Palace, was held in London in 1851. The model on display in the Museum of London shows a very large functional edifice resembling a Lego creation. Queen Victoria gave Prince Albert all the credit for the London Exhibition and after his death in 1861 she commissioned the Albert Memorial featuring many Exhibition references, now standing opposite the Albert Hall. The memorial is by Gilbert Scott, more famous for the magnificent St Pancras station and hotel, and the statue is by Dubliner John Henry Foley.[1] A smaller statue of Prince Albert also by Foley stands near the site of the Dublin Exhibition.

The Hyde Park 1851 Exhibition drew six million visitors, Dargan being one of them, and made a healthy profit of £186,000.[2] The Irish contribution was small but included a model of the railway viaduct over the Nore at Kilkenny, exhibited by Captain Moorsom. On his return from London Dargan proposed holding a similar event in Dublin to his colleague Cusack Roney.[3] Cork got in first with its exhibition in the Corn Market and Corn Exchange in 1852, promoted by Mayor John F. Maguire MP.[4] Dargan subscribed £25, displaying sugar from the Irish Beet Sugar Co.'s plant at Mountmellick with which he was involved. He also attended the opening ceremony and enjoyed it mightily, according to W.R. Le Fanu who wrote in his diary: 'Dargan got gloriously drunk.'[5] The attendance at the Cork Exhibition was a modest 138,000 but the event broke even.

The bronze statue of Prince Albert by John Foley dates from 1872 and is a fine piece of work. It is discretely domiciled against the wall of the Natural History Museum where it is unlikely to cause antipathy as the only people who see it are TDs and Senators using Leinster Lawn as a private car park.

The Irish Crystal Palace

Dargan was elected a life member of the Royal Dublin Society (RDS) in November 1851, proposed by M.M. O'Grady MD and H. Kemmis QC.[6] The RDS headquarters were in Leinster House and every three years the Society held an exhibition or show on Leinster Lawn to promote Irish agriculture and industry. Dargan proposed the Society should hold an expanded exhibition in 1853, which he would fund with a donation of £20,000. The conditions were that the RDS allow Dargan to build an exhibition hall on Leinster Lawn, that he would choose the chairman, deputy chairman and secretary of an executive committee and that the building became his property when it closed. If the proceeds were less than £20,000 plus 5 per cent interest Dargan would receive all the receipts. If the surplus was greater he would receive £20,000 plus 5 per cent and if it made a loss he would cover it.[7] All such projections proved academic as the substantial loss was ultimately borne by Dargan.

Naturally the RDS was keen to accept the deal as it faced no financial risk and stood to benefit from much reflected glory. It lost no time in printing a special letterhead inscribed 'Great Industrial Exhibition of 1853 in Connexion with the Royal Dublin Society'.

Dargan's committee appointees were Sir Edward McDonnell, chairman of the Great Southern & Western Railway, George Roe and George Woodcock with no fewer than eighteen others. The design competition drew twenty-nine entries for the building whose budget was £15,000 and the judges were three railway engineers: Charles Lanyon, George Millar and George Hemans. The winner was John Benson from Sligo who designed the Cork Exhibition building.[8]

Benson's design was very fine, being a central hall of glass and iron supporting the main dome between two side halls, each with a smaller dome. *The Illustrated Magazine of Art* described Benson's building as a 'mixture of oriental with what might be called the modern style'.[9]

The committee sent invitations to every exhibitor at Hyde Park and to the mayor of every town, city and borough in Ireland and Britain, explaining that the purpose was to showcase the very best of Irish manufactured goods and to allow Irish people to see the finest artefacts from other countries. In one week in July 1852, 18,000 letters went out.[10] Armed with an introduction from the Secretary of State for Foreign Affairs in Whitehall, Cusack Roney made a grand tour of European capitals after which King Leopold of Belgium promised to send a naval vessel to Dublin laden with exhibits. Most exhibits came from Britain and France with others from Holland and Zollervein (a commercial confederation of German states). The *Weekly Freeman* trenchantly described the essential purpose of the Exhibition was not to be a 'raree show – a holiday toy invented to gratify the curious or annihilate the ennui of fashionable do-nothings' but to 'promote employment in Ireland, to exhibit to the world the capacity, the high intelligence, and the persevering industry of a neglected people'.[11]

Copy letter of 29 September 1852 from Dargan to Exhibition Secretary, C.P. Roney, offering the committee an extra £6000 in addition to the £20,000 he had already donated towards the costs of the event.

OPENING OF THE DUBLIN GREAT INDUSTRIAL EXHIBITION

The Dublin Exhibition building on Leinster Lawn, Merrion
Square, as portrayed in the *Illustrated London News*.

Even before the building went up there were some dissenting voices: the
Evening Mail lauded Dargan's generous gesture but said the location (close to
148,000 square ft of exhibit space on a six-and-a-half-acre site) was too small and
wrongly sited on the RDS grounds with no possibility of extending the area or the
period it was open. The paper was also scathing about the excessive influence
of the RDS and the 'intrusiveness of every member ... [which was] sufficient to
annihilate any project'. The Society, it said, claimed full credit for Dargan's event
to which it 'does not subscribe sixpence, or incur the least risk or responsibility.
It merely sanctions, in the largest possible spirit of patriotism, with its name, the
splendid edifice erected with that gentleman's money.'[12] Although there is some
truth in this it is a little harsh in that the RDS had been running smaller scale
events for years.[13]

Another critic was Robert Travers, librarian at Marsh's Library, who wrote begrudgingly to a friend in England that Dargan's gesture was far from one of self-less generosity but that he stood to gain 6 per cent on his investment, 'twice what the money is worth', and on closure would acquire the building at a price deter-mined by his own appointees on the committee. With the sale of refreshments he claimed Dargan stood to make a handsome profit under the guise of public benevolence.[14] This too is a jaundiced view as claims about self-interest masked as philanthropy could only be an issue if the Exhibition made a substantial profit, which it did not. Dargan's frequent capital injections into the project make his motives clear and suggest he knew it would not return a large surplus.

Dargan's men began staking out the building on 18 August 1852; that day he attended a reception in Athlone station where Lord Eglinton praised his generosity and raised a cheer for him. A month later the ribs of the main hall were up and when Eglinton came to the site in October he struck the first iron girder with a tiny mallet before remarking the burden of governing Ireland would be a lot easier if there were many more Dargans.[15] He also promised to ask Queen Victoria to send part of her art collection, to which the *Freeman's Journal* added that she should send 'something new' and not just items displayed in Hyde Park and that she might also visit to 'look after her goods', which indeed she did.[16]

The *Dublin Evening Post* described Dargan's engineering methods at the site, saying they resembled building a railway.[17] There was a tramway of three parallel lines, each carrying a crane in a ballast wagon. The centre crane raised the girders bolted to the exterior uprights while the two outside cranes raised the wooden uprights 38 ft (12 metres) in the air and the metal pillars 18 ft (5.5 metres). As each upright was raised and workmen secured it to the ground they then raised the middle girder, which was riveted at each end while the pillar went into its socket.

The frontage onto Merrion Square was 300 ft (90 m), the main hall 425 ft long and 100 ft wide (130 x 30 m) with a single-span roof of rolled and fluted glass 105 ft high (32 m) that gave a cool, grey-green tone to the interior, to minimize light damage to artworks. The inside was painted light blue, the ribs in buff picked out in scarlet. The two side halls were 50 ft (15 m) wide, each dome being 65 ft (20 m) high.[18] It was a very elegant structure.

The committee believed the event would be self-financing and relying on Dargan's guarantee, with great optimism but poor foresight, said it would not accept cash donations. By the autumn of 1852 the building costs had risen steadily and Dargan's £20,000 was spent. The committee proposed a public subscription but Dargan offered a further £6000 on the same terms as before. This became a pattern as the works ate into the available capital until it reached the point where Dargan had provided £88,000. This was a substantial sum and represented a considerable strain on his resources. Nor was construction problem-free: a storm on Christmas Eve 1852 caused great damage, bringing down part of the unfinished structure while a scaffolding collapse the following April killed three workmen. The Exhibition accounts show the men's families received compensation of £275 10s 10d, minuscule by today's standards but extremely generous for the time when men worked almost entirely at their own risk. Sproule commented afterwards that 'there were very many inefficient persons in every department' of the works but unfortunately does not elaborate further.[19] It could be that with a very large committee involved this was one project Dargan did not monitor closely, to his cost.

Declining to Be Sir William'd

In one of his final acts before returning to England, Lord Eglinton offered Dargan a knighthood, which he declined. This was one of many gentrification offers Dargan received around this time, all of them respectfully turned down. There has been speculation as to why Dargan refused such titles, some suggesting he did so from inherent nationalist or egalitarian motives, or as a protest at the execution of his two uncles during the 1798 rebellion. There is no evidence to support such theories and the true explanation is more likely that if he became Sir William or Lord Dargan it would have been difficult for him to continue in business, commerce not being considered a suitable occupation for the aristocracy.

Exhibits began to arrive from all over Europe and part of the southern hall became a bonded warehouse. Excise officers logged items arriving and no duty was payable if the goods were re-exported at the end of the Exhibition. The first scheduled event was the Spring Cattle Show in early 1853, which Dargan allowed the RDS to hold in the incomplete Exhibition halls. In March season tickets went on sale at two guineas for gentlemen and one guinea for ladies and boys – girls did not feature on the tariff list. Advance sales of 10,039 tickets were healthy and produced revenue of £14,438 but all RDS members enjoyed free entry through their own door under the southern gallery. This over-generous privilege was widely taken up by the very people of affluence who were most able to pay an entry fee, representing the loss of a great deal of revenue to the organizers and ultimately to Dargan.

The Exhibition Opens

Opening day was set for 12 May 1853 and the night before Dargan gave a dinner at Mount Anville for a large group of friends and business associates. Among them were W.R. Le Fanu, Sir Joseph Paxton, designer of the Hyde Park building, Sir Edward McDonnell, GS&WR chairman, Dargan's contracting partner William McCormick and William Fairbairn, a close colleague whose Manchester engineering firm supplied many steam engines to Dargan including the stationary 50hp one that powered the Exhibition machinery.[20]

At 8 am the next day Dargan was in the Exhibition building 'quietly pacing from place to place ... and seeming unconscious of being observed'.[21] At 11 am a long procession set out from the Mansion House for Merrion Square led by the latest Lord Lieutenant, Earl St Germans.[22] Troops lined the streets and following in the procession were the Knights of St Patrick in full regalia, then the full complement of aldermen and city councillors, few of whom had hand, act or part in creating the Exhibition.

The parade reached its destination at noon where bands played 'God Save the Queen' as they made their way to the crimson dais holding two chairs of state. The dolly mixture of dignitaries included Viscount Gough, Earls Granville and Meath, the Marquises of Kildare and Drogheda, Samuel Holme, Mayor of Liverpool (a friend of Dargan's from his Bury Railway days), the Peruvian minister, the Mayor of Manchester, the US consul and Archbishop Paul Cullen. Dargan did not join this group but stayed with the crowd of onlookers, 'his ample proportions half concealed behind a pillar' as the *Edinburgh Evening Post* put it.[23] But when George Roe presented him to St Germans there was a burst of applause 'that even a sovereign might envy' as Sproule's memoir of Dargan described it in the official catalogue. The Earl referred to Dargan's liberal and patriotic effort and then knighted Cusack Roney and Benson.

The ponderous music programme began with 'God Save the Queen' again (twice), the 'Hallelujah Chorus' (twice), Haydn's 'The Heavens are Telling', 'The Hundredth Psalm', Handel's 'Coronation Anthem', Mozart's 'O, God when thou Appearest', Mendelssohn's 'Hymn of Praise' and the march from 'Athalia'. The Liverpool Philharmonic performed at the opening although the organ lent by an Oxford college was built by the Dublin firm of Telford & Telford. At the top of the main hall was a statue of Dargan by Jones with this inscription: 'Erected to William Dargan Esquire, by the persons on the staff of his various undertakings, as a tribute to his great and inestimable qualities, not only as a public employer, but as a benefactor of his country. 12 May 1853.' (This is not John Foley's statue that stands outside the National Gallery today.) Most agreed Jones' statue was not a great likeness and its defects excluded it from the fine arts section.[24] Its present location is uncertain. Dargan's engineering colleague George Hemans asked if Landseer could do a portrait of him or his wife, Jane, adding he was doubtless teased about all his portraits and busts.[25]

Medal struck to commemorate the Exhibition. On one side is an unusual image of Dargan in profile while on the reverse is the façade of the building with the text: 'Great Industrial Exhibition In Connexion with the Royal Dublin Society. Erected at the sole expence of WILLIAM DARGAN. Opened the 12th of May 1853 Sir J. Benson Archt. Woodhouse Fecit.'

The Illustrated Magazine of Art vol.1 published a full page picture of this bust of Dargan in classical guise, the editor using a 'species of pious fraud or gentle violence' to extract biographical information from 'the least egotistical of men. Copies of the bust were on sale around the time of the 1853 Exhibition.

The evening of the opening there was a dinner at the Mansion House attended by many who had positioned themselves so prominently at the opening. Although Dargan was one of the chief guests of honour his name appears far down the long litany of toasts. Replying, he praised his 1500 workmen for finishing the job within a tight schedule without any disruption. Later he described his men thus: 'I gave them good wages, I paid them regularly, and they acted as Irish men always do when fairly treated – they stood by me and I will stand by them.'[26] A few days later St Germans offered to knight Dargan which he again declined, the Earl asking him to keep the offer secret. Dargan did, however, agree to Lord Howth's suggestion that he become a Deputy Lieutenant of Dublin, a largely honorary title, and so from 1854 his entry in *Thom's Directory* appears with DL after his name. He also accepted honorary life membership of the Royal St George Yacht Club from the Commodore, Marquis Conyngham of Slane. Dargan's acceptance letter is suitably effusive but there is no record of him participating in leisure maritime pursuits.[27]

Many visitors were from Britain and one party chartered a steamer, the *Fire Fly*, travelling from Ardrossan to Dun Laoghaire but slept on board their ship because, it was said, they believed there was nowhere to stay in Dublin.[28] Of course they may just have been thrifty. However, as well as dispelling such illusions the arrival of so many visitors threw a welcome light on the true condition of the country, recovering from the Famine that had ended just four years before. Attendances in the first week were steady if not spectacular. Two days into the week just 400 people paid the hefty 5s entrance fee on the first two days but a week later there were almost 4000 paying visitors on one day, rising to 5000 the following day.

Among the early visitors to the Exhibition and Mount Anville were the travel writers Mr and Mrs Hall, who eulogized both.[29] The *Liverpool Chronicle* remarked that Dargan was 'one of those clever and energetic men who, in any part of the world, would convert the wilderness into a garden'. His achievement, the paper added, was all the more remarkable in a country where the 'selfishness of its landlords and capitalists is patent to the world'. This latter group had debased the value of peasant labour, condemning them to virtual slavery in 'hovels unfit for human shelter and the possession of miserable patches of land worthy of a nation of kangaroos'.[30] Among other visitors was Mr Punch.[31]

Mr Punch Visits Dargania

Punch *magazine, though notorious for its jaundiced if not racist view of Ireland, feted the Exhibition in a whimsical review. The editor, Shelley Brooks, sent Dargan a copy with the offer of a free subscription hoping 'through its pages to do some good by making truth fly a little faster with the aid of feathers'. Mr Punch's visit began when 'two gigantic policemen ... spun him into the building gratis' where his two beautiful guides, Honora and Grace, chided him for sometimes saying 'rather severe things about Ireland' whereupon he humbly promised to refrain from further criticism.*

As all eyes turned to a newcomer, Mr Punch greeted him this: 'This is your work ... Don't say it is not, WILLIAM DARGAN, and because England knows it too and holds your name in honour accordingly.' Mr Punch enjoyed 'being shot into Dargania' and urged readers who wished to please him to 'have the goodness to run over to Dublin to see the Exhibition'.

Sunbeams of Royal Favour

Victoria was always rather fearful about visiting Ireland, hardly surprising since several of the attempts on her life were made by Irishmen. However, the

Exhibition organizers knew that a royal visit would draw large crowds and bring it vital publicity. Her presence at the opening would have been ideal but failing that a visit half way through would be highly beneficial. The royal party eventually arrived at Dun Laoghaire on 29 August 1853. Dargan was among the crowd and she travelled in the special coach built by the Kingstown Railway for her 1849 visit.[32] From Westland Row she went to the Vice-Regal Lodge (now Áras an Uachtaráin) where she stayed for the week. She thought it 'very comfortable' with 'pretty terraced gardens'.[33] Socially the visit was low-key, its main purpose being to visit the Exhibition and 'to shed sunbeams of royal favour on the noble enterprise of Mr Dargan' as the Cork Examiner put it.[34] John Mitchel was more acerbic in his anticipation of the visit: 'It is understood that her majesty will visit the west. The human inhabitants are expected by that time to have been sufficiently thinned and the deer and other game to have proportionately multiplied. The Prince Albert will then take a hunting lodge in Connemara.'[35]

Several papers reported an imaginary visit by Victoria to Dargan's house on the day she arrived in Ireland, saying when the queen arrived there was no one at home. The tale was repeated by a number of other sources and is total fiction.[36] A visit had been planned for that day but heavy rain caused its cancellation.

Dargan Meets Victoria

The queen's first visit to the Exhibition took place the day after her arrival. First royal impressions were mixed: she thought the building was 'ugly on the outside but very fine in the interior' but she was comparing it to the one credited to her beloved Albert. After the usual lengthy welcome speeches, she responded, referring to the project as having 'no pecuniary aid but that derived from the patriotic munificence of one of my Irish subjects'.[37] She asked to meet Dargan and when Lord Granville introduced him, congratulated him and reached out as if to shake hands. When he hesitated she laid her hand on his arm and shook it warmly, drawing a burst of cheering from the crowd.

An instance of youthful royal tetchiness followed when the young Prince Edward (later to be Edward VII, much later) refused to accept a copy of the Exhibition catalogue because it was less elaborate than the one presented to Victoria. The spurned edition is preserved in National Library with a brief description of the incident inscribed on one of the pages.[38] Victoria then went on a visit to the halls. She thought them 'extremely well arranged and the people gave us a most kind and cordial welcome' and she admired the modern art collection in particular.[39]

A view of the frontage to Mount Anville with the distinctive tower designed by railway architect John Mulvany, a colleague of Dargan's.

That afternoon the queen made her celebrated visit to Dargan's house, Mount Anville. Three carriages set off from the Phoenix Park going at a fast pace through the windswept city and onto the Donnybrook Road. Fears for the queen's safety dictated a brisk pace and although many passers-by turned their carriages to follow, the royal party was going so fast they were unable to keep up.

The queen arrived at Mount Anville at about 5.30 pm, took tea, and admired the fine views across Dublin bay from the distinctive tower Dargan had built to John Mulvany's design.[40] It was rare for any British monarch to visit a commoner (other than for a tryst) and Victoria's account is thoroughly wholesome whereas Prince Albert's is more forthright.

Victoria Calls on Dargan

'The day continued deplorably showery but still, we ventured out for a drive, and opened the carriage several times. The Boys and Ly. St. Germans were with us. We drove through and on beyond Dublin, to a Mr Dargan's house, who has built a tower, much in the same style as those at Osborne – commanding a view of the whole country. The rain *had just ceased and enabled us to see the really fine view of Kingstown Harbour, Howth, the Dublin and Wicklow Hills, with the 'Sugar Loaf'. Mr Dargan has risen from being a labouring man, originally a road maker, and has accumulated an immense fortune. He has built the whole Exhibition at his own expense, and is touchingly simple and modest. I would have made him a Baronet, but he was anxious that it should not be done. Mrs Dargan is a very good-natured kind of woman.'*

Turning down the offer of a title must have taken some courage.[41] Prince Albert's description of Dargan is more forthright than the queen's and less diplomatic with the tone of someone visiting a foreign country, which presumably it was for him, although it is hardly accurate to describe Dargan as ever having been a common labourer.

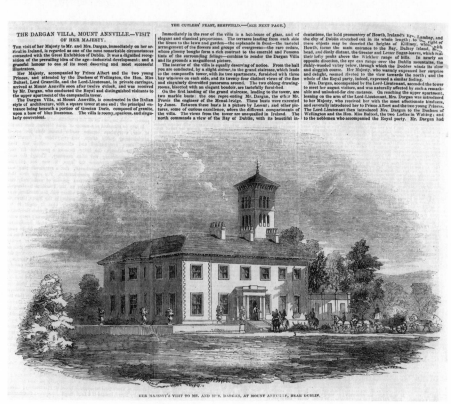

The *Illustrated London News* reports Queen Victoria's visit to Mount Anville with a fine engraving of the house. The reporter noted Mrs Dargan was overcome by the visitation being 'naturally affected by such a remarkable and unlooked for circumstance' and was obliged to lean on the Lord Lieutenant for support. The house and gardens 'combine to render the Dargan Villa and its grounds a magnificent picture'.

Prince Albert on Dargan

'Mr <u>Dargan</u> is the man of the people. He is a simple, unobtrusive, retiring man, a thorough Irishman, not always quite sober of an evening, industrious, kind to his workmen, but the only man who has by his own determination & courage put a stop to every strike or combination of workmen, of which the Irish are so fond. All he has done has been done on the field of Industry & not of politics or Religion, without the Priest or factious conspiracy, without the promise of distant extraordinary advantages but with immediate apparent benefit.

The <u>Exhibition</u>, which must be pronounced to be very successful, has done wonders in this respect. A private undertaking, unaided by Govt. or any Commission with Royal Authority, made and erected at the sole expense of a single Individual, & this an Irish Road contractor, not long ago a <u>common labourer</u> himself, who had raised himself solely by his own industry & energy, – it deserves the greatest credit & is looked upon by the Irish with infinite self-satisfaction as an emblem of national hope.'

Albert also recorded an anecdote told by the Duke of Leinster over dinner in the Vice-Regal Lodge about a Cork cab driver who said 'Dargan is the man for us; he has put plenty of money into our pockets and never took any out of them.'[42]

The party stayed at Mount Anville for half an hour during which Victoria offered Dargan busts of herself and Albert, to be designed by an artist of his choosing.[43] The next day she made her second visit to the Exhibition without the public present and inspected a controversial dessert service by Kerrs of Worcester with characters from *A Midsummer Night's Dream*. Writing in the *Freeman's Journal*, 'Excelsior' was critical of plans to present this service to the departing Lord Lieutenant: 'Doubtless Lord Eglinton has his merits, he also has had his rewards', the paper said, suggesting Mrs Dargan was a more suitable recipient.[44]

The next day, 31 August 1853, was bright when Victoria visited the Exhibition to see the sculptures, linen, lace, Griffith's Geological Survey of Ireland and the Shakespeare dessert service mentioned above. Also on display was a fine coach from the Dublin firm of Thomas Hutton that became the Irish State Coach; 'a state carriage built for me' as the queen described it somewhat acquisitively.[45] The exterior was black and blue with gilt decoration and a blue damask interior. Fire badly damaged it in 1911 but it was fully restored in 1989 and is now on display in the Royal Mews, Buckingham Palace. The queen bought some pictures in the Exhibition gallery and although the public arrived as she was leaving she was relieved to note they 'behaved very well'.[46]

A Worcester presentation plate from c.1852–62 features a view of Mount Anville and heads of Thomas Moore, Patrick Sarsfield and Brian Boroihue (sic) around the edge. Although 'distressed' it sold at auction and is now valued at appx. €1200. Image kindly provided by Kevin Curry.

A Staffordshire pot lid with an illustration of the 1853 Dublin Exhibition building in transfer print. Image kindly provided by Kevin Curry.

The Irish State Coach built by the Dublin firm of Thomas Hutton was presented to Queen Victoria at the 1853 Exhibition. It underwent extensive refurbishment after fire damage in 1911.

A military review in the Phoenix Park that evening was cut short when two cavalrymen were injured after their mounts stumbled. St Germans gave a dinner in the Vice-Regal Lodge for twenty-six, including William and Jane Dargan and their niece, Louisa Haslam, the daughter of Jane's sister Frances Arkinstall and her husband Dr Joseph Haslam. At the ball that followed the queen remarked: 'There certainly is much beauty in Ireland of a peculiar character, fine eyes and hair, brilliant complexions.'[47]

The next day Victoria was at the Exhibition by 9.30 am, 'a deplorable day, thick mists and fine rain', she noted. She was escorted round by Dargan with Alderman Roe and Lord Talbot de Malahide, inspecting a machine for weaving Balbriggan socks and one for rearing farmed salmon using an artificial current in the water. The queen's fourth and final visit was on Friday, 3 September to see the china collection and the view from the upper gallery before leaving to plant four trees at the Vice-Regal Lodge and to call on Lord Howth.[48] Victoria left for Westland Row station, noting anxiously that although the route was crowded there were no troops lining the streets. The royal visit was reported at length in the Irish and British papers and Victoria concluded the exhibition raised the feeling of enterprise among the people: 'Mr Dargan's own life and lifestyle they are likewise inclined to study and reflect upon.'[49]

A crude jug made to commemorate the 1853 Exhibition. Image kindly provided by Alistair Smeaton, Dublin City Libraries and Archives.

The Exhibition Draws to a Close

Attendances peaked during Victoria's visit and declined sharply thereafter so that by 10 October receipts were only £100 a day. When the entrance fee dropped to 6d the daily takings rose again to £400 and T.D. Jones, the Committee's Finance Officer, admitted it was a mistake not to have made the reduction earlier. As the closing date approached, Monday 31 October, the number of visitors rose again. Entry on the final day rose to half a crown and 12,500 went to see the Exhibition for the last time.

The closing ceremonial was as elaborate as the opening: Dargan and the Committee greeted Earl St Germans and his military escort and the musical programme ('gone through', as *The Times* indelicately put it) was as substantial as before. St Germans wished Dargan health and prosperity and declared the Exhibition closed, calling for three cheers for Dargan and one cheer more. The great bell tolled the closing hour at 4 pm and the last visitors were gone by 5 pm.

With honourable motives but poor timing some members of the Committee and others were reluctant to close up shop, a delegation calling for a two-day post-ponement to reduce Dargan's loss and with the harvest over to allow farm labourers to visit it. But exhibitors were already removing their goods and Roe commented it would look very odd if the day after the Lord Lieutenant closed the Exhibition they declared it open again. The Committee chairman said it was unsafe to admit visitors while goods were being removed and their proposal was too late, as reopening would expose them to the 'charge of unpunctuality'. At this 'the deputation and other citizens ... silently withdrew'. The Darganaeum was to remain closed.[50]

There was one concession. With all exhibits removed, the RDS agreed to Roe's proposal to open the main hall as a winter garden. By 10 November the side sections were coming down as workmen dismantled the interior divides and counters leaving just the main hall, which now lay empty, a fairly dismal site. Some of the first new residents were feathered when Dargan's assistant, William Mackie, allowed the Amateur Poultry Society to exhibit their fowl in December. In January 1854 the RDS allowed the Winter Garden to open on certain evenings from 8–10 pm provided there were fire precautions and enough police to prevent 'disorderly or improper conduct' in the shadowy alcoves of the hall.[51]

The week before the Winter Garden was to close in mid March 1854 there were military bands and a light display similar to modern lasers – a 'series of pris-matic tints were cast upon the spectators and surrounding objects'. Jane Dargan asked that the hall remain open for St Patrick's Day when once again military bands played to a small audience. The hall was then closed for the last time. Clearing the site went on over some months, judging by the many requests the RDS made to Dargan to clear Leinster Lawn and forward the proceeds from entry to the Winter Garden to which it was apparently entitled.[52]

Closing the Accounts

T.D Jones, Exhibition Financial Officer, prepared the statistics and the final accounts. The event drew 1,149,369 paying visitors with sales of 50,123 catalogues giving a total income of £69,232. Expenditure came to £90,143, including £1930 dismantling costs, leaving a net loss to Dargan of £20,911, 'which he may be said to have bestowed on the Irish people', as Jones put it.[53] Dargan's subvention was in fact greater, as being the contractor he effectively subsidized the works and obtained the materials at a preferential rate. Jones said he charged £59,871 to put up the building whereas the commercial rate for a similar construction job would have been closer to £100,000. The loss was a serious blow to Dargan but not the crippling one some commentators have suggested, given the scale of his operations at this time.

Two days after the closure there was a banquet in Dargan's honour in the Round Room of the Mansion House with sales of 500 tickets plus a hundred for guests. Ladies, including 'Mrs Dargan and her friends', were on the balcony and the room decorated with plants from the RDS gardens, flags from the Exhibition halls and a number of busts of Dargan. George Roe mentioned that Victoria's most popular act while in Ireland was to honour Dargan adding that Dargan had told him he was perfectly satisfied with the financial outcome; the main toast was to him. Responding, Dargan rose to prolonged cheering and spoke of the Exhibition's success, the hard work of all involved and commenting that no other project had given him more pleasure. The final toast was to Mrs Dargan and the party broke up at 1 am.[54]

Was the Exhibition a Success or a Failure?

The various titles of the Exhibition suggest a certain confusion of purpose. It was known as the Great Industrial Exhibition, the Dublin Industrial Exhibition and the Exhibition of Art-Industry, the last the most accurate. There were very few exhibits of mass-produced Irish-made goods, probably because there was little such industry in the country. Irish manufacturers showed cabinets, furniture, picture frames, linen, Celtic-style jewellery and a state carriage. The *Times* noted the great interest in the building itself and the picture gallery, regretting there were not more industrial exhibits. One anonymous visitor said there were few Irish goods apart from the first doll made in Ireland and groups of men making buttons and sweets.[55] The same person did however see a fine group of girls at the refreshment table and heard the Dargan Polka and the Dargan Gallop. Among the few Irish-made railway items were a small locomotive from Grendon's of Drogheda, a double signal post and a high-pressure pump from the Inchicore railway works to power the fountains.

Table 6.1: DUBLIN 1853 EXHIBITION, INCOME AND EXPENDITURE ANALYSIS

Income

Receipts at the door	£28,981 6s 6d
Season tickets	£18,238 10s
Catalogue sales	£2,928 0s 3d
Railway excursion/day tickets	£2,182 3s 1d
Refreshment rooms rent	£550 0s 0d
Cloakroom/retiring room charges	£318 0s 4d
Sale of ticket cases	£23 1s 4d
Sale of medals	<u>£11 12s 0d</u>
	£53,232 13s 6d
Value of building and fixtures	£16,000
Total	£69,232 13s 6d

Expenditure

Salaries and wages	£8,442 12s 9d
Travelling expenses, goods transport	£4,982 11s 4d
Printing and advertising	£4,537 5s 10d
Office expenses	£1,740 2s 6d
Furnishing Exhibition & offices	£3,314 16s 6d
Police wages	£2,889 14s 7d
Corporation for pavements, water	£526 11s 11d
Gas supply	£303 3s 0d
Music	£1,510 0s 5d
Payment to bereaved families	<u>£275 10s 10d</u>
	£28,342 9s 8d
Construction of building	£59,871 2s 1d
Total	£88,213 11s 9d
Excess of expenditure over income	£18,980 18s 3d
Dismantling costs	£1,930 7s 10d
Final loss met by Dargan	£20,911 6s 1d

The ratio of industrial to artistic exhibits is revealing: of thirty classes, twenty-nine were fine art with just one manufacturers class. Among the latter were crude products from workhouses and prisons such as flannel, tweed, towels, linen and frieze, a coarse woollen cloth, 'unattractive articles ... the rudest form of industrial effort' as Sproule described them.[56] One catalogue noted that 'excepting some objects of minor importance Irish manufactures cannot as yet enter into competition with those of other countries'. Ó Gráda described the exhibition trenchantly as one of Irish industrial decline, although industrial stagnation might be more accurate.[57]

If not financially, on a personal level the Exhibition was a tremendous success for Dargan. It showcased some fine works of art and however limited in content was a statement of national self-confidence at a time when the country needed such a boost. The international focus, limited as it was, was also welcome.

Another benefit was that many exhibitors agreed to leave their items behind when the event closed. Robert Kane's Museum of Irish Industry offered to take all minerals and agricultural products while even before the opening the RDS had invited every exhibitor to donate their exhibits after the closure, enclosing a printed consent form with the letter of invitation. The response was very positive judging by the number of completed forms the RDS received, the expense of packing and shipping goods home being a further incentive towards philanthropy.[58]

The Dargan Institute and the National Gallery of Ireland

Efforts to sustain the ethos of the Exhibition focused on two core ideas: an industrial training school and an art gallery, each to have some link to the Dargan name. Out of these disparate proposals was born the National Gallery of Ireland, tracing its origins to calls for public acknowledgment of Dargan's generosity in funding the Exhibition. In June a requisition with 2000 names went to the Lord Mayor of Dublin calling for public recognition of Dargan's contribution. The names covered almost a full page of one newspaper and included the Duke of Leinster, the Earls of Kildare and Bandon, seventeen bishops of various denominations, baronets, aldermen and newspaper editors.[59] A meeting in the Mansion House on 14 July 1853 sought to honour Ireland's 'most distinguished individual' who, it said, had laid the foundations for the country's future prosperity. Among the speakers was Sir William Rowan Hamilton, discoverer of quaternion equations, who admitted he was a poor judge of Dargan's achievements but recognized the intellectual and moral attributes that created them and stressed that Dargan needed emulation rather than more praise.

By September 1853 the Dargan Institute Committee, chaired by James Perry, was meeting weekly in Commercial Buildings and inviting subscriptions to mark Dargan's philanthropy. The Regular Sawyers Society sent £10 as a token of the business Dargan had brought its members, while the Midland Great Western Railway donated £200. Dublin pawnbrokers raised £100, Dublin publicans gave £64 while William Kirk MP, Dargan's Newry friend, sent £10. But the Marquess of Westmeath told the Committee in January 1854 that the amount collected, £6000, was £4000 shy of the minimum needed to establish the Dargan Gallery.

The existence of a rival gallery scheme, the Irish Institution and a degree of confusion about the aims of the Dargan proposal (some people believed their donations went to reducing Dargan's loss on the Exhibition) added to the lack of progress. One project would have to be abandoned or the two should merge. When the two groups met in the summer of 1854, edging towards the establishment of a national gallery, the Dargan faction spelt out terms for any marriage. Dargan's name was to appear over the main door, Catterson Smith's portrait of Dargan was to hang in a prominent position and there was to be a memorial with an inscription to Dargan on the exterior wall.[60] Unfortunately there was no formal agreement on these conditions leading to later tensions. The planned relocation of Marsh's Library within the gallery complex and the need to clarify the role of the RDS were further complicating factors.

Parliament passed the National Gallery of Ireland bill on 10 August 1854 and George Mulvany became Hon. Secretary of the Gallery Board. He was a brother of Dargan's architect colleague, John Skipton Mulvany, and painted the very fine portrait of Dargan that now hangs in the CIÉ boardroom at Heuston station. The estimated cost of the building was £11,000 with funds coming from parliament, the Dargan Institute and the Treasury. Cockburn & Son won the building contract and the foundation stone was laid on 29 January 1859. Part of the project was to cast another statue of Dargan (this time in bronze) by Thomas Farrell RHA. It arrived from London at the North Wall in May 1863. The statue is 3.3 m high standing on a pedestal of granite and Dargan is shown with left leg slightly forward. The pedestal bears the one word, 'Dargan' and the statue stands in front of the National Gallery close to the site of the Exhibition building.

What made the statue unique was its installation while the subject was still alive. Most comments were positive but the *Dublin Builder* magazine said it was 'by no means a graceful outline' and criticized the use of Aberdeen granite for the plinth, although it was in fact sourced in Roscommon.[61] James Stephens, author of *The Crock of Gold* and a Registrar of the Gallery, voiced his whimsical dislike of the statue in a 1924 letter to the Director: 'I wish you would command me to have a bomb slung at the Dargan statue on our Lawn, that man's frock coat, and the general imbecile complacency of his rear-view comes between me and happiness.'[62] The statue is quite hard to see and like Stephens most people only spot it from the rear when coming out of the Gallery.

Dargan was not present at the statue unveiling and opening of the National Gallery by the Earl of Carlisle on a perishing day in January 1864. At the ceremony his friend and later his executor, Alexander Boyle, formally handed over responsibility for the Gallery to the new board of trustees. Among Jane Dargan's papers is an undated handwritten note, probably in her writing: 'Mr Dargan gave a donation of £2000 to the National Gallery which was not made public until after his death' confirmed by Gallery records.[63] Dargan later told George Mulvany, the first Director, he planned to increase his donation 'if his health and prosperity were spared'.[64] At the opening Mulvany said the Gallery had already bought seventy-one pictures, thirty-one more came from the National Gallery in London, twenty-five were gifts and 104 were bequests. In the first two weeks 9649 people visited while in the following ten months there were 167,698 visitors who bought 8119 copies of the first catalogue.

The Dargan statue, 'the man with his hand in his pocket', stands in front of the original entrance to the National Gallery close to the site of the 1853 Exhibition.

One of the main rooms, as it is today, was the Dargan Wing and until recently Catterson Smith's rather bland portrait, costing £320, hung near the Merrion Square entrance. On the front wall near the statue of a pensive George Bernard Shaw and close to where the main hall of the Exhibition stood is a plaque with this inscription:

National Gallery of Ireland, Founded AD 1864,
Erected by the contributions of the fellow-countrymen
of William Dargan Esquire,
Aided by the Imperial Government,
In commemoration of his munificent liberality
In founding and sustaining the Dublin Industrial Exhibition of 1853.

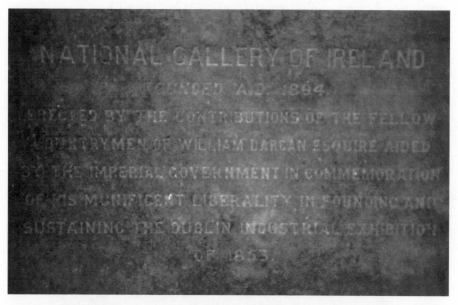

A plaque set into the wall of the National Gallery explains Dargan's role in its creation. With the new entrance from Clare Street few people notice this, or indeed the Dargan statue nearby.

The Exhibition Legacy

There is little physical trace of the Exhibition today. Much of Leinster Lawn now serves mundanely as a car park for Oireachtas members. It is likely that Dargan removed some of the large entrance gates for use in his gardens at Mount Anville. Another survival from the Main Hall is the three-tiered seven-metre fountain by architects Baird & Thomson. It stands in front of the former Masonic School in

Ballsbridge, now Bewley's Hotel. Dargan also used iron girders from the Exhibition for the platform canopy at Waterford station. Sadly the original station was demolished some years ago and replaced with a fairly hideous block of zero artistic merit. John Foley's rather fine 1872 statue of Prince Albert lurks discretely in shrubbery next to the wall of the Natural History Museum where nobody sees it or can take umbrage with it.

The three-tier fountain that stood in the Centre Hall of the Exhibition building is a composite effort. The Glasgow firm of Ferguson, Miller & Co. made it to a design by architects Baird & Thompson, with figures by Messrs Mossman and ornament by J. Steel. It is one of the few survivals of the Exhibition and stands in the grounds of the former Masonic School, Ballsbridge, now Bewley's Hotel.

The *Freeman's Journal* made the telling observation that Dargan's success had changed the negative perception of industrial enterprise as a career as up to then the 'stain of industry polluted the blood to the third and fourth generation'.[65] Meanwhile Dublin Municipal Council failed to agree on a testimonial that it felt should be national, not confined to Dublin.[66] The same paper suggested Mayor Robert Kinahan should stand down as MP in favour of Dargan: 'Certainly we could well afford to sacrifice either of the distinguished men who now represent Dublin for such a successor.'

One of the initial problems was choosing the most suitable type of building to house the Exhibition and whether it should be a temporary structure or adapted for other use after the event. Paxton's Hyde Park building (one of the first prefabrications in the world) was taken down and re-erected in even larger format in a public park at Sydenham, south London, giving its name, the Crystal Palace, to an area of the city and indeed a football team.[67] Curiously when Jane Dargan moved back to England as a widow she settled in Penge, only a short walk from the Crystal Palace. Queen Victoria opened the building twice, once in Hyde Park and again in its new location; for thirty years it drew two million visitors each year to its concerts, plays, flower and dog shows, fireworks displays and exhibitions. The Crystal Palace burned down in November 1936, an event overshadowed by the abdication of Edward VIII a few days later and the progression towards World War II. Nothing is left apart from some large exhibit models of dinosaurs that serve as a climbing frame for children. Back in Dublin, as some had predicted there was no possibility of retaining Dargan's Exhibition building on Merrion Square as the RDS needed to use the Leinster Lawn site for other purposes.

Fourteen years later Dargan was a director of the company that ran the 1865 Dublin Exhibition in a specially constructed building on Earlsfort Terrace and Iveagh Gardens. Later adapted for use by UCD, the building now houses the National Concert Hall. Among the remains of another similar event, the 1907 Exhibition in Herbert Park, is the ornamental pond and a dacha-like kiosk now in use as a summerhouse in a Dartry, south Dublin garden.

Table 6.2: STATISTICAL COMPARISON OF 1853 AND 1865 DUBLIN EXHIBITIONS[68]

	1853	*1865*
British exhibitors	1555	770
Foreign/colonial exhibitors	288	1544
Works of art	1493	2072
Total receipts	£53,000	£45,000

SEVEN

Dargan's Own Line: The Dublin & Wicklow Railway

The railway line most closely identified with Dargan as contractor, engineer, director and investor is the Dublin & Wicklow Railway (D&WR) whose headquarters were in the former railway station in Harcourt Street. Dargan won some of the early small D&WR contracts between the city and Dundrum, including the nine-arch Dodder viaduct at Milltown and the retaining walls at Ranelagh. This embankment runs at the end of my garden: I can visualize Dargan talking to his foremen as the sound of chisel against stone rings out in the morning air, while skilled stonemasons cut and shape the dark grey limestone blocks to the required dimensions. The smooth bevelled cut marks in each block are as clear today as when they were made 160 years ago. The Harcourt Street line is now part of the Luas.

In February 1852 Dargan won the contract to build the 31 miles (50 km) from Dundrum and Dun Laoghaire to Wicklow for £308,000. A year later he made a substantial investment in the company, buying 9763 forfeited shares (on which investors had paid a deposit) but lost them when they then failed to pay the balance due.[1] Dargan continued to buy up shares in this way and accepted a large part of his fees in debentures. A 20,000 share stockholding made him a powerful force in the company, provoking objections from at least one proprietor, a Mr Palmer, who claimed Dargan had put his own people on the board and was effectively acting as chairman.[2]

To make this investment Dargan needed to use shares in the D&WR and other lines such as the Midland Railway valued at £200,000 to secure heavy borrowings from the Bank of Ireland. These loans totalled £100,000 on which he was paying 5 to 6 per cent, plus a management fee. Dargan wrote quite deferentially to the bank saying this loan would place him 'in a position of perfect financial independence'.[3] The truth was that he did indeed have a lot of influence on the D&WR board.

Dargan finished the 9 miles (14 km) from Dundrum to Bray in July 1853. After a VIP trip to Bray (the town became in time one of his abiding projects, see Chapter 8), there was a reception in Quinn's Hotel. But unusually Captain H.W. Tyler RE, the railway inspector, was highly critical, discovering many flaws in Dargan's work, or possibly that of his subcontractors.

Tyler's complaints were not trivial: the Balally cutting was too steep and quite dangerous; several bridges were incomplete; Dundrum station was unfinished and train drivers could not see the signal box; Carrickmines Road bridge was hazardous and the level crossing had no gates. While at Shanganagh the line was so close to the highway that road carriages had to pull onto the track to pass one another.[4] One possible explanation for this lack of attention is that Dargan was at this time building the Waterford & Limerick Railway, the Tramore Railway and the Midland line to Cavan, and was under some pressure to finish the Exhibition building in time for the official opening in May, combined with the company's anxiety to have the line complete to tap into the anticipated extra traffic generated by the Exhibition. Dargan made good these snags on the Wicklow Railway and in due course the line opened for traffic.

One example of Dargan's influence was the link-up or virtual merger between the D&WR and the Dublin & Kingstown Railway whereby the former company built the line from Dun Laoghaire to Dalkey and then ran the train services. Despite some vocal opposition Dargan assured proprietors their stock could only rise as a result and the EGM eventually backed the union.[5] At another celebratory dinner in Breslin's Restaurant in Bray station,[6] James Perry having replaced Edward Septimus Codd on the D&WR board and thus being a director of both companies, spoke of Dargan's positive role in the negotiations. Dargan replied he was delighted to help bring these two companies together, one of which he was himself the sustainer and the other of which had sustained him, a neat reference to his first railway contract with the D&KR and his current role with the D&WR.

By the end of June 1854 Dalkey to Bray was nearly ready and Dargan built a temporary terminus at Harcourt Road using materials from the carriage court of the Exhibition building.[7] Col. Wynne inspected this section and after lunch in Bray station with company officials, the group travelled at some speed to Dundrum; this time the verdict was positive. Sped on their way by army bands at Harcourt Road the directors travelled on a special train to Bray on 8 July 1854 and the line

Harcourt Street station then in use as an office building in pre-Luas days when there was a contra-flow for road traffic.

Bray station was built as a long, low single-storey platform, 'a very satisfying building combining elegance with functionalism',[8] probably by George Wilkinson, who designed Harcourt Street. Years later Samuel Beckett grew up in Foxrock and regularly took the train to Harcourt Street. He also wrote a radio play set in Foxrock station, *All That Fall*. Economy demanded that many of the D&WR stations were modest in design, employing tricks such as building the signal cabin on the passenger footbridge to avoid the need for a separate raised cabin. Wicklow and Rathdrum stations are examples of this. None of the GS&WR architectural extravagance here. Dargan and Le Fanu inspected the works and on 6 December 1854 they walked the route together around Bray Head.

Dargan received his next payment of £50,000 in company bills for although the D&WR secured a £100,000 government loan funds remained tight for the railway and its contractor. By summer of 1855 Dargan had almost finished converting the Dalkey atmospheric line (see Chapter 3) to normal traction and was pressing the Board of Works for permission to continue towards Wicklow. In July 1855 the directors walked from Bray to Dun Laoghaire with Dargan and then invited the railway inspector to call.[9] The board renewed some of Dargan's bills, adding that if the funds were not there when they fell due he would have to accept their further renewal. But the line south of Bray, which severely challenged the great English engineer Isambard Kingdom Brunel, continued to be an engineering headache.

Dargan was involved at least partly in building this difficult section. Honeycombed with tunnels and perched high above the sea, the track crossed several inlets on narrow timber bridges and to this day suffers the steady onslaught of storms and landslides. It is said the company chose a coastal route over the more obvious and much easier inland one because Lord Meath donated the land. In 1867, six months after Dargan's death, a train came off one of these timber bridges at a spot near the Brandy Hole: there were only two fatalities but twenty-three people were injured. Trains on this stretch of line still proceed slowly and viewing it from the cliff-top path between Bray and Greystones shows what a difficult piece of engineering it was. The ruins of huts where linesmen were posted to check for rock falls and sea damage are still visible while at several points erosion has forced the line inwards leaving short abandoned tunnels and track sections standing in splendid isolation.

By contrast the line south of Bray Head and beyond Greystones is quite flat but proved equally troublesome. This scenic stretch runs along the shoreline where the ravages of the sea were a problem right from the start and continue to be so. Once again the line was relocated inland using more and more sea defences of massive concrete blocks and nets of giant boulders. Building on or near water was attractive to railway engineers because it avoided costly land purchases – but many such cost saving measures were short-sighted. Other similar examples are the line south of Merrion towards Monkstown and the Sligo line running alongside Lough Owel near Multyfarnham.

The directors took a trial run along Dargan's line from Bray to Wicklow on 13 October 1855 with another dinner in Breslin's Restaurant. Eleven days later Colonel George Wynne passed it as safe to open. But when the Dublin Grand Jury criticized a number of Dargan's road bridges, rail traffic between Dundrum and Bray stopped so he could make the repairs (some of which he handed over to his engineering colleague Purdon, using his plant and workmen) such as ballasting the Dundrum section and finishing the double line to Bray with points and crossings.[10]

As company engineer it was part of Brunel's job to sign and pass Dargan's invoices for the sections of the line he was building. At the end of 1855 Brunel estimated Dargan had received £369,000 and was due £49,235, a figure which Dargan disputed, believing he was owed considerably more. Like much of his business correspondence Dargan's letter to the board in January 1856 is forthright, concise and shrewd:

> And although this sum is greatly below what I believe is justly due me, circumstanced as I am in the company, I am not disposed to quarrel with the decision of your engineer or with yourselves. You will observe, however, that under the terms of this contract I am entitled to be paid the sum due to me in cash on demand, which mode of settlement would be most acceptable.[11]

This was enough to warrant creating a special D&WR committee early in 1856 including two of Dargan's allies, James Perry, his Quaker friend and supporter and Alexander Boyle who later became Dargan's sole executor and Joseph Gaughan. Dargan was also at the meeting that agreed a complex system of paying him an additional £50,000 over and above Brunel's statement and twenty-five bonds of £2000 each, payable in two years at 5 per cent, a month later. Part of the agreement was that the D&WR would maintain the extremely difficult section from Bray to Wicklow while Dargan would manage that from Bray to Dublin.[12]

Dargan Joins the D&WR Board

With his accounts almost settled, the February 1856 directors' meeting invited Dargan to join the board. Although he could not take D&WR construction contracts he became involved in every aspect of running the company including the engineering. He sat on finance, working systems and officers' duties committees and mediated complaints from the D&KR about unequal competition and even passenger fares. He invited his friend W.R. Le Fanu to apply for the position of consulting engineer at £100 per annum. He too was very involved with the D&WR at this time and often met Dargan at Mount Anville and on site.[13]

Dargan joined a delegation to Dublin Castle to seek interest relief on a £100,000 loan and requesting a further advance. He secured a £25,000 personal overdraft from the Royal Bank of Ireland via his friend, Charles Copeland and the company later took out a £30,000 overdraft from the Bank of Ireland at a hefty 8 per cent.[14]

Throughout 1856 Dargan attended almost every one of the weekly board meetings, many of which discussed his substantial portfolio of D&WR bonds. One meeting on 8 August 1856 noted Dargan had received interest on his bonds from the company amounting to £3347. It is worth noting that he managed this while at the same time building the lines to Cavan, Foynes, Banbridge, Monaghan, Ennis and Tralee as well as the Liffey Graving Dock and being involved in running his mills at Chapelizod. His energy and capacity to manage show the extraordinary ability of the man: any one of these projects would have been a full-time job and despite keeping all these projects on the go Dargan dedicated a huge amount of time to the D&WR, much more than he did with any other railway. In addition his financial support kept the company afloat through lean times, in turn putting a strain on his own finances – using railway shares as security he borrowed heavily from several banks, in particular the Bank of Ireland.

The lofty five-arch viaduct built by Dargan at Bride's Glen stands just south of the current Luas terminus. It will come into use if the Luas line extends to Bray.

Such was the Bank of Ireland's hold on his finances that for several years Dargan needed its proxy to vote at D&WR shareholders' meetings. Some of the latter were trying, such as one in mid 1856 when a shareholder named Flood asked who was paying for defective bridgework at Dundrum. The deduction came out of Dargan's account, the chairman Frederick Ponsonby assured the meeting, to which Dargan replied with some irritation: 'And I may as well tell you, Mr Flood, it was a most unjust one,' as the person responsible was no longer working on the bridge, presumably a reference to a deficient subcontractor.[15]

Dargan gave yet another dinner in Breslin's in September 1856 for the directors, some shareholders and Charles Copeland of the Royal Bank of Ireland. He used the occasion to comment on the company's finances in a speech that explains much about how he and the other directors ran the D&WR. Receipts of £1500 a week would cover all salaries, working expenses, wear and tear on rolling stock and rental due under the Kingstown Railway lease agreement. Every £100 over that would give the shareholders a 1 per cent dividend, a prospect they greeted enthusiastically. A few days later the company published a healthy set of returns for the week ended 9 September 1856: the total received was £2240, well above Dargan's benchmark figure of £1500.[16] Unfortunately the accounts did not always remain that healthy.

The D&WR Hits Choppy Waters

Renewal or replacement of Dargan's bonds and debentures was often on the D&WR agenda with a complicated series of court judgements against the company issued in favour of Dargan in 1856–8. While it is certain Dargan was not suing his own company with a view to threatening its viability or even forcing it into bankruptcy, the actual purpose of these judgements is unclear. It is possible that Dargan's own creditors, in particular the Bank of Ireland, were forcing him to go down the legal road to ensure he had enough capital to meet the repayments on his own loans. A study of Bank of Ireland loan applications, approved overdrafts and loan renewals for the years 1854–66 reveal extremely heavy borrowings: in August 1860, for example, Dargan's loans totalled over £100,000.

Company engineer W.R. Le Fanu was busy at this time dealing with a wall collapse at Harcourt Road and a hundred-ton earth slip at Bray Head; he was also a regular visitor to Mount Anville.[17] Shareholder meetings could be stormy, and one from 17–19 November 1858 at Westland Row was particularly so. During a discussion about bond and bill transactions a row broke out between two investors over a closed window. A Dr Fulton complained the meeting room was like the black hole of Calcutta and insisted on opening a window, over the vocal objections of another shareholder who slammed it shut. Dr Fulton then took the matter into his own hands and smashed three panes with his stick. Company officials had to summon the railway policeman to restore order. Press coverage of the incident was extensive whereas the company minutes barely refer to it.[18]

The meeting was held over several days and one of the main disputes was over the appointment of Joseph Hone and Dargan's friend, Alexander Boyle, to the board amid bitter complaints about the poor performance of D&WR shares. Dargan spoke at some length about the company's share prices, accompanied by calls for the dismissal of the entire board. The wrath of the shareholders focused on the fact that they were receiving almost no dividend with many calling on the company to abandon plans to extend the line further south until it was in a healthier state. The next day's meeting was even more heated. Discussions began about an extension to the Avoca copper mines, costed by Le Fanu at £6000 per mile, which he said could generate up to 100,000 tons of rail freight per annum.[19] There was strong opposition to the chairman's suggestion that Dargan would provide half the capital for the extension. One shareholder, Martin Burke, accused Dargan of being far from impartial and said 'someone so deeply interested in getting the shareholders' money' should not even be a director, provoking calls of 'order, order'. Dargan responded saying his only motive was to increase the value of D&WR shares and thus his own investment. There followed a heated discussion about the other directors, attempts to restructure the board and shareholder delegations. Dargan then reminded the meeting that receipts barely covered expenses, only preference shares paid a dividend and that the Gorey extension was vital, adding that such discord could only damage the company. He was then called to chair the last part of the meeting which he did.[20]

Bray Head was and remains a constant headache for railway engineers, being an extraordinarily difficult route to build and maintain. Note the original trackbed on the seaward side of the tunnel entrance.

Dargan was a major financier of the DW&WR. This is one of his many share certificates, a 5 per cent preference share for £50 issued on 2 March 1865 when he had moved to 2 Fitzwilliam Square.

The new Harcourt Street terminus took a few years to complete and is the design of George Wilkinson who also designed Ballinasloe station and a number of hospitals and workhouses. Maurice Craig describes Harcourt Street as 'a beautiful example of the blending of materials and textures, no less than of forms. ... As a composition in masses it is excellent'.[21] When Captain George Ross inspected the high level terminus in January 1859 he ordered the demolition of the temporary building at Harcourt Road and allowed just a single line to open. He shrewdly commented on a major hazard in the new terminus: three lines ran into one platform with just a timber buffer between the turntable and the outer wall over a steep drop into the street, a flaw which led to the 1900 accident.[22]

Valentine's Day Accident, Harcourt Street, 1900

On 14 February 1900 Captain Ross' fears came horribly true. A heavy cattle train entering Harcourt Street station was unable to stop before hitting the buffers. It smashed through the end wall and came to a stop suspended over Hatch Street. The fireman, Peter Jackson, leapt to safety but thinking he could halt the slow-moving train by putting the engine into reverse, the driver, William Hyland, bravely but foolishly stayed on the footplate. He was injured in the crash and his arm was later amputated.

Hyland told of applying the brakes leaving Ranelagh and despite the poor traction on greasy rails said his speed was just 6 mph. While the exhaustion of the crew – they had worked over twelve hours with almost no break, a standard working day – the weight of the train and slippery rails contributed to the crash but the real culprit was the dangerous station layout, spotted by Ross forty-one years before. Inbound goods trains also had to run along the single passenger platform before reversing into the siding, at best an inefficient arrangement, at worst dangerous. The company later gave the injured driver a desk job in its depot and by 1919 the Railways Executive had imposed an eight-hour working day for railway workers.

South from Wicklow and a New Company Name

By February 1859 the shareholders accepted the need to extend the line towards Wexford and the company received four tenders to build the section from Wicklow to Rathdrum. Thomas Edwards won the contract with his £100,000 tender and by the end of the year had a thousand men at work.[23] The company also opened its own hotel at Rathdrum station, the Royal Fitzwilliam, possibly on the site of an industrial school. Dargan invested £5000 in the hotel that was run by the Breslin family from Bray and managed by Joseph Softlaw, formerly of the Bridge Hotel, London but was never an outstanding success. It is a fine building and still standing though unused at the time of writing. Around this time the company decided it needed a newer more comprehensive name to reflect its territorial ambitions, becoming the Dublin Wicklow and Wexford Railway (DW&WR). By July 1861 the line to Rathdrum was nearly complete and Le Fanu and Dargan travelled the route on one of the latter's engines. This section opened on 20 August 1861. Le Fanu kept meticulous accounts of his DW&WR fees as well as detailed notes of his fishing exploits: before catching the 9.35 am train one morning to meet Dargan at the DW&WR board he landed twenty-eight trout from the Dargle river.[24]

In 1863 the railway company opened a hotel beside Rathdrum station, the Royal Fitzwilliam, run by two ladies named Breslin, relations of Edward Breslin who ran the catering at Bray station. The hotel was renamed the Railway Hotel but was never a great success. It was vacant until recently.

Dargan remained very involved in every aspect of managing and promoting the interests of the DW&WR. He persuaded the directors to double the Dundrum-Bray line and pressed for the Gorey extension, as well as helping to secure a £100,000 government loan. More mundane matters included fare levels, fines for negligent staff and economies such as reducing the number of station masters and locking level crossings to employ fewer crossing keepers.[25]

Attracting passengers to the railway was obviously paramount and Dargan understood early on that while most companies preferred first-class passengers, substantial profits could to be made from third and fourth class passengers, even with fares as low as a farthing a mile (a farthing was a quarter of a penny, approximately one eighth of a cent). A railway carriage, as the name suggests, was basically a horse-drawn vehicle adapted for railway use and often built by the same firms that built road vehicles, such as John Dawson of Phibsboro. Around forty could squeeze into a third-class carriage, sometimes just a wagon with seats open to the elements, whereas a first-class carriage of the same size would hold twelve to fifteen at most. It was also much more expensive to build. When the Kingstown Railway successfully began wooing third-class passengers in the 1840s with cheap excursions, early morning workmen's tickets and other concessionary fares, William Galt commented ungrammatically: 'the company carried, without any increase in expenditure, 478,117 more passengers than what they did in 1840'.[26]

The earliest surviving carriage in Ireland is Dublin & Kingstown Railway no.48, built in the 1830s, and now on display in the Ulster Folk and Transport Museum outside Belfast. Now beautifully restored it was a DW&WR third-class carriage, which resembles a goods vehicle with half the side walls removed and the roof retained (see p.162). Seating consisted of plain wooden benches with a shoulder-high partition between sections and a single oil lamp. Travelling any distance in such a carriage, exposed to seashore wind and rain as well as smuts and sparks from the adjacent engine must have been very uncomfortable, but these were the accepted conditions for third-class passengers.

As part of his lobbying activities, Dargan obtained permission from the city engineer of Dublin Municipal Council to extend the Westland Row (Pearse) station terminus over Great Brunswick and Cumberland Streets, on condition that the railway '(which I have no doubt they will) do as little damage to the street they propose to arch over as possible'.[27] Planning procedures were a lot simpler in those days.

In January 1863, 1400 men and 200 horses were at work on the Rathdrum to Enniscorthy section. Among the engineers was James Dargan, William's nephew. He did much work on the bridges and travelled regularly on the works engine, the *William Dargan*, a Bury locomotive that Dargan may have sold to engineering colleague Edwards.[28] Le Fanu was also busy on this stretch and in May he and Dargan travelled to London to promote a parliamentary bill for a further extension southwards. A few months later Le Fanu resigned from the DW&WR after 'ten years which were the busiest of my life'; he then assumed the less demanding role of Public Works Commissioner.[29]

The financial status of Dargan's railway remained precarious as it struggled to complete further extensions. As part of his financial duties Dargan continued to negotiate additional loans for the DW&WR from the Bank of Ireland, often with some difficulty, despite providing personal guarantees from the directors.

Dargan's health was failing when the board elected him deputy chairman on 12 February 1864 but a week later he declined the post, proposing Frederick Ponsonby instead. Ponsonby in turn proposed him as chairman and this time he accepted. Dargan's rather shaky, spidery signature appears at the end of the company minutes, in sharp contrast to the strong confident signature of earlier days. His physical deterioration can be tracked by comparing his signature at the end of the minutes of each board meeting. Occasionally it is strong and clear with the word 'Chairman' added as in March 1864 but more often it is weak and almost indecipherable.[30] In May that year he told a shareholders' meeting that with the line now open to Enniscorthy the company was seeking to place a bill before parliament for extensions to Wexford and Waterford. Despite his own difficult financial situation Dargan offered to take £25,000-worth of the new preference share issue in January 1865.

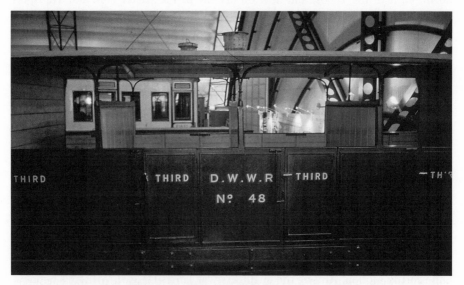

This third class DW&WR carriage built by D&KR dates from around the 1860s and reveals the Spartan conditions endured by passengers who travelled exposed to the elements. It is preserved in the Ulster Folk and Transport Museum.

The 1865 State Inquiry into Irish Railways

While his physical health may have been in decline in the mid-1860s Dargan was very far from incapacitated as shown by accounts in the minutes of his vigorous chairing of company meetings. An even clearer sign of his great stamina is that he travelled to London in June 1865 to give lengthy evidence before the Royal Commission of Inquiry into Irish Railways. What makes this surprising is that just six weeks before Dargan had a serious fall from his horse that left him concussed, and for several days it was believed he was close to death. But he rallied and a few weeks later made the arduous journey to London. He was in London again on 5 July and 19–28 July 1865, suggesting he was on the mend.[31]

The Commission's brief was to conduct a thorough investigation into the accounts, operations and works of Irish railways with a view to seeing what state aid, if any, was appropriate to put them on a sound footing. Most of the senior figures in Irish railways appeared before it and Dargan's lengthy and detailed evidence gives a comprehensive picture of the status of all lines. The questions were wide-ranging and focused on the varied financial and other problems facing Irish railways, allowing the respondent to make detailed replies without an adversarial approach.[32] The extent and quality of his evidence reflect an extraordinary mental vigour.

The main points Dargan made were that Irish lines could be worked for 40 per cent of gross receipts, compared to 50 per cent in England and that lower fares were not a railway panacea: when the D&KR did this, traffic increased but not revenue. As things stood, reduced third class fares would not induce labourers to use the train, he believed, because they had little need to travel, unlike traders and shopkeepers. It made more sense, he said, to develop and use existing lines before expending capital and energy constructing new ones and estimated the total expenditure on Irish railways at £26 million with their current worth £22 million.[33]

Dargan presented three radical options to the Commission:

1. Reduce running costs and duplication, amalgamate all Irish railways into three companies or even one large company;

2. Provide substantial state investment through loans set at 1–1½ per cent below current rates; or

3. Outright state purchase of all railways with the option of leasing them to private concerns.

These proposals were full of insight and over the following decades, all three solutions were applied in varying degrees. Low cost state loans did encourage railway construction and in the early twentieth century most lines were merged to form Great Southern Railways. Outright state purchase followed a few decades later. The option of leasing lines to private companies was not tried in Ireland but privatization has been government policy in Britain for some years. This has had very poor results for the travelling public, with high fares, inadequate service and ongoing massive state subsidies provided to private transport companies.

Turning to the DW&WR Dargan said it was 120 miles (193 km) long and cost £80–85 per mile per annum to maintain, describing his role thus: 'Our railway is peculiar. At the commencement probably the only capital in it was what I had myself' and each section as far as Enniscorthy was built on borrowed money. The Avoca mines contributed 120,000 tons per annum in goods traffic. If the DW&WR received £1.5 million in state investment, he added, it could reduce some rates by up to 30 per cent and provide a good return on that investment.

Referring to Irish railways in general, Dargan developed some of the points he made in a letter to William Pole, the Commission Secretary written in November 1865 and published as an Appendix to the report.[34] He compared roads that paid no taxes to railways that paid high taxes, contributed to poor rates and reduced pauperism by giving employment. A state loan to Irish railways of £2 million per annum for three years at 3½ per cent would allow all companies to cut third class fares and redeem higher rate loans, the 'heavy incubus on their resources, caused by exorbitant rates' as the Irish Railway Reform Committee put it.

Above all he argued that promoters of new lines must be able to prove the viability of their projects before receiving parliamentary approval to begin construction. In these three options he anticipated the twenty-first-century issue for public transport that requires it to be valued according to its overall contribution to public wellbeing and the environment and not simply on the profit and loss yardstick beloved of so many dismal scientists.

Back in Dublin Dargan continued as chairman, attending most DW&WR board meetings in summer 1865. His signature remained strong until August when again it appears spidery. Dargan took £35,000 in preference shares at 5 per cent and issued a two-year IOU for 3000 shares in the name of Robert Gray, with a further £40,000 in 5 per cent preference shares, transferred into the names of Dargan and Waldron and held in trust until redeemed. At the same time he was negotiating a £20,000 loan for the company from the Public Works Loan Commissioners.[35]

A Financial Storm

Following on from the era of frantic railway investment in the 1840s known as the 'railway mania', the second half of 1866 was a period of great financial turmoil as regards railway stock. Bubble speculation in railway shares was rampant and fortunes won and lost, mainly lost. On Black Friday, 11 May 1866, British banking firm and major railway financier Overend, Gurney & Co. collapsed with debts of £18 million, causing widespread panic as railway shares plummeted, the ripple effects touching every railway in Britain and Ireland. As a direct result, two of Britain's leading contractors, Samuel Peto and Edward Betts, faced financial disaster and were unable to continue repaying their debts of £4 million.

In the light of this crisis and because its financial well-being was now very much tied in with Dargan's, the DW&WR was particularly concerned about the number of IOUs and promissory notes he had issued for its shares. The collapse in share values hit Dargan hard and thus the DW&WR. Given his declining health the directors were therefore extremely anxious when they learned of Dargan's decision a few months later in November 1866 to hand responsibility for his business affairs to two trustees, fearing the implications of insolvency or a complete financial collapse on the part of their chairman and principal shareholder.[36] (See Appendix 1 for a listing of Dargan's bank loans and overdrafts over a thirteen-year period.)

Dargan did not attend the board meeting on 22 November 1866 and after several meetings the directors decided their only option was to offer their personal security to draw down a loan of £84,700 from the Royal Bank of Ireland via Charles Copeland and to ask Dargan to transfer all his DW&WR debts to them. This drastic step was, they believed, the only way to restore confidence in the company.[37] At a special shareholders' meeting on Christmas Eve 1866, the directors explained the seriousness of the crisis: this was the last time Dargan signed the minutes and, his health declining even further, he attended his last board meeting three days later on 27 December.[38]

In mid-January 1867 the Royal Bank of Ireland gave a temporary cash advance of £18,000 to meet the D&KR half-year rent, promising further weekly advances of £1000. At the same time the Wicklow company served notice on Dargan, a few weeks before he died, that it would hold him liable for any loss it incurred if any of his IOUs or promissory notes totalling £84,700 failed.[39]

Maintaining solvency and keeping the company afloat remained difficult as a year later Copeland said the DW&WR's overdraft was much greater than expected and that the Royal Bank of Ireland planned to sell forty £500 debentures unless company Secretary Edward Maunsell could suggest an alternative.

As Dargan's final illness brought his business connection with the DW&WR to an end the company recognized his great contribution despite its lingering anxiety about the implications of his financial difficulties for the railway's future (see Chapter 9). Of course the company survived and in due course built its line to Wexford and eventually the connection to Waterford.

EIGHT

A Man of Many Parts: Wexford Sloblands, Bray, Hotels, Sugar Beet, Flax, Whiskey, Chapelizod Mills

Dargan is chiefly known for his railway engineering as well as canal and road construction. However his career took in a remarkably wide range of other projects including town development, hotels, sugar and flax production, a distillery, land reclamation and a large thread mill in Dublin. While some were quite successful, many were less so, possibly because he did not give them the attention they needed and therefore suffered some financial losses.

Reclaiming Wexford

This project was similar to the reclamation Dargan completed with great difficulty on the Foyle (see Chapter 4). John Macneill, his engineering colleague, prepared plans to improve Wexford harbour in 1845. With John Redmond and two former MPs Dargan set up the Wexford Harbour Embankment Co. in 1846 using a £7000 loan from the Bank of Ireland to build 8 ft (2.5 m) high embankments enclosing a large area of land, with a view to draining it and turning it to agriculture.[1] The other purpose behind the works was to improve Wexford harbour by narrowing the channel of the Slaney, improving the tidal scour and deepening the channel approach to the harbour. A pumping station built at Drinagh has been restored as a sloblands interpretive centre.

Work began at the north end in 1847 and by May the following year Dargan's men had reclaimed 1400 acres at Beggarin and Garrygibbon. The project went on for three years, enclosing 2400 acres valued at £36,000, which were then ploughed into ridges, laid out in 50–100 acre sections and drained. The next year Prof. William Sullivan reported the land was sufficiently free of salt to grow wheat, oats, barley and beans and by 1851, 650 of the 800 acres planted were doing well.[2] In 1854 Le Fanu was involved in the second phase, the south slobs, though it was not as successful as the soil never hardened enough to become truly fertile. These were valuable assets once the land was under cultivation and Dargan used the lands at Wexford to raise an £18,000 mortgage when he was under financial pressure in 1864.[3] William's nephew, James Dargan, also visited the slobs a week after his uncle's death in February 1867.[4]

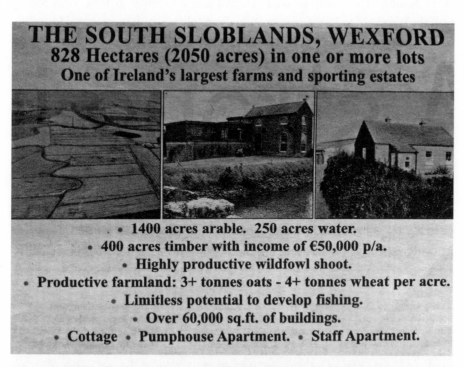

THE SOUTH SLOBLANDS, WEXFORD
828 Hectares (2050 acres) in one or more lots
One of Ireland's largest farms and sporting estates

- 1400 acres arable. 250 acres water.
- 400 acres timber with income of €50,000 p/a.
- Highly productive wildfowl shoot.
- Productive farmland: 3+ tonnes oats - 4+ tonnes wheat per acre.
- Limitless potential to develop fishing.
- Over 60,000 sq.ft. of buildings.
- Cottage • Pumphouse Apartment. • Staff Apartment.

In 2004 there was an auction of 828 hectares of the sloblands Dargan had reclaimed in south Wexford, described as productive farmland.

Bray: I Do Like to Be Beside the Seaside

The traditional seaside resort holiday was very popular in Britain in the pre-package tour era. Resorts like Blackpool, Skegness, Minehead, Llandudno and above all Brighton once drew large numbers who were not in the Grand Tour league or chose not to go abroad. When the Wicklow Railway opened to Bray in July 1853, Dargan recognized that being within easy reach of Dublin and Britain, Bray could become one of these popular resorts. Prior to this Bray was a very poor fishing village: St John Joyce described it as having heaps of sand, shingles and dunes with two cottages at Bray Head known as 'the Rat Hole'.[5]

Lord Meath of Kilruddery House owned much of the land around Bray and supported Dargan's development plans and with John Quinn, a local businessman, Dargan bought sections of land near the shore.[6] As the *Dublin Builder* put it he then removed the 'unsightly huts of fishermen and bathing women', compensated the occupants and then built the seafront esplanade, which is now one of the delights of the town. Bray Town Commissioners were suitably grateful and planned to raise a subscription to provide seats but Dargan asked 'that the matter should be left in his hands'.[7] The Commissioners elected him a member in 1861. Lord Meath gave the leasehold to Dargan for an annual rent of one shilling, provided he 'paint, repair, maintain and keep the paling or fence' in good condition and the ground 'sewn with grass seeds and mown or clipped at all proper seasons'.[8]

Dargan built this group of houses on Quinsborough Road, Bray. Originally called Dargan Terrace it was in later years renamed Duncairn Terrace.

G.R. Powell's 1860 *Official Handbook to Bray, Kingstown and the Coast* is dedicated to Dargan and details many of his Bray developments.[9] The first is Dargan (now Duncairn) Terrace on Quinnsborough Road, dating from 1854 with centre blocks of six houses and alternating smaller blocks of two houses, each two bays and three stories over basement. The terrace faces south towards Bray Head and each house cost £1800 to build (happily one of the end of terrace houses is named Dargan House).[10] He was also involved in building Ravenswell Road and a bridge under the railway.

An unusual venture of Dargan's in Bray was his Turkish baths. He thought such places were a boon to health after a visit to a similar establishment in Killarney and considered building one in Portrush but settled on Bray. The official opening took place in Breslin's Hotel where a Dr Barker of Blarney gave a lecture on the baths' therapeutic benefits.[11] The source of the baths' Moorish overtones was the design by John Benson, the architect of the Exhibition building on Leinster Lawn. They had an arched roof with stained glass windows and a 'circular ottaman, with an octagon mirrored pillar rising from the centre of the cooling rooms'.[12] A Dr Haughton was in charge. The baths opened from 6 AM to 11 PM daily (closed on Sundays from 10 AM to 3 PM) and a single public session cost two shillings or twelve sessions for eighteen shillings including bathing sheets and towels; 'shampooing' was sixpence extra. Turkish baths were new to most people at the time and to overcome public reluctance to use them Powell advised visitors to forget travellers' tales of 'boilings, scrubbings, steamings' inflicted by 'Moorish attendants grinning like sable familiars on their trembling victims' or 'joint-cracking, socket wrenching, chest-jumping inquisitors'. Bray's Turkish baths were intended to be a much more pleasant experience.[13] Connected to the baths was the Galtrim House hydropathic establishment.

There was much building work around Bray in 1860–1 as a result of Dargan's efforts, including a mile-long seafront road. He laid out a common, a fair green and a market place, helped to install gas lights and removed the harbour bar.[14] He was also a major investor in a large new hotel on Quinnsborough Road, down from Dargan Terrace. The four-storey International Hotel designed by Edward O'Kelly was the largest hotel in Ireland at the time. It had a fine set of stone steps leading to a portico supported by Ionic columns and boasted (shared) bathrooms on every floor, a well-stocked wine cellar and lights and fires at no extra charge. It was much needed to establish Bray's credentials as a major resort and opened in May 1862.[15]

At the opening banquet Dargan expressed his confidence in Bray's future and said Wicklow was 'unsurpassed for scenic beauty in the whole of the civilized world. It has sea and mountain beautifully planned ... Nature has done much for Bray and it remained for them to still further beautify and improve it.'[16]

But the hotel was not a resounding success, perhaps because Bray was not sufficiently known or developed to support such a large establishment. Two years later Edward Breslin who owned the Marine Hotel in Dun Laoghaire (Dargan was also an investor in what is now the Royal Marine Hotel) bought the International for just £7000; it was said to have cost £24,000 to build. Many years later a fire destroyed most of the International, the remainder was demolished and a bowling alley now stands on the site.

Among Dargan's other properties disposed of after his death were fourteen acres on Main Street, sold for £11,000, five acres of the Carlisle Grounds (now home to Bray Wanderers football club[17] (£1420) and 10–12 Prince of Wales Terrace. Another property he was associated with was Killarney House, although it appears he leased this as there is no title deed recording its purchase. Dargan also leased a piece of land in Bray to Cardinal Paul Cullen for 900 years at an annual rent of one shilling.

Writing in 1861, Cusack Roney sums up Dargan's improvement works in Bray, saying that having withdrawn from many of his other business ventures he was now concentrating on Bray and the DW&WR:

> Although the works of William Dargan may be seen in almost every part of Ireland, it is at Bray he has of late years concentrated his energies. ... Under his guiding eye, and by the judicious investment of his abundant capital, a small and comparatively obscure village has been rapidly transformed into a charming marine outskirt of Dublin.[18]

Dargan did have a number of other projects going at this time, having only just completed the Portarlington to Tullamore and Mallow to Fermoy lines for the Great Southern & Western Railway and the Athenry & Tuam Railway. He was also very involved in running the thread mills at Chapelizod with his partner, Benjamin Haughton.

Bray gave due recognition of all Dargan did for the town when in November 1992 the Urban District Council hosted a seminar on Dargan's legacy, attended by some of his descendants, the late Herbert Dargan SJ and the late Daniel Dargan SJ as well as Mary Dargan Ward. Part of the event was the unveiling of a bust of William in the refurbished Heritage Centre and an exhibition on the railway and Dargan's influence on the town. The two local history societies have also done excellent work to ensure Dargan's name is not forgotten.

The late Herbert Dargan SJ speaking at the unveiling of an exhibition on William Dargan in Bray Heritage Centre in November 1992. His brother, the late Daniel Dargan SJ, is standing behind him to the right. The Heritage Centre is closed at present.

The dinner menu at the Dargan Conference held in Bray in November 1992. It is signed by four members of the Dargan family: Herbert Dargan SJ, Daniel Dargan SJ, their sister-in-law, Breda Dargan and their niece, Tessa Dargan.

Dun Laoghaire and Malahide Hotels

As well as the International Hotel, Dargan also invested in two other coastal hotels, neither venture particularly successful. The Dublin & Drogheda Railway promoted the Grand Hotel, Malahide, that opened in May 1844 but four years later the investors wound it up. Among the shareholders were John Macneill, Dargan's colleague and engineer to the D&DR, William McCormick, Dargan's contracting partner on several lines, coachmaker John Dawson, bookseller George Grant, the ubiquitous Charles Copeland of the Royal Bank of Ireland, the equally ubiquitous James Perry who was almost Dargan's mentor throughout his career and Pierce Mahony of the Dublin & Kingstown Railway. A group of four, including Dargan, took over the assets of the hotel and soon after agreed to sell it for £9702 to one of the group, James Fagan MP, who made a down payment of £1732 and issued 5 per cent promissory notes for the balance. Outstanding liabilities were £1000 to the D&DR, £2740 to the Royal Bank of Ireland and £267 to McCormick.[19]

In 2005 the Royal Marine Hotel, one of Dun Laoghaire's signature buildings, closed its doors and held an auction of all its furniture and fittings. Happily the hotel was refurbished and has since reopened.

Another of Dargan's hotel ventures was in Dun Laoghaire, the Royal Marine and it was equally disappointing. In its May 1863 prospectus the company behind it offered 20,000 £5 shares recently acquired from Thomas Gresham.[20] He owned the hotel of that name still operating on O'Connell Street, Dublin and it will be recalled he fiercely opposed the extension of the railway into the centre of Dun Laoghaire, receiving a silver plate for his efforts from the relieved citizens of the town. Dun Laoghaire (Kingstown as it was known) was then one of the main ports of entry to Ireland as well as being a fashionable residential area so a comfortable hotel should have done well. Dargan's name appears first on the prospectus and he chaired the board meeting at 113 Grafton Street on 10 July 1863.[21] The architect was John McCurdy and the contract worth £50,000 went to Cockburn builders. The plan was to develop the grounds in front of the hotel, lay out gardens and a promenade with terraced walks, statues, flower displays and a covered colonnade running down to the mailboat pier.

Work began in the summer of 1864 but soon after the hotel company scaled down its plans considerably and reduced the workforce so that one writer to the *Dublin Builder* who signed himself 'Not a Victim', said he rarely saw more than half a dozen men 'shovelling earth from one spot to another'.[22] But a few weeks later Cockburn's men were more active, filling in the 'unsightly hollow' running down to the railway to make lawns. The October 1865 issue of the *Dublin Builder* has an illustration of the new wing and central tower of this 'important and troublesome undertaking', with an 850-foot frontage, completed for £25,000, half the original cost.[23] A year later the hotel company had an £18,000 mortgage from the National Bank, secured by twenty-three acres of land and from then its fortunes went steadily downhill. By 1867 it was in liquidation but Mr Dargan was no longer concerned or involved, having passed to that bourn from which no traveller returns. The Royal Marine has some fine interiors and plasterwork and reopened a few years ago after extensive refurbishment.

Dargan the Improving Farmer

William Dargan, being a son of Carlow, was more than just an industrialist and civil engineer; he was also a farmer who engaged in producing sugar beet, flax and wool. Again, many of these agricultural experiments weren't always completely successful. It appears Dargan was also involved in the Irish Waste Land Improvement Society whose goal was to secure five-acre holdings of underused land to be given to industrious tenants.[24] He was an early director of Matthew Barrington's Farmers' Estate Society, although it appears did not play a very active role in it.

The Society recognized that land insecurity was the basic cause of rural unrest. Such insecurity, said Barrington, 'renders the Irish peasant reckless, inconsiderate and improvident', all the more so as the Famine was at its height at this time.[25] The press welcomed the idea and Barrington promoted his scheme through the years of the Famine.[26] The *Freeman's Journal* commented: 'We can never be at peace in Ireland until the mass of the people shall have a fixed, permanent right of property in the soil.'[27] The Society's aims were highly honourable but largely unfulfilled. It sought to buy landed estates as they became available and resell them to occupying farmers in lots of between 25 and 100 acres. Purchasers were to repay the loan on easy terms with low interest.

The first meeting of the Society took place at the Dublin offices of Barrington Jeffers (Dargan's solicitors) in Ely Place on 30 October 1848 but little action followed and a year later questions were asked in the press about accounting procedures and the running of the Society.[28] The Society seems to have had only limited success, possibly because those most in need were least able to commit to repaying a loan no matter how easy or extended the terms.

Dargan was listed as a director of the International Financial Society, set up to make advances on landed estates. He was also a member of the Royal Agricultural Improvement Society (RAIS), proposing a subscription to fund the annual cattle show to be held in August 1851.[29] He took the Duke of Leinster's place at a dinner in the Railway (later Great Southern) Hotel in Galway on 19 August 1852, which heard he had won first and second prize (5 and 3 sovereigns) and a medal for butter produced on his farm at Moyvoughly, Moate, where he also grew flax (see below). The press was less complimentary about the food at the dinner: it was cold, cost 10s a head including a pint of wine and was 'as good as under the circumstances could have been provided'.[30]

Later with Pierce Mahony Dargan proposed holding the 1853 cattle show in Killarney and offered a £500 guarantee against any loss, travelling there on a special train with Edward McDonnell, chairman of the GS&WR.[31] Dargan chose the slightly unusual venue of an RAIS banquet in Killarney to make a speech about the importance of labour to the economy and society in general. Labour, he said, sustained rich and poor alike and industrial success depended on labour skills and the country's ability to employ every able-bodied man. Dargan concluded by saying it was in the interest of every property owner to 'advance the intelligence, the capabilities and the producing power of every man in his employment'.[32] Ideas like these were ahead of their time and while lauded were generally not acted upon.

Dargan attended the Rathdown Union Farming Society dinner at Quinn's Hotel, Bray, in late 1852 where he mentioned sending a consignment of butter to the Smithfield Cattle Show. Mount Anville was in effect a small farm and James

Byrne, Dargan's talented gardener, won many prizes for flowers, vegetables and fruits between 1852 and 1855. In April 1852 his flowers won first prize at the Royal Horticultural Society Show and six months later first prize for grapes, peaches, nectarines and the Hamilton Prize for the best collection of fruit, plus awards for celery, cauliflower and kidney beans. He also won awards at the Royal Horticultural Society of Ireland Spring Shows in April 1854 and at Salthill in July where, suitably, the Dublin & Kingstown Railway sponsored the prizes. More awards followed from the Rathmines Floricultural Society.[33]

Around this time Dargan became involved in promoting peat bogs as a source of energy.[34] By 1851 the Irish Peat Co. was making paraffin from turf harvested at Cloney bog, Athy and built its own narrow-gauge bog railway at Derrylea, near Portarlington. Dargan suggested he would invest £50,000 in the company if it seemed viable but it did not deliver on its early promise and a year later there were only four men working there.[35]

Cork Linen: Kildinan Flax Mill

A more substantial project was Dargan's heavy investment in a flax mill at Kildinan, Co. Cork, producing the raw material for making linen. He had seen the industry at close hand when working on various projects in the north and realized that managed properly, flax could generate an income for many marginal farmers. In 1849 he acquired 2000 acres from Edmund Burke Roche MP (later Lord Fermoy) who lived at Trabolgan House, a Georgian mansion near Whitegate, Co. Cork, demolished some years ago. The two became friends: Roche asked Dargan to be godfather to his son in August 1851, hoping the child would emulate 'the first Irishman of our day in energy, ability and integrity'. He also hoped Jane Dargan would accompany him to the christening.[36] Together the two men set about draining the land to plant flax and build a flax mill. Dargan told a meeting in Mallow courthouse that he believed no other industry in the south could generate the same prosperity as in the north. This is borne out by Sir Robert Kane's research from the early 1840s which estimated there were 100,000 acres under flax, all of them in the north of Ireland, producing 30,000 tons of linen valued at £50 per ton.[37] He quoted an 1839 report, which said there were 9000 people in forty mills earning an average of 2s 9d per week. The industry was indeed extensive but these are very low wages although Dargan never paid his workmen less than nine shillings a week. Most millworkers were women or children whose health suffered greatly from the harsh conditions of the mills.

In 1850 when Dargan brought his engineering colleague William Le Fanu to see the flaxfields he was thoroughly impressed to see them thriving in 'the most luxuriant and highly cultivated manner'.[38] That summer a *Cork Examiner* reporter visited the fields and published a detailed account of the Kildinan farm. There were 2500 acres in the estate: 1000 were under cultivation, 500 were partly reclaimed and 1000 were mountain. The manager's name was Rosborough and the farm employed 113 men and 87 women using new drainage methods intended to bring the land swiftly into cultivation.[39] The reporter also approved of the smoking ban among the workers, 'an indolent habit which only requires a little firmness in the employer to entirely efface'. Roche told a meeting of the Cork Flax Society in December 1850 he was fortunate that Dargan had agreed to set up a plant that would take all the flax he could grow. Dargan was a committee member of the Royal Society for the Improvement and the Growth of Flax in Ireland, contributing £40 in 1841–50 and £30 in 1852.[40] At a meeting in the Devonshire Arms Hotel, Bandon on 14 January 1851 local farmers spoke of the encouragement which Dargan's adviser A.C. Davidson gave them, some earning £4 per ton of flax supplied. On behalf of the Flax Society Dargan also presented a selection of linen tableware to the Lord Lieutenant on 29 October 1851.

A new type of production, the Chevalier Claussen method, introduced at the factory in 1851, was about to reduce the production time from six days to several hours. It involved metal rollers crushing the raw flax, dropping the seeds into a receiver while the plant itself steeped in six huge vats. On the floor upstairs workers cleaned the flax by hand, passing it through a winnowing machine. The sixty workers earned £50 weekly in total.

A few years later Dargan expanded his flax growing to Moyvoughly, near Moate, sowing fifty acres there, but already some were questioning Kildinan's viability. A press report in a northern paper speculated that the Kildinan experiment was in trouble even though Robert Kane had told a Flax Society meeting in Belfast that Dargan was working to increase output. This took place amid accusations of mismanagement and incompetence aimed, Kane said, at sinking the project and forcing Dargan's withdrawal.[41] It is unclear who was behind these charges as seemingly the only group that would benefit from the collapse of Kildinan were the northern producers. But as the output from Cork was relatively small it is unlikely it posed a major threat. Dargan's letter of reply dated September 1851 to the *Northern Whig* is as usual concise and to the point: 'Your correspondent has been misinformed. I have not given up my flax mill or farm in the County of Cork. I am working both with as much energy as I can. Yours truly, Wm Dargan'.[42]

Roche planned further expansion and sought a state loan to build forty-eight stands and extra space for breaking, cleaning and packing flax, much of the output going to England. The Cork Exhibition of 1852 sold thirty-five tons of Roche's flax at between 4s 9d and 11s a ton with a further ten tons from Dargan's mill sold at the Cork flax market after it opened in February 1853.[43] Flax production continued to grow with the acreage rising from 58,312 in 1847 to 175,000 in 1853 and 301,700 in 1864.[44]

Despite this increasing output and the best efforts of Roche and Dargan the flax experiment was in difficulty and it appears the mills were often idle for lack of flax. Le Fanu suggests that although Dargan supplied the seed to farmers and guaranteed to pay the current Belfast market price for flax, the project perished on the rocks of rural conservatism and reluctance among farmers to switch to a non-food crop on their modest holding as well as concerns that growing flax would exhaust their land.[45] Poor management may well be another reason: the 1850s were exceptionally busy for Dargan and with so many railway and other projects in progress he may not have had the time to sustain a large business like this. What-ever the reasons, by 1862 Dargan was on the verge of disposing of his imaginative and initially successful but ultimately ill-fated flax project at Kildinan.[46] Ironically within a few years the outbreak of the American Civil War increased the demand for cotton from the Union states and reduced its export to Europe, while at the same time increasing demand for linen as a substitute.

Unlikely Bedfellows: Karl Marx and William Dargan

Dargan's Kildinan flax mill receives an unwelcome mention in Das Kapital, *first published in 1867, the year Dargan died. In it Marx discusses the causes of industrial accidents, focusing on the flax industry in Ireland and in particular the mill at Kildinan:*

> The reader knows that during the last 20 years, the flax industry has very much extended, and that, with that extension, the number of scutching mills in Ireland has increased. In 1864 there were in that country 1,800 of these mills. Regularly in autumn and winter women and 'young persons', the wives, sons, and daughters of the neighbouring small farmers, a class of people totally unaccustomed to machinery, are taken from field labour to feed the rollers of the scotching mills with flax. The accidents, both as regards number and kind, are wholly unexampled in the history of machinery. In one scotching mill, at Kildinan, near Cork, there occurred between 1852 and 1856, six fatal accidents and sixty mutilations; every one of which might have been prevented by the simplest appliances, at the cost of a few shillings.[47]

Sugar Beet and Whiskey

Estimated annual sugar consumption in Ireland in 1852 was 50,000 tons, worth £2 million, almost all of it imported.[48] Anthony Marmion calculated an acre of beet produced twenty-five tons of sugar and cultivating it would cost £11, leaving a profit of £5 5s, and since 32,000 acres would keep a hundred sugar factories in production the potential market for home-grown sugar was enormous. In April 1852 Dargan travelled to Mountmellick with Thomas Bergin, Secretary of the Dublin & Kingstown Railway to visit the Irish Beet Sugar Co. factory that was just starting production. The town had strong Quaker connections and Dargan's involvement with this and other ventures confirm the close links he maintained with the Society of Friends throughout his working life, as a contractor, investor and in many cases a partner. His actions and behaviour suggest he shared many of their values of hard work, self-motivation and integrity in business, if not so much their traditional sobriety.

Dargan became a director of the company and later his railway partner, William McCormick, also took shares in it. The firm brought a William Hirsch from Valenciennes to modernize the factory, which then employed 150 people. Dargan estimated with all overheads paid the factory produced a ton of sugar for £6, which sold for £7 10s, a good profit. By autumn 1852 output was twenty tons a week and a dividend of 4 per cent was anticipated.[49] Dargan exhibited sugar from this factory at the 1852 Cork and 1853 Dublin Exhibitions.

Difficulties arose in the autumn of 1854 as the Crimean war was said to have caused a fall in the market price of sugar and thus the price paid to farmers, who switched to more profitable crops, failing to deliver their agreed beet quota to the factory. Added to this Hirsch said there were still serious production problems. By October 1854 the plant had been sold to John Adair of Bellegrove.

Like sugar, nineteenth-century whiskey production and consumption were substantial with much of the output exported. Another short-lived and rather unusual venture of Dargan's was his investment in a distillery near Belturbet, Co. Cavan. The Lough Erne end of the Ulster Canal is not too far from this town so it is possible Dargan saw the potential while he was finishing the waterway in the early 1840s. With partners Alexander Dickson and James Dunlop he bought a corn and flour mill at Strahagland for £7000 in 1843 on land owned by 'Brindsley Butler, Earl of Lanesboro, a lunatic' as the legal papers put it, somewhat bluntly.[50] To set up the distillery Dargan acquired part of an old infantry barracks in January 1846 consisting of houses, gardens, bogs, two islands, a dam, officers' quarters and a house known as Riversdale with 5½ acres, as security against an investment of at least £3000. But the partnership foundered and within a few months Dargan secured a judgement against Dickson in the Queen's Court for £8000 plus costs.[51] Dickson died soon after making his will in September 1852 and the distillery's affairs were in some disorder as Dargan tried to disentangle his late partner's mortgage deeds held by the Ulster Bank. The legal correspondence went on for some years and in a settlement finally reached in April 1854 Dargan estimated he was still owed over £4000.[52] It is uncertain how much whiskey, if any, the distillery ever produced.

Running Aground on the Dublin Graving Dock

Another of Dargan's tricky projects was the graving dock built for the Corporation for Preserving and Improving the Port of Dublin (CPIPD), more commonly known as the Ballast Board. The chairman was Thomas Crosthwaite who was President of the Chamber of Commerce, 1857–70, Dargan's partner in the Chapelizod thread mills (see below) and later his neighbour in Fitzwilliam Square. A graving dock is a dry dock, essential for cleaning and repairing a ship's hull and for many years ship owners had bemoaned the lack of such a facility on the Liffey. In 1848 the Chamber of Commerce commissioned George Halpin, William Cubitt and John Macneill to prepare a report and a year later Halpin senior had completed the plans.[53] The Dublin Steamship Association, of which Dargan was a member, lobbied the Chamber to oppose tolls for any such dock and diplomatically queried the latter's competence to decide its dimensions: 'While the Association entertain the highest respect for that influential and useful body [the Chamber of Commerce] they may be permitted to doubt the soundness of their opinion.'[54]

The first graving dock in Dublin Port as Dargan completed it in 1860; from a drawing in *The Engineer* magazine.

The graving dock in the 1990s, watered but rarely used. Sadly it has since been filled in.

The cost estimate was £63,000 and Dargan's bid of £60,000 in 1853 was the third-highest of nine tenders from firms in Dublin, Cork, Limerick, Glasgow and Gosport but he still won the contract – something he had reason to regret. His sureties of £6000 were from his former partner William McCormick, now of Park Square, London, and William Coates of Belfast. The Board asked Dargan to extend the dock by 100 ft to be paid pro rata and he began work at the East Wall Road site in April 1854. Dargan built a short railway to remove the earth from the dock site, unlike at Belfast Harbour where he could dump spoil near the Down shoreline; there would be no Dargan's Island in the Liffey. By July he had a steam pile driver, pumps and good-quality stone on site. But there were many extended delays for a variety of reasons, many of them Dargan's fault. Thomas Codd wrote to the Ballast Board to say they 'had given a preference to Mr Dargan, even at a higher price than other parties had demanded, under an impression that the work would be done not only in the most effective but in the promptest manner' but there was little progress.[55] The Board wrote to Dargan reminding him of the 1 June 1855 completion date and followed up with a threat of legal action. Dargan was suitably penitent. 'Whatever may have been the delays and mistakes in the works ... (and I admit there have been some)' he promised George Halpin, the Board's engineer, that he would now finish the job promptly.[56] Meanwhile the cost had risen to over £100,000.

Dargan's finances must have been under some pressure as optimistically he sought regular payments and a loan of £15–20,000 from the Ballast Board against security of a promissory note and railway shares. In March 1857 Dargan told the Board he was almost finished and asked for early settlement of his accounts. Relations between the two had become very strained, over the pumping costs. Six months later dealing with Halpin's assistant, Bindon Blood Stoney, Dargan said he would cease running his pumps, making it impossible for the Board to work on the dock gates.[57] By the end of the year Dargan estimated he was owed £8600 with interest of £3500, against which the Board offered just £2000.[58] Conflict was imminent.

Drawing on his experience of the Ouzel Galley's arbitration work (see Chapter 9), in January 1858 Dargan suggested inviting the distinguished English engineer, William Cubitt, to arbitrate in the dispute.[59] The Ballast Board agreed, provided Dargan dropped his interest claim and he and Halpin were the only witnesses called. The Board foresaw a long, costly affair and that proved to be the case. Cubitt agreed to mediate (but in London not Dublin for health reasons) and said the process would take nine months to complete. Both disputing parties were surprised at how seriously he took the task, referring to it as his 'Court of Inquiry'.[60] Halpin reported after a meeting in Cubitt's Clapham house that the old man insisted both parties sign a deed accepting his verdict in advance, whatever it might be. Each side put their case after which Cubitt sent his son to Dublin to inspect the graving dock before taking sworn evidence from each side. He would accept written submissions provided both parties saw them. Halpin then accused Dargan of bad faith in March 1858 when the latter insisted on the return of a set of papers the same day they were delivered, before Halpin had a chance to study them: 'unpleasant and invidious', he said. Cubitt too said he was surprised at 'Dargan's mode of proceeding'.[61]

The proceedings gathered legal momentum with Cubitt's lawyers cross-examining Dargan and Halpin on such details as the kind of cement used in the dock. Three weeks later in November 1858 Cubitt announced he had reached a verdict, which he would deliver once each party had paid half his quite considerable fee of £603 to his solicitors. When the payments were made he pronounced in favour of Dargan who was to receive £10,177 by the year end. He had won but his immediate claim for payment drew a cold response from the Ballast Board: 'An answer to be sent to Mr Dargan calling his attention to the last clause in the award', namely that payment was not due until 31 December.[62] On 31 December the Board paid Dargan £9876 2s, retaining £301 8s paid to Cubitt.

The graving dock finally opened the following year on 9 February 1860 and the first ships into it were the *Agnes Anderson*, a 1100-ton clipper owned by Messrs Martin, and the *Connaught* of the City of Dublin SP Co.[63] It was a low-key ceremony with only a few of the commissioners present; there is no record of Dargan attending. In a final, curious twist, the Chamber of Commerce, which had campaigned so long for a graving dock, offered its congratulations not to the Ballast Board but to merchants and shipowners.[64] The *Engineer* magazine described the dock thus in 1867: 'one of the most excellent specimens of material and workmanship'.[65]

Dargan's letter to William Lees of the Ballast Office, 28 January 1857, agreeing to arbitration by the great English engineer, William Cubitt, on condition that he (Dargan) be allowed to submit his claims for interest to Cubitt.

Chapelizod Flax and Thread Mills

In the midst of a number of creditworthy but by no means completely successful commercial ventures, Dargan's mills at Chapelizod village on the site of an artillery barracks in west Dublin, are a notable exception. The firm was originally called William Dargan & Co. and he put up the seed capital of £6000 with Benjamin Haughton from Antrim, first as general manager and then as Dargan's partner. By mid 1856 the five-storey mill was 140 ft long, 40 ft wide and 60 ft high (43 x 12 x 18m) spread over five acres and employing 900 workers, two-thirds of them women.[66]

It was thus a big operation and several events throw light on how Dargan and Houghton ran the plant, two of them court cases. In confirmation of Karl Marx's criticism of industrial safety standards at Kildinan, in 1856 a spinning master named McCracken caught his arm in machinery while changing a drum belt, resulting in amputation. He earned 15 shillings a week and while in hospital said the firm promised to look after him for life. On his return to work he received a lower-paid job and then became a night watchman before being fired. Giving evidence in the court of Queen's Bench Haughton denied making any promise to the injured man but confirmed the company did pay his wages while he was in hospital. The verdict divided liability, saying the company was at fault for not having better safeguards but McCracken was also at fault for not following safety procedures. The court awarded him £200 but just sixpence in costs.[67]

Four weeks later the company was again in court summoned by the Capel Street police office for running machinery half an hour after 2 PM on several Saturdays in July 1856, the working week being five-and-a-half days (as it remained right up to the 1960s). The factory inspector did not accept that the act governing Saturday work allowed an extra hour to make up for water shortages (the mills being driven by water wheels which took their power from a channel of the nearby River Liffey). He argued that with 900 people the extra half hour's work meant enormous gains for the company. The company was convicted but the fine was modest: a shilling for each offence, hardly a serious deterrent. That the case came to court at all suggests a degree of industrial vigilance that seems rare for the time but the nominal fine also suggests the offence was not considered a heinous one. A third case against Dargan in 1855 (but not related to the Chapelizod mills) concerned a £500 contract with the English and Irish Telegraph Co. to lay wires in the streets of Dublin, which he sub-contracted to a James Hickey for £219. Hickey sued him successfully at the Queen's Bench for non-payment in 1855.[68]

Day Trip to Bray

One event shows a level of concern for the welfare of the employees in Dargan & Houghton, which was also unusual for the time. The mills closed on Saturday 28 July 1860 for the factory outing to Bray. That morning 700 men, women, girls and boys marched behind the factory band from Chapelizod alongside the Phoenix Park and the River Liffey as far as Harcourt Street station where they squeezed into a special DW&WR train of sixteen carriages, which left at 9.45 AM.

On arrival at Bray they marched to Galtrim House where long lines of tables were set for a substantial dinner with plenty of stout and beer. The ladies ate first at 1 PM followed by the men, with dancing afterwards to a military band. The party returned to Dublin at 7 PM and made the long trek back to Chapelizod, a visitor commenting on the absence of drunkenness, in contrast to similar outings in Britain. Dargan planned to be there but went north on pressing business; this may have been the Banbridge Junction Railway, which he had completed the year before.

Between the second court case and the works outing a serious incident occurred when a fire broke out in the mechanical department of the Chapelizod mills early on the morning of 7 August 1858. An unnamed constable, no.192D, spotted the blaze and a range of fire tenders came from the Hibernian Military School in the nearby Phoenix Park with youthful firefighters aboard, from the police and from three insurance companies: the Royal Exchange, the National and the West of England. In those days insurance firms often ran their own horse-drawn fire tenders to reduce fire damage claims but of course only attended fires in their clients' premises. Insured buildings often bore a metal plate on the outside wall to indicate a particular firm covered them. The factory also had its own fire engine but it was in poor condition and the water pressure was very low 'as usual'. So lines of local people, doubtless many of them employees who lived close to the factory, formed a bucket chain from the river. Their efforts were well meaning but probably ineffectual against a blaze in a five-storey building full of highly combustible material.

Later that day William and Jane Dargan visited the devastated site where the cost of the damage was put at £10,000 although fortunately the building was well insured (hence the three fire tenders). He and Haughton rebuilt the factory and by 1860 it was back in production. But by 1863 the factory was for sale, largely because of the over-supply of thread from England, according to Le Fanu's diary and also possibly because Dargan wanted to liquidate some of his assets to channel his finances into the DW&WR. As part of the sale were forty-eight delightful two-storey cottages still to be seen in the village of Chapelizod, including a hall, library and reading room and a manager's house and office. Dargan's engineer friend Robert Hoey showed an interest in acquiring the mills but they were bought in time by Distillers Co. of Edinburgh who converted the building to a distillery, producing 25,000 gallons (114,000 litres) of spirits a week. In 1875 it was valued at £66,552 and as well as the main building 'the greater part fireproof' happily, there were various outhouses, stores and warehouses.[69] In addition there were two steam engines from the Manchester engineering firm of Fairbairn, with whom Dargan had many dealings over the years.

Dargan's sundry enterprises may not have been stellar successes but the agricultural ones pass the test set by the curmudgeonly Dean Swift when he said: 'Whoever could make two ears of corn or two blades of grass to grow upon a spot of ground where only one grew before, would deserve better of mankind, and do more essential service to his country than the whole race of politicians put together.'[70]

NINE

Sic Transit:
Dargan's Later Years

In the late 1860s Dargan appeared to scale down many of his business commitments other than the Dublin Wicklow & Wexford Railway (DW&WR). There is also a degree of obscurity about some aspects of Dargan's career when his civil engineering and contracting days were coming to an end. Overstating matters somewhat Cusack Roney said in 1861 Dargan was 'removed almost entirely from the active pursuits in which he was engaged for upwards of 30 years'.[1] For a man who had done so much work it is hardly surprising he wanted to take things a little easier.

Some have suggested that this withdrawal from public life or semi-retirement masks a dark secret, which forced him to become almost a recluse and while Dargan may no longer have been personally building railways he remained a bedrock of the DW&WR and was lauded as the originator of the National Gallery, with his statue erected beside the building during his lifetime. The Victorians were nothing if not respectable so all this would have been very unlikely if there was a large skeleton waiting for the cupboard door to swing open. In an era without computers, phones or e-mail, when a letter was the fastest means of communication (albeit with same day delivery in Dublin), he had lived a very demanding life, which would take its toll on the physical stamina and mental agility needed to keep a large business going. Someone of lesser calibre might well have slipped into total retirement, especially given that even for a middle-class person at the time, surviving well into their sixties was an achievement.

In that period of Dargan's life and the years following there were attempts to analyse the reasons for his success, apart from his innate abilities, his straightforward way of dealing with people and his enormous capacity for hard work. In his memoir of Dargan in the 1853 Exhibition catalogue, Sproule attributes his success to his skilled choice of assistants and other senior staff and a very well-run office.[2] This seems very plausible but without information on either, it is impossible to confirm or deny. Dargan himself was never one to issue statements explaining his commercial success but he did offer two maxims, which he said he followed throughout his life: 'You catch more flies with a spoonful of honey than a pint of vinegar' and 'Never show your teeth unless you can bite.' [3]

Such was his public profile that as early as 1851 Dargan was receiving invitations to stand as an MP, in this case for Newry. He refused all such requests, probably for the same reason he refused to accept a baronetcy from lords lieutenant and Queen Victoria: to do so would have made it difficult to continue running his businesses. Other less prominent honours he was more willing to accept: he became a deputy lieutenant of Dublin (a purely honorary position), honorary life member of the Royal St George Yacht Club, vice-president of the Dublin Literary Society and Hibernian Athenaeum, member of the Dublin Chamber of Commerce (1854–66), crew member of the Ouzel Galley Society to which he was elected on 16 November 1853, membership no.237 (see below),[4] an honorary member of the RDS and the Royal Society of Antiquaries produced a medal in his honour bearing his image. There was also professional recognition of his abilities: in an unusual gesture the Institution of Engineers of Ireland twice elected Dargan an Associate but not an Associate Member.[5]

Serving Aboard the *Ouzel Galley*

In 1853 Dargan was proposed for membership of the Ouzel Galley Society, an honour for any businessman at the time. A precursor of the present-day Dublin Chamber of Commerce the Society had a curious history.

'Ouzel' is an old English word for a blackbird and the original Ouzel Galley, *a trading ship, left Dublin port in 1695 bound for the eastern Mediterranean. Such voyages were hazardous and the limited communications of the time meant it was not surprising to hear nothing of her for some months. However after several years passed she was presumed lost or seized by pirates, along with her cargo and all her crew. She was quite well insured and so policies were honoured, grieving spouses came to accept their sailor husbands were lost and after a time there was no*

further mention of the Ouzel Galley. *Until one day in 1700, five years after she departed, up the Liffey came the good ship* Ouzel, *a little storm-tossed, but with her crew aboard and a valuable cargo in her hold. There was great surprise and delight at her return but once the novelty had worn off a bitter dispute arose between the original owners of the ship, whose wares she was carrying, and the insurers over who owned her and her cargo and whether the original payout should be returned. There was also the delicate issue of women thinking they were widows who had married again.*

To overcome the commercial recriminations and avoid a series of lengthy lawsuits a group of merchants agreed to arbitrate the conflicting claims. Happily in 1705 all accepted their compromise solution on the ownership of the vessel and her cargo. Out of this resolution came the Ouzel Galley Society. The 1859 Rules and Regulations stated the Society arbitrated on 'all disputes to them referred, relating to Trade and Commerce; the expenses whereof are appropriated to the benefit of decayed Merchants'. The Society met in the Commercial Buildings in Dame Street where a Portland stone plaque of the Ouzel *was set over the south door.*

Like many similar bodies the Society had its share of quaint customs. The officers took naval titles, so for example Thomas Crosthwaite was Captain, George Pim was Boatswain (sporting his special whistle) and Charles Halliday was Master. Other officers were the Gunner and the Carpenter and the remaining members were hands. In later years the Society was better known for its dinners than its arbitration work and it was dissolved in the late 1880s. A painting of the Ouzel Galley *hangs in the Dublin Chamber of Commerce offices and the Portland stone plaque is still in position on Dame Street near the Central Bank.*

There is an unconfirmed tradition that Dargan enjoyed fox-hunting, a popular pastime in his native Carlow that he may have shared with his architect friend, John Mulvany. The open country around Mount Anville would have given plenty of scope to exercise a pack of hounds. Dargan was a busy man but that does not mean he did not have a social life, especially around the time of the Exhibition. Happily some of the personal correspondence kept by his wife Jane has survived, giving us a glimpse into this side of his life. Among his professional colleagues, W.R. Le Fanu often called to Mount Anville for breakfast, dinner or to stay overnight as his diaries relate.[6] On 21 January 1855 only a Mr and Miss Bell were there but on 21 January 1856 Croker Barrington made for a lively dinner. On 12 February that year in Dargan's absence Le Fanu escorted Jane Dargan and Miss Allen to a ball in Dublin Castle and as he says 'Mrs Dargan left me home at 2'.[7] Mary Allen was a niece of Jane Dargan's and when she married George Phillips, an income tax official, on 23 September 1856, the wedding reception was at Mount Anville. Phillips became very involved with the Dargans and was present when William died.

The rear of Mount Anville house

Fine ornate garden gate at Mount Anville

After he bought Mount Anville from a Judge Burton, Dargan employed his architect friend, John Mulvany, to make substantial changes to this Italianate villa-style house. He built very pretty gate lodges and an elaborate granite gateway with Mulvany's distinctive flat pediments, repeated in the fine tower providing views all over south Co. Dublin, as Queen Victoria noted. Inside the house is bright and airy with a large glass-roofed central hall – it is likely Mulvany designed a number of these interior changes.

There were frequent visitors to Mount Anville such as the Mayor of Melbourne in 1858 and Queen Victoria in 1853. On one occasion Lord Gough sent a gift of Irish oak furniture from his house, St Helens, down the hill from Mount Anville. Many others came to see the gardens, the view from the tower or to seek patronage for a position or support for various causes. One Alfred McClintock sought a position in the Rotunda Lying-in Hospital; Josephine Roy More thanked Jane Dargan for a recent visit with a basket of of fruit; Walter Berwick appealed to Jane for help to keep his music academy going; and J. Emmerson Tennent asked William if he could bring a friend the next day to view 'the beauties of Mount Anville'.[8] Among the other causes the Dargans supported was a fund for French flood victims, joining a committee with James Perry in June 1856. He also contributed generously to a dinner on 22 October 1856 for 3000 soldiers returned from the Crimean war. It took place in Stack A, the tobacco warehouse beside George's Dock built by John Rennie in the 1820s. It was a substantial feast comprising 250 hams, 230 legs of mutton, 250 pieces of beef, 500 meat pies, 100 venison pasties, 100 rice puddings, 250 enormous plum puddings, 200 turkeys, 200 geese, 2000 rolls, 3500 lbs of bread, 3 tons of potatoes, 8500 quart bottles and 3500 pint bottles of port, the latter said to be the donation of Dublin wine merchant, Henry Brennan. The leftovers went to the city workhouses and mendicity institutes and the £1000 surplus invested in government stock, the interest going to the pupils of the Royal Hibernian Military School in the Phoenix Park, now St Mary's Hospital.[9] Up to 1000 guests paid ten shillings (gentlemen) or five shillings (ladies) and ate in a gallery overlooking the main concourse. The interior of this very fine building resembles the platform roof of Heuston station and is now part of the Dublin Docklands development.

Dargan's Accident

On 1 May 1865 Dargan was riding along the Stillorgan Road when he was thrown from his horse near Booterstown Avenue, suffering a serious concussion. He had been talking to Mr Hornsby, Secretary of the Board of Works, when it is said a woman shaking a cloth startled the horse. Mr Vernon of Mount Merrion brought the unconscious Dargan in his cab to Mount Anville. There he was treated by, among others, Dr Dominic Corrigan, one of the leading doctors of the day and honorary physician to Queen Victoria. Well-wishers included the Lord Lieutenant and Dargan's nephew James Dargan who called frequently to see his uncle although he was often unable to receive visitors.[10] James' regular visits recorded in his diary give a fairly consistent picture of his uncle's movements and health: on 15 August he told him to come back the next day and when he asked for a clerkship for 'Tom' in the Ballast Office, William said he could not arrange it and agreed his nephew should think of moving to England; James did indeed move across the Irish Sea as a few weeks before his uncle's death he was living in Wrexham.[11] Dargan was able to sign the DW&WR minutes taken at subsequent board meetings even though he himself was not present.

By the end of May a correspondent, John Nevinson of Castle Saunders, Belturbet, wrote how glad he was that Dargan had rallied so well after his accident.[12] However writing not long after Dargan's death, R.S. Joby thought the effects were more long term and that he never recovered fully from the trauma of the fall and the concussion he suffered, which led to a crippling depression.[13] It is also likely that when treating the effects of this illness the symptoms of Dargan's liver cancer emerged, the disease that eventually led to his death.

The accident, his heavy alcohol consumption and increasing ill health left Dargan unable to run his business but did not incapacitate him. Barely five weeks after his injury Dargan made the first of several trips to England – a journey not for the fainthearted, even though railways had made it a lot easier. The first of these was to testify before the Royal Commission of Inquiry into Irish Railways on 14 June 1865 (see Chapter 7). His detailed and lengthy evidence on a host of topics including traffic, rates, trends, profitability and the long-term prospects for railways in Ireland reveal a man well briefed, articulate and in full possession of his faculties. He visited England three weeks later and again from 19–28 July, a lot of travelling even for someone who was fully fit and well.[14]

Leaving Mount Anville

In the mid 1860s Dargan took a very desirable residence in central Dublin, 2 Fitzwilliam Square East, where he stayed from time to time. One of his neighbours was his business partner from the Ouzel Galley, Thomas Crosthwaite, who lived a few doors away at 9 Fitzwilliam Square East and witnessed Dargan's will. Another, was engineer W.R. Le Fanu who lived at number 59 on the north side of the square. Financial difficulties, the effects of his accident and perhaps a desire for less travelling pushed Dargan to give up his beloved house at Mount Anville with its splendid gardens in 1865 and move into town.[15] When he put his mansion up for sale a group of Sacred Heart nuns looking for a convent in the south of the city set their sights on it. However they could not meet Dargan's asking price and a further obstacle was Jane Dargan's strong opposition to selling to a Catholic religious order.

Written in French, the unpublished *Lettres Annuelles de la Societé du Sacré Coeur de Jésus* and the *Journal de la Maison de Mount Anville* recount the tactics of these formidable ladies:

> One of the most difficult problems was to persuade M Dargan, the owner of the only property which appeared altogether suitable, to negotiate with us. Up to that it had been impossible to arrange a meeting and we did not know what his real intentions might be. Happily on the 19th of the month [July 1865], the much desired meeting took place, and the owner, without being prepared to reduce his price, seemed willing to deal with us on the sale of the house. One can imagine how this pleased us. ... All the same, when every-thing seemed to be going well, urgent business required M Roche, who was working for us, to be away. ... With all our heart we put up a spontaneous cry to St Joseph and he responded, sending us a true friend in M Vincent Scully, a man who knew M Dargan and was the perfect person for us. He negotiated a sizeable reduction, but the price was still beyond our means. So we made a fresh appeal to St Joseph and he answered us again. Indeed, last Wednesday ... we learned we could have the property at the original offer price. Everyone was amazed but we knew who we were indebted to: St Joseph.[16]

The arrival of Monsieur Scully, who persuaded Dargan to lower his price, was not entirely the result of heavenly intervention. Scully was a relation of the supe-rior at the Sacred Heart Convent in Glasnevin, Mother Julia Scully, who is listed in the 1866 *Thom's Directory* as the owner of Mount Anville.

The sisters later observed Jane Dargan's opposition to the sale:

> The Glasnevin community moved into Mount Anville in 1865. It was Mother Roche's father who negotiated the purchase of this magnificent house in great secrecy for the owner's wife was a very committed Protestant who would not consider selling to religious, no matter what the price.[17]

Dargan sold Mount Anville to Anna Butler and Susan Martin, 'spinsters' with an address in Glasnevin, for £10,000 on which they paid £53 stamp duty. The property consisted of over fifty-four acres and the sisters were delighted with their purchase, which included all trees, shrubs, crops and plants, greenhouses and conservatories.[18] They described the gardens at their summer best in tones of rapture as 'a paradise':

Everywhere you look you see something to delight the eye. Beautiful trees abound, arcades with bushes on each side, plants of every kind, rows and rows of lovely flowers. There are exquisite fruits in glasshouses, one of which has a 35-foot vine, while the others are for flowers. M Dargan very graciously made a gift of them to us and we can now sell them for a good price. ... You can gaze on cows and sheep in the fields and two vegetable gardens give us plenty of fruit and vegetables while there is a fine farm with a good hen-run and an abundance of fowl: hens, a cock, geese, ducks, turkeys and pigeons everywhere. Add to this the wonderful view of the mountains and Dublin Bay and you have an idea what Mount Anville is like.[19]

But when the nuns arrived to take over their new home on 18 August 1865 – the previous occupants very much still in residence – they faced scenes of chaos:

The servants, above all, appeared not yet ready to leave. A great deal of furniture was still in the rooms and there was disorder everywhere. What could we do under the circumstances, give them a few more days? Our superior didn't think so, for they had had two weeks already since they learned we were moving in. So we had to show we had come to stay and this approach worked. The servants hurried up and carpets, curtains and furniture, everything was packed up. ... At the end of the day when we were sure everybody had gone we thought about security for the night. Doors and driveways were closed and the little colony of five people settled down for their first meal. Holy poverty was the order of the day for some time and we had many privations but we faced everything with joy.[20]

William and Jane Dargan then moved permanently to 2 Fitzwilliam Square, a magnificent and beautifully proportioned four-storey-over-basement house with a courtyard and coach house. Fitzwilliam Square is unique in that it is the only private square in Dublin still reserved for residents. Having vacated 62 South William Street, the house also became an office. Dargan lived here for the rest of his life.

Handing Over Control to Others

Following on from his accident, the painful symptoms of his liver cancer and being forced to give up his beloved Mount Anville, financial events in Britain were to deal a further blow to Dargan. For many years following the railway mania of the 1840s and the seemingly endless expansion of the rail network, most railway shares had risen steadily in value. In early 1866 a financial crisis erupted in Britain as confidence in overpriced railway shares evaporated amid revelations of sharp business practices, causing a panic in the market.

Front view of 2 Fitzwilliam Square East, where William and Jane Dargan moved after the sale of Mount Anville. The plaque next to the door reads: 'William Dargan 1799–1867, Founder of Irish Railways and National Gallery lived here'.

Opposite: A 1937 map, 6 inches to the mile (15 cm:1.6 km) showing the area known as Mountanville Callary and the extent of Dargan's former estate, marked as 'Convent of the Sacred Heart'. The area was at the time completely rural.

195

'Frightful disclosures' appeared about irregularities on major British lines such as the London Chatham & Dover, the North British and the Carmarthen and Cardigan Railways. Among the UK casualties was George Hudson, an MP, contractor and speculator, dubbed the 'Railway King'. When his illegal business dealings came to light – such as paying dividends from company capital – he fled to France and on his return went on trial, spending three months in jail. Others affected were prominent British railway contractors Thomas Brassey, Samuel Peto and Edward Betts who often worked together on shared contracts and were unable to repay debts of £4 million. As mentioned in the context of the DW&WR, on Black Friday 11 May 1866, the UK bank Overend, Gurney & Co. collapsed with debts of £10 million (about 1 billion today). The effects rippled through the Irish and British railway world for over a year, causing a market crash with share values plummeting even further.[21]

Dargan was badly hit by this meltdown. He had secured many of his bank loans with railway shares whose value in many cases dropped by 50 per cent or more and those banks in particular were concerned that his business would fail. By the end of the year Dargan's health was deteriorating further and he decided he could no longer manage his enterprises. He therefore appointed two trustees to handle all his financial affairs: Valentine O'Brien O'Connor of Beresford Place and Richard Martin of Merrion Square. This was a major step, not something arranged overnight, galling for an entrepreneur like Dargan and quite a responsibility for the two individuals concerned. When news broke that he had signed over his business via a deed of trust on 19 November 1866 with a list of his assets and property in Bray, Portrush and Wexford, it caused great anxiety among his creditors and his fellow DW&WR directors who set up a committee to assess the implications.[22]

One UK paper at the time, the *Daily Express*, said Dargan's actions were no cause for alarm and reflected no discredit on him. Rather the causes lay in 'reckless speculation, and worse than reckless railway mismanagement in England, for the exposure of which the year 1866 will long be memorable'. It was 'bearing, bulling, financing, cooked accounts and depravity of all kinds' that caused the crisis in railway investment and it said Dargan's estimated debts of £150,000 could be met by his 3000 £100 DW&WR shares, worth £120,000 at the time but likely to recover. The deed of trust was 'for the purpose of obtaining time to realize the assets, and converting scattered securities into ready money'.[23] Robert Peel, Chief Secretary for Ireland from 1861–5, was quick to offer help in this letter to Dargan, a kind gesture.[24]

Whitehall, 3 December 1866

My Dear Sir,

Permit me to express the heartfelt sympathy with which as a sincere admirer I have heard of the temporary bankruptcy which has overtaken your affairs.

Having learned during a residence of some years in Ireland what your noble energy has already accomplished in promoting works of ... national enterprise, I sincerely hope that you may be enabled shortly to assume your labours in that field which has borne much abundant fruit to the benefit of your country. Indeed, I rejoice to hear it confirmed upon what appears to be reliable sources of information, that the pressure is but temporary.

When national expressions of sympathy would assume a tangible form I should feel honoured in being foremost to take a part.

I am, dear sir, yours very faithfully,

Robert Peel

This is an appropriate place to scotch firmly once and for all the oft-repeated statement that Dargan died a bankrupt. He did not and when the trustees and executors had completed their work there was a healthy surplus remaining, as will be detailed later.

Making a Will

Being aware that his illness was very serious and that he did not have much longer to live, Dargan turned his mind to drafting a will. On 22 January 1867 he called in his solicitor friend Croker Barrington of Ely Place who, given the potential complexities of the estate, in turn briefed a barrister, D.C. Heron. In the first draft filed with the papers of the legal firm Barrington & Jeffers, Dargan intended to leave his wife Jane £500 per annum for life, £500 to Jane's niece Louisa Haslam, the daughter of her sister Frances Arkinstall who was married to Dr Joseph Haslam and £300 each to his nephews James Boland and James Dargan.[25] Heron advised that 'Mr Dargan must see that it does not provide for the disposal of one tenth of his property and does not appoint any residuary legatees.' Heron said the purpose of a will was 'to name all the objects of the testator's bounty and to include the disposition of all the property so as to prevent an intestacy'. Some of his client's relatives could make a claim against such a will and he had 'the greatest objections that such a will should be approved of by me as the will of William Dargan. However Mr Dargan has the right to make any will he pleases and I will draft the will according to his instructions.'[26] It seems likely that Dargan's mind, once so acute, was sadly becoming enfeebled as his life drew to a close.

The second draft of the will prepared four days later was more comprehensive:[27] 'Testator now desires that the annuity to Mrs Jane Dargan, (his wife), shall be increased to £600 per annum, paid quarterly and to leave her a legacy of £3000 together with the testator's plate, pictures, carriages, horses.' The legacy to Louisa Haslam was doubled to £1000 payable within six months for 'attention' and Dargan's sister Selina was also to receive £500. Alexander Boyle, the will's executor, would inherit £2000 and an unspecified amount was to go to Dublin charities. The draft concluded: 'My … wish and direction to my solicitor is that my friend Mr Croker Barrington should act professionally in carrying out the trusts of this my last will.' Heron asked that the executor, Boyle, should have full powers to deal with the property and to 'dispose of it as he shall think best'. The will was finalized the same day.

THE HIGH COURT OF JUSTICE (IRELAND)
PROBATE AND MATRIMONIAL DIVISION, DUBLIN.

I William Dargan of Fitzwilliam Square in the City of Dublin being weak in health but sound in mind do make this my last Will and Testament and inasmuch as I have already executed two trust deeds for the benefit of my creditors whereby I assigned all my real and personal estate to Trustees for said purposes and I am only entitled to the residue of said property after payment of said debts I now in the first place ratify and confirm said deeds I next give devise and bequeath all my real and personal property estate and effects to Alexander Boyle Esquire of Earlsfort Terrace in the City of Dublin as Trustee for the purposes hereinafter mentioned and in the realising and winding up of my estate I give to the said Alexander Boyle full power to deal with the property as he may think fit and to retain or dispose of it as he shall consider best and to be the sole judge of the propriety of such retention or disposition and I direct the said Alexander Boyle out of said property to pay the annuity and legacies in this my Will mentioned and to dispose of the residue according to the directions herein contained I leave and bequeath to my dear wife Jane Dargan all my Plate linen furniture pictures carriages and horses as used by me at my house in Fitzwilliam Square I further leave and bequeath to my dear wife Jane Dargan an annuity of six hundred pounds per annum for the term of her life payable quarterly and I charge all my real and personal property estate and effects with the payment of said annuity and as the first charge thereon with power of distress as to the real estate Next subject to the payment

The first page of the copy of William Dargan's will of 26 January 1867, completed a few weeks before his death.

There is a poignancy in the opening lines of the final unsigned copy will dated 26 January 1867, just twelve days before Dargan's death, in which he describes himself as being physically weak but mentally strong.[28]

High Court of Justice (Ireland): Probate and Matrimonial Division, Dublin

I, William Dargan, of Fitzwilliam Square in the City of Dublin, being weak in health but sound in mind do make this my last Will and Testament and in as much as I have already executed two trust deeds for the benefit of my creditors, whereby I assigned all my real and personal estate to Trustees for said purposes and I am only entitled to the residue of said property after payment of said debts I now in the first place ratify and confirm said deeds.

I next give, devise and bequeath all my real and personal property, estate and effects to Alexander Boyle Esquire of Earlsfort Terrace in the City of Dublin as Trustee for the purposes hereinafter mentioned and in realising and winding up of my estate I give to the said Alexander Boyle full power to deal with the property as he may think fit and to retain or dispose of it as he shall consider best and to be the sole judge of the propriety of such retention or disposition and I direct the said Alexander Boyle out of said property to pay the annuity and legacies in this my Will mentioned and to dispose of the residue according to the directions herein contained.

I leave and bequeath to my dear wife Jane Dargan all my plate, linen, furniture, pictures, carriages and horses as used by me at my house in Fitzwilliam Square. I further leave and bequeath to my dear wife Jane Dargan an annuity of six hundred pounds per annum for the term of her life, payable quarterly, and I charge all my real and personal property, estate and effects with the payment of said annuity and as the first charge thereon with power of distress as to the real estate.

Next, subject to the payment of said annuity and to keeping up and maintaining a sufficient fund for the payment thereof, which I direct my Executor to do, I give and bequeath the following legacies. To my said dear wife, Jane Dargan, Three thousand pounds. To Miss Louisa Haslam, as a token of my affection for her and for her great attention to me, one thousand pounds. To my sister, Selina Dargan, five hundred pounds. To said Alexander Boyle, two thousand pounds in consideration of his trouble in carrying out the trusts of this Will and acting as Executor thereof and also as a token of my esteem and affection for him.

And I appoint my Nephews, James Boland and James Dargan my Residuary devisees and Legatees and I give, devise and bequeath to them all the residue of my real and personal property. I direct that my Executor shall pay all the said Legacies clear and above Legacy duty. I direct that said Legacy of one thousand pounds payable to said Louisa Haslam shall be paid within six months after my death and in priority of the other legacies. In case of a deficiency of my estate the said legacies of Three thousand pounds, Two thousand pounds and five hundred pounds are to be rateably reduced.

I appoint said Alexander Boyle[29] my sole Executor and I direct him to distribute the sum of two hundred pounds amongst such Public Charities in Dublin as he may select. My wish and direction to my said Executor is that my friend Mr Croker Barrington should act professionally in carrying out the trusts of this my last Will.

In witness whereof I, the said William Dargan, have hereunto set my hand this Twenty sixth day of January one thousand eight hundred and sixty four [1867] _____ Wm Dargan.

Signed and declared by the Testator as and for his last Will and Testament in presence of us present at the same time who at his request and in his presence and in the presence of each other have hereunto subscribed our names as witnesses.

_____ Croker Barrington   _____ Thos B. Crosthwaite

Be it known that on the Seventh day of June 1867 the last Will and Testament hereunto annexed of William Dargan, late of Fitzwilliam Square in the City of Dublin, Esquire, deceased, who died on or about the 7th day of February 1867 at same place, was proved and registered in the Principal Registry of Her Majesty's Court of Probate and that the administration of all and singular the personal estate and effects of the said deceased was granted by the aforesaid Court to Alexander Boyle of Earlsfort Terrace, Dublin, Esquire, the sole Executor named in the said Will, he having been first sworn well and faithfully to administer the same by paying the just debts of the deceased and the legacies contained in said Will so far as he is thereunto bound by law and to exhibit a true and perfect inventory of all and singular the said estate and effects and to render a just and true account thereof whenever required by law so to do.[30]

The Final Curtain

In late January 1867 Dargan telegrammed his nephew James Dargan, then living in Wrexham, asking him to return to Dublin. James' diaries record this on 22 January: 'To Fitzwilliam Sq. saw Uncle who told me come again before I returned. Think he won't live.'[31] As his diaries indicate James was a regular visitor to the house during his uncle's final weeks. When he and James Boland called on 30 January Dargan's nephew, Fr John Boland a curate in Tullow parish, Co. Carlow and the son of one of his sisters, was there and it is believed that Dargan received the last rites of the Catholic Church from him in his final days.[32] The Mount Anville nuns were particularly pleased that Dargan returned to the Catholic Church on his deathbed: 'Even though he was a long time away from the practice of his religion, his death was consoling. He consented to have a priest and to receive the last sacraments.'[33] Before returning to Wrexham the next day James Dargan wrote of his uncle: 'No one has any hope of his recovery.'[34]

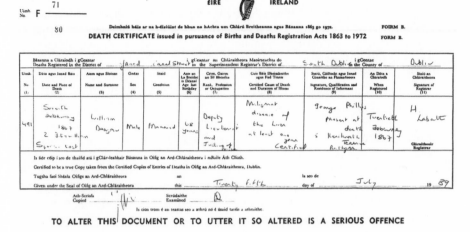

Dargan's death certificate giving the cause of death as 'malignant disease of the liver at least one year certified'. His occupation is given as Deputy Lieutenant and Justice of the Peace.

Dargan's health declined further and he died at 2 Fitzwilliam Square at 7.10 PM on Thursday 7 February 1867, aged 68, the cause of death being 'malignant disease of the liver, at least one year certified'. This painful disease is often linked to cirrhosis and given the medical knowledge of the time, was untreatable. One newspaper suggested the cancer had spread to his kidneys. The notification of the death was made by George Phillips, surveyor of taxes, of 5 Kenilworth Terrace, Rathgar, the husband of Jane's niece Mary.[35] He was present at the death. James Dargan was then back in Wrexham and heard of his uncle's death the next day, leaving for Dublin on the night mail. He spent many of the following days at the Fitzwilliam Square house.[36]

One of the first people to offer practical help was George Fitzgibbon, a barrister of 10 Merrion Square who wrote to Louisa Haslam: 'Can I be of any use to Mrs Dargan? If I can, let me know, if not, you need not take the trouble of writing an answer.'[37]

A special board meeting of the Dublin Wicklow & Wexford Railway passed the following resolution a few days later:

> The directors of the DW&WR Co. desire to express in the strongest manner their unanimous feeling of profound regret at the loss which they have just sustained with the death of their late Chairman, William Dargan. ... They wish to record the ... sense of the great services which he rendered to this undertaking, which for many years was the object of his unwearying exertions and for which he made many sacrifices.[38]

The directors sent a copy of this resolution to Jane Dargan and the next day the company secretary, E.W. Maunsell, wrote to her: 'I can hardly describe the blank that is left by the removal of one whom I always looked up to and revered – and who has proved a kind, considerate, and may I say, affectionate, friend to me for the last 18 years.'[39]

The Funeral

The Dublin firm of Patrick Beakky, 39–40 Stafford Street, handled the funeral arrangements. Dargan's body was placed in a suite of coffins, the outer one of polished oak with brass mountings and an inscription on a gilt shield: 'WILLIAM DARGAN, Died 7th February, 1867, Aged 68 years'. The funeral was set for the following Monday 11 February, a cloudy day, fine with a WSW wind according to W.R. Le Fanu who did not attend.[40] Also absent was William Fairbairn of the Manchester engineering firm whose engines Dargan bought on many occasions. He penned a perceptive profile of Dargan when he wrote to Jane the day before the funeral commiserating on the death of her

> highly respected husband and my excellent and kind-hearted friend ... but for a severe attack of illness from which I am slowly recovering I would have been one of the first to have followed the remains of my respected friend to the grave. That cannot be but I shall cherish his memory as one of my first and best friends, a man of strict honesty of purpose and a true patriot to his country. Few men have done so much with less attention for the interests of the community of Ireland.[41]

On the morning of the funeral James Dargan arrived at 2 Fitzwilliam Square at 8.30 AM where a large crowd had gathered and the cortège set off soon after 9 AM. Four black horses pulled the hearse with two for each of the three mourning coaches. The protocol at Victorian funerals did not encourage the widow or indeed any women to attend and there is no mention of Jane Dargan being there. In the first coach rode James Dargan, James Boland, Dr Joseph Haslam (married to Jane's sister, Frances) and George Phillips. In the second were Rev. James Boland and Rev. Patrick Boland, John Dargan and H. Simmonds and in the third Valentine O'Brien O'Connor, Richard Martin, Croker Barrington and Robert Hoey. Then came the coaches of the Lord Mayor, Sir John Gray MP, the Chancellor, Chief Justice Monahan and many dignitaries, business associates and other acquaintances. The list of mourners reveals representatives from three banks: Charles Copeland of the Royal Bank of Ireland, Edward Hudson Kinahan, David Mahony and M. Costello of the National Bank and John Quain of the Union Bank. There is no mention of a representative from the Bank of Ireland with whom Dargan had many dealings in his later life.

Funerals are always large affairs in Ireland and in the Victorian era they were even more so. *The Irish Times* described the funeral as 'the largest public funeral which has taken place in the city for many years'. A large number of DW&WR workmen walked in front of the hearse all the way to Glasnevin, the numbers quoted were between 300 (*Evening Mail*) and 500 (*Freeman's Journal*). There was also a great avalanche of carriages at Dargan's funeral and estimates of the numbers vary between 150 (*Saunders News-Letter*) and 250 (*The Irish Times*), see Table 9.1.[42] A curious custom at Victorian funerals was the notion of sending one's carriage, which might be occupied by the owner but often was not. The crest on the door was meant to identify the mourner.

Table 9.1: PRESS ESTIMATES OF NUMBER OF PRIVATE CARRIAGES AND DW&WR WORKMEN AT DARGAN'S FUNERAL[43]

	Evening Mail	Daily Express Times	Irish Journal	Freeman's Newsletter	Saunders Gazette	Bray
Carriages	200	150	250	250	150	150
DW&WR workmen	300	400	400*	500	300	300–400

* This paper noted there were an additional 300 men present from other railways connected with Dargan.

The route of the cortège was Fitzwilliam Street, Merrion Square East, Nassau Street, Grafton Street, College Green, Westmoreland Street, Carlisle Bridge, Rutland Square East, Frederick Street, Blessington Street to Glasnevin where Rev. Michael Gibney, Catholic chaplain to the cemetery, received the coffin. A group of DW&WR men carried it into the mortuary chapel where Fr Gibney said the office of the dead, accompanied by Canon Lee, PP of Bray, Canon Pope, Rev. Francis Murphy SJ[44] and Rev. Brennan, PP of Rostrevor. Dargan's body was then buried in a plot donated by the cemetery near the O'Connell circle, a position of some honour in the Glasnevin mortality league.[45] Afterwards the family returned to the city, as James Dargan recounts:

> Back with Jas Boland until 3 then to FitzWm Sq. to hear will read. Mrs D. is left 600 per year + 3,000. Miss Haslam £1,000. Alexr Boyle executor 2,000. Dublin charities £200 and Aunt Selina £500 and I and Jas Boland residuary legatees. Went to Barrington Jeffers saw state of account.[46]

Dargan's grave in Glasnevin cemetery, recently restored. Dargan's grave bears all the stylistic hallmarks of architect John Skipton Mulvany and was almost certainly designed by him.

SIR JOHN MACNEILL
C.E. FRS MRIA.
BORN DUNDALK, IRELAND 1793
DIED LONDON, 2 MARCH 1880
CIVIL & STRUCTURAL ENGINEER
DESIGNER OF ROADS & RAILWAYS
FIRST PROFESSOR OF ENGINEERING
TRINITY COLLEGE DUBLIN

THIS TABLET ERECTED 20 JULY 2001 BY THE
INSTITUTION OF ENGINEERS OF
IRELAND & TRINITY COLLEGE DUBLIN

The plaque marking the simple grave of Sir John Macneill, Dargan's engineering colleague, who died in poverty in 1880 and is buried in Brompton Cemetery, London.

Jane Dargan sent this black-edged envelope to solicitor Croker Barrington, probably in the days after Dargan's funeral in February 1867. The note reads: 'Saturday. My dear Sir. Will you be kind enough to come over here I think Mr [James] Dargan expected you at 10 Oclock. Yours very sincerely Jane Dargan'. Barrington's office in Ely Place was a short distance from 2 Fitzwilliam Square.

James Dargan spent the next few months sorting out his uncle's business affairs with the trustees, the lawyers and William's widow Jane and visiting property around the country. He was busy: one day in August 1867 he called on solicitors Barrington Jeffers, then met the DW&WR board at Westland Row (now Pearse) station, followed by a creditors' meeting at the solicitors again.[47]

Paying Tribute

As well as the DW&WR several companies passed resolutions of sympathy, among them the Royal Insurance Co. where Dargan had been a director since around 1864.[48] Lord Cloncurry, the chairman, wrote to Jane of the loss of 'an esteemed friend' and 'a valued advisor' as did B. Stride, the company secretary.[49]

In the Victorian style, the newspaper tributes were fulsome if occasionally repetitious. The following are some of the more interesting ones:[50]

> *Dublin Evening Mail*: 'He will be remembered not as a talking philanthropist, but as a man who conferred substantial benefits upon Ireland ... by promoting industry among the people, providing a large amount of employment for many years, and raising the price of skilled labour.'

> *Freeman's Journal*: 'Humble to all below him, William Dargan passed with the crowd as a man devoid of ambition and destitute of pride. Yet, few men

were more ambitious, and few possessed more of that self-respecting and self-sacrificing pride which enables the really great mind to despise the small ambitions of life that meaner natures crave. ... Often ... was he complimented for his desire to elevate the labourer by advancing his wages and increasing his comforts. But Dargan always replied that it was true economic policy, not maudling philanthropy, that influenced his course. His doctrine was, that the well-paid labourer became self-respecting, and, though high-priced, became the cheapest to his employer.'[51]

Ulster Observer: 'He was generally regarded as a plain, blunt man, who carried out contracts with rugged fidelity, and who was fortunate in making rough calculations. This is a very erroneous estimate of a really great man. Dargan was more than a contractor. He was an engineer of great abilities ...'

The Times, London: 'The amount of business he got through was something marvellous. The secret of his success, as he once said himself, consisted in the selection of agents on whose capacity and integrity he could rely, and in whom he took care not to weaken the sense of responsibility by interfering with the details of their business, while his own energies were reserved for comprehensive views and general operations.'

Daily Express: 'He was a self-made man in every sense of the word, and formed a striking example of what may be accomplished by persistent energy, devotion to a particular pursuit, strict integrity, fair and honourable dealing, intensity of purpose, and decision of character.'

The Irish Times: 'He was of the people, and he remained by choice among the people. Wherever there is an Irish railway there is his monument, more noble than any pyramid. And yet his best record is in the hearts of his countrymen ... who will tell their children how much one man has done for the progress of his country.'

Liverpool Mail: 'A true Irish patriot, an energetic and indomitable worker, and not merely an eloquent talker, has been called to his rest. ... With rare simplicity and singular abnegation he gratefully declined honours ... and tacitly rebuked Irish fondness for glitter and gee-gaw, for titles and honours, preferring to remain plain WILLIAM DARGAN and to be remembered as a real "Friend of Ireland".'

Illustrated London News: 'William Dargan ... was the son of a respectable farmer in the county of Carlow, and raised himself to the high position he ultimately reached by his own enterprise and energetic character.'

Belfast Newsletter: 'Mr Dargan was pre-eminently one of the men of the time, and his honored name will live in the history of Ireland. ... His name will ever be associated with the great improvements effected in our port and harbour; and many of the iron roads in Ireland were constructed under his superintendence.'

'Great Roads He Planned and Splendid Crystal Halls'

The Dublin Builder *of 1 March 1867 carried an unusually lyrical tribute for a journal dedicated to the building sciences. It was in the form of an acrostic based on Dargan's name. Although not great poetry it has a rather more sincere note than some of the patronizing doggerel written about Dargan during his life:*

> **W**eep, sons of Erin, ye have lost a friend,
> **I**n heart munificent and genuine worth;
> **L**oved by his countrymen, his deeds commend,
> **L**et Ireland glory that she gave him birth;
> **I**n acts so useful his life he spent,
> **A**nd needed not a title or vain ornament;
> **M**ay heaven reward him better far than earth.
>
> **D**ublin laments her patron, ever kind,
> **A**nd all those generous acts and words recall;
> **R**ich thoughts spring from his ever-fertile mind,
> **G**reat roads he planned, and splendid crystal halls;
> **A** noble man of nature, wide his fame,
> **N**e'er shall we look upon his like again.

Amidst all the eulogy, some queried the role of banks and financial institutions in Dargan's business difficulties and 'An Inquirer' wrote to one paper:

Many assert that he died prematurely of a broken heart, and that the cause of his untimely end was the pressure of his financial position, owing to the difficulty of realising securities during the late panic. It is also stated that his total engagements are brought within very narrow limits, compared with what they were in former times, and that his assets in real property and other valuable securities are not only ample to pay all engagements but will show a large surplus. ... If this be the case, is it not a reflection upon our great banks (some of which at one time got the character, whether rightly or wrongly, of sustaining foreign enterprise), that none of them came to the relief of Mr. Dargan in his late difficulty, when, as it is stated, they could do so without the least risk of loss, and, at the same time, [help one] whose great enterprise has been to Irishmen a source of national pride and wealth.[52]

Around the same time another correspondent, Thomas Edwards of 84 Pembroke Road, Dublin, said that one bank where Dargan was not a customer offered to help him and invited another bank to join a rescue bid, but Dargan died before they could act. With a degree of perception lacking in many others Edwards added that, 'It will be found on the wind up of his affairs that he died possessed of a considerable surplus after providing for all liabilities.'[53] Joby suggests Dargan believed himself bankrupt when he died 'although he was probably solvent, if only just'.[54]

A Sordid Little Dispute

Dargan's grave is a fine limestone vault set behind iron railings and is almost certainly the work of his architect colleague John Skipton Mulvany whose career covered stations, private houses and hotels all over the country. The vault he designed in Mount Jerome for their mutual friend, James Perry, bears a strong resemblance to Dargan's so it is fairly certain he designed this one also. The Glasnevin grave is a simple, pedimented limestone tomb on a plinth with a low chain-link railing painted in black and gold.

Some months after the funeral and before the vault was completed, an unpleasant sectarian dispute broke out over the choice of scripture text to be used on the grave, 'Whoever believes in me shall have eternal life', John 3:36. Jane Dargan wanted the Protestant King James version and through George Phillips stated this was her firm wish in a letter to the Glasnevin Cemetery Committee in June 1867.[55] Canon Farrell of the same Committee insisted on the Catholic version, the Douai Bible, so that the stonecutters, Fitzpatrick & Molloy, were unable to proceed. The issue went as far as Rome when Mgr L. Forde reported on it to Cardinal Cullen the following month, blaming the disagreement on Laurence Waldron, a colleague of Dargan's on the DW&WR board.[56] At the next meeting of the Cemeteries Committee Charles Coyle read a letter from George Phillips on behalf of Jane Dargan offering to omit the biblical quotation entirely and thus it was completed without holy writ:[57]

William Dargan,
Died 7 February 1867, aged 68 years.
RIP[58]

Launching an Appeal

As the sole executor, the task of carrying out Dargan's wishes fell to Alexander Boyle. The two had known each other a long time and had friends and business acquaintances in common. Boyle was a partner in stockbrokers Boyle, Low & Pim, who were much involved in the Kingstown Railway. Boyle gave architect John

Mulvany one of his first jobs when he asked him to redesign his Killiney house, Belle Vue. With James Pim, James Perry and others they formed what O'Dwyer calls the group of interrelated entrepreneurial Quaker families who were such a driving force in the economy of nineteenth-century Ireland.[59] Dargan had chosen his executor well. His immediate priority was to deal with the pressing creditors, mainly banks. As the deed of trust and Dargan's will confirm they had first claim on the estate and until they were settled Jane Dargan could not receive a penny. As the illustration of the black edged note makes clear (p.205), Jane was not at the funeral but she was involved in these matters.

Under the terms of her husband's will, Jane Dargan was left quite well off, if not luxuriously so. As well as all his property, Jane was to receive £3000 with a pension of £600, not quite on the level of today's politicians perhaps but an income that would allow her to live in comfort for the rest of her days. There was a general belief that Dargan was almost penniless when he died and so to provide her with an income, a group of Dargan's friends led by Richard Martin, one of his original trustees, launched an appeal to set up a fund for Jane. A number of replies to the appeal are extant, such as that from the Duke of Leinster who wrote to Martin on 23 March 1868 enclosing 'a draft for one thousand pounds towards the purchase of an annuity for the widow of the late William Dargan. I am your obedient servant, Leinster.'[60] This was a very generous donation, even for a landed duke. Other donors, albeit rather less generous ones, included Lords Mayo, Talbot de Malahide, Howth and Fermoy, Arthur Guinness and the Lord Chancellor. Lord Mayo wrote from the Irish Office, London, offering to help 'any movement to relieve the unfortunate position in which Mrs Dargan is placed'.[61]

James Neil McKenna responded positively from 84 Lancaster Gate, London, sending £100 and agreeing to join the committee as did Arthur Guinness: 'there has not been alive for the last twenty one years one to whom Ireland is more indebted than Wm Dargan'.[62] William Kirk, Dargan's former colleague in Banbridge sent £20, adding 'if you think this is not enough let me know and I will increase it'.[63] Lord Malahide also agreed to meet an unnamed nephew of Jane's at the Kildare Street Club to help him find a position. An appeal to Queen Victoria was less successful: she did not help individuals and there were no exceptions but the Prince of Wales stretched the royal purse and donated a modest fifty guineas.[64]

A few days after the funeral the DW&WR board agreed to a request from Barrington Jeffers & Co., Dargan's solicitors, to allow the £600 annuity to Jane Dargan to be paid and to give the firm access to the minutes and resolutions that approved acceptance of Dargan's IOUs for shares. But the Bank of Ireland kept its distance from the annuity and a month later ordered the sale of DW&WR stock provided as collateral for Dargan's borrowings.

The appeals continued with one to the British prime minister, Disraeli. His successor, Gladstone, met a delegation of Irish MPs on 11 March 1869 about securing a civil list pension for Jane, commenting he had never seen a 'more influential memorial'.[65] It appears that through her husband's friends and colleagues she was able to reach the most powerful in the land.

Writing in 1868 in *Personal Recollections of English Engineers* F.R. Conder was scathing about the idea of appealing to people in England to help Mrs Dargan:

> It is melancholy to reflect that ... an appeal has appeared in the English journals, on behalf of the destitute widow of Mr. Dargan. Under every possible aspect the matter is one for regret. ... That any Irishman, who is not by profession a mendicant, should not have felt called on, in the name of patriotism and of self-respect, to do his utmost to prevent such an appeal from being made to the sister country, above all at a moment when Irish politics have been made the engine for bringing public business to a dead lock, is something neither to be explained, nor to be comprehended.[66]

Meanwhile parcels of Dargan's lands in Bray and Wexford and other property went on the market in June 1869, showing clearly the extent of his property holdings.

Table 9.2: SALES OF DARGAN'S PROPERTIES, JUNE 1869[67]

Lot	Property	Annual rent	Sale price	Purchaser
1.	357 acres Wexford Harbour North	£460 3s 11d	Withdrawn at £7000	
2.	107 acres Wexford Harbour South	£744 2s 7d	No bids	
3.	149 acres Wexford harbour North	£82 13s 5d	£950	Robert Hoey
4.	14 acres Bray Main St, houses, premises	£1147 4s 9d	£11,000	R. MacRory
5.	Five acres Carlisle Grounds, Bray	£256 5s	Withdrawn at £1420	
6.	Marine Hotel	—	Sold prior to auction	
7.	10 Prince of Wales Terrace, Bray	£90	£1090	R H Dordan
8.	11 Prince of Wales Terrace, Bray	£90	£1050	W F Little
9.	12 Prince of Wales Terrace, Bray	£100	£1100	W H Jackson
10.	Houses, gardens, Terrence Tce, Bray	£278	Withdrawn at £1800	

Two and a half years later, Edward Purdon, Lord Mayor-elect of Dublin, bought a large parcel of Dargan's reclaimed lands in Wexford for £20,000.[68]

The work of sorting out the estate continued for some years. When Alexander Boyle died in 1870 William's nephew James Dargan (now living at 2 Cambridge Road, Rathmines) took over the job of executor in March that year. Boyle had done his work so well that the unadministered assets were less than £300.[69] However James Dargan himself did not have long to live. He had become a permanent way superintendent on the Cork & Bandon Railway, living at Arundel Terrace, Blackrock Road, Cork and died there three years later on 11 February 1873, just six years after his uncle's death. The executors of his estate valued under £450 were his unmarried sister Jane Dargan and James Boland. After all debts and bequests were met, James Dargan left 3 per cent of the residue of his estate to the St Vincent de Paul Society.[70] Since William and Jane Dargan did not have children most of the recent generations of Dargans (the late Herbert Dargan SJ, Daniel Dargan SJ and William Dargan SJ) are William's great-grandnephews, descended from James, William's brother, his wife Jane Walsh and their son, also called James.

Jane Dargan's Final Years

Jane did not stay in Ireland long after William died. Reports suggest she was somewhat disgruntled and she decided to move back to England but it is uncertain exactly when. By late 1868 she had moved out of 2 Fitzwilliam Square East and it appears lived at 8 Dargan Terrace, Bray for some months.[71] Among Jane's papers is a letter posted to her in April 1869 to 5 Claremont Buildings, Shrewsbury, not far from her original home at Adbaston. The 1871 Census in England records her as an 'annuitant' (recipient of an annuity) living with her brother, Henry Ackrintall (sic), an unmarried retired farmer of sixty-six and her niece Louisa Haslam, aged forty-four. By then Jane had her civil list pension of £100 (awarded in 1870) and by 1875 she had moved to London. Croker Barrington's legal practice was the firm of Barrington Jeffers and its papers contain an empty envelope postmark dated 23 February 1875 at Castlewellan and addressed to 'Mrs Dargan, Anerley Park, Anerley, Surrey', but no indication of the sender or contents.

She settled in a house called Glenmore at 21 Anerley Park, Penge, London SE20 where she lived until her death in 1894. It is not clear why she picked this area. A clue may be that fact that Anerley Park is a short distance away from Crystal Palace Park where Paxton's Hyde Park Exhibition of 1851 relocated after its closure. The buildings stood there until destroyed by fire in 1936. Could it be that someone involved in Dargan's 1853 Dublin Exhibition or the Hyde Park event found this house for her?

Glenmore, 21 Anerley Park, Penge, London SE20, where Jane Dargan spent her final years. When this photo was taken in April 2012, and for several years prior to this, the house was in at least six flats and rather down at heel. Note the cypress tree to the right, similar to the trees that were such a remarkable feature of Mount Anville.

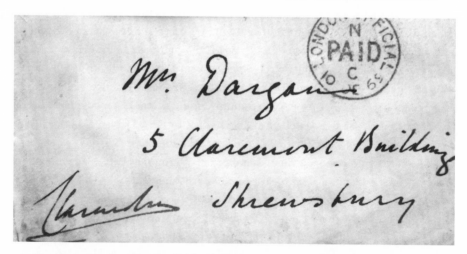

Letter posted to Jane Dargan in March 1869 to an address in Shrewsbury two years after her husband's death, suggesting Jane had already left Ireland by this time.

At the time the photo opposite was taken, in April 2012, the house was in several flats and quite run down. One is immediately struck by the tall, mature cypress tree in the front garden, unlike any other house on the road: this tree bears a remarkable resemblance to those planted by William at Mount Anville and it is possible Jane planted it to remind her of her former gracious home. Indeed while in London, Jane gave her address as 'formerly of Mount Anville House, Dublin'. Her niece, Louisa Haslam, came with her from Dublin and lived for many years at Anerley Park where her household consisted of two servants and a cook.[72]

On 26 June 1875 Croker Barrington wrote to Jane Dargan in London with a positive – and for a lawyer – remarkably concise and coherent statement of her late husband's financial status:[73]

10 Ely Place

Mr Dargan died on the 7th February 1867 having by deeds dated 19th November 1866 assigned all his property of every description, real and personal, to trustees for payment of his debts. The Trustees, on the 21st November 1867, filed a bill in the Court of Chancery to carry out the Trust under the direction and control of the Court. ... Claims for debts were sent in amounting to £225,287 13s 8d. Of these claims on investigation before the Court there was disallowed, or not proved, the sum of £50,955 19s 4d, showing net amount of debts due £174,351 14s 4d. This amount together with interest was paid by the Trustees and all legacies of the late William Dargan were also paid leaving a surplus of close on £30,000.

The net worth of Dargan's estate was over £204,000 (very approximately 25 million today) which covered all his debts and his legacies. Even though it took seven years to complete, the trustees did an excellent job in finalizing his affairs. After paying all debts and legacies to family and friends there was a very healthy balance of £30,000 (about 3.75 million today). This was more than enough for Jane to live comfortably for the rest of her life.

Almost nothing is known of Jane Dargan's last twenty years in Anerley Park. Presumably she brought her furniture and other possessions from Dublin and she kept a large folder of press cuttings to do with William's career, with the occasional comment written in the margin. She also maintained a folder of letters and cards, mainly to do with social events such as parties and dinners. Any of William's business papers she took to London have not survived. Jane Dargan made her own will on 20 April 1893: it gives valuable information on her relations, many of whom took the middle name Dargan.[74]

This is the last Will of me JANE DARGAN Glenmore Anerley Park Surrey widow of the late William Dargan of Mount Anvell [sic] Dublin I wish my furniture and all my property in Glenmore to be sold And all my property to be realised I bequeath to my nephew William Dargan Haslam two hundred

213

pounds To Bertie Pearce Haslam One hundred pounds To Frances Maud Haslam One hundred pounds To my niece Mary Phillips wife of George Phillips of Hollingbourne in the county of Kent One hundred pounds To my nephew John Allen Egham One hundred pounds To my nephew Thomas Allen One hundred pounds

The residue of my property to the said William Dargan Haslam EXEC-UTOR of this my will

To my second EXECUTOR Edward Boyce twenty pounds Date April 20th 1893 – JANE DARGAN –

Witnessed by J SIDNEY TURNER Surgeon 81 Anerley Road S E – LOUISA HASLAM Spinster 21Anerley Park S E

Affidavit of due execution filed –

On the 20th day of August 1894 Probate of this will was granted to William Dargan Haslam and Edgar Bois the Executors

The bequests in Jane Dargan's will amounted to just £700 to be met from her own resources and the sale of her house, Glenmore. The chief beneficiary was her nephew, William Dargan Haslam. A curious aspect of the will is that it appears Jane did not leave anything to Louisa Haslam, who witnessed it. It is probable that she made provision for her before she died although Louisa was clearly not staying on in the house after her aunt's death. Another interesting aspect is that Jane left nothing to her Dargan in-laws in Ireland, suggesting there may have been some distance other than geographical between them.

Jane Dargan died on 22 June 1894, aged ninety-one, the cause of death being diabetes asthenia, certified by her neighbour, J. Sidney Turner MRCS who lived in Anerley Road and had witnessed her will. The death certificate gives her occupation as 'Widow of William Dargan, Railway Contractor'.[75] The *Times* of 26 June 1894 carried a brief notice of her death on page 1 (the front page in those days was entirely dedicated to death notices) and on 28 September 1894 an advertisement from W.H. Waller Solicitors inviting anyone with a claim on her estate to contact them. Two local papers, the *Crystal Palace Advertiser* and the *Beckenham Journal*, carried a death notice: 'Dargan: On the 22nd inst., at Glenmore, Anerley Park SE, in her 92nd year, Jane, widow of William Dargan, late of Mount Anville House, Dundrum, County Dublin'.[76]

Jane was not interred with William in Glasnevin and despite making considerable efforts to discover where she was buried, writing to twelve cemeteries in the Croydon area and contacting several local Anglican churches, I have been unable to locate her grave.[77] She appears not to have been active in her local Anglican church in Penge, nor in Taney Church of Ireland parish when the Dargans lived at Mount Anville. It is possible Jane's body went back to her birthplace of Knighton in Adbaston, Staffordshire for burial. Jane's niece, Louisa Haslam, is buried in St

Mary's churchyard, Market Drayton, Shropshire, north of Adbaston, where her grave is inscribed: 'Louisa H. Haslam, daughter of Joseph Haslam, died 22 April 1906, aged 82'.[78] The absence of any mention of a husband in the inscription suggests Louisa was single although the 1881 census describes her as married, aged fifty-six and staying with Jane at the house of Jane's sister Frances Haslam and brother-in-law Dr Joseph Haslam in Stafford Street, Drayton Magna, Market Drayton. When probate was granted three months later Jane's effects in Ireland amounted to £931 9s 11d.[79]

Jane Dargan's Relations

Jane's nephew and executor of her will, William Dargan Haslam, was Louisa Haslam's brother, their parents being Frances Haslam née Arkinstall and Dr Joseph Haslam. William Haslam was an artist who married Agnes Eleanor Pearce and lived at 3 Ashburnham Gardens, King's Road, Chelsea. Their son, Bertie Pearce Haslam, born on 27 June 1877, was seventeen when his great-aunt died leaving him £100 and provides a valuable direct connection with the present day Dargans. Bertie Pearce Haslam, an active freemason, was a stamp dealer with a shop on the King's Road, Chelsea. He inherited the magnificent portrait of William Dargan that presumably once hung in Mount Anville and later Jane's house in Penge. It is by George Francis Mulvany, who was closely involved in the creation of the National Gallery of Ireland and became its first director. He was also a brother of John Skipton Mulvany, the architect who worked closely with William Dargan and designed his grave. Bertie Pearce Haslam very kindly donated the picture to CIÉ in the early 1960s.

Bertie Pierce Haslam wrote to Mary Dargan Ward on 16 August 1963 about a visit he made to Dublin, including Mount Anville and Kingsbridge (Heuston) station as it was then, where he saw the restored portrait of his grand-uncle:

> I am now 86 and as I was living alone I had to sell everything and I thought Ireland might like the picture. They have had it nicely cleaned up and I could only wish it was in your beautiful Picture Gallery where so many more could see it. He was often talked about by those of us who knew him.[80]

It is indeed a great pity the portrait is not in the National Gallery as few people ever view it in the CIÉ boardroom. Bertie Haslam retired to a masonic home, Davidson Lodge, Addiscombe, South London and died in Queen's Hospital Croydon on 1 September 1966, aged eighty-nine. He could not have met William Dargan who died about ten years before he was born; perhaps he meant his family talked about him although apart from Bertie there is no record of any of the later Haslams visiting Dublin. After a post-mortem Bertie Haslam was cremated and his ashes interred at location 195, Garden of Remembrance, Mitcham Road Cemetery, Croydon. [81]

TEN

The Heritage of William Dargan

William Dargan was one of the major figures of nineteenth-century Ireland. It is the premise of this book that he was arguably the greatest railway engineer and one of the leading industrialists and entrepreneurs of his day. His input to the development of the country was, and remains, enormous in a career that embraced roads, canals, railways, cross-channel steamers, land reclamation, harbour and reservoir construction, town development, sugar beet and peat production, flax farming and thread manufacture

Dargan also achieved success in England, competing successfully against major British contractors such as Thomas Brassey. He built and funded the 1853 Dublin Art–Industry Exhibition as a showcase for Irish art and manufacturers. The Exhibition cost him £20,000, but was a significant boost to national morale a few years after the Famine and out of it arose the National Gallery of Ireland.[1] He built approximately 830 miles (1335 km) of railways, financing lines himself when investors were slow to appear or the company was unable to raise the capital.[2] Communication boosts trade and industry and the effect of Dargan's work on the Irish economy was electrifying: as the driving force behind this transport and industrial revolution, during an era blighted by the horror of the Great Famine, he did indeed change the face of Ireland.

This is all the more remarkable when considering Dargan's background. He was not born with a silver spoon in his mouth but nor did he come from an impoverished family. His working career began in Britain and then he returned to Ireland; many aspiring entrepreneurs did things the other way round. He was lucky to receive a good education in construction and engineering from Thomas Telford and William Provis who recognized their exceptional trainee. Dargan learned many of his skills building the Holyhead Road with Telford, a Scotsman working on a Welsh road to improve communication between England and Ireland.

From there Dargan's career developed on two foundations: hard work and his reputation for quality and fair dealing, something many of his contracting rivals lacked. These qualities brought him more and more contracts until his name became a byword for straightforwardness and integrity.

His career really took off in the mid 1840s when he had contracts worth over £1 million in total so that by the early 1850s Dargan was a very rich man. He was also a person of influence in the business and social world of the time but remained relatively unaffected by his success. Writing a year after Dargan's death Conder said he was 'singularly modest and quiet, in abode, in dress, in manners'. He declined to be recruited into the lower orders of the nobility, nor to accept a sinecure seat in the Commons, nor any of the other titles, honours or positions that could have limited his business activities or set him apart from other men. The only significant title he ever accepted and used was the honorary one of Deputy Lieutenant of Dublin. Conder relates the tale of an English engineer seeking Dargan's support for an appeal on some matter or other to Dublin Castle:

> 'I came to ask you … if you cannot spare the time to go to Dublin with me, to write to the Lord-Lieutenant, to say … that you strenuously recommend him to do what I ask, as it is of great importance to the prosperity, and even the peace, of the country.' 'What!' said Dargan, opening his eyes in unaffected surprise. 'Me! Me write to the Lord-Lieutenant, me dear Sir! I daur not. I never took such a liberty in me life.' [3]

A remarkable aspect of his career and key to his success is the fact that Dargan inspired trust and confidence not just among those who awarded him contracts but also amongst his employees. He paid good wages, on time, and dealt with his men firmly but fairly. In 1848 Dargan claimed he employed 50,000 men, a substantial portion of the entire working population in Ireland at the time.[4] This was a commercial transaction but Dargan's paternalistic approach was ahead of its time and won him great loyalty and genuine affection from his men.[5] However, in keeping with the industrial policy of the time he would not tolerate a strike, or combination as it was then called, and rarely re-employed men who downed tools for higher wages, an attitude very much in keeping with the labour practice of that era.

A fine mahogany writing desk inscribed 'To William Dargan Esq'; in private ownership.

A contemporary portrait of Dargan resting on the desk
with his name inscribed.

This is the only known photo of William Dargan taken against the traditional artificial background; note the very real top hat on the right.

Dargan was always prepared to negotiate for the sake of harmonious relations with a client, and rarely did a disagreement turn into a dispute. There was a steely side to his character and when faced with a patent injustice (such as his clash with the Ballast Office over construction of the Dublin Graving Dock) he did indeed show his teeth and was in time vindicated.

The extraordinary thing about Dargan's success was that he managed to accumulate a fortune and yet retain those humanitarian characteristics that other self-made men seem able to shed effortlessly. Do you have to be ruthless to succeed in business? Dargan proved the answer to that question is no, although he paid a heavy price in enduring financial insecurity during his last years

Dargan's Heritage: New Uses for Old Railway Lines

While many of Dargan's lines are still in use, quite a number are abandoned. Railways tend to stay on the level and follow a straight line with gentle curves, often running through scenic areas, and so when closed make a superb walkway and cycle path available to all at quite modest cost. Unlike France, Spain and the UK Ireland has been slow to capitalize on reusing abandoned railways as a leisure amenity, a notable exception being the beautiful and very successful Greenway route from Westport to Achill, Co. Mayo.

Among other lines that are ripe for this type of development are:

Clidfen-Galway: *a line running through some of the most beautiful, unspoilt scenery in the country, much of it far from any roads.*

Dromod-Ballinamore/Belturbet/Arigna: *this line traverses the very pleasant drumlin country of south Leitrim and Cavan.*

Tralee-Dingle: *one of the most spectacular routes in Ireland that crosses the Dingle peninsula.*

Bray-Greystones: *This is a delightful cliff walk running above and parallel to the railway as it passes through a honeycomb of tunnels below. Further south from Greystones towards Wicklow the old railway route is also a walkway running along the shore with the relocated railway on the land side.*

Despite his achievements and public profile, Dargan was essentially a private individual. For example, little is known about his thirty-eight year marriage to Jane nor the impact on the couple of not having children, unlike one engineering colleague. W.R. Le Fanu tells of going fishing one day and chatting to a water bailiff named McClelland about the number of children each had. 'Isn't it strange how the

Lord would give you and me, that can't afford it, such a lot? And look at Mr Roe and Mr Dargan and other rich men that hasn't one. But I suppose … the Lord takes some other way of tormenting them'.[6] Dargan stayed well clear of those two social mine-fields, politics and religion, refusing to ally himself with any political cause and was seemingly removed from any religious practice until close to death. However those who claim he turned down the offer of a baronetcy for political or even nationalist reasons are wide of the mark. Dargan did not shun Queen Victoria during the 1853 Exhibition, in fact he greeted her respectfully and escorted her round the building. Likewise he could easily have avoided receiving her at Mount Anville (even in those days such events did not happen without considerable planning) but did not do so and when she was leaving Ireland after her 1861 visit he was at Westland Row station to speed her on her way to Dun Laoghaire.[7]

One personal detail is fairly certain: Dargan appears to have been a heavy drinker – at least from the 1840s onwards – a habit which must have had a serious impact on his business and family life. For example, in his diaries William Le Fanu refers several times to Dargan being drunk at various social occasions, while writing a year after his death F.R. Conder who worked as engineer on lines in Waterford and Cork has a fairly trenchant account of the effects of Dargan's drinking habits and their link to his premature death. His description suggests a man close to alcoholism:

> The lovers of Ireland would have done well to present to Mr Dargan a butt or two of that pure Amontillado sherry, the habitual use of which is the best protection against the undue use of inferior wine. He was killed by Irish sherry. He would stop, in his rapid drives across the country, to change the horse in his gig, and would drink a bottle out of the neck for refreshment. Human nature has its limits, and the well-knit frame, and well-organized brain, of the active man, were unable to withstand this method of keeping up the steam.[8]

At Limerick in 1853 Dargan spoke at some length about the need for an educated labour force in Ireland, a radical notion for the time and one of the few recorded occasions when Dargan ventured into discussion of issues of economic or social policy and development. He made two significant points: first that while forced emigration was a great evil it had some benefits in that it allowed working men seek better pay outside Ireland and would ultimately raise wages at home as the supply of surplus labour declined. And second, that the contribution of women in industry and agriculture was unrecognized and greatly undervalued. He quoted Madame de Staël's reply when Napoleon asked her how to make France a great nation: 'Educate the mothers'.[9]

Early in his career Dargan understood that the future of transport lay in railways rather than canals and he quickly and easily made the switch. He took a gamble in determinedly seeking the first railway contract in Ireland, the Dublin & Kingstown, or 'Quaker line' that opened two years before the first passenger railway in London. Had it failed, the advent of railways to Ireland might have been delayed by twenty years, but it was an outstanding success and in time became the busiest and most profitable line in Ireland. Dargan thus established a solid reputation among the business community and the government as its pioneering builder. Two other reasons for his success during the 1840s were his early concentration on the more industrial north-east of the country and his successful tender for the massively lucrative GS&WR contract to build the line to Cork and the equally substantial MGWR contract from Mullingar to Galway.[10] And it has to be said, Dargan was lucky.

Although Dargan was expected to retire and live off his accumulated fortune from these large contracts – which he could well afford to do – he was more inclined to invest in many other projects, such as the 1853 Dublin Exhibition and committed himself fully as contractor, investor, director and finally chairman of the DW&WR. Without his efforts to promote the DW&WR through the difficult economic conditions of the 1850s, construction of the line would have stalled, possibly for good. Returns on his investment were slow and Dargan's ill-health from about 1864, combined with his riding accident, forced him to assign all his business interests to trustees. In 1863 James Dargan overheard a conversation with a stranger on the Rathdrum to Dublin train about his uncle.[11] He said Dargan senior was 'from the plough … very clever', one for 'grand projects' but 'useless for detail' and 'has bills dishonoured for £15 through careless management'.[12] The point was doubtless overstated but the comments suggest a man whose business might have fallen into some disorder.

From Dargan's well-documented behaviour and sense of fair play throughout his life, we can surmise it must have been a painful decision to accept a 'temporary bankruptcy' as Robert Peel described it, inaccurately.[13] The British financial crisis of 1866 dealt a further blow when the value of railway stock crashed in Ireland and Britain as investors scrambled desperately to recover some of the money they had put into speculative railway shares. It may well be that as W.R. Le Fanu said, he 'died comparatively poor, and, to use his own words, "of a broken heart"'.[14] This is a curious phrase to use when discussing someone's business affairs. Perhaps Le Fanu knew more than he was telling, but it is unlikely Dargan died thinking he was on the verge of bankruptcy. Alexander Boyle, his trustee, would have reassured him and Dargan would not have made such generous provisions in his will if he thought there was nothing in his estate to meet them.[15] The two trustees, with his friend and solicitor, Croker Barrington, worked hard for several years after

Dargan's death to put his affairs in order and as noted, finally revealed his estate had a healthy surplus after meeting all debts, liabilities and bequests.

In his humorous, anecdote-laden and somewhat stage-Irish memoirs, William Le Fanu offers this perceptive pen-portrait of Dargan, someone he worked along-side for years and knew very well:

> I have settled, as engineer for different companies, many of his accounts involving many hundred thousand pounds. His thorough honesty, his will-ingness to concede a disputed point, and his wonderful rapidity of decision, rendered it a pleasure, instead of a trouble, as it generally is, to settle these accounts; indeed in my life I have never met a man more quick in intelli-gence, more clear sighted and more thoroughly honourable.[16]

Not a bad epitaph for anyone.

Selected Bank of Ireland Loan Applications, Overdrafts and Renewals, Dargan/D&WR, 1854–66

Date	Amount	WD or D(W)&WR	Security/terms	Approved
7 Feb 1854	Renew £50,000 loan	WD	5 per cent half yearly	Yes
17 July 1855	£10,000 bill	WD	Warning on o/d size	Yes
5 Apr 1856	£27,500 bills discount	WD	Govern'r to meet D	
12 Aug 1856	Renew £10,000 o/d	WD	3 months	Yes
6 Feb 1857	£10,000 o/d	WD	–	Yes
14 Apr 1857	£10,000 o/d	WD	–	Yes
21 Apr 1857	£20,000, new a/c	D&WR	Board's notes	Yes
26 Oct 1857	£30,000	D&WR	8½ per cent	Yes
6 Nov 1857	£20,000	WD	–	Yes
26 Jan 1858	£40,000	WD	6 per cent pref. shares	Yes
27 Apr 1858	£30,000 discharged	D&WR	£10,000 cash, £20,000 promissory notes	
16 Nov 1858	£5000 o/d for six weeks	WD	–	Yes
12 Apr 1859	£70,000	WD	6 month extension sought*	

15 May 1860	£10,000	WD	Yes	
7 Aug 1860	£20,000	WD	Shares	Yes
31 Dec 1860	£10,000, three months	WD	Securities	Yes
3 June 1862	£5000, three months	WD	Securities	Yes
16 Sep 1862	£5000, three months	WD	–	Yes
25 Nov 1862	£5000, three months	WD	–	Yes
26 Jan 1864	£16,700, four months	WD	DW&WR shares	Yes
26 Jan 1864	£5000 o/d	WD	'	Yes
2 Aug 1864	£10,000 o/d	WD	'	Yes
9 Aug 1864	£20,000, six months	DW&WR	Directors' notes	No
22 Nov 1864	£400	DW&WR	–	Yes
17 Jan 1865	£10,000	WD	DW&WR shares	Yes
5 Dec 1865	£12,000	WD	DW&WR shares	Yes
3 May 1866	£10,000	DW&WR	DW&WR bonds	No
7 Aug 1866	£13,000	WD	£30k R stock**	Yes
4 Dec 1866	£13,000	Dargan trustees***	To hold shares	No
11 Dec 1866	£10,000	WD	DW&WR preferences	No

NOTES

*The Bank sought £20,000 in extra D&WR shares as additional security.

** Dargan and Alexander Boyle also offered their personal securities.

*** A fortnight after Dargan's death the Bank declined to offer a loan to Jane Dargan in response to a request from Barrington & Jeffers, Dargan's solicitors and a few weeks later decided to dispose of £30,000 of DW&WR stock in Dargan's name.

A Chronological Listing of Dargan Projects

Start date	End date	Project	All or part
1819	c.1824	Holyhead road	Part
1824		Barrow Navigation	All
1824?	c.1825	Howth Road	All
1828		Swords turnpike	All
1828	1831	Dunleer turnpike	All
1828	c.1835	Birmingham & Liverpool Junction canal, surveyor	Part
1829	1832	South Circular Road, Dublin	All
1829	c.1832	Carlow road	All
1830s		Shannon at Limerick	All
1831	1834	Banbridge town centre, market house	All
1832?	1833	Middlewich canal, England	Part
1833?	1835	Kilbeggan canal	All
1833 Feb	1842 May	Ulster Canal	All
1833 April	1834 Dec	Dublin & Kingstown R.	All
1836 May	1837 May	Extension to Kingstown	All
1838 Feb	1840	Bann reservoir	All
1839 Apr	1842 Jan	Belfast harbour 1	All
c.1839	1848	Ulster R. Lisburn to Armagh	All but 7m
1840	1850	Newry–Liverpool steamers	All

1841 Feb	1844 Mar	Dublin & Drogheda Railway	Part
1841 Apr	1854	Foyle reclamation	All
1841 May	1843 summer	Solitude reservoir, Belfast	All
1842	1844 Mar	Dalkey atmospheric railway	All
1844 Nov	1846 Aug	GS&WR, Dublin to Carlow	Most with Wm McCormick
1845	1847 May	Howth branch	All with Wm McCormick
1845 Oct	1848 May	Waterford & Limerick R. Limerick–Tipperary	All
1845 Oct	1849 Feb	Dundalk & Enniskillen R. 1	All with Wm McCormick
1846	–	Grand Hotel Malahide	partner
1846	c.1853	Belturbet distillery	shareholder
1846 Feb	1848 Nov	Liverpool & Bury R.	All with Wm McCormick
1846 Feb	1848 summer	Belfast & Ballymena R.	All
1846 Aug	1854	Newry & Eniskillen R.	All
1846 Oct	1849 May	Newry Warrenpoint & Rostrevor R.	All
1846 Oct	1849	Glenstal Castle	subcontractor
1846 Nov	1850 Nov	GS&WR, Thurles–Cork	All
1847		Dublin & Belfast Junction R. Newry–Portadown	All
1847	1853	Wexford sloblands	partner
1847 early		Dundalk & Enniskillen R.	part, from Coyle & Atkinson
1847 Jan	1848 July	Irish South Eastern R. Carlow–Bagenalstown	All
c.1847 Mar	1850 May	Manchester & Leeds R.	Parts with Wm McCormick
1847 Apr	1849 July	Belfast harbour 2	All
1847 Apr	1850 Apr	Belfast & Co. Down R.Belfast–Holywood	All
1848		Farmers Estate Society	member

1849	1862	Kildinan flax mill	with Lord Fermoy
1849 Feb	1855	Dublin & Drogheda train services	All
1849 Jun	1850 June	Cork Blackrock & Passage R.	part, from Moores
1849 June	1850 Apr	Newry Navigation	All
1849 summer	1851 Aug	Midland Great Western R. Mullingar–Galway	All
1849 Nov	1855 May	Newry Warrenpoint & Rostrevor R. train services	
1850	1858	Galway–US ships	partner
1850?	1852	Craigmore viaduct	All
c.1848	1850 Nov	Irish South Eastern Railway Bagenalstown–Kilkenny	All
1850 Sep/ Oct	1853 April	Waterford & Limerick R. Tipperary–Waterford	All
1851		Royal Agricultural Improvement Society	member
1851		Moyvoughley flax	promoter
1852 Feb	1854 July	Dublin & Wicklow R. Dublin–Bray	All
1852 Spring	1853 July	Killarney Junction R.	part
1852 Apr	1854 Oct	Irish Beet Sugar Co.	director
1852 June	1854 Mar	1853 Dublin Art–Industry Exhibition	All
1852 Dec	1853 Sept	Waterford & Tramore R.	All
1853	1853	*SS Great Eastern*	investor with I.K. Brunel
c.1853	1856 July	Midland Great Western R. Inny Jun–Cavan	All
1853 July	1864 Jan	National Gallery	donor
1853 Sept	1855 Nov	MGWR Mullingar–Longford	All
1853 Dec	1855 Nov	Belfast Ballymena, Ballymoney & PJR	All
1854?	Oct 1855	Dublin & Wicklow R. Bray–Wicklow	All
1854 May	1858 Apr	Limerick & Foynes R.	All
1854 July	1860 Feb	Dublin graving dock	All

1854 July	c.1861	Chapelizod thread mills	owner with Houghton
1854 Oct	1859 Mar	Banbridge Junction R.	All
1855	1858 Apr	Portadown & Dungannon R.	from Fox Henderson
1856 Feb	1858 May	Ulster R., Armagh–Monaghan	All
1856 Feb	1864 Mar	Dublin & Wicklow R.	Director
1855 Spring	1856 Oct	Randalstown–Cookstown	All
1856 May	1859 July	Tralee & Killarney R.	All
1856 Sept	1859 July	Limerick–Ennis	from Johnson & Kinder
1858	1861	Foynes/Kilrush ships	All
c.1858	1860 May	Great Southern & Western R. Mallow–Fermoy	All
1858 May	1859 Sept	Great Southern & Western R. Portarlington–Tullamore	All
1858 Jun	1866 July	Bray development	All
1859 Apr	1860 Sept	Athenry & Tuam R.	All
1863 July	1867	Royal Marine Hotel	Partner
1864 Mar	1867 Feb	Dublin & Wicklow R.	Chairman

Bibliography

1. MANUSCRIPT SOURCES

A. General

British Library

Griffin, A., *Handbook of Contemporary Biography*, 'William Dargan', ADD MS 28,509

_____, William McCormick, ADD MS 38,381

_____, John Macneill, ADD MS 28,511

Peel Papers, MS 40,588, f.128; 40,547, f.282

Vignoles, Charles, Journals, 1830–62, ADD MS 35,071, 34,530

British Library of Political and Economic Science

Charles Hadfield Papers

Dublin City Archives

Dublin Municipal Council, Minutes, 1863, vol.C2/A1/23

Dublin Diocesan Archives (RC)

Cullen Papers and Correspondence, Cullen File II, 1865, 327/1,2; File IV, 1866, 327/5; File V, 1867, 334/4

Dublin Port Archives

Ballast Board (Corporation for Preserving and Improving the Port of Dublin), correspondence, 1855–58

Engineers Ireland Archives

Macneill, Sir John, Letter Books, 1827–44

General Register Office, England

Jane Dargan's will

Jane Dargan's death certificate

Glenstal Abbey, Co. Limerick

Barrington Papers

House of Lords Record Office

Belfast & Ballymena Railway, manuscript evidence to SC, April 1845

Belfast Harbour Act and plans: 1831 1&2 Wm 55, deposited plans: 1 V 76 1837

_____, deposited plans, 1837: 1 Vic 76

Belfast & Holywood Railway, deposited plans, 30 November 1836

Belfast Waterworks, deposited plans, John Macneill: 1840 3&4 V.79

Dublin to Carlow road, deposited plans and estimates by William Dargan, 1829: 10 GIV 75

Dublin & Drogheda Railway, William Cubitt's plans and estimates,

_____, Report of William Cubitt to Provisional Committee, 9 January 1836

_____, Deposited plans, 17 May 1836

_____, Share subscription lists and Book of Reference, 1836

_____, manuscript evidence to SC, July 1840

Dublin and Kingstown Railway, deposited plans and estimates, 1831: 1 & 2 Wm IV 69

_____, bill from western pier, Kingstown harbour, May 1833

_____, deposited map and plan of Kingstown extension, 28 April 1834

_____, Book of References: 1834 4&5Wm IV 27

_____, Correspondence and papers, 28 February 1843: 1843 (62) L.197

Dublin and Kingstown Ship Canal, Memorials and maps, HC 1833 (603) xxxv.85

Great Southern & Western Railway, Estimates and subscription contract, June 1844

_____, manuscript evidence before SC, June–July 1844

Holyhead road, deposited plans and map of Menai bridge and road from straits to Holyhead: 1819 59 GIII 48, Pub

Howth to Dublin road, Further estimates for improvements, C.W. Flint: 1824 (56.57) xxi.28.38

Howth road, deposited plans, estimate and map: 1816 59 GIII 71

Midland Great Western Railway, manuscript evidence to SC, June 1846

Ulster Canal, deposited plans: 6&7 Wm 72, 1836

Ulster Railway, deposited plans for Ladybridge–Armagh extension, 30 November 1835

_____, Folder Book of Reference and estimate of William Bald, 6&7 Wm IV 33

_____, House of Commons SC on Extension Bill, MS evidence, 19 May 1845

_____, Report of Capt. Simmons to Office of Commissioners of Railways

Waterford, Wexford, Wicklow & Dublin Railway, evidence before Select Committee: 1850 (85) XXI.1; 1850 (119) XXI.19

_____, Return of share capital: 1850 (79) XXI.35

Institution of Civil Engineers Archives, London

Telford Papers, Lib 11/67

Kilruddery House, Co. Wicklow

Meath Papers

Kings Inns, Dublin

Registry of Deeds, abstract volumes, 1820–75

Chapelizod Distillery, Surveyor's report, Francis Beatty, Dublin, 20 July 1875

Incumbered Estates Court, Index

_____, Queen's County Rental, 1850

Marsh's Library, Dublin

Robert Travers correspondence

Mount Anville Archives, Dublin
'Journal de la maison de Mount Anville', 1865
Mount Anville Convent House Ledger, August 1865

National Archives, Dublin
Calendar of Grants of Probate and Letters of Administration, 1867, 1870, 1873, 1894,
Chief Secretary's Office, Index to Registered Papers, 1853–67, 12,992–20,214
_____, Registered Papers Abstract Book, 1854
Dublin to Howth road, plan for the, William Duncan [Dargan], Board of Public Works, 1823, V20 7/4/23
Elliott, Samuel and William Allen, Tithe Book for Queen's County, TAB 24/51
Grants of probate and letters of administration made in the principal registry, calendar, 1867, p.78; 1870, p.125; 1873, p.152
Incumbered Estates Court, Queen's County Rental, July–August 1850
_____, Proceedings, vols.1–5, 1849–51
Landed Estates Court, Rentals Index, 1867–85
Meath Papers, Bray leases, 1861–66, C/1, Boxes 18 & 35
Midland Great Western Railway, Notice re lands to be acquired, Mullingar to Galway, 18 December 1849: M5677/1A–3/4–80; PW file 3044/60
Pembroke Estate Papers, Railways, 1826–67, 1011/6/77; 1011/9/2; 1011/13/2; 1011/3/41
Public Works, Commissioners of: Richard Osborne to Drainage Commissioners, OPW Registers 296/47, 24329/47
_____, Barrington & Jeffers, correspondence with Alexander Stewart/ Edward Hornsby
OPW Correspondence files, 8820/58; 16214/59
_____, Roads and Bridges Minute Books, 1825–36, National Archives, OPW/I/7/1/1–I/7/1/6
_____, Commissioners of, Letter Books, 1825–72, National Archives, I/7/2/1–I/7/2/12
_____, Roads and Bridges, Letter Books, 1827–40, National Archives, OPW/7/2/1–7/2/7
_____, correspondence with Dublin & Kingstown Railway, 1842, PW 1067/77
_____, Railways correspondence, 1842–60, OPW/25,952/53–14,067/77
_____, Dublin & Kingstown Railway correspondence, 1844–48, PW/12/24,329,47
_____, Box files, Railways, canals, roads, drainage, 1847–58, OPW/24,329/47–2605/57
_____, Engineering correspondence files, 1850–68, 471/50–12,366/68
_____, correspondence with Dublin & Wicklow Railway, 1853, PW 26,016/53; 1854, PW 11845/54 and PW 13,039/54
_____, Buildings, roads and railway Registers, 1854–67, 5/14/12–5/14/23
_____, Dublin & Wicklow Railway, 1856 Registers, OPW/5/14/15
_____, Ulster Canal correspondence, 1861, OPW/14,276/64
_____, Royal Marine Hotel, 23 July 1863, OPW 11476/63
_____, Royal Marine Hotel correspondence, July 1863, OPW/11,476/63
Vignoles, Charles, Letter Books for Railway Commissioners, December 1836, 2D/59/54
Wills, Abstracts of, 1894

Ena Dargan Papers
Jane Dargan Papers

National Archives, London
Dublin & Drogheda Railway, Report of Capt. Simmonds to Board of Trade, 28 May 1847, MT6/4/9
Godwin, John, letter to Secretary, Railway Department, Board of Trade, 9 January 1842, MT6/1/108

Holyhead Road Journals 1819–27, MT27: 57–62, 74

Index to Railway Inspectors' Reports

_____, 1842, MT6

_____, 1843, MT6

_____, 1847, MT6

_____, 1848, MT6

_____, 1849, MT6; MT29

_____, 1850, MT6; MT29

_____, 1851, MT29; MT29

_____, 1853, MT6

_____, 1854, MT6; MT29

_____, 1855, MT6

_____, 1859, MT29

Portadown–Belfast, Report of Maj.–Gen. Pasley to Privy Council for Trade, 18 November 1843: MT6/2/3

Ulster Railway, Portadown to Armagh, Report on, 2 February 1848: MT6/5/124

Public Record Office, Northern Ireland

Ballymena, Ballymoney, Coleraine and Portrush Junction Railway, Portrush land leases, UTA2/B/2

Bann Reservoir, Agreement with Dargan, 12 February 1838, D1632/6/2

Belfast & Ballymena Railway, articles of agreement with William Dargan and bond, 4 February 1846, UTA8

Belfast Ballast Board and William Dargan, Articles of Agreement, 28 February 1839, T.2433/1

Belfast harbour, bond between William Dargan, James Perry and Wright Pike, 28 February 1839, T.2433/2

_____, Articles of Agreement, 28 February 1839, T.2433/1

Caledon Papers, D2433

Dargan, William, last will and testament, High Court of Justice, T.1034

Dorgan [Dargan] Papers, Belturbet distillery and Barrington Jellett, 1843–53, D.1905/2/17A/3

Downshire Papers, D671/C

Grand Jury, Co. Down, Presentment Books, 1829–42, DOW4/2/11A–15

_____, Treasurer's Presentment Books, 1830–37,DOW4/5/6–7

Kirk Papers, 1853

Newry & Enniskillen Railway, Moore Bros. works contracts, n.d., UTA56/A

Portadown & Dungannon Railway, correspondence, plans and sections, 1856–1919, COM.9/155/224

Portadown, Dungannon & Omagh Junction Railway, plans and works, 1856–64, T.877/819–27

Reilly Papers, William, correspondence with William Dargan, 1831–40, D.671/C/56/1–23

National Library of Ireland

Barrington & Jeffers Papers, 12.994

Richard Boyse Osborne, Diaries, 1808–97, ms.7888–7895

Private collections

James Dargan Diaries, 1863–70

Royal Archives, Windsor Castle

Prince Albert, memorandum, 28 February 1853

Queen Victoria, Journals, 1834, 1853

Society of Friends' Library, Dublin
Quaker Pedigree Sheets

Society of Friends' Library, London
Registry of Births

St Alban's Parish, Liscard, Merseyside
Death Register, 26 May 1846

Trinity College, Dublin, Manuscript Library
Donoughmore Papers
Le Fanu, Diaries 1846–67
Midland Great Western Railway, Requisition letter, 'Liffey branch and Longford deviation', 1845

B. Company/institution minute, committee and letter books
Allied Irish Bank Archives
Royal Bank of Ireland, Directors' Minutes, vol.10, 11 1843, 1853–4, 1858–69
_____, Charles Copeland private letter book, 1868

Bank of Ireland Headquarters, Dublin
Bank of Ireland, Court of Directors' Minutes, vol.10–22, 1830–70,

Belfast Port Archives
Belfast Harbour Commissioners, General Board Minutes 1839–48
_____, Committee Minutes 1830–50

Church of Ireland Representative Body Library, Dublin
Baptism, marriage and burial records, Carlow parish, 1744–1835; Tullow parish 1696–1825

CIÉ Archives, Heuston Station
Barrow Navigation Company, Board Minutes
Dublin & Drogheda Railway, Board Minutes, vols. 1–6, 1835–53
_____, Executive Committee Minutes, vol.1, 1846–7
_____, Works Committee Minutes, 1844–46
Dublin & Kingstown Railway, Board Minutes, 1832–45
_____, Land Committee Minutes, 1833–45
_____, Letter Books 1–5, 1833–35
Dublin & Wicklow Railway (later Dublin, Wicklow & Wexford Railway), Board Minutes,
      vols I–VII, 1845–67
Great Southern & Western Railway, General Board Minutes, vols 1–6, 1843–54
_____, Finance Committee Minutes, 1845–8
Midland Great Western Railway, Board Minutes, vols 1–3, 1844–60
Waterford & Limerick Railway, Board Minutes, vol. 1, 1845–52

Dublin City Archives, City Hall
Dublin Municipal Council Minutes, 1853–67, C2/A1/17, 18, 21–3

Fingal County Archives, Dublin

Dublin and Malahide Turnpike Trust, Board Minutes, 1826–51

Dublin to Carlow Turnpike Trust, Board Minutes, 1829–55

Dunleer Turnpike Trust, Board Minutes, 1820–52

Glasnevin Cemetery

Dublin Cemeteries Committee, Minutes Book 9, March 1867

_____, Rotation Committee, Minutes Book, vol.10, 1867

Institution of Civil Engineers, London

Manchester and Leeds Railway, incomplete contract, undated

Liverpool Record Office

Liverpool Dock Committee Minutes 1811–21

National Archives, Dublin

Ballast Board (Corporation for Preserving and Improving the Port of Dublin), Minute Books 1–20 to 1–24, 1850–61

_____, Letter Books, 1859–61, DBPB 2–1

Chief Secretary's Office Registered Papers, Lord Gosford to William Dargan, private index 2/102/30

_____, Dargan to the Lord Lieutenant, 6 February 1854, CSORP 1854/12992

Dublin Chamber of Commerce, Minutes of Council Proceedings, vols 6, 7, 1845–74, 1064/3/5–1064/3/9

_____, Minutes of Proceedings of General Assemblies, 1820–75, 1064/2/1

Public Works, Commissioners of, Engineering Minute Books, 1841–5, III/1/3/1–III/1/3/5

_____, Roads and bridges, Minute Books, 1825–27, OPW/I/7/1–I/7/1/6

_____, Inland navigation, Journals of Directors General, 1811–31, OPW/II/5/2/3–II/5/2/5

_____, Navigation Letter Books, 1849, OPW/I/5/2/5

Ulster Canal, OPW Register, 14276/64

National Archives, London

Birmingham and Liverpool Junction Canal, Board Minutes, 1826–40: Rail 1075/83

Lancashire and Yorkshire Railway, Minutes of Proprietors and Directors, 1847–50, Rail 343/17–18

_____, Land and Construction Committee Minutes, 1846–51, Rail 343/523

_____, General Purposes Committee, 1846–7, Rail 343/488

Liverpool and Bury Railway, Board Minutes, 1845–6, Rail 368/2

_____, New Schemes Committee, 1845/4, Rail 368/4

_____, Committee of Management Minutes, 1845–46, Rail 368/3

_____, Finance Committee Minutes, Rail 368/5, 1845–46

Manchester and Leeds Railway, Land and Construction Committee Minutes, 1846–48, Rail 343/523, Public Record Office, London

National Gallery of Ireland Archives

National Gallery of Ireland, Minute Books I, II, 1854–80

_____, Letter Books I, II, 1854–76

_____, Donation of Trust, 1859

Public Record Office, Northern Ireland

Ballymena, Ballymoney, Coleraine and Portrush Junction Railway, Board Minutes, 1853–61, UTA2/A

_____, Contract plans, 1858, UTA26/A/2

Banbridge Junction Railway, Board and Finance Committee Minutes, 1852–61, UTA18/A/1

_____, Board Business Book, 1854–59, UTA18/C/1

_____, Shareholders' Minutes, 1859–77, UTA18/B/1

Bann Reservoir Company, General Minutes, 1836–41, D1632/1/1

Ballymena, Ballymoney, Coleraine and Portrush Junction Railway, Board Minutes, 1853–61, UTA2/A

Belfast & Ballymena Railway, Board Minutes, 1857–61, UTA28/A/1

Belfast & County Down Railway, Board of Directors and Committee Minutes, 1845–56 UTA20/A/1; UTA20/A/2

_____, Half-year reports, 1847–78, UTA20/AE/1

_____, Shareholders' Minutes, 1846–66, UTA20/AD/1

_____, Journal 1845–52, UTA20/EK/1

Belfast Spring Water Commissioners, Board Minutes, 1807–55, Wat 1/1A/5

Belfast Water Commissioners, Board Minutes 1840–46, Wat 1/2AD/1–1/2AD/2

Lagan Navigation, Letter Books, 1830–50, COM1/2/7–1/2/9B

_____, Financial Records, 1809–39, COM1/3/2/1

_____, Day Book, 1839–51, COM1/3/2/2

Londonderry & Coleraine Railway, Board Minutes, 1845–55, UTA1/A/1

Londonderry & Enniskillen Railway, Board Minutes, 1844–54, UTA13/A/1

_____, Shareholders' Minutes, 1853–64, UTA13/B/1

Newry & Armagh Railway, Board Minutes, 1861–7, UTA16/A/1

Newry Navigation, Board Minutes, 1839–65, D.934/20–21, 79

_____, Letter Books, 1843–58, D.934/2–934/5

_____, Journal, 1831–96, D.934/5/1

_____, Shareholders Minutes, 1832–1937, D.934/9/1

Newry Warrenpoint & Rostrevor Railway, Board Minutes, 1845–61, UTA15/A/1

Portadown, Dungannon & Omagh Junction Railway, Rough Minutes, 1859–64, UTA17/B/1

_____, Correspondence, plans and sections, 1856–1919, Com.9/155/224; D.847

_____, Plans and works, 1856–64, T.877/819–827

Ulster Canal, Letter Books, 1833–35, COM 1/2/8

Royal Dublin Society Archives

Minutes of Council, 1851–7

Letter Book I, 1853–4

Royal St George Yacht Club Archives, Dun Laoghaire

Committee Minutes, 1853

Trinity College, Dublin, Manuscript Library

Board Minutes, 1830–41

Waterford & Limerick Railway, Chairman's Reports, 1858, Donoughmore Papers, H/18/21–12

2. PARLIAMENTARY AND OFFICIAL PAPERS

A. House of Commons printed papers

Accidents to labourers employed on construction of railways or public works 1846–7, abstract returns from coroners of Ireland: HC 1847 (355) xxxvii.273

Anglesea road, First Report of the Select Committee on the: 1819 (217) v.121

_____, Second Report of the Select Committee on the: 1819 (217) v.121

Anglesea road and Menai bridge, Report of progress on the: 1821 (574 & 575) x.229

Birmingham & Liverpool Junction Canal, Report of the SC: 1826 (309) IV.631

Combinations of workmen, First and second Reports from SC: 1837–8 (488) VIII; 1837–8 (646) VIII

Dublin & Kingstown Railway, Report to the SC: HC 1833 (291) xxxv.517

Dublin and Kingstown Ship Canal, Report of the Select Committee on the: HC 1833 (591) xvi.451

Galway railway, Return of the total cost: 1854 (15) XIX.425

Great Southern & Western Railway Commissioners for loans to public works on the, report of James Walker: 1847 (459) LXIII.289

Holyhead and Liverpool roads, Report to the Committee to inquire into sums expended: HC 1830 (224) CCLXXIII.131

Holyhead road, Journals of the House of Commons, 9 February 1825; vol.86, 1&2WmIV, 24 June 1831

House of Commons Journals, 1820–37

Land in Ireland, (Devon Commission), Commissioners of inquiry into the state of law and practice in respect of the occupation of :HC 1845 (606) xix

London to Holyhead Road, First Report from the SC on the: 1819 (78) v.115

_____, Second Report: 1819 (217) vi.12

_____, Third Report: 1819 (256) v.135

_____, Fifth Report: 1822 (417) vi.115

London to Holyhead road, First Report of the Commissioners to further improve the, 6 May 1824: 1824 (xxi)

Payment of wages in goods, Report of SC to inquire into the law which prohibits: 1847 (471) IX.125

Post Office communication with Ireland, Report of SC: HC 1842 (373) IX.343

Public Works in Ireland, Commissioners of, First and second reports of SC on advances made by: HC 1835 (575) xx

_____, Correspondence between James Pim and the Commissioners,: HC 1833 (291) xxxv.517

Railway audits, Third report of SC: 1849 (21.13) X, vol.4

Railway bills in Ireland, Report from SC: 1845, vol. X

Railway Commissioners appointed to consider a general system of railways for Ireland, First Report, evidence of John Macneill, 20 May 1837: HC 1837 (75) xxxiii

Railway Commissioners appointed to consider a general system of railways for Ireland, Second Report of: HC 1838 (145) xxxv

Railway Labourers, Report of the SC: HC 1846 (530) xiii.411

Railway subscription contracts deposited in the Private Bills Office of the Commons: 1837 (95) XLVIII.1

Railways and canals amalgamation, First Report of the SC: HC 1846 (200) xiii.85

Railways in Ireland, First and Second Reports of Commissioners appointed to inspect the accounts and examine the works of, minutes of evidence, William Dargan, 14 June 1865, Q.5453–5724: 1867 (3844–II) XXXVIII Pt 2

_____, letter from Dargan, 6 November 1865, Appendix AY

Return of amount expended in construction and working of all railways in Great Britain and Ireland, 1841, 1844, 1847: 1847 (278) LXIII. 63

Return of number of persons employed on all railways under construction on 1 May 1847: 1847 (579) LXIII.101

Shrewsbury and Bangor Ferry Road, First annual Report of the Commissioners: 1820 (127) vi.351
_____, Third report: 1822 (126) vi.361
Shrewsbury and Holyhead road, Fourth annual report of the Commissioners for: 1824 (157) ix.281
Shareholders in railways, list of persons, with index of names: 1837 (40) IX.1
_____, list of persons subscribing £2,000 or more in Private Bills Office: 1845 (317) XL.1
_____, list of person subscribing under £2,000 in Private Bills Office: 1845 (625) XL.153
_____, alphabetical list of persons subscribing £2,000 in Private Bills Office: 1846 (473) XXXVIII, 1
_____, list of all persons with shares in Irish railways on 1 February 1847: 1847 (54) XV.483
Telford, Thomas, First report to Holyhead Road Commissioners, 5 June 1820: HC 1820 (126.279) vi.287
Turnpike roads in Ireland, Report from the SC: 1832 (xvii) 645
Wexford, Carlow & Dublin Junction Railway, House of Commons SC, printed evidence, June 1845

B. House of Lords printed papers

Audit of railway accounts, third Report of Lords SC: 1849 (21.13) X
Bann Reservoir Act and Plans: 1836 6&7 Wm 95
Dublin & Drogheda Railway, Report of Lords Committee on the Bill, 1836: 1836 (247) XII.81
_____, Minutes of evidence, Lords Committee on the Bill for, 1836 (241) XXXIII.445
Management of railroads, Report of Lords SC: 1846 (489) IX. 217
Waterford, Wexford, Wicklow & Dublin Railway, Report of Lords SC: 1851 (206) XIX.481; 1851 (242)
        XIX. 483

C. Other official papers

Atmospheric Railway, Report on, 15 November 1843, Public Record Office, London: MT6/1/316; see also
        1842 (368) XLI.381
Census of Ireland 1841: 1843 (504) XXIV.274–5
Public Works in Ireland, Annual Reports of Commissioners: 1833 (75) xvii
_____, First,
_____, Second
_____, Third
_____, Fourth
_____, Eighth
_____, Ninth
_____, Tenth

D. Statutes and bills

Birmingham & Liverpool Junction Canal Act: 7 Geo IV, cap.95, 26 May 1826
Employment of the labouring poor for a limited period in distressed districts of Ireland, Bill to facilitate:
        1846 (649) (672) III.133.143
Employment of the people by the encouragement of railways in Ireland, bill to stimulate the prompt and
        profitable: HC 1847 (41) III.485 mf.51.21
Great Southern & Western Railway, Act, 7 & 8 Vic c.c; 8 & 9 Vic c.cxxiv
Limerick and Waterford Railway, Act, 7 Geo IV, CXXXIX, 31 May 1826
Midland Great Western Railway, Act authorising advance of money out of the consolidated fund to, 28
        July 1849: 12 & 13 Vic c. 62; 17 & 18 Vic c. 124
_____, Act, July 1854, 8 & 9 Vic c.cxix

National Gallery of Ireland act: 17–18 Vic. C.99;

_____, Act to provide for the establishment of a National Gallery of paintings: HC 1854–5 (117) IV.549; 1865 (203) III.113; 1864 (336) XXXIV.25

Payment of wages in goods in Ireland, Bill to prohibit: 1850 (76) IV.567

Railways in Ireland, bill to authorise the advance of money out of the consolidated fund for loans towards defraying the expense of making: HC 1847 (343) III.503 mf.51.21

Relief of distress, Bill to render valid certain proceedings for the relief of distress in Ireland by employment of the labouring poor: 1847 (9) II.129

Ulster Railway, Act, 6&7 Wm IV C. xxxiii, 19 May 1836

_____, Act: 18 Vic cap.CXXI, 15 June 1855

3. CONTEMPORARY NEWSPAPERS AND PERIODICALS

Advocate, The

Albion, The

Aris's Birmingham Gazette

Art Journal

Belfast News Letter

Bray Gazette

Carlow Sentinel

Cork Constitution

Cork Examiner

Croydon Times

Crystal Palace District Advertiser

Daily Express

Daily Post

Dublin, Builder, The

Dublin Evening Mail

Dublin Evening Post

Edinburgh Evening Post

Engineer, The

Evening Packet

Exhibition Expositor and Examiner

Finn's Leinster Journal

Freeman's Journal

Galway Vindicator

Gentleman's Magazine

Globe, The

Illustrated London News

Illustrated Magazine of Art

Imperial Magazine

Institution of Civil Engineers, Proceedings of

Institution of Civil Engineers of Ireland, Transactions

Irish Builder, The

Irish Farmers' Gazette

Irish Railway Gazette

Irish Railway Telegraph

Irish Times, The
Limerick and Clare Examiner
Limerick Chronicle
Limerick Recorder
Liverpool Chronicle
Liverpool Mail
Liverpool Mercury
Liverpool Times
Locomotive, The
Londonderry Sentinel
Morning Advertiser
Morning Chronicle
Morning Herald
Newry Examiner
Newry Telegraph
Northern Whig
Railway Times
Royal Gazette
Saunders News-Letter
Times, The
Tipperary Vindicator
Tralee Chronicle
Ulster Gazette
Ulster Observer
Weekly Freeman

4. CONTEMPORARY PUBLISHED SOURCES

Atlas to the Life of Thomas Telford, Payne & Foss, London, 1838

Bailey, Lt C., 'Parishes of Co. Tyrone II', Ordnance Survey Memoirs of Ireland, 1835, Angelique Day and
    Patrick McWilliams (eds), Institute of Irish Studies, Belfast with Royal Irish Academy, Dublin,
    1992, p.3

Barrington, Sir Jonah, Personal Sketches of his own Time, vols I–III, George Routledge, London, 1869

Barrington, Sir Matthew, letter on Farmers' Estate Society to Sir Robert Peel, 28 October 1844

Barry, Frederick, Dublin Metropolitan Railway, 1864

Bateman, John, 'Description of the Bann reservoirs of Co. Down', Minutes of the Proc. of the Institution
    of Civil Engineers, vol.VII, sess.1848, pp.251–89

Battersby, W.J., Glories of the Great Irish Exhibition, Battersby's Repository, n.p.,1853

Bennett, George RE, 'Parishes of Co. Down III', Ordnance Survey Memoirs of Ireland, 1833–8, Angelique
    Day and Patrick McWilliams (eds), Institute of Irish Studies, Belfast with Royal Irish Academy,
    Dublin, 1992, pp.24–5

Bentinck, George, 'Railways in Ireland', House of Commons speech, February 1847

Bergin, Thomas, 'Observations on Lt Col. Sir Frederick Smith's and Prof. Barlow's report on the
    Atmospheric Railway', 1843

Bermingham, Thomas, Statistical evidence in favour of state railways in Ireland, Dublin, 1841

Berry, Henry, A History of the Royal Dublin Society, Longman Green, London, 1915

Boase, George Clement, Dictionary of National Biography, Smith Elder, London, 1909

Brief sketch of a new line of communication between Dublin and London, 1836

Burgoyne, Sir John, Fox, Life and Letters, Richard Bentley, vols I&II, London, 1873

Carbery, John, Observations on the grand jury system of Ireland, James Ridgeway, London, 1831

Carlow to Wexford Railway, Report of the SC, privately printed evidence, 1845, Halliday Pamphlets,
      Royal Irish Academy

Carlyle, Thomas, Reminiscences of my Irish Journey in 1849, Sampson Law, London, 1882

Casebourne, Thomas, 'Description of a portion of the works of the Ulster Canal', Minutes of the
      Proceedings of the Institution of Civil Engineers, vol.2, 1842

C.E., A, Personal Recollections of English Engineers, Hodder & Stoughton, London, 1868, Public Record
      Office, London: ZLIB 1/11; see also F.R. Conder, 1868.

Chambers' Repository and Miscellany, W.&R. Chamber, London, 1855

Cloncurry, Valentine Lord, Life and Times, James McGlashin, Dublin, 1849

Conder, F.R., The Men who built the Railways, (published in 1868 as Personal Recollections of English
      Engineers), David & Charles, Newton Abbot, 1983 edition

County Londonderry, Ordnance Survey Memoirs of Ireland, VII, 1834–5, facsimile reprint, Angelique
      Day, Patrick McWilliams, Noirín Dobson (eds), Institute of Irish Studies, Belfast in association
      with Royal Irish Academy, Dublin, 1994

Cotton, Charles P., Manual of Railway Engineering in Ireland, Edward Ponsonby, Dublin, 1861

Cotton, Edward J., Guide to the Belfast & Northern Counties Railway, B&NCR, Belfast, 1896

Crory, W.G., Treatise on the Industrial Resources of Ireland, Dublin, McGlashan & Gill, 1860

Cusack, M.F., The Liberator: His Life and Times, Longmans, London, 1872

D'Alton, John, History of Drogheda with a Memoir of the Dublin & Drogheda Railway, Dublin, 1844
      _____, A Memoir of the Great Southern & Western Railway, Alex Thom, Dublin, 1846

Dawson, William, Plan for a Complete Harbour at Howth Town, Dublin, 1805

Day, James, Practical Treatise on the Construction and Formation of Railways, John Weale,
      London, 1839

Devey, Joseph, Life of Joseph Locke, Richard Bentley, London, 1862

Disraeli, Benjamin, Lord George Bentinck, Routledge, London, 1858

Dublin Almanack 1835, 1836, Pettigrew & Oulton, Dublin

Dublin Chamber of Commerce Annual Reports, 1851–66

Dublin Directory 1831

Dublin and Cashel Railway, statement on behalf of the Grand Canal Company, 1844

'Dublin and Chapelizod Distilling Co.', Wine Trade Review, vol. XIII, October 1873

Dublin & Drogheda Railway, Minutes of evidence taken before the HC Committee on the, privately
      printed by J.L. Cox & Sons, 75 Great Queen Street, Lincoln Inns Fields, London, 1836, Halliday
      Pamphlet no.1660, Royal Irish Academy
      _____, Report of William Cubitt to Provisional Committee, 9 January 1836
      _____, Half-year reports 1839ff

Dublin & Kingstown Railway, 10th Annual Report, March 1842

Dublin terminus of the Cashel or Great Southern and Western Railway, Remarks on, 1845

Dundalk & Enniskillen Railway, half-year report, 29 August 1850

Dundrum, Foxrock and Kingstown Junction Railway Bill, April 1865, privately printed evidence,
      Halliday Pamphlets, Royal Irish Academy

Exhibition of Art–Industry in Dublin, Virtue & Co., London, 1853

European and American Steam Packet Co., Prospectus, 1851

'Fairbairn, Sir William, Memoir', Mins of Proceedings of Institution of Civil Engineers, vol. XXXIX,
      1874–75, Part 1, pp.251–64

Fleming, J. & J.H., The Post–Chaise Companion, Dublin, 1803

Flynn, Henry, A glance at the question of a ship canal...connecting...Kingstown with...Dublin, 1834

Foster, Thomas Campbell, Letters on the Condition of Ireland from The Times, Chapman and Hall, London, 1846

Fullerton, A., Parliamentary Gazetteer of Ireland, Dublin and London, 1846

Gashin, J., Vice-Regal Speeches and Addresses of the Earl of Carlisle, McGlashin & Gill, Dublin, 1866

Gibson, C.B., History of Cork, vol.2, Cork, 1861

Graving Docks, Report on the importance of, Dublin Chamber of Commerce, 1849

Great Leinster and Munster Railway, half-year report, 1 August 1838

Great Southern & Western Railway, Irish Railway Charts: Dublin–Carlow, James McGlashan, Dublin, n.d.

Grierson, Thomas, 'Enlargement of Westland Row terminus with a sketch of the early history of the D&KR', Transactions of the Institution of Civil Engineers of Ireland, vol.XXVIII, 1887

Guide to Belfast and Adjoining Counties, Marcus Ward, Belfast, 1874

Guinness, Arthur, Is Agitation Useful?, Dublin, 1848

Hall, Mr & Mrs Samuel, Hall's Tour of Ireland 1840, Virtue, London, 1841, Sphere Books, London, edition of 1984

Hardy, P. Dixon, 'Thirteen Views of the Dublin and Kingstown Railway', Dublin Penny Journal, 1834, Carraig Books facsimile reprint, 1981

Head, Francis, A Fortnight in Ireland, 1852

Hemans, George, Report to the directors of the MGWR on the port of Galway as a packet station., 30 October 1850

_____, 'Account of the construction of the MGWR in Ireland', Proc. of the Institution of Civil Engineers of Ireland, vol.IV, part 1, 1849–50, 1851

Helps, Arthur, Life and Labours of Mr Brassey, Bell & Daldy, London, 1872

Henderson's Belfast Directory 1846–7

Hibernian Bank, Proprietors' Annual Report, 1848

Illustrated Magazine of Art, vol.1, John Cassell, London, 1853

Inglis, Henry, A Journey through Ireland, Whitaker, London, 1834

Irish Catholic Directory 1867

Irish Railway Reform Group Committee, Proceedings, Dublin, 1866

Irish Railways: Government Loans, Memorial of railway companies to the Treasury, Limerick, April 1866

Irish Tourist's Illustrated Handbook, James McGlashan, Dublin, 1852

Irwin, George O'Malley, Handbook to the County of Wicklow, Newman & Co., London, 1844

Jones, J.E., Dublin & Drogheda Railway Plates, 1844

Jones, T.D., Record of the Great Industrial Exhibition, 2nd ed., John Falconer, Dublin, 1854

Joyce, W. St John Weston, The Neighbourhood of Dublin, 1912, Gill and Macmillan edition, Dublin, 1976

Kane, Sir Robert, Industrial Resources of Ireland, Dublin, 1844

Kelly's Penge, Anerley and Beckenham Directory, 1888–89, London

Kennedy, Maj. John P., Report to the proprietors and shareholders of the W&LR, Calcutta, 1849

Kingstown canal, Report of a committee of gentlemen, merchants and traders held in Dublin on 11 August 1833 to promote ... a ship canal from Kingstown harbour to Dublin, 1833

Lacy, Thomas, Home Sketches on both sides of the Channel, Hamilton Adams, London, 1852

Laws of excavation and embankment upon railways, a practical inquiry, Saunders & Ottley, London, 1840

Le Fanu, W.R, Seventy Years of Irish Life, Edward Arnold, London, 3rd edition, 1894

Lewis, Samuel, A Topographical Dictionary of Ireland, 2 vols, London 1837, facsimile edition, Kennikat Press, New York and London, 1970

Londonderry & Coleraine Railway, privately printed summary of evidence before House of Commons Select Committee, 1845

Lowry, Mary, The Story of Belfast, Headley, London, 1912

MacCartan, H.A., The Glamour of Belfast, Talbot Press, Dublin and T. Fisher Unwin, London, 1921

Macneill, John, Report on a proposed Line of Railway from Dublin to Cashel, 1844

_____, Report on the present state of the Grand Canal, 1844

_____,Report on the state of and improvements to the Grand Canal Co's docks at Ringsend, 1846

Maguire, John F., The Industrial Movement in Ireland as illustrated by the National Exhibition of 1852, Cork, 1852

Mallet, Robert, Report on the railway constructed from Kingstown to Dalkey upon the atmospheric principles, 1844

Marmion, Anthony, Ancient and Modern History of the Maritime Ports of Ireland, W.H. Cox, London, 4th ed., 1860

Martin's Belfast Directory 1841–2

Marx, Karl, Das Kapital, Chapter 15, section 9, 1867

McCarthy, Justin, Sir Robert Peel, Sampson Law, London, 1891

Men of the Time: Biographical Sketches of Eminent Living Characters, London, 1856

MGWR Tourist Guide, Dublin, 1850

Midland Great Western Railway, half-year reports, September 1846 to March 1855

Mines of Wicklow, C.H. Law, London, 1856

Mitchel, John, Jail Journal, M.H. Gill, Dublin, 1913

Moorsom, C.R., Observations to Show the Advantages of Railways, 20 June 1840

_____, Letter to James Perry on railways in Ireland, 1840

Muggeridge, R.M., Notes on the Irish Difficulty, Dublin, 1849

Mullingar, Athlone, Longford Railway, Observations of the Provisional Directors, 1845

Mullins, Bernard, Thoughts on Inland Navigation, Dublin, 1832

_____, Origin and Reclamation of Peat Bogs, Samuel Oldham, Dublin, 1846

Mullins, M.B., 'Historical sketch of Irish engineering', Transactions of the Institution of Civil Engineers of Ireland, vol.VI, 1859–61, pp.1–186

Murland, James, 'Observations on Irish railway statistics', Journal of Dublin Statistical Society, 1849

Newry & Armagh Railway, Half-year reports, June, December, 1861; June 1862

Newry & Greenore Railway, House of Lords SC, 1846, privately printed

Nimmo, Alexander, Description of the Limerick and Waterford Railway, Institution of Civil Engineers, London, 1826

_____, Report to the Directors of the Great Central Irish Railway, 12 October 1836

O'Brien, R.Barry, O'Brien, Thomas Drummond: Life and Letters, Kegan Paul Trench, London, 1889

Observations of the local advantages and security of Holyhead, 1836

O'Connell, Morgan John, Charles Bianconi 1786–1875, Chapman & Hall, London, 1878

Official Catalogue to 1851 Exhibition, 2nd ed., Spicers, London, 1851

Official Catalogue to the Great Industrial Exhibition of 1853, 4th ed., John Falconer, Dublin, 1853

Official Catalogue to 1862 International Exhibition, Truscott, London, 1862

O'Hanlon, J. and E. O'Leary, History of the Queen's County, M. Lalor, 1916

The Ouzel Galley Rules and Regulations, Dublin, 1859

Owen, D.J., History of Belfast, W. & G. Baird, Belfast and London, 1921

Parnell, Sir Henry, A Treatise on Roads, London, 1833

Paxton, Joseph, What is to become of the Crystal Palace?, Bradbury & Evans, London, 1851

Peel, Sir Robert, Speeches of, George Routledge, London, 1853

Peto, Sir Henry, Sir Morton Peto: A Memorial Sketch, 1893

Phillips, George, Ulster Railway Handbook, Belfast, 1848

Phillips, Samuel, Crystal Palace: A Guide to the Palace and the Park, Bradbury & Evans, London, 1854

Pim, James, Letter to Frederick Shaw MP on Irish railways, London, 1839

_____, Letter to Earl Ripon, Board of Trade President, on Atmospheric Railway, 1841

_____, Letter to George Carr, Secretary, GS&WR, 1846

Porter, John Grey, Irish Railways: A Few Observations, 1847

Post Office Directory 1832, 1838

Powell, G.R., Official Handbook to Bray, Kingstown and the Coast, McGlashan & Gill, Dublin, 1860

Practical inquiry into the laws of excavation and embankment upon railways, Saunders & Ottley, London, 1840

Principal railways executed, in progress and projected, a few general observations, Longman, Liverpool, 1838

Provis, W.A., History and descriptive account of the suspension bridge constructed over the Menai strait, London, 1828

Punch, vol.XXV, 2 July 1853, pp.1–2

Rennie, Sir John, Autobiography, E&F.N. Spon, London, 1875

Rickman, John (ed.), Life of Thomas Telford, Hansard, London, 1838

Robinson, Col. Daniel, Report of the Irish Waste Land Improvement Society, 1839

Roney, Sir Cusack, How to spend a month in Ireland, 1861

Royal Agricultural Improvement Society, Report, 1850

Royal Dublin Society, Proceedings of Council, 1851–5

Royal Society for the Promotion and Improvement of the Growth of Flax in Ireland, annual reports, 1851, 1852

Salmond, Thomas, 'River Lagan and the harbour of Belfast', Minutes of the Proceedings of the Institution of Civil Engineers, vol.LV, 1878–9, pp.22–35

Samuda, Jacob, 'The atmospheric railway', Proceedings of the Institution of Civil Engineers, vol.III, 1844, pp.256–83

Slator's National Commercial Directory of Ireland, 1846

Shannon Improvement works, Letter to the Earl of Clarendon on the completion of, 1849

Smiles, Samuel, Lives of the Engineers: Metcalfe and Telford, John Murray, London, 1874

Smith, Charles, Ancient and Present State of the City and County of Cork, Guy & Co., Cork, 1893

Smith, George Lewis, Observations on the Report of the Irish Railway Commissioners, 1839

Smyth, John, 'Historical sketch of work on the Bann reservoir', Transactions of the Institution of Civil Engineers of Ireland, vol.IX

Sproule, John, 'Memoir of William Dargan', Catalogue to the Industrial Exhibition, James McGlashan, Dublin, 1853

_____, The Irish Industrial Exhibition of 1853, James MacGlashan, Dublin, 1854

Tait, A.F., Views on the Manchester and Leeds Railway, 1845, Bradshaw and Blacklock facsimile edition 1971

Tatlow, Joseph, Fifty Years of Railway Life, London, 1920

Taylor, George and Andrew Skinner, Maps of the Roads of Ireland, 1778, 1969 reprint, Irish University Press, Shannon

Telford, Thomas, General Rules for Repairing Roads, J. Taylor, London, 1827

Tennison, C.M., 'The old Dublin bankers', Journal Cork Historical & Archaeological Society, 1894, vol. III, pp.102–6, 143–6, 256–60

Thackeray, William, The Irish Sketch Book, 1843, 1990 edition, Gill and Macmillan, Dublin

Thom's Directory, Alex Thom, Dublin, 1844–71

Thompson, H.S., Ireland in 1839 and 1869, Dorrell & Son, London, 1870

Travels and Sketches of Scenery, from Chamber's Repository and Miscellany, W&R Chambers, London, 1855

Trevelyan, Charles, The Irish Crisis: Measures for the Relief of Distress caused by the Great Irish Famine, Macmillan, London, 1880

Tuck, Henry, Tuck's Railway Shareholders' Manual, Effingham Wilson, London, 1847

University Magazine, 'A visit to Jones' studio', February 1853, vol.XLI, no.CCXLII, pp.140–1

Vignoles, Charles, 'Railways in Ireland', Dublin University Magazine, vol.xix, no.109, January 1842

Vignoles, Olinthus, Life of Charles B. Vignoles, London, 1889

Wallis Healy, F.C., 'William Dargan: A Memoir', Irish Manufacturers' Journal, 1882

Waterford, Wexford, Wicklow & Dublin Railway, Prospectus, 1845, PRO London: Rail 1075/83

Whishaw, Francis, Railways of Great Britain and Ireland, 1842, facsimile reprint, David & Charles, Newton Abbot, 1969

White, George Preston, Letter to Lord John Russell on promoting Railways in Ireland, 1849

Williams, C.W., Observations on the Inland Navigation of Ireland, Vacker, London, 1833

Williams, J.B., 'Parishes of Co. Londonderry VII', Ordnance Survey Memoirs of Ireland, 1835, Angelique Day and Patrick McWilliams (eds), Institute of Irish Studies, Belfast with Royal Irish Academy, Dublin, 1992

Working classes, an appeal to the Lord Lieutenant on behalf of, n.d.

Wrensfordsby, Joseph, Reasons for the government aiding construction of railroads in Ireland, Dublin, 1867

Young, Arthur, A Tour of Ireland, 1780, vol. II

5. SECONDARY PRINTED SOURCES

Aimone, Linda and Carlo Olmo, Les Expositions universelles 1851–1900, Belin, Paris, 1993

Bagwell, Philip, The Railwaymen: The History of the NUR, George Allen & Unwin, London, 1963

Bairstow, Martin, The Manchester and Leeds Railway, Halifax, 1987

Barker, T.C. and C.I. Savage, Economic History of Transport in Britain, Hutchinson University Library, London, 1974

Barrow, G.L., The Emergence of the Irish Banking System 1820–45, Gill & Macmillan, Dublin, 1975

Barry, Michael, Across Deep Waters, Frankfort Press, Dublin, 1985

Bath, Ian, 'The Ulster Canal', Waterways World, February 1993, pp.1–4

Beckett, J.C. and R.E. Glasscock (eds), Belfast: Origin and Growth of an Industrial City, BBC, London, 1967

Bence-Jones, Mark, A Guide to Irish Country Houses, Constable, London, 1988

Biddle, Gordon and O.S. Nock, Railway Heritage of Britain, Michael Joseph, London, 1983

Bielenberg, Andrew, Cork's Industrial Revolution 1780–1880, Cork University Press, Cork, 1991

Binnie, G.M., Early Victorian Water Engineers, Thomas Telford, London, 1981

Black, Eileen, The People's Park: The Queen's Island, Linen Hall Library, Belfast, 1988

Black, R.D.C., Economic Thought and the Irish Question, Cambridge University Press, London, 1960

Boyd, Andrew, The Rise of the Irish Trade Unions, Anvil Press, Tralee, 1972

Boyle, John, Irish Labour Movement in the Nineteenth Century, Catholic University of America, Washington DC, 1988

Brett, C.E.B and Lady Dunleath, Banbridge: Historic Buildings in the Towns of Mid-Down, Ulster
    Architectural Heritage Society, 1974, pp.5, 12

Broadbridge, Seymour, Studies in Railway Expansion and the Capital Market in England, Frank Cass,
    London, 1970

Brooke, David, The Railway Navvy, David & Charles, Newton Abbot, 1983

_____, 'The 'lawless navvy": a study of crime associated with railway building', Jnl of Transport
    History, vol.10, no.2, September 1989

Brookefield, H.C., 'Cobh and Passage West', Irish Geography, II, no.4, 1952

_____, 'Ireland and the Atlantic ferry', Irish Geography, III, no.2, 1955, pp.69–72

Brunicardi, Niall, John Anderson: Entrepreneur, Eigse Books, Fermoy, 1987

Channon, Geoffrey, 'A 19th century investment decision: the Midland Railway's London extension',
    Economic History Review, 2nd series, vol.XXV, no.3, 1972, pp.448–70

Clements, R.N., 'Limerick to Sligo', Journal of the Irish Railway Record Society, no.6, January 1950

Cole, D., Irish Industrial and Contractors' Locomotives, Union Publications, London, 1962

Coleman, Terry, The Railway Navvies, Hutchinson, London, 1965

Collins, Tim, 'The Galway Line in context', Galway Archaeological and Historical Society Journal,
    vol.46, 1994, pp.3–42

_____, Transatlantic Triumph and Failure: The Galway Line, Collins Press,
    Cork, 2002

Cotterell, P.L., 'Railway finance and the crisis of 1866: contractors' bills of exchange and the finance
    companies', Journal of Transport History, NS vol.III, 1975–6, no.1, pp.20–40

Cox, R.C. (ed.), Robert Mallet Centenary Seminar Papers, Institution of Engineers of Ireland and Royal
    Irish Academy, Dublin, 1982

_____, Bindon Blood Stoney, Dublin, Institution of Engineers of Ireland, 1990

Craig, Maurice, Dublin 1660–1860, 1952, Allen Figgis, Dublin, facsimile edition, 1980

Creedon, Colm, Cork, Blackrock and Passage Railway, vol. I, Cork, 1992

Cronin, Maura, County Class or Craft?, The Politicisation of the Skilled Artisan in Nineteenth Century
    Cork, Cork University Press, Cork, 1994

Cullen, L.M., Economic History of Ireland since 1660, Batsford, London, 1978

_____, Princes and Pirates: Dublin Chamber of Commerce, Dublin, 1983

Currie, J.R.L., The NCC, vol.1, David & Charles, Newton Abbot, 1973

Curry, Kevin, 'William Dargan and the Worcester Shakespeare service', Irish Arts Review, vol.17, 2001,
    pp.71–9

D'Arcy, Fergus, 'The artisans of Dublin and Daniel O'Connell 1830–47', Irish Historical Studies, vol.
    XVII, no.66, September 1970, pp.221–43

_____, 'Wages of skilled workers in the Dublin building industry 1667–1918', Saothar, no.15,
    1990, pp.21–37

Davies, A.C., 'The first industrial exhibition: Cork', Irish Economic & Social History Jnl, vol.II, 1975,
    pp.46–59

_____, 'Ireland's Crystal Palace, 1853' in J.M. Goldstrom and L.A. Clarkson (eds), Irish
    Population, Economy and Society, Clarendon Press, Oxford, 1981, pp.249–70

Davies, Mary, That Favourite Resort: The Story of Bray, Wordwell, Bray, 2007

Davis, John, The Great Exhibition, Sutton Publishing, Stroud, 1999

de Courcy, Catherine, The Foundation of the National Gallery of Ireland, National Gallery of Ireland,
    Dublin, 1985

de Varebeke OSB, Dom Herbert Janssens, 'Barringtons of Limerick', Old Limerick Journal, no.24,
    Winter 1988, pp.6–18

Delany, Ruth, Grand Canal of Ireland, David & Charles, Newton Abbot, 1973

_____, A Celebration of Two Hundred and Fifty Years of Ireland's Inland Waterways, Appletree Press, Belfast, 1986

Donnelly, James, 'The Irish agricultural depression of 1859–64', Irish Economic & Social History Journal, vol.III, 1976

Edwards, Lewis, Inland Waterways of Great Britain and Ireland, Laurie None and Wilson, London, 1962

Ellis, Peter Beresford, A History of the Irish Working Class, Victor Gollancz, London, 1972

Fayle, H. and A.T. Newham, The Waterford and Tramore Railway, David & Charles, Newton Abbot, 1972

Ferneyhough, Frank, History of Railways in Britain, Osprey, Reading, 1975

Floud, Roderick and Donald McCloskey (eds), Economic History of Britain since 1700, Cambridge University Press, Cambridge, 3 vols, 2nd ed., 1994

Flynn, Arthur, History of Bray, Mercier, Cork, 1986

Furlong, N., 'History of land reclamation in Wexford harbour', Old Wexford Society Journal, 1969, pp.53–77

Gamer, William, Carlow Architectural Heritage, An Foras Forbartha, Dublin, 1980

_____, Bray: Architectural Heritage, An Foras Forbartha, Dublin, 1980

Garrett, Arthur, Through Countless Ages, All Saints Church, Raheny, n.d.

Gillespie, Vera et al., The Railway Age in Ireland, Ulster Folk and Transport Museum/Northern Ireland Railways, Belfast, n.d.

Gilligan, H.A., A History of the Port of Dublin, Gill and Macmillan, Dublin, 1988

Gilmour, Brian, 'The parents, siblings and early family life of William Dargan', Carloviana, 2009, 103, 159–61

Glasscock, R.E., 'Growth of the port' in J.C. Beckett and R.E. Glasscock, (eds), Belfast: Origin and Growth of an Industrial City, BBC, London, 1967, chapter 9

Goodbody, Michael, Goodbody Family of Ireland, 1980

Goodbody, Rob, The Metals: From Dalkey to Dún Laoghaire, Dún Laoghaire Rathdown County Council, Dún Laoghaire, 2010

Gould, Jack, Thomas Brassey, Shire Publications, Aylesbury, 1975

Gray, Peter, 'Punch and the Great Famine', History Ireland, vol.I, no.2, summer 1993, pp.26–33

Great Southern Hotels, A Centenary Booklet., 1954

Green, E.R.R., 'The Lagan Valley 1800–50', vol.3, Studies in Irish History, 1949

_____, Industrial Archaeology of Co. Down, Belfast, HMSO, 1983

Griffiths, A.R.G., The Irish Board of Works 1831–78, Garland Publishing, New York and London, 1987

Hadfield, Charles, Atmospheric Railways, David & Charles, Newton Abbot, 1967

_____, Canals of the West Midlands, David & Charles, Newton Abbot, 1969, 2nd edition

_____ and Norman Biddle, Canals of North-west England, David & Charles, Newton Abbot, 1970

_____ and A.W. Skempton, William Jessop Engineer 1745–1814, David & Charles, Newton Abbot, 1979

Hall, F.G., Bank of Ireland 1783–1946, Hodges Figgis, Dublin, 1949

Hannan, Kevin, 'Gifts to the citizen', Old Limerick Journal, no. 24, Winter 1988, pp.55–6

Hawke, G.R., Railways and Economic Growth in England and Wales 1840–70, Clarendon Press, Oxford, 1970

Herring, Ivor, 'Ulster roads on the eve of the railway age', Irish Historical Studies, II, 1940–1, pp.160–88

Historic Buildings in the towns of North Antrim, Ulster Architectural Heritage Society, Belfast, 1974

Hone, Joseph, Queen Victoria in Ireland, n.d.

Hoppen, K. Theodore, Election, politics and Society in Ireland, Clarendon Press, Oxford, 1984

Houston, J.H., 'Belfast and Ballymena Railway', Journal of Irish Railway Record Society, no.5, July 1949

Howden, G.B., 'Reconstruction of the Boyne Viaduct, Drogheda', Transactions of the Institution of Civil Engineers of Ireland, 1934

Hughes, Mervyn, 'Telford, Parnell and the great Irish road', Journal of Transport History, vol.VI, no.4, November 1964

Hyde, Francis, Liverpool and the Mersey: Economic History of the Port 1700–1970, 1971

International Genealogical Index, Church of Jesus Christ of Latter Day Saints, Glasnevin, Dublin

Irish State Coach, for details see www.royal.gov.uk/faq/carriage

Joby, R.S., The Railway Builders, David & Charles, Newton Abbot, 1983

Johnson, Stephen, Johnson's Atlas & Gazetteer of the Railways of Ireland, Midland Publishing, Leicester, 1997

Jones, Mark Bence, A Guide to Irish Country Houses, Constable, London, 1988

Kenny, Colum, 'Monster hotel', Standing on Bray Head, Kestrel Books, Bray, 1995

Kinsella, Shay, 'The Alexanders: Milford, Co. Carlow in the 19th century', Carloviana, 2009, 70–93

Knox, William, Decades of the Ulster Bank, Ulster Bank, Belfast, 1965

Leapman, William, The World for a Shilling, Headline, London, 2001

Lee, J.J., 'Construction costs of Irish railways 1830–53', Business History, vol.IX, 1967

_____, 'Provision of capital for early Irish railways 1830–53', Irish Historical Studies, March 1968

_____, 'Railways in the Irish economy', in L.M. Cullen, Formation of the Irish Economy, Mercier Press, Cork, 1969

_____, 'Railway labour in Ireland 1833–56', Saothar: Labour History Journal, no.5, 1979

_____, 'Merchants and enterprise: the case of early Irish railways 1830–55', in L.M. Cullen et P. Butel (eds), Negoce et Industrie en France et en Irlande aux XVIII et XIX Siècles, Centre National de la Recherche Scientifique, Paris, 1978

Lewin, H.G., Early British Railways 1801–44, Locomotive Publishing, London, 1926

_____, The Railway Mania and its Aftermath 1845–62, London, 1936; David & Charles, Newton Abbot, 1969 facsimile reprint

Long, Bill, Bright Light, White Water, New Island, Dublin, 1993

Longford, Elizabeth, Victoria RI, Weidenfeld & Nicholson, London

Loudan, Jack, In Search of Water: History of Belfast Water Supply, William Mullan, Belfast, 1940

Lyons, F.S.L., C.S. Parnell, Weidenfeld and Nicholson, London, 1971

_____, Ireland since the Famine, Weidenfeld and Nicholson, London, 1971

MacLysaght, Edward, Irish Families, Hodges Figgis, Dublin, 1957

_____, The Surnames of Ireland, Irish University Press, Shannon, 1969

MacSuibhne, Peadar, '98 in Carlow, Carlow, n.d.

_____, Paul Cullen and his Contemporaries, vol.I, Leinster Leader, Naas, 1961

_____, Parish of Killeshin, Graiguecullen, n.d.

Mahon, G.R., 'Irish railways in 1853', Journal of the Irish Railway Record Society, 1953

_____, 'Railways and bogs in Ireland', Journal of Transport History, vol.V, no.2, November 1961

Marshall, John, Lancashire and Yorkshire Railway, vol.1, David & Charles, Newton Abbot, 1969

Maxwell, Constantia, Dublin under the Georges, Gill and Macmillan, Dublin, 1979

McCutcheon, Alan, Railway History in Pictures, vol.2 Ireland, David & Charles, Newton Abbot, 1970

_____, Wheel and Spindle: Aspects of Ireland's Industrial History, Blackstaff Press, Belfast, 1977

McCutcheon, W.A., 'Ulster Railway engineering and architecture', Ulster Journal of Archaeology, vol.27, 1964

_____, Inland Navigation of the North of Ireland, 1965

_____, Canals of the North of Ireland, David & Charles, Dawlish, 1965

_____, 'The Newry Navigation', Geographical Journal, vol.129, part 4, pp.466–80

_____, Industrial Archaeology NI, Fairleigh Dickinson University Press, Cranbury NJ, 1984

McDonald, B., 'Newry Warrenpoint & Rostrevor Railway', Journal of the Irish Railway Record Society no.91, June 1983

McNeill, D.B., Coastal Passenger Steamers and Inland Navigations in the South of Ireland, Transport Handbook 6, Belfast Transport Museum, Belfast, 1965

_____, Irish Passenger Steamship Services, vol.1, 1969, vol.2, 1971, David & Charles, Newton Abbot, 1971

Meenan, James and Desmond Clarke, (eds), The Royal Dublin Society 1731–1981, Gill & Macmillan, Dublin, 1981

Milligan, Edward, Quakers and Railways, Sessions Book Trust, York, 1992

Milne, Kenneth, A History of the Royal Bank of Ireland, Allen Figgis, Dublin, 1964

Mitchell, B.R., 'Coming of the railways and UK economic growth', Journal of Economic History, vol. XXIV, September 1964, no.3, pp.315–36

Mitchell, James, 'Father Peter Daly', Journal of Galway Archaeological and Historical Society, vol.39, 1983–4, p.57

Mulligan, Fergus, One Hundred and Fifty Years of Irish Railways, Appletree Press, Belfast, 1983

_____, See Ireland by Train, Appletree Press, Belfast, 1986

_____, General Index to Dublin Historical Record, Old Dublin Society, Dublin, 2004

_____, The Trinity Year: A Portrait of Trinity College Dublin, Gill & Macmillan, Dublin, 2009

Murray, Kevin, 'William Dargan', Jnl of the Irish Railway Record Society, no.2, 1950–51

_____, Ireland's First Railway, Irish Railway Record Society, Dublin, 1981

_____, 'William Dargan-Industrialist', n.d., unpublished paper for Irish Society for Industrial Archaeology

National Gallery of Ireland: Summary Catalogue, Gill & Macmillan, Dublin, 1981

Newham, A.T., Cork, Blackrock and Passage Railway, Oakwood Press, Headington, 1970

Nevin, Martin and Norman Macmillan, 'William Dargan: Ireland's greatest capitalist and industrial king', unpublished paper, n.d.

Nowlan, Kevin, (ed.), Travel and Transport in Ireland, Gill & Macmillan, 1973

O'Brien, John, 'Agricultural prices and living costs in pre-Famine Cork', Journal of Cork Historical and Archaeological Society, part 1, vol.LXXXII, no.235, January-June 1977, pp.1–10

Ó Cleirigh, Noel, 'The Great Eastern and the Arklow connection', Arklow Historical Society Jnl, 1983

Ó Cleirigh, Nellie, 'Dublin International Exhibition 1865', Dublin Historical Record, vol.XLVII, no.2, Autumn 1994, pp.169–82

O'Dwyer, Frederick, Lost Dublin, Gill & Macmillan, Dublin, 1981

_____, 'The architecture of John Skipton Mulvany', Irish Architectural and Decorative Studies, vol.III, 2000, pp.10–75

O'Dwyer, Michael, 'Building the Waterford & Limerick Railway', Reflections on Munster Railways, Limerick Museum, 1984, pp.15–24

Ó Grada, Cormac, 'Industry and communications', in New History of Ireland, T. W. Moody, F.X. Martin, F.J. Byrne (eds), vol.V, Oxford, Oxford University Press, 1982

_____, Ireland: A New Economic History 1780–1939, Clarendon Press, Oxford, 1994

Ollerenshaw, Philip, Banking in Nineteenth Century Ireland, Manchester University Press, Manchester 1987

O'Meara, J., 'Athenry & Tuam Railway', Journal of the Irish Railway Record Society, no.108, February 1989

O'Neill, Siobhan 'Bray', Irish Independent 19 February 1960, 6

O'Sullivan, John, 'Aspects of the architectural heritage of Bray', in John O'Sullivan (ed.), The Book of Bray, Blackrock Teachers' Centre, Dublin, 1989

O'Sullivan, T.F., Goodly Barrow, Ward River Press, Dublin, 1983

O'Toole, Jimmy, The Carlow Gentry, Carlow, 1993

Ó Tuaithaigh, Geáróid, 'The air of importance.... Aspects of nineteenth century Galway', in Diarmuid Ó Cearbhaill, Galway: Town and Gown 1484–1984, Gill & Macmillan, Dublin, 1984

Patmore, J.A., 'Knaresborough: a navvy gang of 1851', Journal of Transport History, vol.V, 1961–2

Patterson, Edward M., Great Northern Railway of Ireland, Headington, Oakwood Press, 1986

_____, Clogher Valley Railway, David & Charles, Newton Abbot, 1972

_____, Belfast & County Down Railway, David & Charles, Newton Abbot, 1982

Pearce, Rhoda M., Thomas Telford, 1973

Pearson, Peter, Dun Laoghaire, O'Brien Press, Dublin, 1981

Penfold, Alistair, Thomas Telford: Colossus of Roads, Ironbridge Exhibition Catalogue, 1981

Pollins, Harold, 'Railway contractors and the finance of railway development in Britain', Journal of Transport History, vol.3, 1957–8

_____, 'Aspects of railway accounting before 1868' in M. Reed (ed.), Railways in the Victorian Economy, New Abbot, London, 1969

Priestly, J.B., Victoria's Heydey, Heinemann, London, 1951

Reid, Malcolm, 'Speculation', Oxford Companion to British Railway History, Oxford University Press, Oxford, 1997

Rolt, L.T.C., George and Robert Stephenson, Longmans, London, 1960

_____, Thomas Telford, Penguin, Harmondsworth, 1985

_____, Navigable Waterways, Penguin, Harmondsworth, 1985

_____, Isambard Kingdom Brunel, Penguin, Harmondsworth, 1989

Rookes, Nancy, Liverpool's Historic Waterfront, Royal Commission on Historic Monuments, series 7, London, 1984

Root and Branch: AIB Yesterday, Today, Tomorrow, Allied Irish Banks, Dublin, 1979

Russell, Iain F., Sir Robert McAlpine & Sons: The Early Years, Parthenon, (private publication), n.d.

Rynne, Colin, The Industrial Archaeology of Cork City and its Environs, Dúchas-The Heritage Service, Dublin, 1999

Sheaff, Nicholas, Iveagh House, Department of Foreign Affairs, Dublin, 1978

Sheehy, Jeanne, Kingsbridge Station, Gifford & Craven, Gatherum Series no.1, Ballycotton, 1973

_____, 'Sir John Macneill and the railway to Carlow', Carloviana, 1972, pp.42–3

Shepherd, W.E., Midland Great Western Railway of Ireland, Midland Publishing, Leicester, 1994

_____ and Gerry Beesley, Dublin & South Eastern Railway, Midland Publishing, Leicester, 1998

Simpson, Noel, The Belfast Bank 1827–1970, Blackstaff Press, Belfast, 1975

Smith, Hazel, The B&I Line, Gill and Macmillan, Dublin, 1984

Storne, Margaret, 'The man who built the Antrim coast road', Geographical Magazine, January 1971

Sweetman, Robin, 'Development of the port' in J.C. Beckett et al., Belfast: The Making of the City 1800–1914, Appletree Press, Belfast

Sweetman, Robin and Cecil Nimmons, Port of Belfast 1785–1985, Belfast Harbour Commissioners, Belfast, 1985

Tierney OSB, Mark, 'Sir Matthew Barrington', Old Limerick Journal, winter 1988, no.24

_____ and John Cornforth, 'Glenstal Castle', Old Limerick Journal, winter 1988, no.24

_____, Glenstal Abbey: A Historical Guide, Glenstal Publications, 1990

Vignoles, K.H,. Charles Blacker Vignoles: Romantic Engineer, Cambridge University Press, London, 1982

Walker, Brian (ed.), Parliamentary Election Results in Ireland, Royal Irish Academy, Dublin, 1978

White, James, National Gallery of Ireland, Thames & Hudson, London, 1968

White, Terence de Vere, The Story of the Royal Dublin Society, The Kerryman, Tralee, n.d.

Wilson, Maureen, 'Sir John Macneill', Tempest's Annual, 1973, pp.12–22

Woodham Smith, Cecil, The Great Hunger: Ireland 1845–9, London: Hamish
Hamilton, 1962

Theses

Bielenberg, Andrew, Industrialisation and Decline in the Cork City region 1780–1880, M Litt thesis,
University of Dublin, Trinity College, 1989

Harrison, Richard, Dublin Quakers in Business, M Litt thesis, University of Dublin, Trinity College, 1987

Lee, J.J., Economic History of Early Irish Railways, MA thesis, University College Dublin, 1965

Mulligan, Fergus, William Dargan 1799–1867: A Business Life, PhD thesis, University of Dublin, Trinity
College, 2002

Murphy, Paula, Thomas Farrell: Dublin Sculptor 1827–1900, University College, Dublin, Ph D thesis, 1992

O'Reilly, Brenda, Introduction to Victorian railway architecture in Ireland, BA thesis, University College
Dublin, 1983

Notes

1. Introduction

1. It is difficult to give the modern day euro equivalent of nineteenth century currency to take account of inflation and the cost of living then and now. For a very approximate conversion, multiply by 100.

2. The sources for this information on Dargan's addresses include correspondence, company records and various directories. *Thom's Directory*, published annually, has a vast amount of information about nineteenth century Ireland. Others include the *Dublin Directory, Dublin Almanack, the Post Office Directory, Pettigrew & Oulton's Directory, Martin's Belfast Directory, Henderson's Belfast Directory, Salter's National Commercial Directory* and the *Irish Almanack*.

2. Dargan's Early Life and Career

1. MacSuibhne, n.d., 139–40

2. Gilmore, (2009), 159–61, and Julie Parks; gravestone information courtesy of Brian Gilmore

3. *Men of the Time* (1856)

4. Incumbered Estates Court, Deed 510839, 6 December 1819 between Patrick Dargan and Thomas Dargan and William Dargan, Registry of Deeds

5. For a detailed discussion of all the possible variables in Dargan's early life, including his birthplace, see Mulligan (2002), *William Dargan: A Business* Life, unpublished PhD thesis, 1–3

6. *Carlow Sentinel*, 9 February 1867

7. Incumbered Estates Court, Queen's County Rental, 1850

8. See endnote 4

9. House of Commons Select Committee on Carlow Wexford Railway, 3 June 1845, pp.83–4

10. I never met William Dargan SJ but had several meetings with Herbert Dargan SJ and Daniel Dargan SJ. Herbert was based in Northern Ireland and we met at PRONI where I was researching William's Northern projects. Towards the end of his life Daniel was based at the Jesuit house in Ranelagh where I called on him from time to explain why this book on his great ancestor was taking so long to finish.

11. Griffin (c.1853). In this collection of manuscripts each one has been corrected and proofread with substantial additions.

12. *Illustrated Magazine of Art*, vol.I (1853), 25–6

13. Commissioners of Irish Education Inquiry, Appendix to the Second Report, Queen's County, 764–5

14. Wallis Healy (1882); Murray (1950–1), 94

15. *Dublin Evening Post*, 2 November 1852; *Dublin Exhibition Expositor*, May 1853, 4; *Illustrated Magazine of Art* (1853), 26

16. Begun in 1790, this mill was by the 1840s 'one of the most extensive and celebrated in Ireland'; Hall, Mr and Mrs Samuel (1841, 1984 ed.), p.134. Louis Cullen described it as 'the first major industrial building in Ireland': Cullen, (1972), 93

17. Smiles (1874), 252–3; Hughes (1964), 207

18. For a description of the more blatant abuses of the system see Black (1960), 168

19. For a very readable biography of Telford, see Rolt (1985) and for an account of his life published a few years after his death, see Rickman (ed., 1838).

20. House of Lords SC on the Dublin & Drogheda Railway, 4 June 1836, privately printed

21. Holyhead Road Journals 1819–27, MT27: 57–62

22. In 1887, seven years after Macneill's death, the *Irish Builder* carried an emotive account of his last days and the indifference of his engineering colleagues to his poverty. The author was fellow engineer, John P. Doyle of Highfield Road, Rathgar, berating his professional colleagues who drew their knowledge and wealth from training under Macneill but now showed little concern for their master's fate. Quoted in Jeanne Sheehy, Kingsbridge Station , Gatherum Series no.1, 1973, 12

23. Parnell (1833), pp.100ff

24. First Report of the SC on the London to Holyhead Road: 1819 (78) v.115; Second Report of the SC on the London to Holyhead Road: 1819 (217) v.121

25. Second report of SC on the Anglesey Road: 1819 (217) v.12. For plans of the road see *Atlas to the Life of Thomas Telford CE*, Payne and Foss, London, 1838. Plate 66, figure 6 shows the Stanley Sands embankment and no.70 is the Menai bridge, which opened 30 January 1826. Plate 79 is Holyhead harbour and plate 80 Howth harbour. See also the act and plans, 1819, 59 Geo III 48, HLRO

26. *Report to the committee to inquire into sums expended on the Holyhead and Liverpool roads*, 30 May 1830, evidence of Telford, quoted in Appendix IV; Parnell noted that after seven years the embankment was 'in a perfect state', Parnell, op.cit., p.369; Smiles, op.cit., pp.255–6

27. *Report on progress on Anglesea road and Menai bridge*, May 1821, pp.1,3: 1821 (574 & 575) x.229; Holyhead Road Journals, March 1818-August 1819, MT 27/57; August 1819-July 1821, MT 27/58; December 1819-May 1822, MT 27 57–59, PRO London. The journal keepers made regular complaints about the quality of some of the works and the infrequent presence of the contractors, Gill & Hodges.

28. He noted 'this new piece has been rather heavy in winter' but would settle well and that 108 men on average had been working in 1823. John Aird to Telford, 13 February 1826, Telford Papers, UK Institution of Civil Engineers, LIB 11/67, T/Ho. The foreman, Ellis Williams, later transferred from Anglesey to work on the Howth road along with Dargan: *Fourth report of the commissioners for the Shrewsbury and Holyhead road*, 22 March 1824, p.5: 1824 (157) ix.281

29. Journals of Charles Vignoles, 17 April 1832, ADD 35,071; Vignoles, K.H. (1982), 23

30. Quoted in Joyce (1976 facsimile of 1912 ed.), 321

31. Plan for the Dublin to Howth Road (1823), NA V20 7/4/23; First Report of the Commissioners to further improve the London to Holyhead Road, 1924 (56.57) xxi 28.38

32. Parnell (1833), 381

33. Unfortunately Howth harbour was already silting up badly and even as Dargan completed the road there were plans to move the packet station to Kingstown.

3. Dargan's First Contracts

1. Telford to Dargan, 23 October 1824, Jane Dargan Papers. The minute books for the Barrow Navigation have not survived although the directors included Thomas Crosthwaite whose path crossed with Dargan many times.

2. Minutes of the Dublin and Malahide Turnpike, 27 December 1827, 111; 25 March, 21 May 1828, 122, 126–8

3. 10 Geo IV 75, 1829, HLRO

4. Minutes of the Dublin to Carlow Turnpike, 12 August 1829, p.19

5. At first he signed the minutes 'Clerke' and in October 1829 in the Downshire Arms, Blessington, he changed the spelling to 'Clarke'. When those minutes were passed a week later he opted for 'Wm Dargan, Clerk': ibid. 12 October 1829, 25, 28.

6. Ibid., 30 March 1830, pp.33, 34, 37, 38

7. Ibid., 7 April, 10 June, 6 July 1830, 6, 41–2 46–8

8. A set of drawings and estimates for the road was prepared not by Dargan but by a surveyor named H.T. Provis who earned a guinea a day. He was almost certainly a kinsman of William Provis, Dargan's supervisor at Anglesey and on the Birmingham & Liverpool Junction canal.

9. Report from the SC on turnpike roads in Ireland, 1832 (xvii) 64, lvii

10. Minutes of the Dunleer Turnpike Trust, Drogheda, 15 March 1828, 22 December 1828, 15 February, 1 June 1829, Fingal County Archives

11. Ibid., Dargan to Robinson, 19 February 1829

12. Dargan to James Cawley, 8 Lr Merrion Street, 31 January 1831; Robinson to Dargan, 16 March 1831: copy letters, Dunleer Turnpike Commissioners

13. Robinson to Dargan, 8 April 1831: copy letters, Dunleer Turnpike Commissioners. Despite this the Commissioners asked Dargan to estimate for new sections of road at Julianstown and Balrothery: rough minutes, Dunleer Turnpike Commissioners

14. Dunleer Turnpike Commissioners, rough minutes, 21 April 1831

15. Ibid., 11 May, 12, 14 July 1831

16. Dargan to Dunleer Turnpike Trust, 1 August 1831; rough minutes 6 August 1831

17. Ibid., 6 August 1831

18. Robinson to Dargan, Dunleer Turnpike Trust, rough minutes, 7, 28 September, 11 October 1831

19. Dunleer Turnpike Trust, rough minutes, 19 December 1831

20. Minutes of evidence taken before the Commons Committee on the Dublin & Drogheda Railway, privately printed by J.L. Cox, London, op.cit., evidence of William Dargan, 4 June 1836

21. Hadfield (1969), 188–9; B&LJC Minutes, 16 July 1830

22. The act is 7 Geo IV c.95, 26 May 1826; Birmingham & Liverpool Canal SC, 1826 (309) IV.631. See also Hadfield (1969), 183–9; Rolt (1985b), 188; Aris's Birmingham Gazette, 22 July 1826

23. Minutes of evidence taken before the Commons Committee on the Dublin & Drogheda Railway, evidence of William Dargan, 4 June 1836.

24. Rolt (1985b), 190

25. A Newport colleague, W.A. Pim wrote to Dargan in 1831, reporting good progress. More significant was his request for patronage in his brother's career, suggesting Dargan had a certain social and commercial influence: Pim to Dargan 16 October 1831, Jane Dargan Papers.

26. Diary of Charles Vignoles, 10 September 1833. .

27. By this time there was already mention of a plan to convert it into a railway and he added the canal was very deep and wide with an excellent towpath allowing goods to go much faster than on most other waterways: First report of SC on railways and canals amalgamation, evidence of Robert Scott MP, p.61, q.559: HC 1846 (200) xiii.85.

28. See 7&8 Geo IV.c.102; Hadfield (1969), 181–2, 300–1; Hadfield and Biddle (1970), 136–7

29. Extract from the parish register of Adbaston church, courtesy of the former minister, Rev. Pamela Freeman and Staffordshire County Record Office. I am very grateful to the parish council and the churchwarden of St Michael's, Jenny Muddimer, who very kindly showed me around the church in April 2011.

30. St Thomas' church, with a façade based on Palladio's Redentore in Venice, was destroyed in the Civil War in 1922. A new church with the same name but in the Byzantine style opened in Cathal Brugha St in 1931–2. For photos of the original church see O'Dwyer (1981), 68

31. Ms Dictionary of Biography, BL Ma Add 28,509, f,407, 512; Lewis (1832), 176–7

32. Dargan to Reilly, 1 May 1832, Downshire Papers, PRONI 671/C/56/1-23

33. Bennett (1833–8, 1992 ed.), 124–5

34. Brett and Dunleath (1974), 5, 12, 14. For a 20th century illustration of the cut see McCutcheon (1984), plate 17/4.

35. Dargan to Reilly, 19, 24 February 1833, Downshire Papers, PRONI 671/C/56/1-23

36. Ibid, 10 April, 27 May 1833

37. Ibid, 17 September 1833

38. Ibid., 30 June 1834

39. Ibid., Dargan to Reilly, 8 March, 13 April, 20 July, 12 August 1840; Dargan to Thomas Parry, Turnpike board, 4 January, 29 July, 19 November 1840

40. Second report of the commissioners for extension and improvement of public works in Ireland, HC 1833 (75) xvii, 25

41. HL Committee on Dublin & Drogheda Railway, 4 June 1836, privately printed, 372–4

42. Quoted in Delaney (1973), 178

43. On the Liverpool & Manchester Railway George Stephenson acted as both engineer and contractor, an arrangement that Thomas Telford thought highly unsatisfactory.

44. In the early 1900s my great-granduncle, Hugo Prior, thought little of walking from Ballinamore, Co. Leitrim to Greenore to catch the boat to Glasgow to work the summer on a Scottish farm, returning the same way a few months later.

45. *Journals of the House of Commons*, 9 February 1825

46. The act was 7 Geo IV, c.cxxxis, 31 May 1826; Williams (1833), 14

47. William Cubitt, Report on the Dublin and Kingstown Canal, HC 1833 (591) xvi.451; Flynn (1834); see also Report from the HC Select Committee on the Dublin & Kingstown Canal, HC 1833 (591) xvi.451 and Memorials and Maps relating to the Dublin & Kingstown Canal, HC 1833 (603) xxxv.85.

48. *HC Select Committee on the Dublin & Kingstown Railway*, 17 May 1833, p.25: HC 1833 (291) xxxv.517

49. *Journals of the House of Commons*, vol.86, 1831, 1&2 Wm IV, 24 June 1831.

50. D&KR Board Minutes, 16 March 1832; Grierson (1887) 101. Telford declined to cost the line pleading ill health and so Stephenson, the great English railway pioneer, took on the job.

51. Board Minutes, Trinity College, Dublin, 29 March 1831. Trinity also opposed William Aher's intrusive plan of the 1840s to build a railway viaduct across College Park. Its attitude to the iron horse has mellowed since then, allowing the 1891 loop line to curve over the north-east corner of the campus.

52. Grierson (1887), p.128; *Pettigrew and Oulton's Dublin Directory 1836*, p.186

53. Thirteen Views of the D&KR, *Dublin Penny Journal*, 30 August 1834

54. John Macneill to Major Donald Macneill, 23 December 1830, John Macneill Copy Letter Books, vol. II, book 19, Engineers Ireland Archives

55. Pim to CPW, 14 September 1831, HC 1833 (291) xxxv.517

56. *Journals of Charles Vignoles*, 1 January 1833, British Library MS Add. 35,071; Vignoles, Olinthus (1889),177–92

57. D&KR Board Minutes, 11 January 1833; Vignoles, K.H. (1982), 49

58. Journals of Charles Vignoles, April 1832, vol.III, 11–12, 21, British Library MS Add.34.530

59. Harrison, Richard (1987), *Dublin Quakers in Business*, unpublished M.Litt thesis, Trinity College, Dublin, 478. Quakers also played a major role in financing railways in England. One of the original financial backers of the Liverpool & Manchester Railway was the wealthy Quaker businessman Joseph Sanders.

60. Lee describes Perry as 'pushing, devious and very able' and his later life does indeed show he was prepared to cut corners when needs be: Lee (1965), Chapter 2.

61. D&KR Board Minutes, 28 December 1832, 6. Being on the board was no sinecure: there were weekly meetings at 6 am in Salt Hill House, followed by a walking inspection of the line with fines up to a guinea for directors who were late or failed to attend.

62. A copy of the tender document is in Grierson (1886–7), 64–140

63. Vignoles, Olinthus (1889), 178–9

64. Marmion (1860), 129–30

65. *Saunders News-Letter*, 5 March, 2 April 1833; Rolt (1960), 196–200

66. Pembroke Estate Papers, National Archives, 1011/6/77, 15 December 1832; 1011/13/2 28 January 1832; 1011/3, 2 February 1833

67. Hodgens to Dargan, 8 November 1833, D&KR Letter Book no.2, 341; D&KR Letter Book no.3, 343

68. D&KR Land Committee Minutes, 10, 24 December 1833; D&KR Board Minutes, 3, 7 January 1834, 367, 368

69. Grierson (1867), 86

70. *Dublin Evening Post*, 4 June 1833

71. D&KR Board Minutes, 9 August 1833; Vignoles to the D&KR board, D&KR Letter Book no.2, 2 August 1833; Journals of Charles Vignoles, 3 August 1833

72. D&KR Board Minutes, 14 October 1833, 303

73. Commissioners of Public Works in Ireland, First and Second Reports, HC 1835 (575) xx

74. Dublin Penny Journal (1834)

75. Minutes of evidence taken before the Commons Committee on the Dublin & Drogheda Railway, evidence of William Dargan, 4 June 1836

76. Grierson (1887), 89–90

77. Ibid., 98–101

78. Vignoles to the D&KR Board, 8 November 1833, D&KR Letter Book no.2; Journals of Charles Vignoles, 15, 25 December 1833

79. Journals of Charles Vignoles, 5, 6, 7, 26 January 1834; D&KR Board Minutes, 17 January 1834

80. D&KR Land Committee Minutes, 29 January, 4 February 1834; D&KR Board Minutes, 7 February 1834. The iron roof design is similar to Liverpool Lime St station, both being the work of the Dublin firm of William Turner.

81. Journals of Charles Vignoles, 12 February 1834; Vignoles to Dargan, 12 February 1834, D&KR Letter Book no.3

82. Vignoles, K.H. (1982), 59

83. D&KR Board Minutes, 13, 20 June, 4 July 1834, 495, 500, 508

84. Journals of Charles Vignoles,, 13 July 1834; Vignoles, K.H. (1982), 175

85. D&KR Board Minutes, 31 October 1834, 586

86. In 1851 the Manchester firm of William Fairbairn, run by Dargan's friend, built another bridge over

the Dodder at Lansdowne Road (since replaced) and over the Suir at Cahir (still in use) when Dargan was building the Waterford & Limerick Railway.

87. D&KR Board Minutes, 8, 10 December 1834, 622–3

88. The meal cost £43 14s, directors and 12 shareholders each paying a guinea, leaving a balance due of £21 13s 0d; D&KR Board Minutes, 2 January 1835.

89. Journals of Charles Vignoles, 18 December 1834. The engineer's grandson commented: 'Her death could only be a release to them both', Vignoles, K.H. (1982), 61.

90. Third Annual Report of the CPW (1835), 14

91. John Macneill to Thomas Graham, 16 December 1834, Copy Letter Books of John Macneill, vol.III, book 28, Engineers Ireland

92. Letter Maria Drummond to her mother, 17 July 1838, quoted in O'Brien, R. Barry (1889), 311, 312

93. *Railway Times*, 25 April 1840

94. D&KR Annual Report, March 1843. This growth made great demands on staff such as train crews, many of whom worked a 100 hour week: Lee (1979), 20

95. For a more detailed account of the workings, see: Mulligan (1983), 22–4; Cox, (1982, ed.), 92–5; Murray (1981), 45–62

96. Hadfield (196),37; Correspondence and papers relating to the D&KR 28 February 1843: HC 1843 (62) L.197; Third report of SC on railway audits 24 May 1849: HL 1849 (21.13) X, vol.4, evidence of James Pim Q.3434–5; D&KR to CPW 10 January 1842; Paine to Trevelyan 22 December 1842, PW 1067/77; D&KR Board Minutes 3 September 1842

97. Index to railway inspectors' reports, report on the atmospheric railway 15 November 1843, PRO MT6/1/316

98. *The Athenaeum*, September 1844

99. O'Malley Irwin (1844)

100. John Rennie, for example, thought its defects could have been remedied easily: Rennie (1875), 420

101. For an excellent and beautifully produced history of the Metals see Goodbody (2010).

4. Northern Waters and Early Railways in Ireland and England

1. Telford to Dargan, 18 July 1833, Jane Dargan Papers

2. Dargan to William Reilly, 19 February 1833, Downshire Papers; Ulster Canal Letter Book no.2, 29 April 1833

3. Rent-roll of the Earl of Caledon, 1833–41, Caledon Papers. Dupré Alexander, Earl of Caledon, was a kinsman of Dargan's early patron, John Alexander of Milford, Co. Carlow. On the main street of Caledon is a row of 2 storey estate houses and Dargan rented one of these. Caledon was described in 1837 as 'a mean village' till the earl developed it: Lewis (1837, 1970 facsimile), 234ff.

4. Second Report of SC on Public Works in Ireland, HC 1835 (573) xx, questions 1586–91, William Cubitt; Lord Gosford to Dargan 7 February 1835, Lord Gosford to Rev. Kennedy 7 February 1835, CSORP private index 2/102/30

5. Letter McCleery to Ulster Canal Committee, 9 April 1835; McCleery to Henry Porter, 10 June 1835, Ulster Canal Letter Book no.2

6. Casebourn (1842), 52–3

7. Caledon to Perry 17 November 1838, Perry-Caledon 21 November 1838, Caledon Papers; Perry to Caledon 17 November 1838, Caledon Papers; Perry to Paine, 24 January 1839, CPW Navigation Letter Books, vol.5, OPW/I/5/2/5, p.262

8. Dargan to Reilly, 12 August 1840, correspondence of Reilly and Dargan, PRONI

9. *Northern Whig* 28 July, 25 October, 26 November 1842, 1 July 1843; *Irish Railway Gazette* 10 May 1847, 254

10. *Saunders News-Letter*, 27 February 1850, 4 January 1851,23; *Irish Railway Gazette*, 9 March 1850, 258-9

11. *Saunders News-Letter*, 1 February 1853

12. Registry of Deeds 1859 Abstract vol.10, AG13, 20 December 1858. The abstract refers to the Dublin & Liverpool Steamship Co. but Macneill (1861) and Mullins (1859–61), 66 are definite it was the Dundalk Co.

13. Macneill (1861)

14. On the agenda for a historic meeting of the North-South parliamentary body in Dublin on 12 October 2012 was the possible reopening of the Ulster Canal. An innocuous discussion item, on a par with promoting motherhood and apple pie, but a start nonetheless.

15. HLRO 1836 6&7 Wm 95 Bann Reservoir Plans; Thomas Handley to Earl of Downshire 2 March 1836, Downshire Papers, PRONI; John Smyth, 'Historical sketch of work on the Bann reservoir', *Transactions of the Institution of Civil Engineers of Ireland*, vol. IX, 51–67. John Bateman, 'Description of the Bann reservoirs, Co. Down' *Minutes of Proceedings of Institution of Civil Engineers*, vol. VII, sess. 1848, 251–89. For a sketch of the Island Reavy reservoir see G.M. Binnie, *Early Victorian Water Engineers*, London: Thomas Telford Publishers, 1981,158

16. Bateman (1848), 259–64

17. HLRO Belfast Waterworks Improvements, 1839 plans by John Macneill CE, 1840 3&4 Vict. 79; Belfast Water Commissioners (BWC) Board Minutes 19 October 1840, 38–9; Loudan (1940), 47

18. BWC Board Minutes 17 May 1841, 111; *Northern Whig*, 20 May 1841

19. Macneill to Dargan 24 February 1842, Macneill to Bournes 24 February 1842, Macneill Copy Letter Books, vol.viii, no.81; BWC Board Minutes 18, 22 July 1843, 381–2

20. McNeill (1971), 183

21. The London North Western Railway acquired the *Hercules* around 1855 and ran her between Holyhead and Dublin. This explains how the Ulster Canal Carrying Co. plate ended up in Holyhead Maritime Museum.

22. Death Register, 26 May 1846, St Alban's Parish, Liscard, Merseyside; *Liverpool Chronicle* 30 May 1846

23. *Liverpool Times* 16 June, 7 July 1846; *Saunders News-Letter* 31 January, 16 July 1851

24. *Saunders News-Letter* 8, 9 December 1854, 26 April 1855

25. Marmion (1860), 311

26. For its history see Delaney (1986), 19–27

27. *Saunders News-Letter* 22 August 1849

28. W.B. Henry-Dargan, Newry Navigation Letter Books, 30 July 1849, 246, PRONI, D.931/4; Newry Navigation Minutes 21 May, 16 July, 23 August 1849; *Irish Railway Gazette* 2 July 1849, 228

29. Newry Navigation Minutes 15, 30 April, 13 May, 12 June, 29 July, 12 August, 7 October 1850; Henry-Dargan, 12 June 23 July 1850, Newry Navigation Letter Book

30. Salmond (1879/9), 22–35

31. Belfast Harbour Commissioners (BHC), General Board Minutes, vol.1, 8 November 1838, 18; 31 December 1838, 18–19; 7,18 January 1839, 20–1; vol.6, 6 February 1839, 10

32. John Burgoyne to BHC, 26 January 1839, Jane Dargan Papers; BHC Board Minutes, vol.6, 6 February 1839, 10

33. The full contract has survived and describes the job in great detail: Articles of agreement, Dargan and Belfast Ballast Board 28 February 1839, PRONI T.2433/1

34. Russell (1910); H.A. MacCartan, *The Glamour of Belfast*, Dublin: Talbot Press, 1921, 135; one has to admire the creativity of the book's title.

35. Black (1988), 6, 35, 42

36. *Martin's Belfast Directory* 1841–4; BHC Board Minutes, vol.6, 4 December 1839, p.137, 15 January 1840, 15. Near Fortwilliam roundabout are Dargan Road, Dargan Crescent and Dargan Drive.

37. *Irish Railway Gazette* 14 September p.555; BHC Board Minutes vol.8, 30 October 1846, 364–5

38. BHC Board Minutes vol.8, 5 November 1848, 384

39. *Saunders News-Letter*, 24 July 1847

40. Macneill to Robinson 2, 12, 27 August 1841; Macneill to Dargan 8 September 1841 (Macneill Copy Letter Books, vol.vii, 72, 73

41. Macneill to Robertson 30 January, 4 February 1842, Macneill Copy Letter Books, vol.ix, book 80. Given Sir John's litigious nature Dargan was lucky he did not sue him.

42. Devon Commission on the occupation of land in Ireland, vol.II, part 1, evidence of John Macneill, 15 December 1843, pp.89–90, q.75: HC 1845 (606) xix

43. HC Select Committee on MGWR, unpublished MS evidence of James Perry, 16 June 1846, 140–44. These are rough, handwritten notes, hence the stilted language.

44. *Railway Times* 16 August 1845,1257; 1 August 1846, 1062; *Irish Railway Gazette* 19 October 1846, 608; L&CR Board Minutes 3 September 1845, 16–17

45. Registry of Deeds 1854, vol.13, abstract 95; 1859, vol.15, ab.203

46. Thomas Carlyle, *Reminiscences of my Irish Journey in 1849*, London, Sampson Law, 1882, pp.257–8. The exiled John Mitchel commented on the visit: 'Ireland ... has had a far more royal visitor. Carlyle has been there again.... I have no doubt he will be delivered of a book on the subject of Ireland soon.' John Mitchel, *Jail Journal*, Dublin, M.H. Gill, 1913, p.204

    HC Select Committee on MGWR, unpublished MS evidence of James Perry, 16 June 1846, 140–44

    Railway Times 16 August 1845,1257; 1 August 1846, 1062; *Irish Railway Gazette* 19 October 1846, 608; L&CR Board Minutes 3 September 1845, 16–17

    Registry of Deeds 1854, vol.13, abstract 95; 1859, vol.15, ab.203

47. *Railway Times* 13 November 1841, p.1192; *Saunders News-Letter* 11 November 1841; for a drawing of an UR overbridge near Lisburn signed by Dargan and John Godwin, engineer, see McCutcheon (1984),106

48. Pasley's report Portadown-Belfast to Lords of Committee of Privy Council for Trade, 18 November 1843, PT6/2/3. The traffic system was quite casual: trains left from each end at the same time and crossed at Moira. The line was single until 1847.

49. Return of number of persons employed on all railways under construction on 1 May 1847, 1847 (579) LXIII.101

50. Report of Capt. Simmons to Commissioners of Railways, UR Portadown-Armagh, 2 February 1848, MT6/5/124 ; Simmons later rose to become Field Marshal Sir John Simmons

51. *Irish Railway Gazette* 30 November 1850, 11 January 1851

52. Cubitt's plans and estimates for the D&DR, 17 May 1836; Report of Cubitt to Provisional Committee of D&DR, 9 January 1836, HLRO. Opposition to such a central location was strong and the company settled for a decidedly less convenient site on Amiens Street.

53. Minutes of evidence taken before the Commons Committee on the Dublin & Drogheda Railway, privately printed by J.L. Cox, London, op.cit., evidence of Dargan, 4 June 1836.

54. John Macneill, Reports for the Commission on Railways 20 May 1837; Second Report of the Railway Commissioners, October 1838, 35ff

55. Macneill-Hemans 7 September 1841 and 1 September 1841, Macneill-Maunsell, Macneill Copy Letter Books, vol.VIII, book 73

56. Evidence of John Macneill, Devon Commission op.cit., part 1, 85–7, q.27,31, HC 1845 (606) xix

57. *Irish Railway Gazette* 5 February, 5 March, 7 May 1849, 44, 79, 166

58. Grey Porter (1847). Porter wandered off the point in his railway pamphlet slightly with an intemperate attack on Church of Ireland clergy.

59. *Official Catalogue to 1862 International Exhibition*, London, Truscott & Son, p.38, item 2316. The rebuilding of the viaduct some 80 years later was almost as complex: Howden (1934), 71–92

60. Articles of Agreement between the B&BR and William Dargan, 4 February 1846, PRONI, UTA8; *Henderson's Belfast Directory 1846-7*, 204; *Slater's National Commercial Directory of Ireland 1846*, 185

61. BBC&PJR Board Minutes 2 August, 8 September 1853

62. *Saunders News-Letter* 9 November 1855; BBC&PJR Board Minutes 26 February, 26 March, 1 September 1856.

63. *Saunders News-Letter* 2 June, 23 September 1856

64. The speech is quoted in the *Irish Railway Gazette*, 1 November 1856, 1318 under the heading 'Ireland for the Irish'.

65. BBC&PJR board minutes 25 May 1858, 18, 31 December 1860, 29 January 1861. The B&NCR was known locally as Big Nancy Coming Running.

66. *Irish Railway Gazette* 26 January, 23 February 1846, 195, 248

67. *Saunders News-Letter* 24 August 1850

68. Index to Railway Inspectors' Reports 1854, D&ER, 15 June 1854, PRO MT6/11/133

69. *Railway Times* 17 January, 14 March 1846, 72, 408; *Irish Railway Gazette* 2 March 1846, 257. A blank undated N&ER construction contract survives: PRONI UTA56/A

70. *Irish Railway Gazette* 28 June 1847, 313; *Railway Times* 28 August 1847, 1106–7; Hugh Boyd-John MacMahon, 18 July 1847, OPW Register of Correspondence

71. NW&RR Board Minutes 17, 21, 25 May 1849

72. *Saunders News-Letter* 24 May, 4, 6 October, 16 November 1849; *Irish Railway Gazette* 23 July 1849

73. Index to Railway Inspectors' Reports, B&CDR, Captain R.M. Laffan, 29 July 1848, MT6/5/134; B&CDR Board Minutes, 3 August 1848

74. Document submitted for B&CDR half-year meeting, 28 August 1849; B&CDR Shareholders Minutes 29 August 1849

75. B&CDR Committee Minutes 11, 18, 25 April, 16, 30 May 1849; Board Minutes 2, 9 May 1849. Special meetings were held on 21, 28 November 1849: B&CDR Committee Minutes, 12 December 1849

76. BJR Board Minutes, 5 July 1854, PRONI UTA 18/A/1

77. BJR Board Minutes, 9 February, 16 March 1859, PRONI UTA 18/A/1

78. McCutcheon 1984, op.cit., p.107. Apart from a book of crudely written rough minutes, contemporary records of this company are sparse.

79. L&BR Committee of Management 2, 26 September, 29 October, 5 November, 10 December 1845

80. L&BR Board 4, 18 February 1846

81. L&BR Board 8 April 1846; L&BR Committee of Management 1 April 1846

82. *Liverpool Mail*, 9 February 1867; George McCorquodale, *Annual Liverpool Directory* 1848

83. *Liverpool Chronicle* 27 March 1847; *Irish Railway Gazette* 29 March 1847

84. *Liverpool Times* 16 November 1848

85. Francis Whishaw, *Railways of Great Britain and Ireland*, 1969 facsimile of 1842 edition, Newton Abbot, David & Charles, 313

86. A.F. Tait, *Views on the Manchester and Leeds Railway*, Bradhsaw and Blacklock, 1971 facsimile of 1845 edition, 7

87. M&LR Land & Construction Committee Minutes 27 April, 20 July 1847; Marshall (1969),248; Broadbridge (1970), 8

88. *Report from SC on railway labourers*, HC 1846 (530) XIII.411, 121. The report was greatly concerned with the workmen's religious welfare but also covered some other aspects of their living conditions such as dwellings, cottages and dormitories. Among the causes of frequent fatalities, the Woodhead tunnel claimed many lives including several of men who took bets over who was able to jump across the tunnel vent openings.

89. Coleman (1965), 20

90. F.R Conder describes working with a tall, good looking foreman on the South Eastern Railway in England who was excellent at his job but had an 'over-fondness for the ale-can' and might have been more content in a land other than one where 'certain prejudices still linger on the subject of monogamy'. Working in different parts of the country this man 'thought a *placens uxor* a proper part of the arrangement for each. Sometimes the different claimants to the title would meet on the same spot, and discord would ensue. Flight was generally the best policy on such occasions.' Conder (1868), 146–7

91. Carlyle to Gavan Duffy 29 August 1846, quoted in Coleman (1965), 20

5. Rails into Munster and Connacht, the Peak of Dargan's Career

1. Craig (1980), 300. An anonymous writer at the time was less impressed, describing it as: 'schizo-phrenic, the terminus being exuberantly classical and the small stations along the line in equally uncompromising Gothic': Remarks on the Dublin terminus of the Cashel or GS&WR, n.a., 1845

2. Williams (1994), 256

3. Cox and Gould (1998) 36

4. He later developed his ideas for financing a railway network 'through this distracted country' by loan guarantees rather than state funding: Letter books of Charles Vignoles for Railway Commissioners, December 1836, NA 2D/59/54; Charles Vignoles, 'Railways in Ireland', *Dublin University Magazine*, vol.xix, no.109, January 1842, 124–36; Half year report, Great Leinster & Munster Railway, 1 August 1838

5. Macneill to Robert Peel 27 January 1844, BL Peel Papers, 40,588, f.128; 40,547, f.282

6. John Macneill, *Report on the proposed line of railway from Dublin to Cashel*, 1844; Evidence of Macneill 2 June 1845, HL Committee on GS&WR, MS evidence book. Mullins later estimated the cost at £16,400 per mile: M.B. Mullins, 'Historical sketch of engineering in Ireland', *Trans of Instn of CE of I*, vol.VI, 1859–61, p.179

7. GS&WR Board Minutes 14 November 1844, vol.2, 106. The company solicitor who drew up the contract deed, Croker Barrington, conducted much of Dargan's legal business.

8. *Irish Railway Gazette* 18 November 1844, 21. The same paper warned readers about the hazards of railway share speculation: 'it is infinitely easier to lose a fortune than to make one by such gambling'.

9. Quoted in Coleman (1965), 70. Peto formed a partnership with Edward Betts and Thomas Brassey dominating railway construction in Britain during the 1850s and early 1860s and working in Canada and the Crimea. Like Dargan he was promoter, builder and financier and shared his concern for his workers' welfare. The 1866 financial crisis brought him down and he was declared bankrupt.

10. One destitute ex-navvy who worked for the Stephensons on England blamed his misfortune solely on truck and tommy shops: Rolt (1960), 227–8

11. Conder (1868: 1983), 89,91–2

12. *Evening Mail*, 17 February 1845

13. *Saunders News-Letter*, 20 February 1845; *Irish Railway Gazette*, 24 February 1845

14. GS&WR Board Minutes 11, 18 June 1845

15. *Irish Railway Gazette* 28 September 1845, 574

16. Dargan to Macneill, 17 June 1845, quoted in GS&WR Board Minutes 18 June 1845

17. George Bentinck, 'Railways in Ireland', House of Commons speech, February 1847.

18. *Report of James Walker to Commissioners for loans to public works on the* GS&WR, 5; 1847 (459) LXIII.289

19. Woodham Smith (1962), 406–7

20. Combination meant 'combining' and covered offences such as going on strike to demand higher wages. Among those accused of striking were John Connor, John Nolan, Thomas Wright, John Cavanagh, James Harrington, Patrick Byrne, Daniel Osborn, Paul Keys, C. Kelly and Edward Downey: *Irish Railway Gazette* 8 September 1845, 586.

21. *Irish Railway Gazette* 28 September 1845, 574; *Saunders News-Letter* 29 September 1845

22. Charles Pasley (he of the gauge issue) was not infallible. Three months later he was inspecting railways in Britain and passed the Dee railway bridge near Chester as safe to open. It collapsed within a year as a train was passing over it causing four deaths. At the inquest Charles Vignoles testified on behalf of the bridge engineer, George Stephenson but Pasley was so agitated by his own poor judgement he could hardly speak: Rolt (1960), 300–2. By contrast Pasley remained utterly cool a few years earlier when he and a colleague nearly drowned inside a diving bell. Using up their air and with no way of alerting those on the surface, the water crept up the inside of the bell until it was at chest level. Pasley chatted away about the most mundane subjects until they were suddenly wrenched from their watery prison to safety by their rescuers.

23. Half-year report, GS&WR, February 1846; GS&WR Board Minutes 7 January 1847

24. Le Fanu (1894), 192–3

25. Returns of the number of persons employed on all railways under construction on 1 May 1847, HC 1847 (579) LXIII.101

26. See D. Cole, *Irish Industrial and Contractors' Locomotives*, Union Publications, London, 1962, 37–8

27. See Lee (1979), 11

28. *Tipperary Vindicator*, 17 November 1847

29. *Irish Railway Gazette*, 6 December 1847, 495; *Liverpool Chronicle*, 27 July 1848

30. Having said that, Tipperary did have a reputation for agrarian and political violence before the Famine and in the 19th century. It may be no coincidence that Séamus Robinson, Dan Breen and Seán Treacy fired the first shots in the War of Independence when they killed RIC Constables MacDonnell and O'Connell at Soloheadbeg, Co. Tipperary on 21 January 1919.

31. W.R. Le Fanu Diaries, 12 August, 22 December 1848.; Conder (1868), 170

32. GS&WR Board Minutes 26 September 1848; Index to Railway Inspectors' Reports, Capt. J. Simmons RE, GS&WR, 15 March, 16 April 1849, MT29/8.

33. Irish Railway Gazette 19 March 1849, 100

34. Diaries of W.R. Le Fanu 16, 17 March 1849

35. Index to Railway Inspectors' Reports, GS&WR, Captain R.M. Laffan RE, 16, 22 October 1849, MT29/8. Captain Wynne was more impressed on his later visit, saying the line was 'well laid and complete'.

36. GS&WR Board Minutes, 8 November 1850. The chairman added later the company had closed the accounts 'with our great contractor... without the slightest difference and to our mutual and entire satisfaction'.

37. Tuck (1847),.211

38. *Saunders News-Letter*, 13 November 1850

39. *Thom's Directory* 1851, 205

40. *Irish Railway Gazette*, 21 June 1847, 304

41. Newham (1970), 8–9

42. Diaries of Richard Boyse Osborne 1809–97, NLI MS 7888–7895

43. Act for construction of the Limerick & Waterford Railway: 7 Geo IV, CXXXIX.31, May 1826; Nimmo (1826)

44. Diaries of Charles Vignoles, 20 August 1845

45. Diaries of Richard Osborne, 15 November 1845

46. Ibid, 7 November 1845

47. One land claims jury risked a spell in jail when the members claimed 15 guineas expenses for their adjudication, a prospect that encouraged these 'avaricious jurors' to settle for 7 guineas each: *Irish Railway Gazette* 19 January 1846, 186. Another paper blamed mean-spirited landowners for the delay in starting the works: *Railway Times*, 14 March 1846, 405–7

48. Osborne to J. Walker, Drainage Commissioners, 5 June 1847; Edward Rupell to J. Walker 4 September 1847, OPW Registers, NA 296/47, 24,329/47

49. Diaries of Richard Osborne, 5 October 1847; W&LR Board Minutes, 16 November 1847, 100

50. Diaries of Richard Osborne, 19 July 1849, 81

51. Major John P. Kennedy, Report to the shareholders of the W&LR, Calcutta, 1849

52. Directors' Minutes, Royal Bank of Ireland, vol.10, 18 August 1853; GS&WR Board Minutes, 18 August, 9 September, 24 October 1853

53. *Railway Times*, 20, 28 January, 25 February 1854, 51, 90, 204; Chairman's reports, 3, 25 February 1858, Donoughmore to John Connolly, 22 February 1858, Donoughmore papers, TCD H/18/2/1–12

54. A condition of the terms of the will was that all his children should stay Catholics: Will of James Dargan, 29 March 1852, information from Brian Gilmore. For some reason the *Hobart Daily Times* also mentions James' death: 7 September 1854; Registry of Deeds, (1854), vol. 12, 323

55. Diaries of W.R. Le Fanu, 15 April 1852; *Freeman's Journal*, 28 September 1852

56. Le Fanu (1894), 194–5

57. For a description of the possible origin of these engines and also a number of anecdotes about the W&TR see Fayle & Newham (1972), 21–2

58. Malcolmson was part of the strong network of Quaker entrepreneurs which included the Perrys, the Pims and the Goodbodys, many of them involved in railways. See O'Dwyer (2000), 46, 53–4, 58

59. Diaries of W.R. Le Fanu, 1 January 1846. The numbers at work varied wildly each week from 700 odd to 4,300 and back to 1,000: *Railway Times*, 20 November 1847

60. Diaries of W.R. Le Fanu, 26 March,12, 30 April, 14, 16 July 1852

61. Diaries of W.R. Le Fanu, 22–25 July 1852. The engineer noted ominously: 'potato blight all through the country'.

62. *Irish Tourists' Illustrated Handbook* (1852), 41

63. Great Southern Hotels (1954)

64. Quoted in *Saunders News-Letter*, 21 November 1856

65. My late uncle, Dr Patrick Logan, travelled on this service after he contracted TB while working in a mining hospital in Newfoundland. In his memoirs he described getting into bed on the flying boat as all the passengers did for the long flight to Foynes. He believed he was coming home to spend his last months in Ireland but lived another 35 years.

66. Diaries of W.R. Le Fanu, 28, 29 September 1853

67. Henry Watson, Limerick to Chief Secretary's Office, Dublin Castle, CSORP, 2 May 1854, 20214

68. Captain H. Tyler, Index to Railway Inspectors' Reports, L&FR, 20 April 1855, MT6/18/4

69. L&FR Half Year Meeting, March 1856

70. *Saunders News Letter* 3 August, 2 October 1860. A kelpie is a Scottish water sprite said to take delight in drowning travellers.

71. For an overview of the line's history see Clements (1950)

72. Index to Railway Inspectors Reports, L&ER, 18 June 1859, MT29/20

73. Tierney and Cornforth (1988), 58; Tierney (1990), 9, 34

74. Kelly to Barrington 3 March 1847, NLI, Barrington Papers

75. Specifications and materials for the Great Tower at Glenstal Castle, 2 August 1858; Kelly-Robert Keys, 23 August 1848; Kelly-Dargan, 24 August, 8 November 1848, Barrington Papers

76. Kelly-Barrington, 27 November 1848, 17 November 1849; Lynch to Barrington, 27 November 1855, Barrington Papers

77. *Saunders News-Letter* 11, 17, 28 May 1858; Index to Railway Inspectors' Reports, GS&WR, Captain H.W. Tyler, 30 September 1859, MT29/20

78. *Dublin Builder*, vol.II, no.18, 1 June 1860, 283

79. MGWR *Tourist Guide*, Dublin, 1850; Craig (1980).300–1

80. List of persons subscribing £2,000 or more in private Bill Office in present Parliamentary session, 1845, 87: 1845 (317) xl.1; James Perry's vault in Mount Jerome cemetery resembles a miniature version of Broadstone station, both designed by John Mulvany.

81. Lee (1965), 30–1

82. Mullins (1846), 180; Bill authorising advance of money out of the consolidated fund to the MGWR of Ireland, 28 July 1849: 1849 (489) I 35; MGWR Half-year reports, 20 April, 28 September 1849, 28 March 1850. The contract included 5 years' maintenance.

83. *Irish Railway Gazette*, 27 August, 7 December 1849; *Saunders News-Letter*, 1 January 1850

84. Mitchell's firm supplied upholstery materials to Dargan for several vehicles; see *Dublin Historical Record*, li 28–9, 31, lii, 101

85. For an excellent, fully illustrated account of Mulvany's life and career, see O'Dwyer (2000), 11–75

86. George Hemans, 'Account of the construction of the MGWR in Ireland', *Proc. Instn of CE of I*, vol. IV, part 1, sess.1849–50, 1851, 48–60

87. Index to Railway Inspectors' Reports, Captain R.M. Laffan, 29 July 1851, MT29/10

88. Hemans (1850); Hemans (1851)

89. Lobbying for Cobh seemed to work. A GS&WR shareholders' meeting in December 1910 heard that 'an influential deputation from Ireland visted the United States in September last, and laid the claims of Queenstown as a Port of Call before the Postmaster-General and other high officials of the United States Government'. GS&WR Report of Directors, 31 December 1910.

90. Eight MGWR directors were also on the board: MGWR Half-Year Report, 28 March 1851

91. For accounts of attempts to establish a Galway-New York route see Collins (1994), 3–42 and Collins (2002).

92. The Atlantic passage could be hazardous with collisions and sinkings commonplace. In 1854 the wooden-hulled Collins Line steamer, *PS Arctic*, sank off Cape Race after colliding with an iron-built French ship, *Vesta*. As the master of the *Vesta* tried to rescue those who abandoned the sinking ship he accidentally rammed and sank several lifeboats, the total loss of life being 322. Two years later another Collins Line vessel, *Pacific*, disappered without trace with the loss of 288 passengers while in 1860 the *PS Connaught*, flagship of the Galway Line, sprang a leak, caught fire and then sank while en route from Boston to Galway. Like *Titanic* there were lifeboats for only a fraction of those on the ship but happily another vessel came alongside and rescued all on board.

93. *Saunders News-Letter* 16, 26 June, 1851

94. Mahony to Dargan 21 August 1851, Jane Dargan Papers

95. Clarendon to Mahony 25 August 1852; Mahony to Jane Dargan 28 August 1852, Jane Dargan Papers

96. For an account of his life see Mitchell (1983–4).

97. Collins (1994), 12

98. Brookefield (1952); Brookefield (1955). Today Galway receives regular visits from cruise liners but until a new harbour is built large ships moor at Mutton Island, somewhat unsuitable as it is now a waste water treatment plant and passengers come ashore by tender, a problem which has persisted since the nineteenth-century.

99. Hemans (1851), 48–60; MGWR Half-year report, 2 September 1853; *Railway Times*, 17 September 1853, 993

6. The Darganaeum: The 1853 Dublin Exhibition and the National Gallery of Ireland

1. J.H. Foley (1818–74) was born in Montgomery St (Monto of notoriety, now Foley St) and was a highly regarded artist. He designed the statues of Daniel O'Connell in O'Connell St and Benjamin Guinness outside St Patrick's Cathedral. Foley is buried in St Paul's cathedral, London. See *Dublin Historical Record*, Vol.XXXII, 42–53

2. For a detailed study of the Exhibition see Davis (1999) and a study of the social implications see Leapman (2001). For a general description of the exhibits see *Official Catalogue*, 2nd ed., Spicers, London, 1851 and a description of the building see Priestley (1972), 62–8, 72–80, 84.

3. Cusack Patrick Roney, a railway colleague of Dargan's, became Secretary of the Exhibition Committee and travelled all over Europe to encourage exhibitors to attend. He is the author of two travel books, *How to Spend Month in Ireland* and *Rambles on Railways*. Earl St Germans knighted him on the Exhibition opening day.

4. See Maguire (1852).

5. Diaries of W.R. Le Fanu, 10 June 1852

6. Proceedings of RDS Council 13 November 1851; Meenan and Clarke (1981), 36

7. Sproule (1854), 5

8. The runners up were Deane & Woodward who built the Museum Building in Trinity College, the Kildare Street Club and Oxford Museum. Third prize went to Richard Turner whose railings grace the outer wall of Trinity College and who built the glass roof at Liverpool Lime Street station as well as working on Westland Row station and the Broadstone station in Dublin.

9. *Illustrated Magazine of Art*, vol.I, 1853, 26–7; *Freeman's Journal*, 24 September, 18 October 1852; *The Weekly Freeman*, 23 October 1852

10. Jones (1854), 18

11. *Weekly Freeman*, 22 October 1852

12. Quoted in *Saunder's News-Letter*, 24 July 1852

13. The Hyde Park Exhibition also had its vociferous opponents, among them Col. Charles Sibthorpe MP, a long time critic of Prince Albert, who said it was 'one of the greatest humbugs, one of the greatest frauds, one of the greatest absurdities ever known'. He claimed large numbers of mature trees would be felled and that the cost of the building, £26,000, would be better spent on famine victims in Ireland. Well to do residents of Kensington feared the Exhibition would turn the park into 'a bivouac of all the vagabonds in London', as *The Times* put it. Quoted in Davis (1999), 73–4

14. Robert Travers to Thomas Jones, 28 May 1853, Travers correspondence

15. *Freeman's Journal*, 12, 26 October 1852. .

16. Ibid.

17. *Dublin Evening Post*, 2 November 1852

18. Sproule (1854), 32

19. Sproule (1854) 11

20. Diaries of W.R .Le Fanu 11, 12 May 1853

21. *Dublin Evening Post*, 12 May 1853

22. Lords Lieutenant, representatives of the British monarch in Ireland, came and went with startling frequency. Being largely a nominal appointment and a sinecure their duties were scarcely onerous. Few 19th century holders of the office are remembered for leaving the country in a better state than they found it.

23. *Edinburgh Evening Post* 18 May 1853

24. *The Exhibition Expositor and Advertiser*, a weekly bulletin published during the Exhibition, has an illustration of the statue, agreeing it was not universally pleasing and its defects might exclude it from the fine arts gallery but said it was a good likeness. 'We cordially hail its presence, with all its faults': Issue no.2, May 1853, 4.

25. Hemans-Jane Dargan, 25 October 1853, Jane Dargan Papers

26. *The Times*, 3 November 1853

27. Howth-Dargan, 2 March 1853; Coyngham-Dargan, 14 April 1853, Jane Dargan Papers; MS Committee Minutes, Royal St George Yacht Club, 12 April, 17 May 1853

28. *Dublin Evening Post*, 12 May 1853

29. Maria Hall to Jane Dargan, 17 May 1853, Jane Dargan Papers

30. *Liverpool Chronicle*, 23 July 1853

31. Shelley Brooks to Dargan, 5 July 1853, Jane Dargan Papers; *Punch*, vol.XXV, 2 July 1853, 1–2

32. Victoria's first train journey from Windsor to near Paddington in June 1842 was a traumatic experience as she feared the excessive speed, 20mph/32 kph, would force the train off the rails. She also had a great fear of being trapped in a burning building.

33. Journals of Queen Victoria, 29 August 1853. The excerpts quoted are taken mainly from her manuscript diaries and available to academic researchers in the Royal Archives, Windsor Castle. I was very courteously received on a research visit there some years ago and it was delightful to see the inside of the distinctive Drum Tower dating from the 12th century and to take tea mid-morning with the staff.

34. *Cork Examiner*, 31 August 1853

35. Mitchel (1913 ed.),.203

36. Three papers described the imaginary visit in some detail only to correct it a few days later: *Dublin Evening Post* 30 August, 1 September 1853; *Morning Chronicle* 31 August 1853; *Evening Packet* 1 September 1853. The story is often repeated, one source being F.C. Wallis, *William Dargan: A Memoir*, reprinted by the author from *Irish Manufacturers' Journal* 1882, 7

37. *Saunders News-Letter* 3 September 1853

38. As one author put it: 'that the future King Edward VII was a difficult child was generally accepted': White (n.d),145

39. Journals of Queen Victoria, 30 August 1853. Victoria kept a diary all her life but unfortunately the journals available to researchers are not the originals. She ordered her daughter Beatrice to rewrite them after her death and destroy the originals. Whatever about rewriting or deleting her personal thoughts it seems unlikely her description of Dargan and the Dublin Exhibition was altered. She also inserted a picture of the Exhibition in her journals. Having had a miserable, loveless upbringing the queen developed an excessive reliance on father figures, above all her beloved German husband and first cousin, Prince Albert. The queen desperately wanted him to be king, something the government would not countenance. After his death in 1861 she went into perpetual mourning wearing only black. and suffering what appear to be decades of depression; hence the oft-quoted: 'We are not amused'.

40. Many papers covered the visit but only as far as the gates: *Evening Post*, 30 August 1853; *Saunders News-Letter*, 31 August 1853; *The Express*, 3 September 1853; *Carlow Sentinel*, 3 September 1853; *Evening Packet*, 3 September 1853

41. In the aristocratic pecking order, baronets are not peers and so cannot sit in the House of Lords. They feature above knights but below (in ascending order of privilege), barons, viscounts, earls,

marquises and top of the pile, dukes. Coincidentally James I created the rank of baronet, selling titles to pay for his Irish wars. Victoria dispensed them as honours to worthy businessmen while at the same time avoiding the risk of cluttering up the House of Lords, as one commentator put it. A baronetcy is hereditary so possibly had William accepted it one of the Jesuit Dargan brothers, the late Herbert or Daniel, could have inherited the title.

42. Memo by Prince Albert made at Balmoral, 28 September 1853

43. Victoria visited Mount Anville again in 1900 on her final trip to Ireland and while there planted a sequoia tree in front of the house. The tree is still there.

44. *Freeman's Journal*, 28 June 1853. The paper's Editor, J. Murphy, later told Jane Dargan that Excelsior was in fact Lord Castlereagh. For illustrations of the service see Curry (2001), 71–9. James McGlashan also published a booklet on the service illustrated by W. Boyton Kirk RHA.

45. The Irish State Coach normally has four horses and is driven from the box seat. For further information see www.royal.gov.uk/faq/carriage.htm. Hutton's factory was in Summerhill and the site is now a depot for Dublin Bus.

46. Journals of Queen Victoria, 31 August 1853

47. Ibid., 2 September 1853

48. Among the exhibits was a chenille tapestry made by Dargan's niece, Louisa Haslam of Market Drayton.

49. Journals of Queen Victoria, 3 September 1853

50. *Galway Vindicator*, 2 November 1853

51. Minutes RDS Council 16 November 1853, 28 January 1854

52. RDS Council Proceedings 12 October 1854, 22 February 1855; William Mackie to RDS 4 July 1854, RDS Letter Books 1853–4

53. For the full Exhibition accounts see Jones (1854).

54. *Dublin Evening Post* 27 October, 3 November 1853

55. *Travels and Sketches of Scenery*, n.a., 9

56. Sproule (1854), 32. It seems a little odd that the official Catalogue should be so dismissive of some exhibits.

57. Ó Gráda (1994), 309

58. William Steele, Asst Sec. RDS to Exhibitors, 25 July 1853, RDS Letter Book I, 1853–4

59. *Saunders News-Letter*, 30 June 1853

60. Minutes, National Gallery of Ireland, Book I, 2 June 1856, 62–5; de Courcy (1985), 13–14. A former director of the National Gallery commented that if it was called the Dargan Gallery it 'might possibly have acquired a more immediate identity, and the name would have gained lustre with the collection': White (1968), 8

61. *Dublin Builder* 1 February 1864, vol.VI, no.99, 17–18. The papers in favour of the statue included *The Irish Times*, *Saunders News-Letter* and *Freeman's Journal* all of 1 February 1864.

62. Quoted in Somerville-Large (2004), 304–6

63. NGI Board Minutes, vol.II, 14 February 1867

64. George Mulvany to *The Express*, 9 February 1867, reproduced in NGI Letter Book I, 11 February 1867; Irish Institution to NGI, 1 November 1864, NGI Letter Book I

65. *Freeman's Journal*, 30 June 1853

66. Dublin Municipal Council Minutes 4, 18 April, 16 May 1853. The city fathers were at this time much more concerned with how best to receive Queen Victoria if she came to Dublin; *Limerick and Clare Examiner* 6 April 1853.

67. See Paxton (1851) which contains a proposal to make it a permanent exhibition centre.

68. *Dublin Builder*, 15 November 1865, vol.VIII, no.142, 270, 273

7. Dargan's Own Line, the Dublin & Wicklow Railway

1. D&WR Board Minutes 4 January 1853, 29. Le Fanu describes this investment by Dargan as financially 'unfortunate': W.R. Le Fanu (1894), 210–11

2. D&WR Board Minutes 29 October 1853, p.69

3. Stocks valued at £200,000 to guarantee a £100,000 loan constituted a healthy risk margin. Court of Directors Minutes, Bank of Ireland, 16 May, 10 October 1854, 382–3, 440

4. Index to Railway Inspectors' Reports, Captain H.W. Tyler, D&WR, 8 August 1853, MT6/10/115

5. D&WR Indenture, Registry of Deeds Abstracts, 17 March 1854, vol.19, Ab.162; D&WR Board Minutes 14 March 1854, 84

6. Breslin also had the catering contract for the 1853 Exhibition.

7. *The Locomotive* 15 April 1944. For a photograph of the railway bridge over the canal see O'Dwyer, (1981), 119. Up to recently the base of the stone supports was still visible on the north bank of the canal.

8. Garner (1980), 32

9. Diaries of W.R. Le Fanu 24, 27 March, 8 May 1855; D&WR Board Minutes 9 February, 8 June 1855, 157, 189

10. D&WR Board Minutes 26 October, 9 November 1855, 12, 17

11. Dargan-D&WR Board, 3 January 1856, D&WR Board Minutes 4 January 1856, 31

12. D&WR Board Minutes 8, 12 January 1856, 33, 37

13. Ibid., 29 February, 27 March, 12, 16, 30 September, 17 October 1856

14. Copeland was a senior figure in the bank and drew a generous annual salary of £1,500.

15. *Saunders News-Letter*, 8 September1856

16. Ibid., 8, 11 September 1856

17. Diaries of W.R. Le Fanu, 16, 22 May, 2 October, 4, 5 November 1857

18. *Freeman's Journal*, 18 November 1858

19. For a brief account of mining in the Avoca area see Shepherd and Beesley (1998), 17–18.

20. Le Fanu had already done a good deal of work for the Wicklow Copper Mining Co.: Diaries of W.R. Le Fanu, 13 August, 8 September, 31 October 1858; *Saunders News-Letter* 19 November 1858.

21. Craig (1980), 301

22. Capt. George Ross, Index to Railway Inspectors Reports, D&WR, 29 January, 2 June 1859, MT29/20. For an illustration and a full account of the crash, see Mulligan (1983), 34–6. On the same day but with no Dargan connection whatsoever a party of Australian schoolgirls had a strange experience while on an outing near Melbourne, immortalized in *Picnic at Hanging Rock*.

23. Diaries of W.R. Le Fanu 30 March 1859; *Dublin Builder* 1 November 1860, p.363

24. Diaries of W.R. Le Fanu 18, 25 January, 17 June, 30 July 1861; summary accounts 1861

25. DW&WR Board Minutes 9, 15, 23 May 1862, 171, 172, 173; *Dublin Builder* 1 June 1862, 141

26. Galt (1843), 28

27. Dublin Municipal Council Minutes 2 February 1863,.232

28. Diaries of James Dargan, 1, 17, 19, 22, 26 August, 7 October, 10 November 1863; *Dublin Builder*, 15 January 1863, p.7; Diaries of W.R. Le Fanu 26 October, 14 November 1862, 20 February 1863

29. Le Fanu (1894), 196

30. DW&WR Board Minutes 12, 17 February, 11 17, 24 March 1864, 303, 291, 293, 294, 298, 303

31. Diary of James Dargan, 6, 19, 25 July 1865

32. In examining the detail of this report, it is worth noting that the 19th century British Parliamentary Papers contain a staggering amount of information and statistics on every aspect of Irish affairs sourced from inquiries, research, investigative committees and highly detailed records of every sort. The British were excellent record keepers. See for example the vast and exhaustive Devon

Commission Report (HC 1845 (606) xix or in this case, Royal Commission on Railways in Ireland, HC 1867 (3844-II) XXXVIII Pt 2, Minutes of Evidence, William Dargan, 14 June 1865, Q.5453–5724, 229–238

33. Royal Commission on Railways in Ireland (1867)

34. Dargan to Pole, 6 November 1865; published as 'Letter from Mr Dargan on Irish Railways', Appendix AY, *Railways in Ireland Commission*, op.cit.

35. DW&WR Board Minutes 20, 28 August, 6 September 1866, 126–7, 132, 137

36. Ibid., 26 November 1866, 170

37. Ibid., 13, 14, 17 December 1866, 181, 183

38. Ibid., 24, 27 December 1866, 187, 190

39. Ibid., 31 January 1867, 203–4

8. A Man of Many Parts: Wexford Sloblands, Bray, Hotels, Sugar Beet, Flax, Whiskey, Chapelizod Mills

1. Minutes of evidence of House of Commons SC on the Carlow & Dublin Jun. Railway, privately printed, 2 June 1845, privately printed, evidence of Macneill; Furlong (1969), 53–77

2. Mullins (1859–61), 98; Dr William Sullivan, *Report to the Museum of Irish Industry*, quoted in Furlong (1969), 71; Lacy (1851), 251

3. Diaries of W. R. Le Fanu 20 January, 3 February, 18 August, 6 September, 22 October 1853; Nevin and McMillan (n.d.), unpublished paper

4. Diary of James Dargan, 14, 15, 19 February 1867

5. St John Joyce (1976 facsimile of 1912), 83

6. Meath Papers, land conveyances, 19 June 1858, 23 March 1861

7. *Dublin Builder* 1 November 1859, 140, 1 November 1860, 359

8. Abstracts Index, Registry of Deeds, vol.38, Ab.108, 21 October 1861

9. Powell (1860), 11, 14. This is a work of *pietas* towards Dargan and a promotion for the Wicklow Railway.

10. Lease details of these and other Dargan properties can be found in Abstracts Index, Registry of Deeds, vols.9, 19 23, 24, 40, 1862

11. Powell (1860), 16–18; Garner (1980), 30; *Saunders News-Letter*, 20 August, 14 October 1859

12. O'Neill (1960), 6

13. There were plans to turn the Turkish Baths into an assembly or concert room but after being put to various uses, sadly the baths were demolished around 1980. Two minarets survived in the garden of local historian, Joe Loughman.

14. *Dublin Builder*, 1 November, 1 December 1860, 360, 380, 1 April 1861, 472

15. *Freeman's Journal* 25 April 1862

16. *Dublin Builder*, 15 April, 15 June, 15 July 1861, 487, 547, 578; 1 June 1862, 138; *Irish Builder*, 15 February 1864, vol.VI, no.100, 30

17. I was at a football match at Dargan's Carlisle grounds between Bray Wanderers and Everton FC in 2004. The Merseyside team were not used to playing on such a small ground and in the pre-match warm-up kept belting the ball over the stand into Quinnsborough Road. At which a wag in the crowd shouted: 'Did youse bring a coupla spare balls?'

18. Roney (1861), 51–2

19. Index of Abstracts, Registry of Deeds, vol.20, Ab.207, 10 August 1848; vol.1, Ab.120, 9 August 1849. In 1856 Dargan and McCormick secured a mortgage on 5 acres of land at Malahide.

20. *Dublin Builder* 15 May 1863, vol.V, no.82, 91

21. *Dublin Builder* 15 July 1863, vol.V, no.86, p.122. The company built only the centrepiece and south wing of McCurdy's design: O'Dwyer (1981), 129

22. Royal Marine Hotel Co. to the OPW Commissioners, 23 July 1863, NA 11476/63; *Dublin Builder* 15 June, 1 July 1864, vol.VI, nos.108, 109, 123, 128

23. *Dublin Builder* 1 October 1865, vol.VII, no.139, 232–3

24. See Report of the Irish Waste Land Improvement Society, 1839; Report of the Devon Commission on the occupation of land in Ireland, evidence of Col. Daniel Robinson, 1845, vol.II, p.1, 5 June 1844, witness 287: HC 1845 (606) xix; 6&7 Will IV.cap.97; Thomas Campbell Foster, *Letters on the condition of Ireland from* The Times, Chapman and Hall, London, 1846, 225, 624, 653

25. Letter from Sir Matthew Barrington to Sir Robert Peel, 28 October 1844, NLI Barrington Papers

26. See *Dublin Evening Mail*, 11 February 1848; *Dublin Evening Post*, 15 February 1848; *Irish Railway Gazette*, 19 July 1847, 335.

27. *Freeman's Journal*, 15 February 1848

28. Letter from 'Patriot', *Saunders News-Letter*, 16 August 1849

29. *Railway News* 23 January 1864, 96; 1850 Report of the Royal Agricultural Improvement Society lists Dargan's subscription as £1.

30. *Saunders News-Letter*, 20, 21 August 1852

31. *Freeman's Journal*, 30 October 1852, 13 August 1853; *Tralee Chronicle*, 1 October 1852

32. *Saunders News-Letter*, 27 June, 13 August, 13 September 1853

33. *Saunders News-Letter*, 26 April, 11 September 1852. Such was the reputation of the Mount Anville garden that the Barringtons of Glenstal asked Dargan to take on a young horticultural apprentice named Ryan: Jonah Barrington to Dargan, 9 December 1854, Jane Dargan Papers

34. Bogs also presented problems for railway builders: for a study of these difficulties see Mullins (1846) and Mahon (1961–2)

35. John Gwynne to Dargan, 20 November 1850, in *Great Irish Peat-Working Company*

36. Letter Fermoy to Dargan, 11 August 1851, Jane Dargan Papers

37. Kane (1844), 314

38. W.R Le Fanu Diaries, 18 June 1850

39. *Cork Examiner* 9 July 1850

40. Most annual subscriptions were a guinea: 11th Annual Report of the Royal Society for the Promotion and Improvement of the Growth of Flax in Ireland, 1851, 76; 12th Annual Report, 1852, 68.

41. Saunders News-Letter, 20 September 1851

42. Letter to the Northern Whig, reprinted in Saunders News-Letter, 20 September 1851

43. James Owens to Commissioners of Public Works, 30 April 1853, OPW Registers 10104/53; Cork Examiner, 20 April 1853; Maguire (1853), 20, 371

44. Donnelly (1976), 45

45. Gibson (1861), 432; John Macneill tried a similar experiment near Dundalk but the factory burned down in 1857: Wilson (1973), 12–22

46. Registry of Deeds, Index of Abstracts 1862, vol.19, Ab.89, 23 May

47. Karl Marx, *Das Kapital*, Chapter 15, section 9

48. Maguire (1853), 383; Marmion (1860), 650–1

49. Ibid. (1853), 24, 395–402

50. Conveyance Dickson and Dunlop to Dargan, 19 October 1843; Declaration of Trust, Dargan and Dickson, 26 January 1846, Barrington & Jeffers/Garrett Papers

51. Registry of Deeds, 1846, vol.6, 26 January, 28 February, Abs.92, 105; Assignment Nicholson to Dargan, 29 March 1849, Barrington & Jeffers Papers. See also PRONI D.1905/2/17A/3 (misfiled under 'Dorgan') which contains Barrington and Jeffers' forwarded legal documents to do with the distillery.

52. James Heron, Ulster Bank, Belfast to Messrs Garrett Solrs, 6 April 1853; John Thompson, Belturbet Distillery to Garrett, Belfast, 24 September 1853; Barrington & Jeffers to Garrett, 1, 15, 18 November 1853; Thompson to Ulster Bank, 4 August 1853, Barrington & Jeffers/Garrett Papers

53. Report on the importance of graving docks, Dublin Chamber of Commerce, 1849, pp.36–8; for an account of the role of the two George Halpins, father and son, see Gilligan (1988), 125, 126

54. Corporation for Preserving and Improving the Port of Dublin (CPIPD) Board Minutes, 9 May 1853, 210

55. Codd to Lees, Minutes of Council Proceedings, Dublin Chamber of Commerce, 17 July 1854, 299–300

56. Dargan to Lees, 7 June 1855, CPIPD Board Minutes 8 June 1855; Dargan to Halpin, 21 July 1855, CPIPD correspondence files

57. Dargan to Lees, 4 June 1857; Halpin to Lees, 12 June 1857, CPIPD Correspondence files; CPIPD Board Minutes 25 September 1857, p.314; Dargan to Board, 25 November 1857, CPID correspondence files

58. CPIPD Board Minutes 1857: 9 October, p406, 16 October, 407, 13 November, 428, 27 November, 435, 4 December, 438, 11 December, 441; Lees to Dargan, 14 December 1857, CPIPD correspondence files

59. Cubitt built a large part of the Great Northern Railway in England and supervised the construction of Paxton's Crystal Palace building relocated from Hyde Park to Sydenham. He also enjoys the dubious credit of being the inventor of the treadmill used in many Victorian jails for grinding or pumping but often as a monotonous and purposeless punishment.

60. Writing from Morley's Hotel, Trafalgar Square, Halpin was already becoming alarmed at the formality of the process: Halpin to Lees, 1 March 1858 (2 letters), CPIPD correspondence files.

61. Halpin to Lees 19 March 1858, CPIPD correspondence files

62. CPIPD Board Minutes, 19 November 1858, 208, 209. Halpin made a desperate attempt to claw back some of the award, accusing Dargan of dredging clay and sand without paying for it but the amount was tiny.

63. CPIPD Board Minutes, 10 February 1860, 133; Gilligan (1988), 127

64. Annual Report of Dublin Chamber of Commerce, 2 June 1860, 30–1

65. *The Engineer*, 8 February 1867, quoted in R.C Cox (1990, ed.), 14. Although filled in the stonework of the graving dock is apparently largely intact.

66. The figures are quoted in a report of a dinner for an ex-foreman, James Smith, held at the Mullingar Hotel, Chapelizod: *Saunders News-Letter* 28, 30 May 1856

67. *Saunders News-Letter*, 24 June 1856

68. The judge remarked Hickey's counsel had argued the case with a degree of zeal worthy of a better cause: *Saunders News-Letter*, 16 June 1855

69. Surevyor's report by Francis Beatty & Co., 18 Bachelor's Walk, Dublin, 20 July 1875; 'Dublin & Chapelizod Distilling Co.', *Wine Trade Review*, vol.XIII, October 1873; Distillers Co. of Edinburgh bought the factory in 1878: *Irish Builder*, 12 September 1901, vol.XLIII, no.1001, 860–1

70. Swift (1726), *Gulliver's Travels*, Chapter 7

9. Sic Transit: Dargan's Later Years

1. Roney (1861), 89

2. Sproule (1853), xi-xii

3. Quoted in Le Fanu (1893), 211. The first saying is attributed to St Francis de Sales.

4. For a record of Dargan's membership see *Thom's Directory* 1854, 784; 1858, 974; 1859, 982; 1860, 1134; 1861, 1174; 1863, 1205; 1864, 1253; 1865, 1305; 866, 1335; 1867, 1303. See also O'Dwyer (1981), 28 and Cullen (1983), 1983, 25–33.

5. I am grateful to Prof. Ron Cox for informing me about this.

6. See, for example Le Fanu's diary entries of 24 August, 31 October 1850, 9–10 September 1851, 27 March, 1 May 1856, 26 December 1861.

7. Diaries of W. R. Le Fanu, 21 January 1855, 20 January, 12 February 1856; Le Fanu records, rather ungallantly, that he spent 4 shillings on champagne in the Castle and tipped Dargan's servant a shilling.

8. Alfred McClintock-Jane Dargan 12, 14 October 1854; Josephine Roy More-Jane Dargan, 3 September 1854; Lord Gough-Jane Dargan, 26 March 1855; Walter Berwick-Jane Dargan, 28 November 1855; J. Emmerson Tennent-William Dargan: Ena Dargan Papers

9. *Freeman's Journal*, 16, 23 October 1856

10. Lt Gen. Knollys to Dargan 10 May 1865, Ena Dargan Papers; Diary of James Dargan 3, 16, 17, 20, 25 May 1865

11. Diary of James Dargan 15, 16 August 1865

12. Nevinson-Jane Dargan, 29 May 1865, Jane Dargan Papers

13. Joby (1983 ed.), 94ff

14. Diary of James Dargan 6, 19, 25 July 1865

15. *Thom's Directory 1863*, pp.1425, 1541. The rateable value was £100 and as there is no deed of sale it seems likely he leased the house.

16. *Journal de la Maison de Mount Anville*, July 1865; my translation. I am grateful to Sr Marie O'Sullivan, Mount Anville Archivist for allowing me access to this journal.

17. 'La communauté de Glasnevin se transporta à Mount Anville en 1865; ce fut le père de Mère Roche qui négocia l'acquisition de cette magnifique propriété en grand secret, car la femme du propriétaire était une très ardente protestante qui n'aurait consenti à aucun prix à la vendre à des religieuses *Lettres Annuelles de la Societé du Sacré Coeur de Jésus*, Seconde Partie, 1924–6, p.15, my translation.

18. Index to Registry of Deeds, vol.23, ab.221, 5 August 1865

19. *Journal de la Maison de Mount Anville*, 18 August 1865; my translation

20. Ibid. Controversy followed the sisters – Sr Margaret Aylward, Dominican superior of the Glasnevin convent which they had just vacated, threatened to sue her sisters in religion for damage to the building, agreeing to Cardinal Cullen's arbitration in the case: Julia Scully to Cardinal Cullen, 5 December 1865, Letters of Cardinal Cullen, 1865, section 327/2, file V, no.18, Dublin Diocesan Archives. A year later the parish priest of Booterstown complained to Cullen again about problems in Mount Anville relating to a carriage for the chaplain, the nuns' interference in children's religious practice, relations with workmen and sundry other matters: L. Forde to Cardinal Cullen, 1866, section 327/5, file IV, no.21, 4 November 1866

21. Joby (1983), 114. For further details of the crisis from a British perspective see P.L. Cotterell (1975–6), 20–41; Pollins (1957–8), 41ff; Reid, 1997, 462–5; for an Irish banking view see Hall (1948).

22. Registry of Deeds, Index of Abstracts, vol.32, Ab.300, 19 November 1866

23. *Daily Express*, 24 November 1866

24. Letter Peel to Dargan, 3 December 1866, Jane Dargan Papers. Curiously, Peel's father, the 2nd baronet and a prime minister, died in 1850 in London following a fall from his horse similar to Dargan's accident. Peel *père* was known as Orange Peel for his strong opposition to Catholic emancipation; he even challenged Daniel O'Connell to a duel over the issue.

25. Barrington Jeffers to Heron, 22 January 1867; early draft of Dargan's will, Barrington Jeffers Papers, NLI 12.994

26. Heron to Barrington Jeffers 23 January 1863, Barrington Jeffers Papers, NLI 12.994. The uncustomary speed of the legal response suggests a certain urgency in finalising the will.

27. Revised draft of William Dargan's will, 26 January 1867, Barrington Jeffers Papers, NLI 12.994

28. This is the only known surviving copy of Dargan's will, made for the Probate Court and is unsigned. It is presumed the original signed will was lost in the fire that destroyed the Public Record Office at the Four Courts during the Civil War. I located the version quoted here in the Public Record Office Northern Ireland. It is dated incorrectly 1864 rather than 1867.

29. Boyle was a longstanding friend of Dargan's and a fellow director of the Dublin Wicklow & Wexford Railway.

30. In the margin of the last page of the will there are a number of administrative references: 'Dargan died Feby 7 1867 £8000'; 'Unad Grant 1870 p.88 and 1873 p.55'; 'reservoir at S.O. 24/7/73 under £45.000.'

31. Diary of James Dargan, 22 January 1867

32. Ibid., 30 January 1867; *Thom's Directory 1867*, 1042; *Irish Catholic Directory 1867*, 43

33. *Journal de la Maison de Mount Anville*, 8 February 1867, my translation

34. Diary of James Dargan, 31 January 1867

35. Death Certificate no.491, 1867, Grand Canal district of south Dublin; *Dublin Evening Post*, 8 February 1867

36. Diary of James Dargan, 8, 9, 10 February 1867

37. Fitzgibbon to Louisa Haslam, 8 February 1867, Jane Dargan Papers

38. DW&WR special meeting, 11 February 1867, 208

39. Maunsell-Jane Dargan, 12 February 1867, Jane Dargan papers

40. It is curious Le Fanu did not attend his friend's funeral and in fact does not mention his death or his funeral in his diaries; he was in bed with sciatica that day.

41. William Fairbairn to Jane Dargan, 10 February 1867, Jane Dargan Papers

42. It is interesting to compare Dargan's last days and his funeral to Daniel O'Connell's twenty years before on 5 August 1847, one so large it virtually paralysed the city. In his last days O'Connell had suffered unspeakable agonies inflicted by over-zealous and incompetent physicians, including painful but useless injections, blistering, bleeding and application of leeches and enemas, all of which increased his final suffering. Adding to his anxiety was a chronic fear of being buried alive: Cusack (1872), 760. The removal of his heart after his death and its burial in Rome, as he requested, made such an eventuality unlikely.

    The *Duchess of Kent*, a 155 ton wooden paddle steamer of the City of Dublin Steam Packet Co. sailed from Birkenhead on 2 August 1847 with O'Connell's body lying in a 'sea chapel' on deck. In Dublin Bay she passed the *PS Birmingham* of the same company, outward bound for Liverpool with a large number of emigrants on board. When the passengers saw the black-shrouded vessel they realised it carried the Liberator's body and raised the most enormous lament, a keening that was heard right across the bay.

    Special trains ran from around the country for the funeral, at least 500 clerics took part in the requiem mass and the funeral was led off by 50 groups of Dublin tradesmen including cartwrights, tallow chandlers, coopers and ropemakers followed by a vast crowd of religious confraternities, nobility, gentry, hierarchy and the citizens of Dublin who made their way through the crowded city streets to Glasnevin. So as not to overwhelm the cemetery, carriages and horsemen were instructed to 'fall out' as the procession reached the Circular Road at Berkeley Street: *Freeman's Journal* 3, 5, 6 August 1847. It is not known if Dargan attended the funeral but it seems unlikely as that Famine summer of 1847 was an exceptionally busy time for him; he was building the line to Cork and working on several projects in the north. For illustrations of O'Connell's funeral, including the vast crowds attending, see *Illustrated London News*, 14 August 1847, 104–6.

43. *Evening Mail*, 11 February 1867; *Daily Express*, 12 February 1867; *The Irish Times*, 12 February

1867; *Freeman's Journal*, 12 February 1867; *Saunders News-Letter*, 12 February 1867; *Bray Gazette*, 16 February 1867

44. Francis Murphy SJ was based in St Francis Xavier's, Gardiner St, Dublin and died in Melbourne in 1898, aged 94. It is not known what direct connection, if any, William Dargan had with the Jesuits although the descendants of his brother James certainly did and at least three joined the Society.

45. Dublin Cemeteries Committee, Minute Book, vol.9, 5 March 1867, 119

46. Diary of James Dargan, 11 February 1867

47. Ibid., March-November 1867

48. Dargan's name first appears in a Royal Insurance advertisement in *Thom's Directory 1865*, supplement p.35; 1866 supplement p.44; 1867 supplement p.33.

49. Cloncurry to Jane Dargan, 13 February 1867; Stride to Jane Dargan; 13 February 1867, Jane Dargan Papers

50. Most of these appeared on either 8 or 9 February 1867.

51. This enlightened policy parallels other significant social changes in Ireland at the time such as the departure for Australia of the last convict ship, the *Hougomont*, laden with Fenians on 12 October 1867, eight months after Dargan's death.

52. *The Irish Times*, 16 February 1867

53. *The Irish Times*, 20 February 1867. This may be the same Edwards who was once an employee of Dargan's and whom he helped set up in business.

54. Joby (1983), .94ff

55. Dublin Cemeteries Committee, Minute Book, vol.9, June 1867, 213

56. Forde to Cullen, 12 July 1867, Letters of Cardinal Cullen, Dublin Diocesan Archives, section 334/4, file V, no.18

57. Dublin Cemeteries Committee, Minute Book, vol.9, 3 July 1867, 220

58. Another oft-repeated myth is that the grave bears just one word, 'Dargan', which any visitor can confirm is nonsense. The confusion probably arose over the statue in front of the National Gallery which has this one word inscription.

59. The Quaker influence on railways persisted well into the 20th century: the GS&WR Half-Yearly Reports for 1902 and 1910 list a James Perry Goodbody among the directors.

60. Leinster to Rushe and Martin 25 March, 20 May 1868, Jane Dargan Papers. The duke also agreed to serve on a committee to help Mrs Dargan.

61. Mayo to Martin, 21 May 1868, Jane Dargan Papers

62. Letter McKenna to Martin, 28 May 1868; Guinness to Martin, 10 June 1868, Jane Dargan Papers

63. Letter Kirk to Gerald Fitzgibbon, 23 June 1868, Jane Dargan Papers. A. Brewster, Merrion Square and Martin Berwick, Upr Merrion Street also said they would join the committee.

64. Buckingham Palace to Martin, 8 June 1868; W. Knollys to Martin, 20 June 1869, Jane Dargan Papers.

65. J. Murphy to Jane Dargan, 13 March 1869, Jane Dargan Papers. The other MPs present were the members for Dublin (Mr Pim), Munster (Mr Murphy), Belfast (Mr McClune), Down (Mr Kirk) and Wicklow (Mr Dick).

66. Conder (1868), 166

67. The *Dublin Builder*, 15 June 1869, vol.XI, no.228, 144, published the details and noted Barrington Jeffers acted as solicitors for the sale. Four lots were bought in trust: no.4 for Thomas Baring, Robert Wigram Crawford, Thomas Hankey, Baron Lionel de Rothschild; no.7 for Elizabeth and Susan Hayman; no.8 for L.D. Carnegie; no.9 for H. Jackson.

68. *The Irish Times*, 23 December 1869, p.5

69. Diary of James Dargan, 15, 16 January 1870. Unfortunately the Diaries cease on 28 November 1870.

70. Calendar of the grants of probate and letters of administration made in the Principal Registry for

1873, p.152, [81]; *The Irish Times*, 23 December 1869, p.5

71. *Thom's Directory 1869*, pp.1490, 1731. Her namesake, Jane Dargan the widow of William's nephew, James Dargan, was living in Belgrave Road, Rathmines as stated: p.1731. The resident at 2 Fitzwilliam Square East in late 1869 was a Mrs Hamil Stewart: *Thom's Directory 1870*, p.1720

72. *Kelly's Penge, Anerley and Beckenham Directory*, 1888–89, 67, 125; 1889–90, 51, 114; 1890–91, 51, 114; 1891–92, 51, 116; 1892–93, 51, 119; 1893–94, 51, 119; 1894–95, 51, 124: British Library. In 1875 Robert Peel agreed to help Louisa Haslam secure a post at St Anne's Asylum; this may not have been successful, for four years later Thomas Fairbairn, a longstanding colleague of Dargan's, declined the same request: Peel to Jane Dargan, 25 July 1875; Fairbairn to Jane Dargan, 19 October 1879, Jane Dargan Papers.

73. Letter Croker Barrington-Jane Dargan, 26 June 1875, Jane Dargan Papers

74. This is an unsigned will and is in the form of a rough printed version, punctuation or lack thereof as in the original: General Registry Office, London.

75. Death Certificate of Jane Dargan, Croydon Sub-District, General Register Office, England

76. *Crystal Palace District Advertiser*, 30 June 1894 and the *Beckenham Journal*, 30 June 1894. The first paper carries a chemist's advertisement promoting cannabis as a cure for corns.

77. There is no record of her burial in the 12 cemeteries in the Croydon area: Bandon Hill Cemetery, Beckenham Crematorium and Cemetery, Bromley Cemeteries, Croydon Cemetery (Mitcham Road), Figgs Marsh Cemetery, Mitcham, Garratt Lane Cemetery, Lambeth Cemetery, Merton Cemetery, Queen's Road Cemetery, Croydon, Streatham Cemetery, Streatham Park Cemetery, West Norwood Cemetery and Crematorium.

78. I am grateful to Ray Thomas, parish archivist at St Mary's, Market Drayton, for drawing my attention to the grave of Dargan's niece and allowing access to the parish records.

79. Abstracts of Wills, 1894, Jane Dargan, 195, [300]

80. Bertie Haslam to Mary Dargan Ward, 16 August 1963, Jane Dargan Papers

81. Superintendant/Registrar, Croydon Cemeteries Office to Fergus Mulligan, 16 September 1994.

10. The Heritage of William Dargan

1. The erection of Dargan's statue outside the Gallery in Merrion Square, a few years before his death, is probably unique in the history of Dublin statuary.

2. This is an enormous amount, even when compared to the 4,500 miles built by Thomas Brassey, the great English contractor who, like Dargan, learned his trade on Telford's Holyhead road and with whom he might be compared. Only 1,700 miles of this mileage were in Britain, the rest across the world: Rolt (1960), 214

3. Conder (1868) 165–6

4. *Irish Railway Gazette*, 28 June 1848, 312

5. During the Famine winter of 1846–7, for instance, while building the GS&WR he kept large numbers on his payroll without imposing wage cuts for shorter workdays or wet weather: *Irish Railway Gazette* 22 November 1847, 480

6. Le Fanu (1894), 265

7. *The Irish Times*, 23 August 1861

8. Conder (1868), 166. Conder was vitriolic about many of his own engineering colleagues, apart from George Stephenson, I.K. Brunel and Dargan whom he met while building railways in Munster. Conder's rambling but fascinating book covers such diverse topics as the role of the press, French inferiority and the baleful influence of the Jesuits.

9. *Edinburgh Evening Post*, 5 October 1853

10. Lee points out that Dargan shrewdly recognised the GS&WR was one of the few solidly financed railways and he was therefore certain to be paid: Lee (1965), 93

11. See, for example, Diary of James Dargan, 14, 15, 16, 17 January, 8 February 1863; 12, 26 January, 15, 22 February, 9, 16 March 1864. James married Teresa Harrington on 8 January 1866; it is not known if his uncle was present.

12. Diary of James Dargan, 1 February 1863

13. See Chapter 9

14. Le Fanu (1894),.211

15. It is interesting the bequests in the final version of his will are so much greater than in the earlier draft, indicating perhaps Dargan acquired a fuller picture of his financial status between the drafting of the two.

16. Le Fanu (1894), 208

Index

Numbers in italic denote illustrations.

279

railway investment speech, 72–3; railway network, 217; railway openings, 6–7; Randalstown viaduct, 71; RDS life member, 128; reasons for success, 187; refuses titles, 132, 134, 138, 187, 218, 222; religion, 10, 200, 203; riding accident 1865, 190–1; runs D&DR services, 69; Salthill Hotel office, 40; schooling, 13–14; sells engines, 91; Shannon steamers, 106–7; signature, 162, 224; silver cup, 46; social life, 188–9; Solitude reservoir, 58; Sproule memoir, 133; statues, 133, 146; steamers to Liverpool, 58–60, 119; sub-contractors, 156; sugar, 178; T&KR, 103–4; Telford's opinion, 20, 218; toll of lifestyle, 186; truck, 4–5, 66, 74, 83; trustees, 165; Tullamore branch, 107–8; Ulster Canal contract, 53–7; UR, 65–7; Vice-Regal Lodge dinner, 141; Vignoles meetings, 34; Walker's opinion, 85; W&LR, 97–101; W&TR, 102; Westland Row terminus, 42, *43*, 48; Wexford sloblands, 166–7, 210; whiskey distillery, 178–9; Wicklow's beauties, 169; women's contribution, 222; work capacity, 187; writing desk, *219*

DART, 6, 37, *38*

Dartry, 150

Das Kapital, 177

Davidson, A.C., 176

Davitt, Michael, 3

Dawes, Rev. Charles, 27

Dawson, John, 96, 113, 161, 172

Day, Christopher, 58

Deane, Thomas, 107

de Grey, Earl, 68

Derenzy, Captain, 23

Derry, 119

de Stael, Madame, 222

Derrylea bog, 175

Devon Commission on Land in Ireland, 64, 68

Devonshire Arms Hotel, Bandon, 176

Dickson, Alexander, 178–9

Dickson, David, ix

Dimsdale, Mr, contractor, 64

Dingle, 221

Disraeli, Benjamin, 210

Distillers Co., 185

Dnieper, River, 33

Dodder river, 45

Dodder viaduct, Milltown, 151

Donegall Arms Hotel, 65

Dooley, Mr, ganger, 92

Dordan, R.H., 210

Drainage Commissioners, 98

Drinagh, 167

Drogheda, 94

Drogheda, Marquis, 133

Dromod, 123, 221

Drummond, Maria, 47

Drummond Railway Commission, 18, 87

Dublin & Belfast Junction Railway: Dargan contracts, 69;

Dublin & Drogheda Railway: bill, 18; Cubbitt's cost estimate, 68; dividend, 66; Dargan/McCormick partnership, 68, 69; Dargan's wage rates, 68; first train, 68; Grand Hotel, Malahide, 172; HL Committee of Inquiry, 24–5, 68; Howth branch, 69; Macneill engineer, 68; O'Connell street terminus, 68; trial run, 68

Dublin & Kingstown Railway: capital, 31; carriage 1860s, 49, 161, *162*; compulsory purchases, 35; construction problems, 47–8; construction schedule, 35; cost estimates, 35; Dargan's tender, 20; dividend, 66; excessive efficiency, 31; extension, 48; fares, 45, 161; first line, 6; first proposals, 30, 31; gauge, 87; injuries, 39; granite sleepers, 48; land valuation,